COMPARATIVE MUSICOLOGY AND ANTHROPOLOGY OF MUSIC

COMPARATIVE MUSICOLOGY AND ANTHROPOLOGY OF MUSIC

Essays on the History of Ethnomusicology

Edited by
Bruno Nettl
and
Philip V. Bohlman

**The
University
of Chicago
Press**
Chicago
and
London

THE UNIVERSITY OF CHICAGO PRESS, CHICAGO 60637
THE UNIVERSITY OF CHICAGO PRESS, LTD., LONDON
© 1991 by The University of Chicago
All rights reserved. Published 1991
Printed in the United States of America
99 98 97   5 4 3 2
ISBN: 0-226-57409-1 (pbk.)

Library of Congress Cataloging-in-Publication Data

Comparative musicology and anthropology of music : essays on the
  history of ethnomusicology / edited by Bruno Nettl and Philip
  V. Bohlman.
     p.   cm. -- (Chicago studies in ethnomusicology)
   Most of these essays are expanded versions of papers read at a
conference entitled Ideas, concepts, and personalities in the
history of ethnomusicology, held at the University of Illinois,
Urbana-Champaign, Apr. 1988.
   Includes bibliographical references and index.
   ISBN 0-226-57408-3 (cloth). -- ISBN 0-226-57409-1 (pbk.) :
   1. Ethnomusicology.   2. Music and anthropology.   I. Nettl, Bruno,
1930-   II. Bohlman, Philip Vilas.   III. Series.
ML3799.C69   1991.   90-38366
780'.89--dc20   CIP
                                                                MN

To the Memory of Alan P. Merriam

We badly need histories, and particularly histories of ideas . . .
Far too few of us . . . know what von Hornbostel really did . . .
(1969)

Contents

      Erich M. von Hornbostel, Carl Stumpf, and the Institution-
        alization of Comparative Musicology   *Dieter Christensen*   201
      The First Restudy of Arnold Bake's Fieldwork
        in India   *Nazir Ali Jairazbhoy*   210
      Marginality and Musicology in Nineteenth-Century Calcutta:
        The Case of Sourindro Mohun Tagore   *Charles Capwell*   228
      Women and the Society for Ethnomusicology: Roles and
        Contributions from Formation through Incorporation
        (1952/53–1961)   *Charlotte J. Frisbie*   244
      The Dual Nature of Ethnomusicology in North America:
        The Contributions of Charles Seeger and George
        Herzog   *Bruno Nettl*   266

IV   NOURISHED BY A VARIETY OF DISCIPLINES
      Recording Technology, the Record Industry, and
        Ethnomusicological Scholarship   *Kay Kaufman Shelemay*   277
      Psychological Theory and Comparative
        Musicology   *Albrecht Schneider*   293
      Interdisciplinary Approaches to the Study of Musical
        Communication Structures   *Doris Stockmann*   318
      Styles of Musical Ethnography   *Anthony Seeger*   342

      Epilogue   *Philip V. Bohlman*   356

      Contributors   361

      Index   365

Acknowledgments

W e owe thanks to many, more than we can name. First, we are grateful to the authors of the studies presented here for their scholarly contributions, for their permission to include their work in this kind of a collection, and for their patience. The essays, or chapters of this volume, developed from papers presented at a conference, "Ideas, Concepts, and Personalities in the History of Ethnomusicology," held in Urbana, Illinois, on April 14–17, 1988. We would like to thank the many units of the University of Illinois at Urbana-Champaign that supported the conference: the School of Music; the College of Liberal Arts and Sciences; the College of Fine and Applied Arts; the George A. Miller Endowment; the Office of International Programs and Studies; the Centers for East Asian and Pacific, Russian and East European, African, Latin American and Caribbean, and West European Studies; the Program in South and West Asian Studies; and the Department of Anthropology; along with the University Scholar Program. To these must be added the Department of Music of the University of Illinois at Chicago.

The conference was organized by a committee consisting of Charles Capwell, Carol M. Babiracki, and the editors of this volume; and they received substantial help from many Illinois graduate students, particularly Frederick Lau, Margaret Sarkissian, Paula Savaglio, and Melinda Russell, and from all of their faculty colleagues in the Division of Musicology at Urbana. Many thanks to them all.

When it came to publication of this volume, we found ourselves particularly indebted to the College of Liberal Arts and Sciences at the University of Illinois at Urbana-Champaign which provided a generous subvention for publication costs from its Annual Development Fund. This subvention was part of an imaginative program of "state of the art conferences" held in various fields, a program initiated by Dean William Prokasy. We are grateful to the University of Illinois Research Board for providing funds to defray in some measure the costs of editorial assistance. And finally, we want to

acknowledge the many kinds of editorial and clerical work provided by
Melinda Russell, who has been with this project beginning with the planning
of the conference through preparation of the manuscript from the time it was
first assembled and on to final proofreading and indexing, and who spent
many hours tracking down bibliographic references in the card catalog and
with our distinguished authors on the long-distance telephone.

B.N. and P.V.B.
1 December 1989

Bruno Nettl
Introduction

I N THE LAST twenty-five years, disciplines in the social sciences and humanities have increasingly turned to the study of their own history. They were stimulated by an increased interest in the history of science and by a kind of disciplinary relativism that emphasizes the understanding of cultural and historical contexts in the reading of scholarship of the past. For ethnomusicology, this interest is of rather recent date, although one of the earliest expositions of its history appeared in Jaap Kunst's landmark, *Ethnomusicology* (3d ed. 1959). But the history of their field has been playing a major role in the work of ethnomusicologists of today. The subject has been featured at conferences (e.g., the International Council for Traditional Music in 1987) and through the publication of anthologies of early writings (e.g., Harrison 1973). The clearest evidence has been the need many ethnomusicologists have felt to specify, in their papers and articles, their intellectual and ideological position.

As the national identities of scholars change, along with their ideologies and their relationships to the people whose music they study, the nature of the scholarship also changes. There is perhaps no field among the humanities which has been so directly affected by changes in social, political, and military history. And thus, ethnomusicologists feel possibly further than other scholars from the thinking of the early figures in their field.

Stephen Blum's assertion tells us in a nutshell why it is important to understand one's disciplinary history: "The terms, questions, and procedures of scholars are developed in response to the specific conditions of social and musical life at a given time and place. Members of each generation reproduce inherited techniques with such changes as may seem to make familiar tools more useful in an altered environment." It is not just that one wishes to avoid reinventing the sewing machine. For us, it continues to be essential to understand how a field such as ethnomusicology could come into existence simply in order to understand the configuration of ideas that are combined in its literature.

Ethnomusicology is, as Alan Merriam noted, a field "caught up in a fascination with itself" (1964:3) in search of an identity where there are no good models. It is clearly a central part of musicology, as that discipline defines itself; but it is, as well, on the outskirts of typical musicological practice in research and teaching, at best a valued minority view. At the same time, it is obviously related to anthropology, but few hard-core sociocultural anthropologists want to know much about it, as it suffers from the general Western attitude toward music as something only musicians can properly understand. There are no disciplines or subdisciplines that parallel it in other arts, no "ethnoartology" or "ethnoliteraturology." Folkloristics does not do for verbal art what ethnomusicology does for music. Indeed, the difference in fundamental orientation and grouping of methods between musicology as a whole and art history and literary scholarship can be traced to its development in which studies ethnomusicological in nature (if not in name) were added to the conventionally historical. Although the majority of the ethnomusicological population comes from formal training in the world of music, the intellectual leadership in ethnomusicology has always drawn heavily on its anthropological component.

The uniqueness of ethnomusicology among humanistic and social fields of learning requires an understanding of its history. Such a work is yet to be written comprehensively, for the small population of ethnomusicologists, past and present, belies the large configuration of ideas, approaches, techniques, ideologies, statements of purpose, and critique that this work would have to take into account. In this volume, we present, as a way station to a comprehensive history, a number of studies that shed light in a large number of ways on the development of ethnomusicology as it has come to exist in the 1980s. Most of them are greatly expanded versions of papers read at a conference entitled "Ideas, Concepts, and Personalities in the History of Ethnomusicology," held at the University of Illinois at Urbana-Champaign in April of 1988. They provide a liberal sampling of the ways in which a scholarly discipline, taken as a unit, may be studied and presented. Their variety reflects the internal diversity of our field.

There are many fascinating areas to be examined. In some of the papers, significant if brief or localized events are scrutinized in detail. Christensen focuses on the roles of two scholars, Hornbostel and Stumpf, who are always included in the ethnomusicological pantheon, in their Berlin workplace. Capwell, on the other hand, tells us about an Indian scholar, Sourindro Mohun Tagore, a man who worked, influential but rarely recognized, in Bengal on the margins of two cultures whose interaction provides some of the essence of ethnomusicology. Jairazbhoy too deals with a major figure in Indian studies, Arnold Bake, and then goes on to explore a unique way of studying intellectual history as well as history of musical culture as he retraces the steps of Bake's field trip. Frisbie deals with the roles of a small number of female scholars, but particularly with those of Frances Densmore and Helen Roberts, in a decade of the history of the Society for Ethnomusicology, the association that has done much to establish ethnomusicology as an independent field, for better or worse.

There are also accounts that cover segments of our field more broadly, covering large geographic areas and spanning upwards of a century. Wong traces the relationship between musicological study and political history in China. Béhague's account of ethnomusicology in Latin America dwells on the complex cultural interrelationship of the area as the basis of the regional character of scholarship. Waterman's study traces three assumptions that have long been held about African music and shows how they have shaped the course of African studies in ethnomusicology. Babiracki's essay narrates the history of a concept peculiar to studies of India, the relationship between "great" and "little" traditions. Elschek surveys developments in Eastern Europe since World War II by focusing on national and regionally comparative research.

The importance of cultural diversity in the development of ethnomusicological studies is exhibited in the essays by Wong, Béhague, Babiracki, Elschek, among others. And the problems specifically of intercultural study, early and recent, are explored by Qureshi, who looks at different types of sources for studying the musical culture of the Indian subcontinent, and by Blum, who shows how the fundamentals of Western musical thought have affected the understanding of the peculiarities of African musical styles. The history of ethnomusicology as viewed against a template of related disciplines and fields—technology, psychology, semiotics, linguistics—is explored in the studies by Shelemay, Schneider, and Stockmann. Shelemay shows how the history of ethnomusicology and the music history of the cultures it studies have been almost completely dependent on technological developments. Schneider analyzes the interaction between musical and psychological studies and points out some of the weaknesses of early research that have sometimes sent us on wild goose chases. Stockmann gives an account of the study of music as communication, drawing on literature from a number of disciplines and comparing the sometimes parallel, sometimes contrastive developments of Central and Eastern European and American scholarship.

It seems that those essays which look back into the most distant past are also the ones that most explicitly carry their findings into the present and extrapolate questions for the future. For example, in a study that extends to the seventeenth century and beyond, Bohlman traces the ebb and flow of certain fundamental concepts and paradigms from the seventeenth to the twentieth. Concentrating on one of these fundamentals, Ringer's essay reminds us of the values of comparative study from a Western perspective and, by implication, recommends a return to earlier values. Seeger, examining the conception of musical ethnography in the works of early thinkers such as Jean-Jacques Rousseau (before 1800) and Richard Wallaschek (a century later), suggests that we have come far but perhaps also that we have not covered all that much ground. In contrast, Qureshi examines the role of outsiders and insiders as guides for research yet to come; and Blum, with a critical if respectful approach to much research of the past—reaching back some two millennia—argues the need for a different future.

Some of the essays provide special views of national scholarly traditions. The fascinating if winding course of research on a particular repertory appears in Porter's examination of change in the study of Anglo-American folk song. Porter, along with Wong, Babiracki, Béhague, Qureshi, and Frisbie, speaks to the question of national and regional schools of research and the degree to which they are conditioned by the cultures by which they are produced. Also, my own chapter tries to interpret the history of American ethnomusicology as the function of two sides of the American character, as illustrated by two influential scholars, Charles Seeger and George Herzog.

Some of the authors have occasion to write about their teachers: Jairazbhoy about Arnold Bake, I about George Herzog, others about the grandfatherly figures of the teachers of their own mentors. Other interesting personal relationships also come to the fore as Christopher Waterman comments on the work of his father, Richard, while Anthony Seeger explains the thinking of his distinguished grandfather, Charles.

There is no history without chronology, and some of our studies trace the sequential development of various components of ethnomusicological activity. Blum concentrates on views and analyses of musical structure presented in historical sequence, while Elschek does the same with types of publications and presentation. Taking periodic soundings, Seeger looks at the ways in which musical ethnography has been carried out in the field, whereas Bohlman takes a similar approach, presenting a sequence of char-

acteristic paradigms in interpretation. Porter is concerned with the idea of
folk music, a concept that is a specialty of European culture through a part
of its history. Shelemay divides the development of recording devices into
overlapping periods. Babiracki, Qureshi, Wong, and Béhague chronicle the
gradual entry of scholars from outside the Euro-American centers onto the
ethnomusicological stage.

A diverse group of studies showing the many things that an intellectual
historian may examine. Yet for all their variety, it would be unwise to stress
this diversity too greatly, as these essays also present a unified view of the
ethnomusicological past. We see certain themes, events, and figures reap-
pearing, in different contexts, throughout the essays of this volume—the
central figures: Stumpf, Hornbostel, Merriam; vexing issues of continuing
controversy: emic and etic, the behemoth of Western culture, "great" and
"little" traditions; influential figures: Béla Bartók, Frances Densmore,
George Herzog; landmark events: the invention of recording, the Cairo Congress of 1932, the founding of SEM; pioneers: G. A. Villoteau, A. J. Ellis,
Charles Seeger; seminal periods: the 1880s and the 1950s. We are not just
dealing with individuals working independently, out of touch and without
common goals but, rather, we are observing what is in certain respects a
grand march that has taken us through various views of the musical and cultural world, from understandable naïveté to substantial sophistication,
from simple to complex technologies, from ethnocentrism to cultural relativism. We have tried to emphasize this unity in the organization of this
book, recognizing four major attributes of the history of ethnomusicology.

What has characterized ethnomusicology most throughout its history is
a fascination with, and a desire to absorb and understand, the world's cultural diversity. Of equal importance is the fact that a group of abiding
ideological and epistemological issues have been with us from the beginning, attacked at various times and places from different viewpoints, but
still with us. Ethnomusicology, like any field, has had its great men and
women, scholars who because of the power of their writing, the interest of
their work, their roles as teachers, or simply their qualities as great leaders
who inspired, determined much of the course of its history. But in a field
with a small and diverse population, the role of individual leadership
looms large. And most characteristic, as already suggested above, ethnomusicology is a field whose fundamental nature results from its association
with several disciplines which have nourished it.

While the chapters in this collection are individual and to some extent
very specialized studies, each one is, in its way, comprehensive. For that

reason we have encouraged their authors to provide copious references to the literature with which they deal, and as a result, the studies are followed by rather long bibliographies. As editors, we considered the advantages of providing a single, integrated bibliography, but in the end we concluded that the reader is better served by separate listings. A number of the bibliographies may well serve as definitive reference guides to the landmarks in a slice of ethnomusicological history—the essays by Stockmann, Elschek, Wong, Babiracki, and Blum in particular.

The authors of the studies in this volume are all in some sense ethnomusicologists, but they differ in background and orientation. They come from various kinds of musical study, from historical musicology, anthropology, systematic musicology. They are specialists in musics of many world cultures, including Europe. Some of them would define ethnomusicology as the comparative study of the world's musics; others, as the anthropological study of music. The majority of these scholars live and have studied in North America, but a few are from Western Europe, Eastern Europe, and Asia. It has been important to the editors that both scholars of many years' experience as well as members of the younger generation be among the authors.

As one might expect, the authors do not always agree, or at any rate, they look at the same thing from greatly different viewpoints. The figure of George Herzog is presented very differently in the essays by Frisbie and Nettl. Hornbostel plays contrastive roles in the studies of Christensen, Ringer, Waterman, Blum, and Schneider; and Charles Seeger, in the chapters by Stockmann, Nettl, Frisbie, and Anthony Seeger. Similar subject matter is placed under different lenses by Babiracki, Capwell, and Qureshi (for South Asia); and by Waterman and Blum (for Africa). The optimistic tones of Stockmann, Seeger, and Bohlman are balanced by cautions and by critiques of recent developments in the essays by Wong, Ringer, and Blum.

We have been observing a grand march and can at least trace the course of the center of the column. But it is a march that has led through detours and byways, past nooks and crannies, over potholes and loose gravel. With these, the authors of the essays deal dispassionately, avoiding advocacy though not eschewing a critical view of what has happened. It is the purpose of these essays to help the scholars and students of ethnomusicology as well as members of other fields—those concerned with all types of musicology, with anthropology, folkloristics, area studies, and more—to appreciate, in its historical context, the scholarship, from raw data to finished interpretation, with which they work.

Works Cited

Harrison, Frank
1973   *Time, Place and Music: An Anthology of Ethnomusicological
        Observations c. 1550 to c. 1800.* Amsterdam: Frits Knuf.
Kunst, Jaap
1959   *Ethnomusicology: A Study of Its Nature, Its Problems, Methods and
        Representative Personalities to Which Is Added a Bibliography.* 3d ed.
        The Hague: Martinus Nijhoff.
Merriam, Alan P.
1964   *The Anthropology of Music.* Evanston: Northwestern University Press.

I

Informed by the World's Cultural Diversity

Stephen Blum

European Musical Terminology and the Music of Africa

1

THE TERMS, questions, and procedures of scholars are developed in response to the specific conditions of social and musical life at a given time and place. Members of each generation reproduce inherited techniques with such changes as may seem to make familiar tools more useful in an altered environment.

Much of the work that proved to be decisive in the formation of the discipline now known as ethnomusicology was carried out by members of the two generations born between the late 1860s and the early 1880s, and between the mid-1880s and early 1900s (table 1). Members of what are termed here the "first and second generations of ethnomusiocologists" established several types of contact with one another, cutting across national boundaries. They developed institutions, ideas, and techniques that have enabled subsequent scholars to investigate a wide range of musical practices and theories. It is the activities of a considerable number of scholars, and the important contacts among them, that justify our calling them the first and second generations of ethnomusicologists.

An outline of the major initiatives taken by members of these generations might emphasize four divergent orientations: those of cultural anthropology in the United States, of musical ethnography in the Russian Empire and the Soviet Union, of musical folklore and national programs of musical research in many parts of Europe and Latin America, and of comparative musicology in Vienna, Berlin, and (to a lesser extent) Paris.[1] These orientations are characterized by somewhat distinctive vocabularies: the sets of terms that enabled scholars to define their work in relation to that of their predecessors and contemporaries in other disciplines as well as in various areas of musical scholarship.

The musics of Africa and their transformations in the New World proved to be difficult subjects of inquiry for early ethnomusicologists

Table 1   Some Members of the First Two Generations of Ethnomusicologists, and Some of Their Precursors

	b. before 1825	b. 1826–45	b. 1846–65	First Generation b. 1866–85	Second Generation b. 1886–1905
ASIA					
Japan				H. Tanabe. b. 1883	Y. Machida. b. 1888
China				Cai Yuanpei. 1876–1940 Wang Kuowei. 1879–1927	Wang Guangqi. 1891–1936 Yang Yinliu. 1899–1984
Indonesia				Paku Buwana X. 1866–1939 Warsadiningrat. 1882–1975 Poerbatjaraka. 1884–1964	Purbodiningrat Sindoesawarno. d. ca. 1965
India, Pakistan, Bangladesh		S. M. Tagore. 1840–1914	V. N. Bhatkhande. 1860–1936		P. Sambhamoorthy. 1901–73 M. Mansooruddin. 1904–87
MIDDLE EAST AND CAUCASUS					
Iran				A. N. Vaziri. b. 1886	A. H. Saba. 1901–57
Azerbaijan				U. Hajibeyov. 1885–1948	
Armenia			N. Tigranyan. 1856–1951	Komitas. 1869–1935.	
Georgia				D. I. Arakishvili. 1873–1953	

Country				
Turkey			S. Ezgi. 1869–1962 R. Yekta Bey. 1878–1935 S. Arel. 1880–1955	M. Gazamihal. 1900–1961
Israel			S. Rosowsky. 1878–1962 A. Z. Idelsohn. 1882–1938	
Egypt			K. al-Khula'i. 1879–1938	M. al-Hifni. 1896–1973
EASTERN AND CENTRAL EUROPE				
Ukraine			F. Kolessa. 1871–1946 K. Kvitka. 1880–1950	M. Beregovskij. 1892–1961
Russia	V. F. Odoyevsky. 1804–69 A. Serov. 1820–71	P. P. Sokal'sky. 1832–87 I. Melgunov. 1846–93 E. Linyova. 1854–1919 A. D. Kastal'sky. 1856–1926 M. E. Pyatnitsky. 1864–1927	S. Kisselgof. ca. 1876–1939 V. A. Uspenskii. 1879–1949 B. Asaf'yev. 1884–1949	V. M. Belyayev. 1888–1968 A. V. Finagin. 1890–1942 Z. Eval'd. 1894–1942 V. S. Vinogradov. b. 1899 E. V. Gippius. 1903–85 F. Rubtsov. 1904–86
Romania	T. Burada. 1839–1923			C. Brăiloiu. 1893–1958 S. Drăgoi. 1894–1968
Hungary		B. Vikár. 1859–1945	J. Seprődi. 1874–1923 B. Bartók. 1881–1945	L. Lajtha. 1892–1963 B. Rajeczky. 1901–89

Table 1 continued

	b. before 1825	b. 1826–45	b. 1846–65	First Generation b. 1866–85	Second Generation b. 1886–1905
Austria, Germany		W. Tappert. 1830–1907	C. Stumpf. 1848–1936 H. Riemann. 1849–1919 R. Wallaschek. 1860–1917 J. Meier. 1864–1953	Z. Kodály. 1882–1967 R. Lach. 1874–1958 E. M. v. Hornbostel. 1877–1935 C. Sachs. 1881–1959	G. Kerenyi. b. 1902 R. Lachmann. 1892–1940 W. Danckert. 1900–1970 W. Graf. 1903–82 M. Schneider. 1903–82 W. Steinitz. 1905–67
Switzerland					J. Handschin. 1886–1955 K. Plicka. b. 1894 K. Vetterl. 1898–1979
Czechoslovakia	F. Sušil. 1804–68	F. Bartoš. 1837–1906	O. Hostinský. 1847–1910 L. Janáček. 1854–1928 L. Kuba. 1863–1956	O. Zich. 1879–1934	
Poland	O. Kolberg. 1814–98			A. Chybiński. 1880–1952 L. Kamieński. 1885–1964	
NORTHERN AND WESTERN EUROPE					
Latvia			A. Jurjans. 1856–1922	E. Melngailis. 1874–1954	
Finland				I. Krohn. 1867–1960	A. O. Väisänen. 1890–1969
Sweden				T. Norlind. 1879–1948	C. A. Moberg. 1896–1978 E. Emsheimer. 1904–89

Norway					O. Gurvin. 1893–1974
Denmark			A. Hammerich. 1848–1931	O. M. Sandvik. 1875–1948	
			T. Laub. 1852–1927	H. Thuren. 1873–1912	
				H. Grüner-Nielsen. 1881–1953	
Great Britain	A. J. Ellis. 1814–90	P. W. Joyce. 1827–1914	A. H. Fox-Strangways. 1859–1948	C. S. Myers. 1873–1946	A. M. Jones. b. 1889
	C. Engel. 1818–82	A. J. Hipkins 1826–1903	C. Sharp 1854–1924	H. G. Farmer. 1882–1965	
			G. Greig. 1856–1914	P. Grainger. 1882–1961	
			H. Balfour. 1863–1939	M. Karpeles. 1885–1967	
			A. Gilchrist. 1863–1954		
Netherlands		J. P. N. Land. 1834–97		J. S. Brandts-Buys. 1879–1939	J. Kunst. 1891–1960
Belgium		V. C. Mahillon. 1841–1924		E. Closson. 1870–1950	A. Bake. 1899–1963
					P. Collaer. b. 1891
France		L. Bourgault-Ducoudray. 1840–1910	J. Tiersot. 1857–1936	B. Carra de Vaux. 1867–?1953	A. Chotrin. b. 1891
			J. Combarieu. 1859–1916	R. d'Erlanger. 1872–1932	A. Schaeffner. 1895–1980
			J. Parisot. 1861–1923	P. Aubry. 1874–1910	
			M. Emmanuel. 1862–1938	L. Laloy. 1874–1944	
				M. Béclard-d'Harcourt. 1884–1964	

Table 1 continued

	b. before 1825	b. 1826–45	b. 1846–65	First Generation b. 1866–85	Second Generation b. 1886–1905
SOUTHERN EUROPE					
Portugal		T. Braga. 1843–1924	J. Leite de Vasconcellos. 1858–1941	P. Barreto. 1878–1921	
Spain			R. M. de Azkue. 1864–1951	F. Pujol. 1878–1945 N. Otaño. 1880–1956	E. M. Torner. 1888–1955 B. Gil García. 1898–1964
Italy		A. Galli. 1845–1919		F. B. Pratella. 1880–1955	A. Bonaccorsi. 1887–1971 O. Tiby. 1891–1955
Yugoslavia		F. Ž. Kuhač. 1834–1911			B. Širola. 1889–1956 V. Žganec. 1890–1969 L. S. Janković. 1894–1974 C. Rihtman. b. 1902 M. A. Vasiljević. 1903–63
Greece					S. Karas. b. 1905
Bulgaria				V. Stoin. 1880–1939	R. Katsarova. 1901–84 S. Dzhudzhev. b. 1902
AFRICA AND THE AMERICAS					
South Africa					P. R. Kirby. 1888–1970 H. Tracey. 1903–77
West Africa					E. Amu. b. 1899
Latin America				F. Ortiz. 1881–1969	M. de Andrade. 1893–1945 V. Mendoza. 1894–1964

Canada, USA				
A. C. Fletcher. 1838–1923	J. W. Fewkes. 1850–1930	F. Densmore. 1867–1957	C. Vega. 1898–1966	C. Seeger. 1886–1979
J. C. Fillmore. 1843–98	T. Baker. 1851–1934	J. A. Lomax. 1867–1948	A. Sás. 1900–1967	H. H. Roberts. 1888–1985
	B. I. Gilman. 1852–1933	N. Curtis Burlin. 1876–1921	A. Carpentier. 1904–80	R. W. Gordon. 1888–1961
	H. E. Krehbiel. 1854–1925	P. Barry. 1880–1937		M. J. Herskovits. 1895–1963
	F. LaFlesche. 1857–1932	C. M. Barbeau. 1883–1969		G. Herzog. 1901–83
	F. Boas. 1858–1941			M. Kolinski. 1901–81
				M. Metfessel. b. 1901
				J. Yasser. b. 1903

NOTE. The division of "generations" by twenty-year spans is a rather arbitrary device, adopted here in order to encourage comparison of the activities of "ethnomusicologists" born at roughly the same time in various parts of the world. I do not mean to suggest that all of the persons named thought of themselves as belonging to these particular "generations"; indeed, further studies of the intellectual history of ethnomusicology will require much more subtle groupings, allowing for ambiguities (e.g., divided loyalties) that I have deliberately suppressed. I have not included persons born in the eighteenth century; obviously, many more names could (and should) be added to this chart.

working in Europe, the United States, the Caribbean, and (beginning in the
1920s) Africa itself. This paper examines a few of the problems that arose
as European musical terminology was applied to African music, particularly in the writings of E. M. von Hornbostel. The principal terms considered are "musical system," "musical thinking," "motive," "melodic
motion" (*Melodiebewegung*), "attention" (*Aufmerksamkeit*), and "heterophony."

2

One consequence of the great diversity in the types of work carried
out by the first generations of ethnomusicologists and their precursors is a
bewildering lack of agreement in vocabularies and modes of discourse. It
is difficult for us to reconstruct the ways in which terms were understood
as synonymous, complementary, mutually exclusive, or implicating one
another in a given environment.

The term "musical system" (or *Musiksystem* in German, *système musical* in French, etc.) may serve as a case in point. In the first half of the twentieth century, it was often the central term used to discuss relations between "the natural" and "the artificial" or "the rationalized" in music
(see, for example, Weber 1921:25–50). For Robert Lach and a number of
other comparative musicologists, "musical system" was in effect synonymous with "tone system." Each system was a product of cultural history,
and comparative musicologists were charged with answering the question,
How has "the human spirit" formed so many different "tone systems"?

> How does a scale originate? How did the human spirit—in var-
> ious lands, various times, among various peoples and races—
> succeed in constructing its musical system, i.e., the sequence of
> individual scale degrees, according to various specific sche-
> mata, or "systems of tonal crystallization," so to speak, which
> differ so fundamentally from one another—as is evident from
> the various scales and tone systems? The solution of this
> problem—one of the most complex, indeed perhaps the central,
> fundamental problem of comparative musicology—is all the
> more complicated and difficult inasmuch as this question be-
> longs to psychology, ethnology, and sociology no less than to
> comparative musicology. (Lach 1924:8)

The question could be seen to challenge fundamental premises of Western
music theory, "slowly developed in the course of centuries" (Riemann
1916:vi). Disturbed by claims that "the same properties of the human ear

could serve as the foundation of very different musical systems" (Helmholtz 1877, tr. Ellis 1885:366), many scholars shared Hugo Riemann's belief that adequate description of most tone systems would show them to be special developments of the universal principles known to Western musicians and theorists.

"Musical thinking," as Riemann used the term, occurs as human beings form "tonal conceptions" (*Tonvorstellungen*) governed by general categories (1916:vi, 112). The dependence of "our musical thinking" upon harmonic *Tonvorstellungen* was acknowledged in several of Hornbostel's first contributions to comparative musicology (Abraham & Hornbostel 1903 and 1904b; Hornbostel 1905, all repr. in Hornbostel 1975)—but only to emphasize the considerable effort required to overcome this dependence and "to concentrate on purely melodic factors" (Hornbostel 1975:65–66, 192, 261). The "theory of pure melody" outlined in several of Hornbostel's papers was an attempt to identify general principles that affect not only the musical practices based on "nonharmonic tone systems" but also the less systematic practices.[2]

In Hornbostel's view, the organization of the earliest tone systems was determined by the physical properties of instruments and by "extramusical" considerations; in singing governed by the principles of pure melody, there was neither need nor occasion to establish systems of stable tones and intervals (1927c:447–49).[3] Whereas harmonic thinking involves selection and combination of tones and intervals, pure melody forms "an undivided unity which [the singer] performs at one stroke as an athlete does an exercise" (Hornbostel 1928b:35). "Human beings who sing melodies rather than combining tones or setting note against note" cannot ignore their motor impulses; the characteristic forms of body movement that distinguish one human group from another, as well as the impulses shared by all humans, enter into the act of singing. "Song, like speech, is sounding gesture, originally not detached from that of the limbs." A listener who does not respond physically, in one way or another, to the singer's motions "hears tones, but not the melody" (Hornbostel 1921:179–81).

Hornbostel's discussion of melody as "an act of motility" (1928b:49) extends from his early essay on Isadora Duncan and "melodic dance" (1904) to his survey of "African Negro Music" (1928b), his contributions to the *Handbuch der normalen und pathologischen Physiologie* (1926a, 1962b), and his reflections on the "inner relationship" of sound and meaning in language (1927b). He was interested in "the physiological connection between the acoustic impulse and the motor reaction"; our inclination "to lift head, arms, legs and thorax" in response to a rising melody is "a kind of reflex . . . [not] completely independent of the character of the stimulus." The fact that similar body movements have accompanied the same melodic motions in different times and places points to the existence of "a unitary acoustic-motor movement as the common root" (Hornbostel 1904, repr. 1975:213, 209; see also Hornbostel 1926a:707 and 1927b: 331, 335). The natural tendency of melody to move downward "from tension to rest," like breathing or striking, is "rooted in the psychophysical constitution of man" (Hornbostel 1928b:34).

The category "melodic motion" (*Melodiebewegung*) is superior or superordinate to both melody and rhythm, not only by virtue of this "physiological correlation," but also because it "dominates a much wider sphere than the purely musical." It is "older and more primordial than melody," encompassing the inflections of *Sprechgesang* and *Sprachmelodie* as well as movement articulated by "fixed differentiated tonal degrees" (1904, repr. 1975:210; 1905, repr. 1975:254). By directing our attention to specific moments in time, melodic motion functions as "one of the elements that determine rhythm" (1904, repr. 1975:210).

With these considerations in mind, Hornbostel argued that the question "How does a scale originate?" was best approached through analysis of the articulation (*Gliederung*) of melodic shapes (*Melodiegestalten*):

> The initial and terminal positions of motives and strophes, the boundaries of the range, the points where melodic direction reverses itself, the centers of gravity of the movement—all these points provide "anchors" for the *Melos,* and it is in their interrelationships (the totality of which determines tonal unity or "tonality") that we must seek the primary form of scales. (Hornbostel 1913a:23)
>
> If the descending direction of the melodic motion be taken into account as well, scansion [*Gliederung*] of the periods into their natural components, the motives, allows us to recognize which tones and tone-relations are decisive for the structure. (Hornbostel 1917:411)

Hornbostel (1913a:13) judged Rameau's well-known claim that "melody is born of harmony" to be accurate with reference to musical thinking in the modern harmonic system, but the opposite of the truth with respect to the evolution of music. The argument was restated by his student Marius Schneider: the melodic motive precedes and determines the tone system

(Schneider 1956:203–4). The "melodic motive" in this sense would seem to involve instinctive or habitual behavior rather than "musical thinking" or "composition," which presuppose a "system" or "language" of tones.[4]

The early "ethnomusicologists" and their precursors joined a series of debates and conversations that had been in progress for well over a century, and we can best understand their vocabulary with reference to the history of these conversations. One of the more common ways of distinguishing either "folk" or "primitive" music was by the apparent absence of relatively developed and autonomous "systems" and "languages." Those students of peasant music who denied the capacity of peasants to think musically had little need for the concept of "folk musical system": Béla Bartók, for example, described the styles—not the systems—that allowed for "spontaneous gratification of the musical instinct or impulse" among the Hungarian peasantry (Bartók 1933:268; repr. 1976:81). Similarly, descriptions of a "low level of musical culture" tended to emphasize the "narrow range of consciousness" (Hornbostel 1928b:38) that had prevented a human group from organizing and utilizing a set of musical resources. The terms "style" and "dialect" did not necessarily imply the same level of organization as did "system" and "language." Terms for categories that could be more narrowly defined—such as "genre," "type," and "schema"—proved useful to many scholars, whether they were concerned with natural, "instinctive" music (Bartók) or with the "science and art" of village musicians (Dzhudzhev 1931:3).

In terminology, methods of analysis, and underlying assumptions, comparative musicology and musical folklore were two areas of inquiry that continued the long-standing European investigation of four interrelated topics: theoretical and practical, natural and artificial music. Discussion of these topics in the late eighteenth century was particularly fruitful in defining some of the issues subsequently addressed by comparative musicologists, musical folklorists, and musical ethnographers. Jean-Jacques Rousseau distinguished two types of musical system, one emphasizing artifice and theory, the other nature and practice. The set of complementary terms used in Rousseau's discussion of this topic includes, among others, "harmonic system," "melodic systems," "melodic inflections," "familiar accents," "signs" or "expressions" of feeling, "language of feeling," and "national music." Rousseau was concerned with the difference between a system that can be analyzed into its component elements (with rules for their combination) and a system of significant melodic inflections, each of them necessarily apprehended and reproduced as a whole.[5] Melodic systems of the latter type are of primary importance in human communication and emotional expression, according to Rousseau and to those who subsequently spoke in similar terms of plainchant, "national musics," and "folk song" (see Blum 1985). Hornbostel's "theory of pure melody" reworked some of the propositions that were advanced in these discussions, holding to the assumption that some modes of perception are more natural and hence more general than others.

In Russian and Soviet musical ethnography, the vocabulary used by Rousseau and his successors (among them Villoteau, Choron, d'Ortigue, and Fétis) seems to have been an important source of a set of terms that includes the Russian and/or Ukrainian equivalents of "musical language" (Yavorsky 1908), "Russian people's musical system" (Kastal'sky 1923), "intonation" and "intonational system" (Asaf'yev 1930, Gippius 1936), "professional folk singers and instrumentalists" (Kvitka 1924), "musical culture" (Uspensky & Belyayev 1928), "folk art," and "national musical art." On the whole, these terms do not correspond to the major concerns of the cultural anthropologists and folklorists in the United States who were interested in music (see below, section 4).

Russian and Soviet musical ethnography, as well as "musical folklore" and programs for national musical research in many parts of Europe, was characterized by creative tension between concepts of "music in general" and concepts of specific "musical dialects," "musical cultures," and "national musics." By its very nature, the "comparative musicology" cultivated in Berlin and Paris, the centers of powerful colonial empires, as well as in Vienna, placed greater emphasis on "music in general."

3

The creation of an approach to the musics of Africa and Oceania assumed a compelling importance to members of the first two generations of comparative musicologists. Part of the impetus to this project may have come from the extraordinary impact of the African and Oceanic art exhibited at the Musée d'Ethnographie du Trocadéro (from 1882) and the Museum für Völkerkunde (from 1886). In the early twentieth century, musicologists could scarcely have hoped to match the achievements of the first French and German students of African art (see Paudrat 1984), given the difference between the paucity of available recordings and the enormous number of African objects in the museums (nearly 10,000 in the Museum für Völkerkunde alone when it opened in 1886). Sound-producing instruments in the collections, together with references to instruments in the ethnographic literature, formed a sizable body of material, which could be studied by the historical and diffusionist methods of Bernhard Ankermann and Fritz Graebner, both of whom worked at the Museum für Völkerkunde. There were also specifically musical reasons for the involvement of Hornbostel and, later, of André Schaeffner with African subjects.

The appeal of African music to Hornbostel was intimately connected with his interest in *Melodiebewegung*. His first study of recordings from sub-Saharan Africa departed from the format of his earlier monographs (e.g., those on Japan, India, the Thompson River Indians, Tunisia), each of which includes a section on *"Tonsystem"* or *"Tonleitern."* Apart from comparing the equiheptatonic tunings of four Burmese and two African xylophones (1911a), Hornbostel did not take up the subject of African tone systems. His analysis of Nyamwezi songs recorded by Weule, Seyfried, and Paasche (1909a) is summarized under the headings "Melos," "Harmonie," "Rhythmus, Aufbau, Tempo," and "Vortragsweise." Similar headings are used in the analysis of one Sukuma song (1910a) and in the monographs on Tessmann's Fang collection (1913b) and on Czekanowski's recordings from Ruanda (1917):

1913b	1917
Melos	Melos
Mehrstimmigkeit	Polyphonie
Rhythmus	Rhythmus
Form	

The discussion of *Melos* in the Nyamwezi songs begins with the assertion that "primitive singers . . . do not retain in the memory a tone system established once and for all"; hence, "they can vary the intonation of intervals within the widest limits according to mood and expressive needs" (1909a:1033). The analyst must first identify the "motives" that the singer "grasps and perceives as unified, undivided wholes." Analysis of the articulation of the melody will reveal functional differences between principal and secondary tones, and the analyst may construct scales as "convenient descriptions" of the melodic tonality—"the totality of (melodic) interval-relations of the principal tones to one another and to the melodically less significant secondary tones" (1909a:1035).[6]

Hornbostel stressed the point that an analyst's decisions concerning scales and articulation of form do not "allow us to draw reliable conclusions concerning the singer's own conception" (1909a:1042). He realized that comparative musicologists would eventually concern themselves with aesthetic judgements expressed in many non-European languages, but few such statements were available to the members of his circle. Among the

rare exceptions were some remarks in Swahili, given by Mwakinyo Makin-
yaga to the Berlin Seminar for Oriental Languages:

> . . . na tena kama wanaimba sauti nnene ao nyembamba, watu
> wanapendezwa zayidi kwimba kwao. Lakini tu kama watu
> watatu wane wanapocheza katikati, watu hawaipendezwa ile
> ngoma.
> . . . and if they then sing with varying degrees of tonal intensity,
> people take even more pleasure in their song. Should only three
> or four persons dance in the middle, people will take less pleasure
> in such a dance. (1909a:1048; tr. made from Hornbostel's Ger-
> man)

A remark in Hornbostel's essay on bird song suggests another criterion by
which to identify what "matters" (worauf es "ankommt") to musicians:
the "direction" (Richtung) adopted in a series of choices.[7]

> If the variation is not altogether random but must follow in a
> definite direction, then clearly the teacher must not merely ex-
> periment playfully but pick and choose from among the sounds
> that he himself produces (in play) or hears from others; or else
> the pupils must choose. If anything, the direction of variation
> must thus indicate what "matters" to the bird himself in his
> songs. Certain birds seem in fact to "improve" their "song" . . .
> (Hornbostel 1911b:125; repr. 1986:99)

In order to interpret the vocabularies and statements of informants, and
to perceive the directions followed in a series of choices, musicologists
needed to develop an exhaustive inventory of the respects in which human
beings are capable of distinguishing one sound from other sounds. Hornbostel addressed this point in his earliest papers, and he tried repeatedly to
list some of the qualities that might "mark" a sound and distinguish it
from what some linguists now call "unmarked" sounds (see Waugh
1982):

> Music arouses attention [Aufmerksamkeit] by various means.
> It attracts attention by a very strong, very high, very low tone,
> by constancy and shifting of tone quality. At present the ulti-
> mate reasons are unfathomable. Besides the aforementioned,
> secondary sense criteria also play a role in attracting attention,
> especially in the reproduction of images [Vorstellungen]. If we
> hear the sounds a b c d, we reproduce previous impressions
> connected with the continued alphabet, so if we expect any-

thing, we expect the continuation of the alphabet; likewise in music. (Abraham & Hornbostel 1903, repr. w. Eng. tr. by Kurath in Hornbostel 1975:64)

Any quality that differentiates one tone from another, including pitch, tone quality, etc., may capture attention and endow the respective pitch with an (subjective) accent (psychological accent). These diverse possibilities of accentuation can be effective in many different degrees, depending on how we are accustomed to regard this or that element of an overall experience. (Hornbostel 1905, repr. w. Eng. tr. by Campbell 1975: 265)

Accents of whatever type "can be substituted for one another, can be combined for support, or, in competition with each other, can be mutually weakened" (Abraham & Hornbostel 1904a, repr. in Hornbostel 1975: 172–73). In a survey of "Psychology of the Phenomena of Hearing," Hornbostel eventually named sixteen qualities or attributes of sounds (table 2).

Table 2   Terms Recommended by Hornbostel for Attributes of Sounds (1926a:730)

Distinctions of *more* or *less*, which appear to allow for quantitative scaling	Distinguished as *either* one quality *or* another	
Helligkeit	Schallfarbe	
Höhe	Tonigkeit	
Größe	Vokalität	
Gewicht		
Dichte		
Lautheit		
Distanz (Schrittweite)	Intervallfarbe	qualities of successive forms
Klangbreite	Akkordfarbe	qualities of simultaneous forms

Total quality of the phenomenon:
Schallcharakter
Intervallcharakter
Akkordcharakter

With more data than were available to Hornbostel, this roster of attributes might have been used to describe systems of marked and unmarked sounds, and also the claims that musicians exert on one another's "attention" by working and playing with such systems. However, several obstacles to the study of "attention" arose from the musical terminology of Hornbostel's time and place. *Heterophony*—as used by Stumpf (1901), Adler (1908), Hornbostel (1909b:302; 1913b:354−66; 1928b:46−47, 49−50, 55), and many others—designated something that supposedly results when musicians have not yet learned to direct their attention toward the potential complementarity (or "harmony" in the older sense) of their sounds.

According to Adler, the definitive type of heterophony is "a polyphony without rules, with cohesion left largely to chance" (1908:21; tr. 1985:628). The ancestry of Adler's concept is made clear by his choice of the word "chance" (*Zufall*): the attempts of German theorists from the fifteenth to the seventeenth centuries to distinguish *sortisatio* from *compositio* (Gurlitt 1942, Ferand 1951). Defined as multipart music in which cohesion is "left largely to chance," heterophony was made to represent one stage or level in the evolution of music: "The original impulse and tendency to play heterophonic music constitutes the basic and leading cause of the origin and development of polyphony" (Adler 1908:27; tr. 1985: 631).

Hornbostel's seminal paper on *Mehrstimmigkeit* in non-European music explicitly rejected all such claims that heterophony has been "the sole" or even "the most important point of transition in the development of polyphony" (1909b:302). Rather than following Adler in making heterophony "the third category of style besides homophony and polyphony" (Adler 1908:27; tr. 1985:631), Hornbostel delineated several possibilities involving attention to simultaneous sonorities that strengthen a melody ("harmony"), or attention to two or more concurrent and more or less differentiated melodies ("polyphony"). The basic categories of the latter were drone and ostinato, each with several subspecies: drones that are rhythmicized, or are ornamented, or alternate between two tones, or shift from one tone to another in parallel with the melody. Certain types are "transitions" between drone and ostinato; similarly, an ostinato sung by a group as "a simplified variant" of the leader's part is a "transition" between responsorial song and heterophony (Hornbostel 1909b:299−302). Hornbostel depicted Africa as a kind of museum or laboratory in which these and other "transitions" might be observed and studied (1909b:301; 1917:412). His typology served as the point of departure for Marius Schneider's writings on African polyphony (1934) and on musical forms produced by leaders and groups in Africa (1937).

In describing African varieties of "heterophony" in which parts "go their own separate ways" (1928b:55) and instrumental ostinati are neither "complementary" nor "parallel" to the vocal part (1928b:47), Hornbostel retained something of Adler's conception that "cohesion [is] left largely to chance" in heterophonic music. Despite his interest in Gestalt psychology, he considered very few possibilities for collective creation and reproduction of musical Gestalts. Hornbostel worked under the crippling assumption that "rhythm and harmony (as far as it exists) in non-European music show characteristics which are the natural outcome of pure melody" (1928b:38). One such "natural outcome" was the desire to reinforce certain points of a melody with "greater fullness of sound" (Hornbostel 1975:51, 263; 1909a:1039, 1041; 1928b:41). Other "natural" developments of multipart music originated in overlapping exchanges between soloist and chorus (1913b:354–55; 1917:403–6). "Rhythmic heterophony" (1928b:55) may arise once clapping or drumming accompanies group singing, and the group repeats the soloist's motive with a different relation to the clapping pattern. According to Hornbostel's interpretation of one such case (musical example 1, from 1917:no. 17 and 1928b:46), the solo, the chorus, and the handclapping present three "metrically related" motives, each of them equivalent to ten eighth notes but beginning at different points in what amounts to a time-cycle of twenty eighth notes. However, no "metrical relationship" between the three so-called motives is apparent to the present writer.

Hornbostel's view of musical evolution justified a concern with linear sequences of sounds ("motives") rather than with the complementarity of interlocking parts. He tended to assume that combination of the "motives" performed by each participant in an ensemble yields accidental, unintended results. In this respect, Hornbostel's approach to musical analysis failed to incorporate the insights gained through his inquiries concerning "spatial hearing" (1926b) and the variable qualities of grounds as well as

EXAMPLE 1. Transcription and analysis of a Hutu women's song (adapted from Hornbostel 1917:409).

of the figures that stand out against grounds (1926a:702–8). His account of drone and ostinato in multipart music (1909b, 1913b, 1917) remained dependent on a conception of "motive." Several decades later José Maceda outlined typical relations of "melody" and "drone" in Southeast Asian music by considering relations of figure and ground rather than "motivic" ideas.[8] Experience of "sound masses" moving between background and foreground also became a central issue in the music of Edgar Varèse, who discussed his own work in strikingly original language (table 3). Hornbostel may not have realized the extent to which comparative musicology would require criticism and revision of the vocabulary used in musical analysis.

Another requirement was criticism and comparison of the stories told about musical evolution. One such story is implicit in Hornbostel's frequently quoted comparison of European and African musicians: "We proceed from hearing, they from motion" (1928b:53). In this view the primordial unity between impulses to motion and the sounds that result (Hornbostel 1927b:331) had in large measure vanished from the experience of Europeans, as aural and tactile perception had become separate domains. Hornbostel described "African drumming" in terms similar to those he had used for "melodic motion" ("leading notes" and "predominant notes"): "Each single beating movement is again twofold: the muscles are strained and released, the hand is lifted and dropped. Only the second phase is stressed acoustically; but the first inaudible one has the motor accent, as it were, which consists in the straining of the muscles" (1928b:53). This interpretation has been often criticized (e.g., Blacking 1955), and it is doubtful that close analysis of the sets of moves employed by drummers would show a regular alternation between "motor accent" and "acoustic stress."

Few subjects are more important in ethnomusicological analysis than the concerns of musicians who play complementary, interlocking parts within rich and complex textures. Students of many practices have found it necessary to criticize common implications of such terms as "motive," "theme," "heterophony," arsis, and thesis. The Indonesian musician and scholar Sumarsam has questioned the use of the terms cantus firmus and "nuclear theme" in the analytic method that Jaap Kunst and his student Mantle Hood applied to Javenese gamelan music (Sumarsam 1975, 1981). Arguing that "the interrelationships among the instruments as one searches for the 'true' melodic motion of composition" is "the most important concept of gamelan music" (1981:57), Sumarsam has also examined

Table 3   The Language of Varèse's Lectures (1917, 1939, 1959, 1962; Excerpts in *PNM* 5 (1) (1966)

Verbs & Processes	⟶ Results	Substantives	Verbs & Processes	Results
"corporealization of the intelligence that is in sound"	⟶ music			
"simultaneous interplay of unrelated elements that intervene at calculated intervals"	⟶ rhythm			
"interaction of attractive and repulsive forces"	form			
emission of sound in many parts of hall	⟶ sound projection			
acoustical arrangements: delimitation by various timbres, different intensities	⟶	Zones of Intensities ("different colors & different magnitudes in different perspectives")	pass over layers penetrate opacities are dilated in rarefactions	
			move, collide ⟶	penetration or repulsion
'oxygenation of chords	⟶	masses		
		planes, layers	shift; transmutations occur, and are projected onto other planes	
			collision, projection ⟶	beams of sound

⟶ = yields, generates

the circumstances of interaction among Dutch and Javanese intellectuals in which the modern Javanese term *balungan* was invented (Sumarsam 1988, 1989). His work provides an excellent model for African musicologists.

4

With the exception of his distinction between "what [the Negro] sings" and "the way he sings" (Hornbostel 1926c:752; 1927a:511), the ideas expressed in Hornbostel's writings on African music are rather far removed from those that were debated with such heat in the United States in the arguments concerning the relation of black music in the United States to African resources, techniques, and values. U.S. intellectual life in the first third of this century was not conducive to scholarly assessment of similarities, differences, and interchange among the musical idioms, systems, and cultures of American Indians, African-Americans, and Euro-Americans.[9] One of the most influential programs for national musical research, that of Oscar Sonneck, reflected firm convictions that "the rural population is and always has been a negligible quantity, in Europe as well as in America" and that both "the Indian's musical system" and the songs of American Negroes were "ethnomusically too different from our inherited European system" to permit meaningful interchange in musical life and musical scholarship (Sonneck 1916:135, 140–41). Discourse along these lines continued for many years to ignore the work of cultural anthropologists and folklorists, as well as the writings on music produced by African-Americans.

Sonneck's reference to "the Indian's musical system" is one of the few instances when American writers on music made brief comparative remarks about "musical systems." The cultural anthropology of Franz Boas and his students, George Herzog among them, placed greater emphasis on *style*, guided by Boas's "principle that context is always part of the human phenomena" (Kroeber 1959:vi). A noteworthy exception is Herzog's study of one West African "system of communication": drum-signaling among the Jabo of eastern Liberia (Herzog 1945). Herzog followed Boas in rejecting the assumption that a "tribal style" must be "an integrated accumulation of songs endowed with the same features." To Herzog, the most evident distinctions were those, not of "tribal styles," but of "different categories of songs in use at the same locality." He predicted that, after more intensive collecting and study, "we shall probably find at least a hundred distinct musical styles on the [African] continent" (Herzog 1934: 412–13).[10]

With respect to the music of black Americans, Herzog found it "possible that African practices still survive in its vocal technic, although little if any of its form, rhythm, and melody can be shown to be of African origin" (1936:52). He approached this question more as a folklorist than as a cultural anthropologist. He seems not to have shared Hornbostel's understanding of the potential importance of the conceptions articulated by performers in their own words (Tedlock 1980). His steadfast effort on behalf of the "scientific" study of primitive and folk music in the United States left him little choice but to dismiss writings that reflected "sentimental" or "purely esthetic" interests and that seemed "biased emotionally" (Herzog 1936:56). Herzog was comfortable with Hornbostel's assertion "that the Negro Spirituals are European songs made and sung by Negroes in America" (Herzog 1935:397; 1936:57; cf. Hornbostel 1926c:751).

Herzog's treatment of this topic had little to offer to African-Americans interested in the past, present, and future of their African cultural heritage. African-American writers of Hornbostel's generation—for example, W. E. B. Du Bois, the Work brothers, the Johnson brothers—were obliged to define their positions against stereotyped conceptions of the capacities of blacks to handle form, harmony, and melody as well as rhythm.[11] Some African-Americans of Herzog's generation—Paul Robeson, for example—explicitly attacked what they saw as excessively intellectualized white interpretations of black emotional experience. The son of a preacher who escaped from slavery at the age of fifteen, Robeson declared that his own studies of West African languages at the University of London had enabled him to understand the "kinship of rhythm and intonation" in African cultural expression on both sides of the Atlantic, as he had experienced it (Robeson 1934). In the mid-1930s, tools that would have allowed scholars to develop, modify, and refine this perception were scarcely available, except perhaps in the Russian-language literature on "intonation."

One of the greatest of the many benefits made available by Melville Herskovits's theory of acculturation was the possibility, at long last, for white scholars to think about the desires and strategies of blacks. As developed by Herskovits and Waterman, the theory of acculturation and syncretism "allows for the conception of a black point of view from which history can be written" (Westcott 1977:129).[12] This achievement lay well beyond the capacities of musical folklore, comparative musicology, and music theory, as cultivated in the United States. The least successful parts of the writings by students and collaborators of Herskovits—Kolinski, Merriam, Waterman—are those that claim an indebtedness to Hornbostel's analytic method, while paying no attention at all to his own concern with "melodic motion" and with attributes of sounds.

5

Although Hornbostel's pioneering studies of African music were not effectively utilized in research on African-American practices, his work as a whole remains an impressive attempt to address some of the problems that have also faced subsequent scholars interested in African music and its New World transformations. One of these problems involves the distinctive attributes of sounds and the creation of "accented" or "marked" sounds. A second is the extent to which one or another idea of "system" is pertinent to the analysis of African and African-American musical practices. A third area of inquiry is the names given by Africans and African-Americans to musical resources, to musicians, and to results of musical action. Scholars have learned to recognize groups or sets of names for resources, actors, and actions (as well as the names given to ensembles and other aggregates).

Implicit in Hornbostel's discussion of attributes of sounds is the possibility that a sequence of vowel timbres may or may not run parallel to the progression of fundamental pitches in a vocal line (Hornbostel 1926a: 709–11). The first study of this topic to use recordings of an African singer is Rouget's analysis of Malinké singing, in comparison to that of the Selk-'Nam (Tierra del Fuego). In his Selk'Nam example, Rouget found that a descending sequence of pitches was reinforced by a sequence of vowels—e, ε, ə—in which the second formant of each vowel is progressively lower; this was not the case in the Malinké example (Rouget 1970). The significance of this variable in the music of some West African vocal ensembles is apparent in Cynthia Schmidt's transcriptions of the Kpelle genre *gbonaŋ*: in one recorded performance (Schmidt 1984: ex. 3, pp. 200–202), the "small [high] voice" sings only the syllables "we ee" as the slightly lower "middle voice" sings "wo oo"; at a later point in the same performance, the middle voice distinguishes its higher and lower pitches with the vowels "ee" and "oo" respectively, as the small voice continues to sing "ee" (Schmidt, ex. 5, p. 205). The harmonic resources of the genre *gbonaŋ* would appear to include several possible associations of specific pitches with the brighter vowel "ee" and/or the darker vowel "oo."

Ruth Stone's analysis of Kpelle musical terminology shows the importance to performers of qualitative differences involving, among others, the features that Hornbostel termed *Gewicht* (light vs. heavy) and *Dichte* (compact vs. diffuse)—for example, *ñóo toôi* ("voice coming out") vs. *ñóo kulâi* ("voice standing/fuzzy") (Stone 1982:77). It seems likely in such cases that performers' conceptions of possible "harmonic relations" among sounds with opposing qualities include assessments of the variable potential of sounds to "move," a potential that is limited by their "weight" and "thickness."

In the first half of the twentieth century, European musical terminology made it easy for scholars to succumb to "the Western fantasy about African rhythm" (Wachsmann 1969:187). "Harmonics" and "rhythmics" were two different areas of theoretical concern with "systems." Myths about the evolution of "harmonic thinking" were so important in the historical self-awareness of European musicians that Africans were presumed to be "incapable" of forming or using musical systems, unless (1) these were "merely" rhythmic systems and/or (2) the tonal systems were universal and not specifically African.

Percival Kirby's work in the late 1920s and early 1930s made a case for "The Recognition and Practical Use of the Harmonics of Stretched Strings by the Bantu of Southern Africa" (Kirby 1932). This marked an advance over Hornbostel's notion that "with its short and hollow tones [the musical bow] is utterly unsuited to directing the attention (*Aufmerksamkeit*) toward the impulses (*Reize*) of consonant simultaneous sounds" (1909a:1041). Obviously, the quality of the cylinders from which Hornbostel worked was largely responsible for this erroneous conclusion. Kirby attempted to synthesize his direct observations of several instruments by listing "the principles of part progression . . . [in] Bantu instrumental practice" and by claiming that these were "completely dependent upon physical laws" (1932:46). Bantu "harmonic systems" (Kirby 1932:31) could thus be seen in Ramellian terms, rather than in terms of a universal Pythagorean "tonality" (Schneider 1934:26–27; 1966a:511). Neither interpretation encouraged analysis of "accents of different loudness and pitch, changes of timbre and sequences of pitches (that is, melody) apart from accent" (Wachsmann 1970:137).[13]

Not until the 1960s did scholarly analyses of African multipart music come to grips with such topics as "simultaneous occurrences of otherwise unrelated sounds made purposely to heighten dramatic tension, to animate a performance, to add to the texture of a piece of music or to provide signals" (Nketia 1967:88). It may prove useful to extend the European concept of "harmonic relations" to whatever sounds "occur simultaneously" in order to "heighten tension," "animate a performance," "add to the texture," or "provide signals." We need not limit the notions of "harmony" and "system" to relations between higher and lower pitches.

It was in the latter sense, of course, that some of the earliest European accounts of African music making spoke of harmony and of concertizing. On Saturday, December 2, 1497, the members of Vasco da Gama's crew were favorably impressed as a crowd of about two hundred South Africans "danced in the manner of Negroes" to the music of a stopped-flute ensemble. Although the chronicler of the voyage noted that "music is not expected of Negroes," he nonetheless used the verb *concertar* to describe the cooperative action of the four or five flutists—some blowing high notes, others low—and the sentence may be one of the earliest examples in Portuguese or Spanish where the verb *concertar* designates the actions of members of an instrumental ensemble (see Spitzer 1963:108–16): "E êles começaram logo de tanger quatro ou cinco flautas, e uns tangiam alto e outro baixo, em maniera que concertavam muito bem para negros de que se não espera música; e bailavam come negros" (Álvaro Velho 1497–99, ed. da Costa 1960:11). It was not uncommon for sixteenth-century travelers to find the sounds of African ensembles "agreeing and according well"; thus, the concept of *musica artificialis,* implying control of harmonic relations on the part of musicians, could be extended to Africa ("Flutes and Pipes, which they sound very artificially," quoted in Stevenson 1968:479, 481).

The motions of performers (whether soloists or members of ensembles) can also "agree and accord well," so much so that the resulting sounds need not always occupy the foreground of a performer's attention (Blacking 1961, Kauffman 1969). Increased understanding of the "systems" or repertoires of moves available to the player of a specific instrument or to each member of a given ensemble enables us to revise Hornbostel's claim that "we proceed from hearing, they from motion"—setting aside his assumptions about "human evolution" and allowing for several types of reciprocity between auditory and tactile sensations.

There can be little doubt that "system" will remain a useful term for describing various sets of moves and of musical resources that are familiar to African performers (e.g., Berliner 1978:57 and Kubik 1979:227). Since the mid-1950s, writings on African music in European languages have examined many types of systematic distinctions that are fundamental to specific musical practices. Major achievements include Joseph Kyagambiddwa's accounts of *okusulika,* a Ganda method of transposition, and of *okukoonera,* a melody that is "methodically constructed" by one xylophonist from two elements in the parts of two other xylophonists (Kyagambiddwa 1956:107, 117). The first of these topics was treated at greater length by Anderson (1968) and the second by Kubik (1960), as one phenomenon within the large class of "inherent" or "resultant" patterns (see also Nketia 1962:51; Jones 1954:35). The importance of Gestalt psychology to ethnomusicological analysis—announced but never demonstrated in Hornbostel's work—is fully realized in the studies of "resultant patterns" (see further Kubik 1979: 223–26, 231–38).

The systematic concern of many African musicians with "resultant patterns" forms one large group of answers to the question, Which of the available possibilities are pertinent in this situation? It is reasonable to assume that many other systematic concerns remain to be identified. The long history of European debate about musical systems has shown that no single model of how musical practices are systematic will prove applicable to all situations. "Musical practice" is a larger concept than "musical system," encompassing as it does many types and degrees of systematization, and many attitudes toward the use of systems. It may be true, in specific cases, that the "rhythmic system" of "a traditional [African] society . . . constitutes, in fact, a closed corpus of polyrhythmic formulas . . ." (Arom 1984:51). It is unwise, however, to assume that any system is necessarily "a closed corpus." Analysis of systems entails analysis of their component subsystems (Arom 1985:879), and we have no reason to assume that performers are incapable of coping simultaneously with the demands of several sets of overlapping constraints.

The early comparative musicologists erred in seeking to explain musical systems in terms of a small number of "musical" and "extramusical" principles. "Absolute pitch" is not necessarily an "extramusical factor," as Hornbostel assumed (see note 3). We have learned that "many tone systems, in fact, are determined by a combination of formative factors resulting from more than one dimension of human experience" (Kubik 1985:45). The point applies to more than just "tone systems," and we should avoid a priori judgments of the "extramusical" as opposed to the "musical" dimensions.[14]

Notes

1. In France, the term *musicologie comparée* has not been as important as *ethnologie musicale*. The latter was the name given to the department of the Musée d'Ethnographie du Trocadéro founded in 1929 by André Schaeffner. In a discussion of the two terms, Schaeffner notes repeatedly that the German comparative musicologists "were inclined to limit the field of comparison" (1956:25).

2. Hornbostel referred more than once to instrumental tunings concerning which "one can hardly speak of a 'system' " (1927c:447). His concept of "nonharmonic systems" was indebted to Alexander Ellis's important paper on "nonharmonic musical scales" (Ellis 1884). The opposition between principles of "distance" and "consonance"—one of the major themes developed by Stumpf and Hornbostel—corresponds to the distinction between "nonharmonic" and "harmonic" systems.

3. In Hornbostel's thought the "principle of distance" is called upon to explain the "oldest" forms of singing and some of the "oldest" instrumental tone systems. Sensations of "distance," like those of "brightness" (*Helligkeit*), involved more sensory domains than the purely auditory; Hornbostel believed that human capacities to perceive pitch-class identity (*Tonigkeit*) and interval-color had developed much more recently (1927c:428). He repeatedly emphasized the importance of "extramusical factors" (such as "absolute pitch" and its cosmological meanings) in the formation of instrumental tone systems (1911a, 1927c, 1928a, 1929). Ultimately, attempts to satisfy the "increasing demands of the ear" for consonant sonorities (1927c:449) proved more decisive for the history of tone systems than did attempts to impose upon the ear the results of cosmological and mathematical speculation (Abraham & Hornbostel 1904b; repr. in Hornbostel 1975:188). Hornbostel acknowledged that in some cases "musical requirements" and extramusical factors had been jointly responsible for determining a tone system (1928a:303–4).

4. According to Schneider, a general "sense of tonality" (*Tonalitätsempfinden*) was the basis on which various peoples had selected melodies with specific structural and dynamic characteristics (1934:26; 1966a:511, 513). Certain structures were more likely than others to restrain the impulses of melodic motion, thus favoring the development of fixed tone systems (Schneider 1966b:549).

5. On the basis of this distinction, Rousseau argued that the modern harmonic system depends on and reinforces an "analytic" or "scientific" way of thinking, which he termed *l'esprit de système*. The modern harmonic system departs from the human norm of "melodic systems" (Blum 1985:351–52) in which the concept of "system" is not carried to extremes, since meaningful melodic shapes are understood without musicians or listeners enumerating their component elements. The larger context in which such arguments have been developed is one of the subjects treated in depth by Gadamer (1972).

6. In his Ruanda monograph of 1917 and in subsequent works, Hornbostel notated scales to descend from the highest to the lowest tone, following "the natural motion of melody." Melodic "tonality," in his usage, is the analyst's conception of "the totality of (melodic) interval relations" (1902a: 1035) heard in one or more specific performances. As a property of the whole, tonality is "established by the function and the mutual relations of the notes" (Hornbostel 1928b:36). For Schneider, in contrast, "tonality" was a far more general concept, underlying the various specialized developments of modes and tone systems (see note 4).

7. Hornbostel also spoke of "direction of variation" in an essay on "U.S.A. National Music": inasmuch as American singers would alter European folk song "in (at least approximately) the same direction," the result would be an "American folk music" (1910b:66).

8. Although Maceda does not discuss Southeast Asian terms for "melody" and "drone" or "figure" and "ground," Mora (1987) has carefully investigated the related concepts *utom* and *tang* among the T'boli people of the Philippines.

9. Stevenson (1970:2–6) contrasts the substantial attention given by Latin American music historians to American Indian music with the lack of any such attention in the histories of music in the United States published between 1839 and 1966.

10. In the mid-1930s Melville Herskovits also observed that, in Africa, "there are as many musical idioms as there are dialects, and more, for each culture has various forms of song" (1935, repr. 1966:169). Only a few years earlier, Hornbostel had described the task facing scholars of African music as the "natural process of differentiating a unity." In this view, generalizations based on a small amount of data would be modified, after further research, "to establish musical dictions and, later on, dialects" (Hornbostel 1928b:39). With the great advances in African musicology that began in the 1950s, questions of "differentiating a unity" have been replaced by hypotheses about the historical processes through which Africans may have varied a number of widely shared principles (see Nketia 1986).

11. Countless European and North American writers on music relied on a narrow conception of rhythm, melody, and harmony as separable areas of "musical talent," with disastrous results: "the [American] Negro is not natively melodic, in the bigger sense. His melodies are largely the evolution of tunes he has absorbed from his white surroundings. His musical instinct is rhythmic first of all" (Grainger 1924:593).

12. Westcott illustrates this point by showing how musical choices made by blues pianists indicate different degrees of interest in specific resources, techniques, and values that were available to them. There are thus several "black points of view," some of them articulated in music that might "cause Whites to syncretize their values with [those of the black musicians], and not the other way around" (Westcott 1977:129). For all of its failings, the theory of acculturation and syncretism helped American scholars to begin examining musical exchange, without confining the discussion to foolish controversies over "borrowing" and "influence."

13. In his approach to the study of African music, Wachsmann consistently bore in mind the points raised in Hornbostel's discussion of *Aufmerksamkeit* and "psychological accent." He pointed out that improvements in recording technology do not inevitably dispel the misconceptions that prevent researchers from recognizing significant differences among sounds. In Wachsmann's view (1969:1876; 1970: 138), the consequences of "the Western fantasy about African rhythm" include numerous recordings that fail to capture details of timbre and pitch that make a difference to African musicians.

14. The author gratefully acknowledges the helpful criticism of this paper by Kay Kaufman Shelemay and other participants in the Urbana conference, and by Sue Carole DeVale and other faculty and students at the University of California, Los Angeles. He is also indebted to V. Kofi Agawu and Jamie Croy Kassler for penetrating comments on the penultimate version of the typescript. Portions of the paper are drawn from a book in progress, *Ideas of Tonality*, undertaken with sup-

port provided by the National Endowment for the Humanities through The New-
berry Library, Chicago.

Works Cited

Abraham, Otto, and Erich M. von Hornbostel
1903   "Studien über das Tonsystem und die Musik der Japaner,"
         Sammelbände der Internationalen Musikgesellschaft 4:302–60; repr.
         w. Eng. tr. in Hornbostel 1975:3–84.
1904a   "Phonographierte indische Melodien," *Sammelbände der
         Internationalen Musikgesellschaft* 5:348–401; repr. w. Eng. tr. in
         Hornbostel 1975:117–82.
1904b   "Über die Bedeutung des Phonographen für die vergleichende
         Musikwissenschaft," *Zeitschrift für Ethnologie* 36:222–36; repr. w.
         Eng. tr. in Hornbostel 1975:185–202.
Adler, Guido
1908   "Über Heterophonie," *Jahrbuch der Musikbibliothek Peters* 15:17–27;
         Eng. tr. in Donald Mitchell, *Gustav Mahler: Songs and Symphonies of
         Life and Death* (Berkeley and Los Angeles: University of California
         Press, 1985), pp. 624–31.
Álvaro Velho
1960   *Roteiro da primeira viagem de Vasco da Gama (1497–1499).*
         Edited by A. Fontoura da Costa. 2d ed. Lisbon: Agencia Geral do
         Ultramar.
Anderson, Lois Ann
1968   "The Miko Modal System of Kiganda Xylophone Music." Ph.D.
         dissertation, University of California, Los Angeles.
Arom, Simha
1984   "The Constituting Features of Central African Rhythmic Systems," *The
         World of Music* 24 (1):51–64.
1985   *Polyphonies et polyrythmies instrumentales d'Afrique Centrale:
         Structure et méthodologie.* Paris: SELAF (Ethnomusicologie 1).
Asaf'yev, Boris
1930   *Muzikal'naya forma kak protsess* [Musical form as process]. Moscow:
         Gosudarstvennoye Izdatel'stvo, Muzikal'noiy Sektor. Eng. tr. in James
         Robert Tull, "B.V. Asaf'yev's Musical Form as a Process: Translation and
         Commentary." Ph.D. dissertation, The Ohio State University, 1976,
         pp. 183–564.
Bartók, Béla
1933   "Hungarian Peasant Music," *Musical Quarterly* 19:267–89; repr. in *Béla
         Bartók Essays,* Benjamin Suchoff, ed. (New York: St. Martin's Press,
         1976), pp. 80–102.
Berliner, Paul F.
1978   *The Soul of Mbira: Music and Traditions of the Shona People of
         Zimbabwe.* Berkeley and Los Angeles: University of California Press.

Blacking, John
1955   "Some Notes on a Theory of African Rhythm Advanced by Erich von
          Hornbostel," *African Music* 1 (2):12–20.
1961   "Patterns of Nsenga Kalimba Music," *African Music* 2 (4):26–43.
Blum, Stephen
1985   "Rousseau's Concept of *Sistème musical* and the Comparative Study of
          Tonalities in Nineteenth-Century France," *Journal of the American
          Musicological Society* 38:349–61.
Dzhudzhev, Stoyan
1931   *Rythme et mesure dans la musique populaire bulgare.* Paris: Librairie
          Ancienne Champion (Travaux publiés par l'Institut d'études slaves, 12).
Ellis, Alexander John
1884   "Tonometric Observations on Some Existing Non-Harmonic Scales,"
          Proceedings of the Royal Society (London) 37:368–85.
Ferand, Ernst T.
1951   " 'Sodaine and Unexpected' Music in the Renaissance," *Musical Quarterly*
          37:10–27.
Gadamer, Hans-Georg
1972   *Wahrheit und Methode: Grundzüge einer philosophischen Hermeneutik.*
          3d ed. Tübingen: J. C. B. Mohr (Paul Siebeck). First published 1960.
Gippius, Evgeny
1936   "Intonatsionniye elementi russkoy chastushki" [Intonational Elements in
          the Russian Chastushki], *Sovetski Fol'klor* 4 (5):97–142.
Grainger, Percy
1924   "What Effect is Jazz Likely To Have Upon the Music of the Future?" *The
          Etude* 42:593–94.
Gurlitt, Wilibald
1942   "Der Begriff der sortisatio in der deutschen Kompositionslehre des 16.
          Jahrhunderts," *Tijdschrift van de Vereniging voor Nederlandse
          Muziekgeschiednis* 16:194–211.
Helmholtz, Hermann L. F. von
1877   *Die Lehre von den Tonempfindungen als physiologische Grundlage für
          die Theorie der Musik.* 4th ed. Braunschweig: Friedrich Vieweg. Eng. tr.
          by Alexander J. Ellis. London: Longmans, Green, 1885.
Herskovits, Melville J.
1935   "What Has Africa Given America?" *The New Republic* 84 (1083):
          92–94; repr. in Herskovits, *The New World Negro: Selected Papers in
          Afroamerican Studies* (Bloomington: Indiana University Press, 1966),
          pp. 168–74.
Herzog, George
1934   "African Songs of the Chewa Tribe in British East Africa," in *Negro: An
          Anthology,* Nancy Cunard, ed. (London: Wishart), pp. 412–14.
1935   Review of Guy B. Johnson, *Folk Culture on St. Helena Island;* and of
          George Pullen Jackson, *White Spirituals in the Southern Uplands,* in
          Journal of American Folklore 48:394–97.

1936   *Research in Primitive and Folk Music in the United States.* Washington,
          D.C.: American Council of Learned Societies (Bulletin 24).
1945   "Drum-signaling in a West African Tribe," *Word* 1:217–38.
Hornbostel, E. M. von
1904   "Melodischer Tanz, eine musikpsychologische Studie," *Zeitschrift der
          Internationalen Musikgesellschaft* 5:482–88; repr. w. Eng. tr. in
          Hornbostel 1975:205–15; repr. in Hornbostel 1986:76–85.
1905   "Die Probleme der vergleichenden Musikwissenschaft," *Zeitschrift der
          Internationalen Musikgesellschaft* 7:85–97; repr. w. Eng. tr. in
          Hornbostel 1975:249–70; repr. in Hornbostel 1986:40–58.
1909a   "Wanyamwezi-Gesänge," *Anthropos* 4:781–800, 1033–52, and 8 pp. of
          musical examples.
1909b   "Über Mehrstimmigkeit in der außereuropäischen Musik," in *Dritter
          Kongress der Internationalen Musikgesellschaft, Wien, 25. bis 29. Mai
          1909, Bericht* (Vienna: Artaria, and Leipzig: Breitkopf und Härtel),
          pp. 298–303.
1910a   "Wasukuma-Melodie: nach der Aufnahme von Dr. J. Czekanowski,"
          *Bulletin International de l'Académie des sciences de Cracovie, Classe des
          sciences mathématiques et naturelles,* pp. 711–13 and 1 musical
          example.
1910b   "U.S.A. National Music," *Zeitschrift der Internationalen
          Musikgesellschaft* 12 (3):64–68.
1911a   "Über ein akustisches Kriterium für Kulturzusammenhänge," *Zeitschrift
          für Ethnologie* 43:601–15; repr. in Hornbostel 1986:207–27.
1911b   "Musikpsychologische Bermerkungen über Vogelgesang," *Zeitschrift der
          Internationalen Musikgesellschaft* 12:117–28; repr. in Hornbostel
          1986:86–103.
1913a   "Melodie und Skala," *Jahrbuch der Musikbibliothek Peters* 19:11–23;
          repr. in Hornbostel 1986:59–75.
1913b   "Musik," in Günter Tessman, *Die Pangwe: Völkerkundliche Monographie
          eines westafrikanischen Negerstammes.* (Berlin-Tegel: Hansa Verlag), vol.
          2, pp. 320–57.
1917   "Gesänge aus Ruanda," in Jan Czekanowski, *Forschungen im
          Nil-Kongo-Zwischengebiet* (Leipzig: Klinkhardt und Biermann), vol. 1,
          pp. 379–412 and 14 pp. of musical examples.
1921   "Musikalischer Exotismus," *Melos* 2:175–82.
1926a   "Psychologie der Gehörserscheinungen," in *Handbuch der normalen und
          pathologischen Physiologie,* A. Bethe et al., eds. (Berlin: Springer) vol. 11,
          pp. 701–30; repr. in Hornbostel 1986:315–68.
1926b   "Das räumliche Hören," in *Handbuch der normalen und pathologischen
          Physiologie,* A. Bethe et al., eds. (Berlin: Springer), vol. 11, pp. 602–18.
1926c   "American Negro Songs," *The International Review of Missions*
          15:748–53.
1927a   "Ethnologisches zu Jazz," *Melos* 6:510–12.
1927b   "Laut und Sinn," in *Festschrift Meinhof* (Glückstadt and Hamburg:
          Augustin), pp. 329–48.

1927c   "Musikalische Tonsysteme," in *Handbuch der Physik*, H. Geiger and Karl
         Scheel, eds. (Berlin: Springer), vol. 8, pp. 425–49.
1928a   "Die Maßnorm als kulturgeschichtliches Forschungsmittel," in *Festschrift:*
         Publication d'hommage offerte au P. W. Schmidt, W. Koppers, ed.
         (Vienna: Mechitharisten-Congregations-Buchdr.), pp. 303–23.
1928b   "African Negro Music," *Africa* 1:30–62.
1929   "Tonart und Ethos," in *Musikwissenschaftliche Beiträge: Festschrift für*
         Johannes Wolf, W. Lott, H. Osthoff, and W. Wolffheim, eds. (Berlin:
         Breslauer), pp. 73–78; repr. in Hornbostel 1986:104–11.
1975   *Hornbostel Opera Omnia.* Edited by K. P. Wachsmann, D. Christensen,
         and H. P. Reinecke. Vol. 1. The Hague: Martinus Nijhoff.
1986   *Tonart und Ethos. Aufsätze zur Musikethnologie und Musikpsychologie.*
         Edited by C. Kaden and E. Stockmann. Leipzig: Philipp Reclam.
Jones, A. M.
1954   "African Rhythm," *Africa* 24:26–47.
Kastal'sky, A. D.
1923   *Osobennosti narodno-russkoy muzikal'noy sistemi* [Characteristics of the
         Russian Folk Musical System]. Moscow: Gosudarstvennoye Izdatel'stvo,
         Muzikal'noiy Sektor.
Kauffman, Robert A.
1969   "Some Aspects of Aesthetics in the Shona Music of Rhodesia,"
         Ethnomusicology 13:507–11.
Kirby, Percival R.
1932   "The Recognition and Practical Use of the Harmonics of Stretched Strings
         by the Bantu of Southern Africa," *Bantu Studies* 6:31–46.
Kroeber, A. L.
1959   Preface to the *Anthropology of Franz Boas*. Edited by Walter
         Goldschmidt. *American Anthropologist* 61 (5), part 2 (Memoir no. 89).
Kubik, Gerhard
1960   "The Structure of Kiganda Xylophone Music," *African Music* 2 (3):6–30.
1979   "Pattern Perception and Recognition in African Music," in *The Performing*
         Arts: Music and Dance, John Blacking and JoAnn W. Kealiinohomoku, eds.
         (The Hague: Mouton), pp. 221–49.
1985   "African Tone Systems—A Reassessment," *Yearbook for Traditional Music*
         17:31–63.
Kvitka, Klyment
1924   *Professional'ni narodni pevtsi i muzikanty na Ukrayni: prohrama dlya doslidu*
         yikh diyal'nosti ta pobutu [Professional Folk Singers and Instrumentalists in the
         Ukraine: A Program for Study of their Activity and Everyday Life]. Kiev:
         Ukrains'koi Akademii Nauk.
Kyagambiddwa, Joseph
1956   *African Music from the Source of the Nile.* New York: Praeger.
Lach, Robert
1924   "Die Musik der Natur- und orientalischen Kulturvölker," in *Handbuch der*
         Musikgeschichte, Guido Adler, ed. (Frankfurt am Main: Frankfurt Verlags-
         Anstalt), pp. 1–26.

Maceda, José
1974   "Drone and Melody in Philippine Musical Instruments," in *Traditional Drama and Music of Southeast Asia*, M. Taib Osman, ed. (Kuala Lumpur: Kementerian Pelajaran Malaysia), pp. 246–73.

Mora, Manolete
1987   "The Sounding Pantheon of Nature: T'boli Instrumental Music in the Making of an Ancestral Symbol," *Acta Musicologica* 59:187–212.

Nketia, J. H. Kwabena
1962   "The Hocket Technique in African Music," *Journal of the International Folk Music Council* 14:44–52.
1967   "Multi-part Organization in the Music of the Gogo of Tanzania," *Journal of the International Folk Music Council* 19:79–88.
1986   "Processes of Differentiation and Interdependency in African Music: The Case of Asante and Her Neighbours," *The World of Music* 28 (2):41–53.

Paudrat, Jean-Louis
1984   "The Arrival of Tribal Objects in the West: From Africa," in *"Primitivism" in 20th Century Art: Affinity of the Tribal and the Modern*, William Rubin, ed. (New York: The Museum of Modern Art), vol. 1, pp. 125–75.

Riemann, Hugo
1916   *Folkloristische Tonalitätsstudien. I. Pentatonik und tetrachordale Melodik im schottischen, irischen, walisischen, skandinavischen und spanischen Volksliede und im Gregorianischen Gesange*. Leipzig: Breitkopf und Härtel (Abhandlungen der Kgl. Sächs. Forschungsinstitut zu Leipzig. Forschungsinstitut für Musikwissenschaft).

Robeson, Paul
1934   "The Culture of the Negro," *The Spectator* (London) 15 June:916–17; repr. in *Paul Robeson Speaks*, Philip S. Foner, ed. (Seçaucus, N.J.: Citadel Press, 1978), pp. 86–87.

Rouget, Gilbert
1970   "Transcrire ou décrire? Chant soudanais et chant fuégien," in *Échange et communications: Mélanges offerts à Claude Lévi-Strauss*, Jean Pouillon and Pierre Maranda, eds. (The Hague: Mouton), pp. 677–706.

Schaeffner, André
1956   "Ethnologie musicale ou musicologie comparée?" *Les Colloques de Wégimont, Ethnomusicologie* 1:18–32.

Schmidt, Cynthia E.
1984   "Interlocking Techniques in Kpelle Music," *Selected Reports in Ethnomusicology* 5:195–216.

Schneider, Marius
1934   *Geschichte der Mehrstimmigkeit, I: Die Naturvölker*. Berlin: Julius Bard. 2d ed., Tutzing: Hans Schneider, 1968.
1937   "Über die Verbreitung afrikanischer Chorformen," *Zeitschrift für Ethnologie* 69:79–89.
1956   "Entstehung der Tonsysteme," in *Gesellschaft für Musikforschung, Bericht über den internationalen musikwissenschaftlichen Kongress Hamburg 1956* (Kassel: Bärenreiter), pp. 203–11.

1966a "Tonalität, A. Ursprungs- und Entwicklungsfragen," in *Die Musik in Geschichte und Gegenwart,* Friedrich Blume, ed. (Kassel: Bärenreiter), vol. 13, pp. 510–14.

1966b "Tonsysteme, C. Außereuropäisch," in *Die Musik in Geschichte und Gegenwart,* Friedrich Blume, ed. (Kassel: Bärenreiter), vol. 13:547–58.

Sonneck, O. G.

1916 "A Survey of Music in America," in *Sonneck, Suum Cuique: Essays on Music* (New York: G. Schirmer), pp. 121–54. Lecture delivered in 1913.

Spitzer, Leo

1963 *Classical and Christian Ideas of World Harmony. Prolegomena to an Interpretation of the Word 'Stimmung.'* Baltimore: The Johns Hopkins University Press.

Stevenson, Robert

1968 "The Afro-American Musical Legacy to 1800," *Musical Quarterly* 54:475–502.

1970 *Philosophies of American Music History.* Louis Charles Elson Memorial Lectures. Washington: Library of Congress.

Stone, Ruth M.

1982 *Let the Inside Be Sweet: The Interpretation of Music Event among the Kpelle of Liberia.* Bloomington: Indiana University Press.

Stumpf, Carl

1901 "Tonsystem und Musik der Siamesen," *Beiträge zur Akustik und Musikwissenschaft* 3:69–138.

Sumarsam

1975 "Inner Melody in Javanese Gamelan." M.A. thesis, Wesleyan University; repr. in *Karawitan: Source Readings in Javanese Gamelan and Vocal Music,* Judith Becker, ed. (Ann Arbor: University of Michigan, Center for South and Southeast Asian Studies, 1984–88), vol. 1, pp. 245–304.

1981 "The Musical Practices of the Gamelan Sekaten," *Asian Music* 12 (2):54–73.

1988 "The Development of Theories of Javanese Gamelan by Indonesian Theorists." Paper delivered at Symposium of the International Musicological Society, Melbourne. To appear in *Cultural Interaction through Music,* Margaret J. Kartomi and Stephen Blum, eds. (Sydney: Currency Press).

1989 "Historical Contextualization of the Term *Balungan* in Central Javanese Gamelan." Paper delivered at 34th annual meeting, Society for Ethnomusicology, Cambridge, Mass.

Tedlock, Barbara

1980 "Songs of the Zuni Kachina Society: Composition, Rehearsal, and Performance," in *Southwestern Indian Ritual Drama,* Charlotte J. Frisbie, ed. (Albuquerque: University of New Mexico Press), pp. 7–35.

Uspensky, V. A., and V. M. Belyayev

1928 *Turkmenskaya muzika* [Turkmen Music]. Moscow: Gosudarstvennoye Izdatel'stvo, Muzikal'noiy Sektor.

Varèse, Edgard

1966 "The Liberation of Sound," *Perspectives in New Music* 5 (1):11–19.

Wachsmann, Klaus P.

1969 "Music," *Journal of the Folklore Institute* (Indiana University) 6:164–91.

1970   "Ethnomusicology in Africa," in *The African Experience,* J. N. Paden and E. W.
          Soja, eds. (Evanston: Northwestern University Press), pp. 128–51.
Waugh, Linda R.
1982   "Marked and Unmarked: A Choice between Unequals in Semiotic Structure,"
          Semiotica 38:299–318.
Weber, Max
1921   *Die rationalen und soziologischen Grundlagen der Musik.* Munich: Drei
          Masken Verlag.
Westcott, William
1977   "Ideas of Afro-American Musical Acculturation in the U.S.A.: 1900 to the
          Present," *Journal of the Steward Anthropological Society* 8:107–36.
Yavorsky, Boleslav
1908   *Stroyeniye muzikal'noy rechi* [The Construction of Musical Language].
          Moscow.

Isabel K. F. Wong

From Reaction to Synthesis: Chinese Musicology in the Twentieth Century

T HIS IS a chronological account of the way in which the Chinese intelligentsia, confronted with Western music and Western views on music, reacted to them, tried to understand them, and eventually took action to adapt them for the reshaping of traditional Chinese music and music scholarship.

Before the twentieth century, China was an agrarian society controlled by a centralized, monolithic government whose bureaucrats were drawn from among the class of "literati." Three components of the state ideology were Confucianism, Legalism, and Taoism. During the nineteenth century, China experienced the challenge of Western commercial penetration, massive social strife, economic stagnation, and explosive population growth. Following the Opium War (1839–42), Britain and other Western powers gained special privileges in five designated "treaty ports," heralding an era of growing Western demands for increased economic and political concessions from the Chinese. Throughout the century after the Opium War, Chinese society was brought into closer contact with Western ideas that challenged, undermined, or overwhelmed every sphere of social and cultural activity of the old order.

Within the space of three generations, institutions, customs, and social relationships were changed or refashioned, the classical Chinese literary language was discarded, and traditional music was first ignored and then reshaped to meet the Western challenge. Before turning to the development of modern Chinese musicology, which too began as a reaction to Western stimuli, let us examine the traditional Chinese views of music and traditional scholarship on music.

According to the orthodox Confucian view of the value of music in education, there were two categories of music: *yayue,* or elegant, cultivated music, and *suyue,* or common, uncultivated music. In a narrow sense, *yayue* denoted ceremonial music which was an integral part of solemn and elaborate state rituals staged to bolster the temporal and cosmological legitimacy of the ruling monarch. To play the ceremonial music in cosmologically correct tuning was of paramount political importance. In a broader sense *yayue* denoted music cultivated by the educated elite, and paramount in this category was music for the *qin,* a zither of high antiquity with seven strings. Because it was the instrument played by Confucius, it was regarded as the instrument par excellence for the literati. More tangentially, the classical musical theater *kunqu* was also included in the fold of *yayue.* Appropriated by the educated elite from a type of folk theater popular in the sixteenth century in the Zhejiang and Jiangsu regions, *kunqu* theater had come to be regarded as a mandatory part of their social rituals and private entertainments, helping them to define and lend social cohesiveness to their leisure activities. The rest of the rich varieties of popular and folk music of the common people, women included, were in the category of *suyue* or "common music." Professional musicians of *suyue* were social outcasts.

Treatises on music were written mainly by members of the literati as an avocation. These works were published either as independent volumes or in encyclopedias, dynastic annals, or personal memoirs. They can be classified under nine topics as follows:

1) *Yuxue* (systematic and historical musicology)
2) *Luxüe* (theories and methods for pitch calculation)
3) Writings on the Confucian or Taoist views on music
4) Records of court institutions of music in various dynasties
5) Bibliographical records of music repertoires
6) Anecdotes about well-known musicians and entertainers
7) Writings exploring the aesthetics and ideology of *qin* music
8) Treatises on *kunqu* music
9) Organological works

There were publications of music as well, most importantly handbooks for the *qin* in *qin* tablatures and anthologies of *kunqu* arias in *gongche* notation.

Having set the stage, so to speak, let us now turn our attention to the development of modern Chinese musicology to provide a broad outline and trace some of the main patterns from its inception in the twentieth century to the present. Six stages of development can be identified: (1) 1912–26, (2) 1927-36, (3) 1937-49, (4) 1950-65, (5) 1966-76, and (6) since 1977.

I. 1912–26

In 1911 the Qing dynasty was overthrown, and although the 1911 republican revolution failed to bring about a nation-state, the subsequent

years saw the rise and fall of all kinds of ideologies, political and social experiments, and utopian schemes, making it one of the most important ger-
minal periods in the realm of Chinese thought. The seed for the modern development of Chinese musicology was sowed during this period. Four
major events stimulated the growth of this field:

1) A traditional music revival movement in general and a *kunqu* theater
   and music revival movement in particular, both launched at the turn of
   the century
2) The "New Literature Movement" launched in 1917
3) The Folk Song Campaign begun in 1918
4) The establishment of the first modern music department at Peking National University

During the turn of the century, as the pace of change hastened under the
impact of reform and the appeal of westernized music became stronger
among the younger generation, proponents of traditional Chinese music,
fearing that the tradition might be forgotten, initiated several revival
movements which included establishing music clubs for amateurs, printing
music in notation, and writing and publishing books on the history of traditional Chinese music. Among these movements, the *kunqu* revival was
the most organized and widely influential. It was initiated by a group of
wealthy literati in the Souzhou area, China's old cultural center. Four areas
of revival activities were implemented:

1) The publication of anthologies of *kunqu* arias; no fewer than eight significant anthologies were published between 1908–25 (Wong 1978)
2) Publication of scholarly articles or books on the history, music, and
   other relevant aspects of *kunqu*
3) Establishment of many amateur singing clubs where old singing masters, hired to be in residence, gave instruction to members, and where
   members also performed together (Wong 1976)
4) Establishment of training academies to train the next generation of actors

The late Yang Yinliu (1899–1984), one of the founders of the field of
modern Chinese musicology, was already active in this *kunqu* revival
movement when still in his late teens, and he continued to do research on
kunqu music in later years.[1] Because of his involvement and influence, and
also because of the prestigious position of *kunqu* in Chinese history, *kunqu*
research has always figured prominently in the field of modern Chinese
musicology.[2] A second impetus came from the "New Literature Movement" begun in 1917 by two professors of Peking National University
(Beida, for short). Although predominantly literary, this movement had a

strong impact on other fields, including music, because of its national importance and because of the important position of Beida in modern Chinese history. Beida was the first modern university established in China and remains China's premier university today. Its first chancellor, Cai Yuanpei (1867–1940), was a remarkable, liberal educator with a traditional Chinese classical education who later also studied Western civilizations and philosophy at the University of Leipzig. Under Cai's campaign for intellectual freedom, all kinds of "new tides" were set in motion.[3] The two leaders of the 1917 New Literature Movement were Hu Shi (1891–1962) and Chen Duxiu (1880?–1942), both faculty of the Literature Department. Together they carried out an iconoclastic attack against the classical literary language and its literature for being too antiquated, difficult to learn, and reclusive. They called for the abolition of the literary language and for its replacement by a simpler, easier vernacular. Their call was widely echoed by the intellectuals, and, thus, within a generation a newly constructed vernacular had become China's national language.[4] Under the impact of this movement, another iconoclastic campaign, the "Folk Song Campaign," was launched at Beida in 1918.

In traditional society, the literary elite had regarded folk song as lowly and seldom paid attention to it. To be associated with folk culture thus represented for the elite a radical break with the past. It is in this sense that the Folk Song Campaign was an iconoclastic movement. It began at first as a movement for the collection of song texts. Its leaders, like those of the New Literature Movement, contended that, since folk-song texts were "the true expression" of the Chinese peasants who formed the majority of Chinese, these texts would be the ideal basis for the construction of a new national vernacular. But in the later phase of this Folk Song Campaign, music too was collected (Hung 1985:1–12).

One of the leaders of the Folk Song Campaign was Liu Fu (1891–1934), a professor at Beida who started his literary career as a "middlebrow" popular romantic novelist in Shanghai, a member of the so-called "Mandarin Ducks and Butterflies School." Liu's interest in folk song was first stimulated by writings on Chinese folklore by foreigners living in China at the turn of the century. In 1918, under the impact of the New Literature Movement, he decided to initiate a folk-song collection movement, and, with financial support and encouragement from Chancellor Cai, he and some of his friends established an office for the collection of folk song. The folk songs collected were published regularly in the *Beida Daily* and attracted interest among Beida students.

It was not until 1919, however, that the Folk Song Campaign began to become a significant intellectual movement. In that year, Li Dazhao (1888–1927), another literature professor at Beida and later cofounder of the Chinese Communist Party, borrowed concepts from the Russian *Narodnik* movement of the 1870s and wrote a famous article called "Youth and Village," calling for Chinese youths to go to the villages to educate the peasants in order to liberate them and uplift China. Heeding Li's call, a group of some forty Beida students formed a "Mass Education Lecturing Corps" to raise the consciousness of the peasants. It was through the process of discovering rural problems that young intellectuals encountered folk songs and folk art, came to recognize their value, and realized that they were important areas for research.

In 1922 Liu Fu established a weekly journal called the *Folksong Weekly* devoted entirely to the publication and discussion of folk songs. At this time he also began to collect the music of folk songs as well. The weekly attracted widespread attention in other parts of China, and soon many journals began to publish special columns of folk songs and folk literature. The Folk Song Campaign became a clarion call for the intellectuals, and folksong collection and research was established as a legitimate field of study from both literary and musical sides (Hung 1985:32–54; 158–80). Later, when the field of musicology proper emerged, folk-song research was included in its scope as a matter of course.

On 4 May 1919 the intellectual and political ferment that had been brewing for some time culminated in a series of student demonstrations led by Beida students as a result of the provocation offered by the award to Japan at the Versailles Peace Conference of the territory in Shandong province leased to Germany. These demonstrations were followed by nationwide strikes by workers, merchants, and students that lasted well into 1922, marking the watershed of modern Chinese history (Chow 1960:84–194). It has become customary to refer to the intellectual and political developments occurring between 1911 and 1922 as the "May Fourth Movement." They therefore include the New Literature Movement and the Folk Song Campaign, actually instituted before 1919. Thus musicology may be properly considered to have been born in the May Fourth era.

Further impetus for the formation of the field of musicology came from the establishment, by Chancellor Cai at Beida in 1916 (*Zhongguo Yinyue Cidian* 1984d), of music-reform study groups, which eventually developed into China's first modern music department in 1922 (*Zhongguo Yinyue Cidian* 1984a). During his sojourn in Germany before World War I, Cai had developed a taste for Western classical music. He was impressed by the accessibility of music education in Germany, as well as the respectability accorded to music by German society, a situation not paralleled in China. Impressed also by the strength and cohesiveness of German society and nation, he concluded that a strong aesthetic education—in which music formed the major component—had contributed to the general well-being of the society, making the country so orderly and its people so civic-minded (Cai 1969). For this reason, he established the Beida Music Reform Group in 1916 in order to reform popular Chinese music by adapting Western musical elements. This Music Reform Group was staffed by Western-trained Chinese musicians as well as by practitioners of traditional music who shared Cai's views on music reform.

One of the musicians of traditional and folk music hired by Cai was Liu Tianhua (1895–1932), a younger brother of Liu Fu, the leader of the 1918 Folk Song Campaign. Liu Tianhua joined Beida in 1922 when the Reform Group was expanded into a music department with the name *Beijing Daxue Yinyue chuanxi Suo*[Institute of Music Transmission and Practice of Peking University], which offered courses on Chinese and Western vocal and instrumental performance. Like his brother, Liu Tianhua was an avid collector of folk music, but he concentrated on instrumental rather than vocal music, and his students also began to collect folk instrumental music. Liu can thus be credited for having enlarged the scope of the Folk Song Campaign, giving it a definitely musical focus (*Zhongguo Yinyue Cidian* 1984d).

An important legacy of Liu Tianhua was his functional rationale for the purpose of folk-music collecting, which stemmed from the belief he shared with Cai Yuanpei that Chinese music needed to be reformed. China, he believed, needed a new national music just as she needed a new national vernacular, and this new national music was to be constructed on the basis of China's folk music mixed with Western elements. Liu himself composed several pieces for *erhu* (a two-string bowed instrument), still performed today, in which a Western-inspired structure, violin tremolo, and vibrato techniques were adapted. More important, this functional approach to folk-music collecting continued to be influential in music circles (*Zhongguo Yinyue Cidian; Liu Tianhua 1930*).

In this formative period of Chinese musicology, then, some characteristic features began to emerge. Besides a modern reexamination of research on *kunqu,* which had been an intellectual concern of old China, and of research on folk music, which was possible only in a modern China, this early stage also saw the emergence of an attitude in which music research was to be applied to reforming Chinese music by borrowing Western elements. Significantly, nationalism was the moving force behind the various foci of research shaping attitudes and approaches which were to be reinforced by events of later years.

II. 1927–36

In 1922 the Chinese Communist Party was established in Shanghai. After that the influence of Marxism-Leninism on Chinese politics and thought increased, and hostility flared up between the ruling Nationalist Party and the Communist Party after 1925. Many of the leaders of the Communist Party were executed in 1927, and the survivors fled into the mountains of eastern China. In 1934 the Chinese Communist Party forces embarked on the famous "Long March" that took them across China's most desolate terrain to the Northwest, where they established a headquarters at Yan'an in Shaanxi province. Meanwhile, Japanese aggression had increased in North China. In 1927 the Folk Song Campaign was forced to move its center from Beida in Beijing to Zhongshan University in Guangzhou (Canton) in the South where it stayed until 1934. These seven years have been regarded as the Golden Age of folk-music research, and the scope of research broadened to include not only rural folk music but also popular urban traditional music.[5] It was also in 1927 that China's first modern conservatory of music, the National Conservatory of Music, commonly called the Shanghai Conservatory, was established. The first director was Xiao Yiymei (1884–1940), a composer trained at the Leipzig Conservatory. Faculty members were largely foreigners or Western-trained Chinese musicians (*Zhongguo Yinyue Cidian* 1984h). The curriculum, modeled closely on that of the Leipzig Conservatory, emphasized training in Western music, although there were a few token Chinese music courses. The establishment of this conservatory at the time was widely regarded as an indication of China's coming of age in her appreciation of "good," that is, Western music. Through the years, graduates of the Shanghai Conservatory, with their Western bias, came to dominate the musical life of the intelligentsia of the treaty ports and to be regarded as authorities for acceptable musical standards and behavior. Although a few Shanghai Conservatory graduates later did do research on Chinese music, the majority generally regarded Chinese music as low culture, and few had any curiosity about it.[6] This attitude continues to prevail today among Chinese students of Western music and parallels the attitude toward folk music held by the old Chinese literary elites.

Now let me turn to an individual named Wang Guangqi (1892–1936), a Chinese law student turned musicologist who studied under Hornbostel and Sachs at Berlin University, where he matriculated in 1927. Wang studied organology with Sachs for three years and worked as his assistant. In 1932 he entered the Ph.D. program in musicology at the University of Bonn, received his doctorate in 1934, and remained in Bonn to teach the music and civilization of China until his death in 1936. Wang was a prolific writer. During his short career as a musicologist he wrote some ten books and scores of articles in Chinese on musicology and comparative musicology for Chinese readers at home. He employed the comparative method in his own research on Chinese music. In addition, he translated many Western works on music into Chinese, among them Alexander Ellis's essay on the cents system.[7] While Wang's works were by no means widely read in China, they had a significant impact on Yang Yinliu, who later employed some comparative concepts in his research. Yang also adapted Ellis's method in his work on calculation of equal temperament (Yang Yinliu 1986b).

After the intellectual breakthrough of the May Fourth period, the fledgling field of modern Chinese musicology did not continue to surge forward in the second period, but remained instead on a plateau. Folk-music research did go on, and Yang Yinliu forged ahead with his reexamination and systematization of traditional topics, now moving toward his research in pitch calculation. The most significant development of this period, however, was political.

With the establishment of the League of the Left Wing Writers, the cultural arm of the Chinese Communist Party in the later twenties, Chinese intellectuals increasingly rallied around it as Japanese aggression and Nationalist appeasement increased. A music study group was founded as part of the League by Lü Ji (b. 1890), a dropout of the Shanghai Conservatory and a Party member who was later to emerge as the chief Party spokesman on policies regarding music (*Zhongguo Yinyue Cidian* 1984f). The members of this Marxist music study group were mainly people interested in music but without much formal training; quite a few were, like Lü Ji, dropouts, for political or financial reasons, from the Shanghai Conservatory. It was this group of musically semitrained Party activists who later shaped the future of modern Chinese music and music scholarship. The aim of the group was to compose songs for the masses on the Soviet model to be sung at political rallies against the Japanese. This process of politicization of music and the arts accelerated as the relationship between China and Japan deteriorated further.[8]

III. 1937–49

When the Sino-Japanese war broke out in 1937, intellectuals of all political persuasions joined the common mobilization effort to resist Japan. During the eight-year war, China was divided into three parts, the coastal section being under Japanese occupation, while the Nationalists controlled the area in the Southwest with Chongqing (Chungking) as the wartime capital, and the Communists controlled the area in Northwest China with Yan'an as the seat of government. Although cultural development in each of the three areas varied, a common feature was the politicization of the arts, a tendency that proved profound and lasting. One of the main reasons for this was the wartime growth in political and cultural status of the Communist-held region, which provided a theater where the cultural authorities in Yan'an could put into practice the theories of the May Fourth Movement. By the 1940s, however, the results of this experimentation had been formulated into a comprehensive cultural policy whose tenets stood in sharp contrast to those of the May Fourth principles. For whereas the activities associated with the May Fourth Movement had been mostly urban and its manifestations, influenced strongly by the West, were produced by the educated for the educated, the revolutionary cultural products prescribed by Yan'an were predominantly rural and popular, produced for a mass audience and modeled after indigenous rural criteria.

During the war, intellectuals outside the Communist zone shared a common sense of political purpose with their counterparts in Yan'an. In the Japanese-occupied area a sense of virtuous resistance to Japan gave impetus to a long-lasting concern with politics, and in the Nationalist area the increasingly corrupt governmental practices contributed to a mood of cynical despair and a heightened sense of political awareness at the same time. Although the three regions were largely isolated from one another, each had an idea of cultural events in the other two. The frustration and despair experienced by intellectuals of the non-Communist zone caused them to look upon Yan'an as the seat of the political and cultural future.

Among the music scholars who migrated to Chonqing, Yang Yinliu deserves mention for his achievements. Under extremely difficult circumstances he completed a book in 1944 dealing systematically with Chinese music history, whose title is translated as *An Abbreviated History of Chinese Music* (Yang Yinliu 1944). It remains one of the most authoritative works on the subject and is a cornerstone of the modern field of Chinese music history. It is also part of an intellectual trend that began during the war of turning back to traditional Chinese culture for inspiration.

In Yan'an, the celebrated "Talk at the Yan'an Forum on Literature and Art" delivered by Mao Zedong in 1942 was widely hailed as the ultimate Chinese Communist pronouncement on the arts;[9] its statement that the arts must be the tool of the state and must serve the people, that is, peasants, soldiers, and workers, by presenting society through their eyes was, in fact, a theoretical summary of Mao's long experiences in political work rooted in the so-called "mass-line" organizational strategy or process for revolutionary change. The mass-line strategy or process has two components. In the first, called "mobilization," the Party must, in order to mobilize the people, discover the specific social issues that are of most immediate concern to them, using these issues as a rallying device to organize a group. This is also called "*from* the masses." The second component, called "organization," dictates that the Party, having discovered the issue which has the greatest potential for eliciting a favorable response from the targeted group, must organize a program relating to this particular issue and persuade the people to adopt it by using musical or literary forms familiar to the targeted group as a means of persuasion. This is also called "*to* the masses" (see Johnson 1968).

In order to make the mass-line strategy function effectively, the Party needed a "cultural army" to collect suitable popular cultural products, which were then to be remolded as means for winning over the hearts of the people. On the musical front, the collection of folk songs was a logical choice as a May Fourth–era precedent already existed. At the direction of the Party, a committee on folk-song collection and research was formed, headed by Lü Ji. Thousands of folk songs were collected, categorized, and recycled for use in specific programs within the mass-line strategy.[10]

In 1941 Lü Ji gave a speech to the cadres of the Folk Song Committee entitled "Guidelines for Chinese Folk Music Research" in which he defined "folk music" and charted out its scope and provided the political rationale for folk-song research. This speech, clearly a major Party policy pronouncement, was later published (1948); its first and second revisions were published respectively in 1981 and 1982 (Lü Ji 1941).[11] I use the term "folk music" here for the Chinese *minjian yinyue. Minjian* means "from the people," and *yinyue,* music. The "people," according to Lü Ji, were the proletariat, urban or rural. *Minjian yinyue*, then, really means the music of the working people.

The scope of folk music, Lü Ji states further, is to include music not only of the majority Han people, but that of the national minorities as well. Eight types of folk music constitute the foci of collection and research: work songs, mountain songs and ballads, musical narratives, musical drama, festival music, dance music, religious music, and instrumental music. The emphasis is on populism; the importance of understanding the contexts in which the music arises is emphasized, because to present the music in a context familiar to the audience is crucial to the success of the mass-line strategy. Finally, Lü Ji states, the ultimate purpose for folk-music research is to discover the broad general principles of Chinese music to be used as basis for the creation of a new national music for the proletariat (Lü Ji 1941). The creation of a new national music had been the aim of the May Fourth generation as well, but Lü Ji's pronouncement adds a clear political purpose not found earlier.

IV. 1949–66

With the establishment of the People's Republic of China in 1949, a period of political consolidation and pervasive change in Chinese society was ushered in. The Party used techniques and strategies developed in Yan'an to implement these changes. Cultural guidelines, designed and prescribed by the Party agency, the Ministry of Culture, were put into practice, with the aim of creating a new national culture by transforming the former elitist culture into a mass culture. In pursuing this new national culture, artists and cultural cadres turned increasingly to Chinese traditional and folk culture for legitimization and inspiration, a tendency that had first surfaced during the war and was further encouraged by the Party until the eve of the Cultural Revolution.

Many new music institutes were founded to train a new army of music workers to carry out the Party's policies on music. Two of the most important were the Central Conservatory of Music in Beijing headed by Lü Ji, established in 1949, and the Institute of Chinese Music Research, headed by Yang Yinliu, established in 1953. A new field for Chinese music research was given the formal name *minzu yinyuexue*, or "musicology of national music" (see Gao Houyong 1980; Lü Ji 1986). The word "national" is used to connote a homogenized music whose ingredients are to come from all ethnic groups in the People's Republic and from all the ages of Chinese music history (Zhao Feng 1983). Musicological research was now to be focused on two distinct but overlapping areas, the first called *gudai yinyueshi* or "ancient Chinese music history." Chinese Marxists divided the history of China into three main periods: *Gudai*, or "ancient period," extending from the ancient, so-called "slave" period to 1842, when China was defeated by Britain in the Opium War; *Xiandai*, or "modern period," from 1842 to the beginning of May Fourth Movement in 1919; and *Jindai*, or "contemporary period," after 1919. For research in pre-1842 music history (*Gudai*), the term *gudai yinyueshi* was used. The second focus of musicological research is called *minjian yinyue*, that is, the scope of folk music defined by Lü Ji in 1941, which focuses on traditional and folk music still existing in contemporary China.

The approaches to research in these two areas differed. For *gudai yinyueshi* the approach, developed primarily by Yang Yinliu, was a combination of traditional Chinese music scholarship, Sinological research, and Western musicological method introduced by Wang Guangqi. For *minjian yinyue*, the method was that developed by the Committee on Folk Music Research in Yan'an led by Lü Ji which emphasized field investigation and the applicability of research for political purposes. But the two subject areas, as well as their methods and approaches, are by no means mutually exclusive. Rather, a true synthesis of the two has emerged over the years.[12]

The turbulent political events in China from 1949 to the eve of the Cultural Revolution are well known. Throughout the period, musicological research was carried on, although intermittently, by dedicated scholars, students, and cultural workers. Systematic archiving and research on musical narratives and musical drama, notably Peking opera and *kunqu*, achieved impressive results. Also impressive was research on the music of the *qin* and on the mouth organ (*sheng*). The various archaeological discoveries of ancient instruments gave a strong impetus to research in ancient Chinese music. Scholarly journals and monographs, some of very high quality, were published. In the 1950s articles on music research carried out by musicologists in the Soviet Union and Eastern Europe were translated; some of the authors also visited China to give lectures.

By elevating Chinese music as a subject of academic research, the Party gave respectability and legitimacy to a subject previously looked down upon. Knowledge gained from research of the complex structure of Chinese music also contributed to its rise in status. Research on the music of the *qin*, *the* instrument of high culture, was carried on side by side with research on Peking opera, a popular theater, resulting in the permanent removal of the barrier separating "high" and "low" culture.

V. 1966–76

It is well known that during the ten years of the Cultural Revolution intellectuals were sent to do physical labor in order to be reeducated, and all schools were closed. Much less known perhaps is the fact that the first signal heralding the Cultural Revolution surfaced in 1963 in the form of an editorial in the newspaper *Wenhuibao,* an official Party paper in Shanghai, on the subject of a Chinese translation of Debussy's *Monsieur Croche Antidilettante* (see He Luding 1981). This editorial, written by Yao Wenyuan, one of the so-called "Gang of Four," was entitled "A Novel and Unique Opinion." In it Debussy's Monsieur Croche was roundly criticized as decadent, arrogant, passive, and obscure. The editorial prompted an answer from He Luding, then Director of the Shanghai Conservatory, who in the same paper urged the writer of the critical editorial to be more objective and to read more books concerning the historical and social context under which the work was written. In the next four months, a dozen articles were published expressing opinions on the subject (He Luding 1981:164–69).

It turned out that Yao's editorial attack on Debussy had nothing to do with Debussy. It was instead a calculated strategy, as Yao later stated, to draw out He Luding and his circle in the Shanghai Conservatory—the citadel of reactionary musical policies—and then systematically to eliminate them during the coming Cultural Revolution (He Luding 1981:183–87).

VI. 1978–PRESENT

Mao's death in 1976 removed a towering figure from Chinese politics and set off a scramble for succession. With the reinstatement of Deng Xiaoping as the leader of the country in 1977, the Chinese leadership moved toward a more pragmatic position in almost all fields. The schools were reopened, and the newly rehabilitated intellectuals immediately plunged into new work.

A five-volume music encyclopedia was launched by the Ministry of Culture in 1979. This is to be a comprehensive reference for work on all categories and genres of Chinese music of all eras. Scholars and music workers of the entire nation have been involved in this gigantic project. Already, two volumes have been published (see Wang Zengwan 1987).

In June 1980 the first National Conference on *minzu yinyuexue,* which was translated by the Chinese themselves at the time as "ethnomusicology," was held in Nanjing, sponsored by the Ministry of Culture. Its participants were some ninety musicologists, music teachers, and cultural workers who came from eighteen provinces, presenting some sixty papers (see

Gao Houyong 1983). A year later, fifty of these were published in two volumes (Nanjing Institute of Arts 1981). As in the case of research papers of the 1950s, the foci, methods, and approaches of the majority of the papers represent a synthesis of a modern adaptation of traditional music scholarship identified with Yang Yinliu and his circle,[13] with the applied approach—with field research—developed in the heyday of Yan'an populism and identified with Lü Ji and his circle.[14] For the first time, there was an article introducing the development of ethnomusicology in the West, mentioning Ellis, Sachs, Merriam, and Hood (see Luo Chuankai 1981).

Four more national conferences were held between 1982 and 1986 (Gao Houyong 1983, 1985; Liu Delu 1986). Already at the 1980 conference, the question was raised regarding the appropriateness of translating *minzu yinyuexue* as "ethnomusicology." Some urged that the approach and method of China's *minzu yinyuexue,* a product of China's history, was distinctly different from Western ethnomusicological methods. As the debate continued, some argued that *minzu yinyuexue* has always been a study of China's own music—as opposed to ethnomusicology in the West, which has always been the study of "others' music," with a special focus on music of "primitive society"—and that therefore "ethnomusicology" ought to be translated in Chinese as "musical ethnography," "anthropology of music," or "musical folklore." The term *minzu yinyuexue,* on the other hand, ought to be translated as "Chinese musicology." Others contended that ethnomusicology in the West has evolved from the study of "others' music" to self-examination as well, and that the stigma attached to ethnomusicology as the study only of "others' music" (presumably more "primitive" than one's own) should be removed. Ethnomusicology is a recognized discipline of the modern world, this argument continued, and China, a modern nation, ought to be participating in the world dialogue.[15]

As a result of this debate many felt that Chinese scholars need to read more Western ethnomusicological works and theories before an objective opinion can be formed. More translations of works by Western ethnomusicologists have been introduced in the last few years. One such example is a book entitled *Minzu Yinyuexue Yi Wen Ji* [Ethnomusicology, a Collection of Translated Essays]. Its contents include excerpts of books or articles by Ellis, Sachs, Kunst, Nettl, Merriam, Hood, Kolinski, and Yamaguti Isamu (Dong Huisong and Shen Qia 1985). In addition to the publication of new articles, monographs, and books, works published prior to the Cultural Revolution have been reissued. A significant new journal called *Musicology in China,* edited and published by the Institute of Music Research, appeared in 1985, its contents reflecting China's increased interest in and curiosity about foreign musics and musical concepts. If the movement toward opening doors continues as promised by the Chinese leadership, then we may perhaps see the return of the May Fourth interest in the Western tradition, but with an important difference. During the May Fourth Movement, Western culture, music included, was used as a vehicle to generate iconoclastic reform. In the 1980s, however, there is a genuine interest among Chinese musicologists in establishing a mutual dialogue with musicologists and ethnomusicologists in the West and in adapting some of the best Western scholarship to the Chinese musicological tradition. Chinese musicologists also welcome Western investigations of Chinese music—not, however, merely as an area study fitted into the Western framework of ethnomusicological research. They feel, rather, that the long history of Chinese musicology documents an intellectual and methodological tradition that can serve as a complement to its Western counterpart (Mao Jizheng 1984).

Notes

1. A group of Yang Yinliu's early writings on *kunqu*, dating from 1925 to 1937, are collected in Yang Yinliu 1986a:1–2. For a biography of Yang, see *Zhongguo Yinyue Cidian* 1984f.

2. Yang Yinliu's *Zhongguo Yinyue Shigang* [Abbreviated History of Chinese Music] consists of a total of 342 pages; of these, 37 pages are devoted to the discussion of *kunqu*. See Yang Yinliu 1944:230–67.

3. For a brief historical survey of the intellectual ferment of this period, see John Fairbank and Teng Ssu-yu 1954:231–34. For a brief biography of Cai Yuanpei (Tsai Yuan-pei) and an English translation of some of his writings, see ibid.:234–39.

4. For a brief biography of Chen Duxiu (Ch'en Tu-hsiu) and an English translation of some of his writings, see Fairbank and Teng 1954:240–46, 251–58.

5. For a detailed account of this later phase of the Folk Song Campaign, see Hung Chang-tai 1985:46–57.

6. For a brief account of the Shanghai Conservatory, see *Zhongguo Yinyue Cidian* 1984c.

7. For a brief biography of Wang Guangqi, see ibid.:1984g. See also Hua Xing and Han Limin 1985. For critiques of Wang's scholarly contributions, see Lü Ji 1984, Li Yadao 1984, and Feng Wenci 1984.

8. A brief account of the activities of the League is found in *Zhongguo Yinyue Cidian* 1984k.

9. For an excellent English translation of Mao's "Talk," with annotation, see McDougall 1980.

10. On activities of the Chinese Folk Music Research Committee, see *Zhongguo Yinyue Cidian* 1984j. On the political use of folk song, see Wong 1984.

11. For information on the political use of folk art, see also Holms 1984. For a firsthand account of events in Yan'an, see Snow 1938.

12. Some of the information provided here was gathered by myself in interviews with Professors Yang Yinliu, Cao Anhe, and He Yün of the Research Institute in Beijing in 1982. See also Gao Houyong 1980, Lü Ji 1985 and 1986, and Zhao Feng 1985.

13. In 1980, three years before his death, Yang Yinliu published a definitive work on the (ancient) history of Chinese music which sums up his life's work. It is modestly titled *Draft History of Ancient Chinese Music* (Yang Yinliu 1980). The contents of the new music journal, *Musicology in China,* inaugurated in 1985, are representative of Yang's approaches.

14. A major music journal in which both Yang Yinliu's and Lü Ji's approaches to music research are applied is *Yinyue Yanjiu.*

15. The information provided here is a summary of the following sources: Dong Huisong and Shen Qia 1982; Qiao Jianzhong and Jin Jingran 1985; Huang Xiangpang 1986; and Wei Tingge 1987.

Works Cited

Cai Yuanpei
1969   "Wenhua jaioyue bu yao wang liao meiyu" [Aesthetic Education
         Should Not Be Excluded From Cultural Education], in *Minsu Congshu*
         [*Folklore Series*], Lou Zikuang, ed., 101:43–44.
Chow Tse-Tsung
1960   *The May Fourth Movement.* Stanford: Stanford University Press. 2d
         ed., 1967.
Dong Huisong, and Shen Qia
1982   "Minzu yinyue wenti" [Problems in Chinese Musicology], *Yinyue
         Yanjiu* [Music Research] 4:33–40.
1985   *Minzu Yinyuexue Yi Wen Ji* (Translation of a collection of essays in
         ethnomusicology). Beijing: Zhongguo wenluan chuban gongsi.
Fairbank, John K., and Teng Ssu-yu
1954   *China's Response To The West, A Documentary Survey 1839–1923.*
         Cambridge: Harvard University Press.
Feng Wenci
1984   "Wang Guangqi di yinyue shixue fangfa he xuefeng" [Wang Guangqi's
         Scholarly Contribution to Musicology and His Philosophy on
         Scholarship], *Yinyue Tansuo* [Exploring Music] 4:12–16.
Gao Houyong
1980   "Zhongguo minzu yinyuexue di xingzhang he fazhan" [The Evolution
         and Development of Chinese Musicology], *Yinyue Yanjiu* 4:8–25. Also
         in *Minzhu Yinyue xue Lunwenji* [Selections In Ethnomusicology]
         (Nanjing 1981), 1:5–20.
1983   "Zhongguo duiyu minzu yinyuexue di yanjiu" [Ethnomusicological
         Research in China], *Luanhe Yinyue* (Hong Kong).
1985   "Zhongguo dui minzu yinyuexue di yanjiu" [Ethnomusicological
         Research in China], *Yinyue Yanjiu* 1:27–29.

He Luding
1981   "Yao wenpi yu Debussy" [The Literary Hack Yao <Wenyuan> and Debussy], in *He Luding Lunwen Ji* [Collected Essays of He Luding] (Shanghai: Wenyi chubanse), pp. 170–82.

Holms, David
1984   "Folk Art as Propaganda: The Yangge Movement in Yan'an," in *Popular Chinese Literature and Performing Arts in the People's Republic of China 1949–1979*, Bonnie S. McDougall, ed. (Berkeley and Los Angeles: University of California Press), pp. 3–35.

Hua Xing, and Han Limin
1985   "Wang Guangqi shengping dashi ji shuyao zhushu nianbao" [Chronology of Wang Guangqi], *Yinyue Yanjiu* 1:8–11; 2:10–16; 3:52–58; 4:27–33.

Huang Xiangpang
1986   "Zhide shenru sikao di jige wenti" [Some Important Points for Consideration], *Zhongyang Yinyue Xueyuan Xuekan* [Journal of the Central Conservatory of Music] 4:3–4.

Hung Chang-tai
1985   *Going To The People*. Cambridge: The Council on East Asian Studies, Harvard University.

Johnson, Chalmers
1968   "Chinese Communist Leadership and Mass Response: The Yan'an Period and the Socialist Education Campaign," in *China In Crisis,* Pingti Ho and Tang Tsou, eds. (Chicago: The University of Chicago Press), vol. 1, bk. 1, pp. 397–437.

Li Yadao
1984   "Jinian Wang Guangqi xiansheng" [In Memory of Mr. Wang Guangqi], *Yinyue Tansuo* 4:9–11.

Liu Delu
1986   "Quanguo minzu yinyuexue di si ci nianhui zai wo yuan juxing" [The Fourth Annual National Meeting of Chinese Musicology at the Central Conservatory of Music, Beijing], *Zhongyang Yinyue Xueyuan Xuekan* [Journal of the Central Conservatory of Music] 4:14.

Liu Tianhua
1930   "Introduction" in *Mei Lanfang Gequpu* [Selections from the Repertory of Operatic Songs and Terpsichorean Melodies of Mei Lanfang], Liu Tianhua, ed. (Peiping).

Lü Ji
1941   "Zhongguo minjian yinyue yanjiu tigang" [Guidelines for Folk Music Research], first delivered orally in 1941. First published in 1948; first revision published in 1981; second revision published in 1982 in *Yinyue Yanjiu* 2:34–39.

1984   "Wang Guangqi zai yinyuexue shang di gongxian" [Wang Guangqi's Contribution to Musicology], *Yinyue Tansuo* 4:3–8.

1985   "Zhongguo yinyuexue, yuexue, he youguang jige genti" [Chinese Historical and Systematic Musicology, and Related Matters], *Yinyue Yanjiu* 1:2–12.

1986   "Duo nian zhoyue di yinyue shixuejia Yang Yinliu xiansheng" [In
          Memory of the Great Music Historian Mr. Yang Yinliu], *Yang Yinliu*
          1986:2–3

Luo Chuankai
1981   "Minzu yinyuexue di yuangge, dingyi, ji qita" [The Evolution of
          Chinese Musicology, Definitions, and Related Matters], in *Minzu
          Yinyuexue Lunwenji*, Nanjing Institute of Art, ed. (Nanjing 1981), vol.
          1, pp. 21–23.

Mao Jizheng
1984   "Minzu yinyuexue de fazhan he cunzai di wenti" [On the Development
          of Chinese Musicology, and Related Problems of the Field], *Yinyue
          Tansuo* 3:28–31.

McDougall, Bonnie S.
1980   *Mao Zhedong's "Talks at the Yan'an Conference on Literature and
          Arts."* Ann Arbor: University of Michigan Press.
1984   "Writers and Performers, Their Works, and Their Audiences in the
          First Three Decades," in *Popular Chinese Literature And Performing
          Arts in The People's Republic of China 1949–1979*, Bonnie S.
          McDougall, ed. (Berkeley and Los Angeles: University of California
          Press), pp. 269–70.

Nanjing Institute of Arts
1981   *Minzu Yinyuexue Lunwenji* Vols. 1–2 (Nanjing). [Essays in Chinese
          Musicology]. Edited by Jianzhong Qiao and Jingran Jin.

Qiao Jianzhong, and Jin Jingran
1985   "Guanyu ethnomusicology zhongwen yiming de jianyi" [Some
          Suggestions for the Chinese Translation of the Term Ethnomusicology],
          Yinyue Yanjiu 3:96.

Snow, Edgar
1938   *Red Star Over China.* New York: Random House.

Wang Zengwan
1987   "Zhongguo minzu yinyue jicheng bianjixue zuotan" [The Encyclopedia
          of Chinese Music Editorial Board Meeting], *Yinyue Yanjiu* 1:56–65.

Wei Tingge
1987   "Bu danchun si ethnomusicology di yiming wenti" [It is Not Just the
          Problem of How to Translate the Term Ethnomusicology], *Zhongyang
          Yinyue Xueyuan Xuekan* 1:98–100.

Wong, Isabel K. F.
1976   "Performing Contexts of K'un-Ch'u: Continuity and Change." Paper
          delivered at the Annual Meeting of the Society for Ethnomusicology,
          Philadelphia.
1978   "The Printed Collections of K'un-ch'u (Kunqu) Arias and Their
          Sources," *Chinoperl Papers* 8:100–129.
1984   *"Geming Gegu:* Songs for the Education of the Masses," in *Popular
          Chinese Literature and Performing Arts in the People's Republic of
          China 1949–1979,* Bonnie S. McDougall, ed. (Berkeley and Los
          Angeles: University of California Press), pp. 112–43.

Yang Yinliu
1944   *Zhongguo Yinyue Shigang* [Abbreviated History of Chinese Music].
        Chongqing.
1980   *Zhongguo Gudai Yinyue Shigao* [Draft History of Ancient Chinese
        Music]. Beijing: Remin yinyue chubanse.
1986a   *Yang Yinliu Yinyue Lunwei xuanji* [Selected Essays on Music By Yang
        Yinliu]. Shanghai: Wenyi chubanse.
1986b   "Pingjunlu suanjie" [Equal-Temperament Calculation], in Yang Yinliu
        1986a.
Zhao Feng
1983   "Minzu yinyuexue di jicheng he fazhang" [Preservation and
        Development of Chinese Musicology], *Yinyue Yanjiu* 1:2–6.
1985   "Zai minzu yinyuexue di san jie nianhui (Shenyang pian) shang di
        kaichangbei" (Opening Speech for the Third Annual Meeting for
        Chinese Musicology in Shenyang), *Yinyue Yanjiu* 1:25–26.
Zhongguo Yinyue Cidian [Dictionary of Chinese Music] Beijing:
        Remin yinyue chubanse.
1984a   "Beijing daxue yinyue chuanxisuo" [Music Institute, Peking
        University], p. 20.
1984b   "Beijing daxue yinyue yanjiuhui" [Music Research Committee, Peking
        University], p. 20.
1984c   "Guoli Yinyue Xueyuan" [The National Conservatory of Music],
        p. 138.
1984d   "Guoyue gaijinse" [Chinese Music Reform Club], p. 138.
1984e   "Liu Tianhua," p. 237.
1984f   "Lü Ji," p. 252–53.
1984g   "Wang Guangqi," pp. 400–401.
1984h   "Xiao Yiymei," p. 427.
1984i   "Yang Yinliu," p. 453.
1984j   "Zhongguo minjian yinyue yangjiuhui" [Chinese Folk Music Research
        Committee], p. 507.
1984k   "Zhongguo zuoyi xijujia lianmeng yinyue xiaozhu" [The League of
        Left Wing Writers Music Study Group], p. 508.

Gerard Béhague

Reflections on the Ideological History of Latin American Ethnomusicology

T HE HISTORY of ethnomusicological thought in Latin America and the Caribbean has been anything but coherent. Many significant factors have contributed over the years to the heterogeneity of ethnomusicology in the Latin American continent, and I will single out a few of them in this essay. I will also identify some of the major problems confronting Latin American ethnomusicology today.

The first students of Native American music were of course the numerous European travelers, missionaries, and scientists who had varying degrees of contact with Indian cultures throughout the colonial period (sixteenth century to early nineteenth century). From the French Calvinist Jean de Léry (who lived in Rio de Janeiro, Brazil, for a couple of years in the late 1550s) and the many Spanish and Portuguese missionaries in Mesoamerica, the Peruvian Andes, Paraguay, Argentina, and Brazil (Juan de Torquemada, in Mexico, Huamán Poma de Ayala in Peru, to name two of the most illustrious), to the Germans Spix and Martius in Brazil in the early 1800s, these writers provided mostly firsthand "ethnomusicological observation" (as Frank Harrison pointed out in his anthology *Time, Place and Music,* 1973). Their reports constitute the most important historical sources of early knowledge of traditional musics of the Latin American continent but, in a true sense, represent the data of remote informants that require the same assessment and analytic treatment as that of any other informant whose cultural outlook deserves close attention. These sources have indeed been treated in that vein in the literature.

The early history of ethnomusicology in Latin American countries, as we now understand the various areas of this field of study, dates back to the late nineteenth century when cultural historians began to recognize the importance of local oral cultural phenomena. This recognition resulted from the strong influence of European and European-related music produced and consumed in Latin America at the time under the control of elite social classes, as a reaction against the domination of that music which tended to obliterate the nationalizing qualities of local musical expressions. At the same time, Latin America, much like other Third World continents, stimulated the same interest in folk and primitive music on the part of comparative musicologists, such as von Hornbostel and Curt Sachs, and ethnologists, such as Koch-Grünberg, all associated with or related to the Berlin School. It was not, however, until the 1920s and 1930s that the first music histories of various Latin American countries were written with specific attention to the traditional, folk, and urban popular music. This attention echoed the nativistic/nationalist intellectual and artistic movements, such as the Mexican postrevolutionary Aztec Renaissance, the *afrocubanismo* trend, the Peruvian/Andean *indigenismo* movement, and the Brazilian *modernismo* with its anthropophagic manifesto. In their search for the identifying factors of nationality, these historians turned naturally to the musical expressions that defined more readily whole groups or cultural areas.

Up to that time both European and native scholars of Latin American music paid little or no attention to actual fieldwork experience. With a few exceptions, it is since about the end of World War II that field research has begun to be undertaken and since about the early 1960s that study in situ has become systematized. Indeed, one of the most innovative factors in ethnomusicological research in Latin America over the last thirty years or so has been the awareness on the part of numerous researchers of the need for firsthand knowledge of and experience in the very musical traditions that they seek to describe and interpret. Such an awareness has made possible a better, more representative account of various aspects of folk and traditional music, but an essentially descriptive approach to such music has continued to operate in most places. This approach has no doubt resulted from the realization of the lack of specific factual data concerning oral musics in general. Whether in organological studies, in the relationships of music, dance, and ritual, or of music and traditional poetry used in various contexts, the great majority of ethnomusicologists and music folklorists have indeed focused on descriptions.

Particularly important for Latin American ethnomusicologists has been the study of origins along the continuum of the triethnic makeup of Latin American music (Iberian, American Indian, African). Naive and simplistic generalizations over this question of origins have frequently resulted from the search for "pure" retention of a given musical trait believed to be attributable without any doubt to a specific primal cultural root. The influential theories of the Argentine folklorist/musicologist, Carlos Vega, (as formulated in his *Panorama de la música popular Argentina,* 1944) bespeak a diffusionist, evolutionist, and neocolonialist attitude. For him, for example, "the musical bow with calabash resonator has all the essential elements of the violin" (ibid.: 25), as he adhered to the concept of "superior" and "inferior" social groups, assigning to the "inferior" group an older, more static cultural evolution than that of the "superior" group, and establishing an evolutionary relationship between the two. Thus, cultural "survivals" are only survivals for the superior groups; from the point of view of the folk groups themselves, they remain as simple current experiences or folkways. "It is fundamental to understand," writes Vega, "that the survivals of today were the folkways of the superior groups of yesterday" (ibid.: 26–27). Therefore, for him folklore (and particularly musical folklore) is "the science of the [cultural] survivals," with its unilinear dynamics, in the sense that the "inferior imitates the superior," or the common people imitate the noble class, although he recognizes that on occasion—but only partially—popular cultural elements ascend to the realm of the higher classes. By extension, Carlos Vega considers folk and "ethnographic" (i.e., primitive) music as part of the "inferior" heritage, old music, alien to the superior cultural environment.

Some of the characteristic traits that he attributes to ethnic music include: the absence of small forms, the lack of harmony, and frequently what he called "an incipient tonal ordering." He further establishes a series of structural contrasts between folk and ethnographic music, that is, folk music being "mensural" with the clear presence of rhythmic feet and brief musical ideas, "generally half motion half rest." Ethnographic music, on the other hand, is "amensural," with a tendency toward periodicity and repetition of its brief rhythmic and melodic schemes, but it is only precursory of the concept of phrase. Whenever rare measured phrases are found, argues Vega, they do not function as articulations of periods. These questions of phrasing generations in primitive and folk music gradually acquired such an importance for Vega that he dedicated two substantial volumes to his study of "phraseology," which oversimplifies rhythmic and formal considerations of both folk and primitive music corpora.

Moreover, in his attempt to explain the popular creative process, Vega naively states: "The act of creation requires, as a foundation and condition, a certain degree of social autonomy of the group to which the individual belongs. It is necessary that people of the inferior classes not be aware of what the superior classes do; it is necessary that the [creative] spirits not assume an imitative attitude. In general, the popular classes keep aspiring, waiting, imitating. And the submissive spirit does not create. The superior classes of the 'new' countries, keep, in turn, imitating what the centers of universal prestige create, and, therefore, upon the ashes of the colonial political regimes, survive our great spiritual colonies." In addition, Vega's criteria in musical classifications aspire to universality on one level, but to regional songsters' characteristics, on the other. Such classifications are based on formal and species-specific criteria, such as the evolutionary approach of a simple to complex continuum of (1) primitive "ethnographic," amensural, nonwritten music; (2) ancient mensural, nonwritten folk music, based on tonal systems, small forms, and an incipient harmony; and (3) modern mensural written music, with tonal systems and great forms, and intensive harmony and polyphony (part of the music history). Tonal subdivisions include the primitive pretonal systems, then the tonal systems, from tritonic to heptatonic, and the posttonal modern systems. Finally, in his identification and classification of South American (particularly but not exclusively Argentine) "*cancioneros*," Vega proposes the following ordering: (1) tritonic, (2) pentatonic, (3) occidental, (a) colonial ternary, and (b) occidental *criollo*, (4) *riojano*, (5) *platense*, (6) oriental (a) colonial binary and (b) oriental *criollo*, and (7) ancient European.

Criteria for such a classification are clearly inconsistent, as they include considerations of both scale formations and geographic origin or location. Moreover, in his brief mention of the primitive *cancioneros*, that is, Indian traditional music, Vega is particularly ethnocentric, when he declares that the "indigenous *cancioneros* of low culture do not define any tonal systems based on common generating principles (such as the circle of fifths etc.). . . . In general, the music of the South American primitive people has entirely remained marginal from all process of the post-Colombian era. Without influencing the European tradition, indigenous music received from it some occasional influence but without true incorporation. The mental gulf that separated one from the other has been and continues to be the guarantee of the lack of contamination. Only some elements of the two high-culture indigenous *cancioneros*—the pentatonic and tritonic . . . had contact with *criolla* music. . . ." One would think that such obsolete ideas would represent only a remote past of South American ethnomusicology. Despite the open criticism of some of these concepts, the most devoted student of Carlos Vega, Isabel Aretz, as recently as 1984 reaffirmed her conviction in these ideas. In her book *Síntesis de le etnomúsica en América Latina,* she relied on the same consideration of phenomenological factors to define musical areas in the Latin American continent. The Andean region, for example, is classified according to (1) music of the jungle population, (2) Aymara *cancionero,* and (3) Inca pentatonic *cancionero.* The south *cone (cono sur)* comprises the Mapuche *cancionero,* the tritonic *cancionero,* the occidental *criollo cancionero,* and the oriental *criollo cancionero,* with various subdivisions. For Mexico, she follows Vicente Mendoza's own iden-

tifications of 1956 *(Panorama de la música tradicional de México)* and recognizes
(1) the music of Indian communities with various degrees of acculturation (or
mestizaje), (2) religious Spanish music of the sixteenth to the eighteenth centuries,
(3) secular Spanish music (of the *romance* type, the lullaby *copies*, children's
songs, and others), (4) music of the *jarabe* and *aires mexicanos*, (5) *corridos*, (6)
canción mexicana, and (7) the *valona*. These types of classification are obviously
of very limited usefulness. Moreover, Carlos Vega's neocolonialist stance remains
strong in the concepts of Isabel Aretz and Luis Felipe Ramón y Rivera in their
search for old European musical practices in twentieth-century Latin American
folk music.

In 1984 Aretz also attempted to reinforce the validity of the strictly analytic approach that is solely concerned with sound-structure phenomena. "At present,"
she wrote, "ethnomusicology is in the hands of two types of professionals: the
one who specializes in the study of purely musical phenomena in a given culture
that must be known thoroughly, and the specialist in the study of one aspect of
the culture, be it social, psychological, philosophical, etc., because of a lack of
knowledge in the transcription and analysis of the music per se. Generally, such a
specialist justifies his or her lack of knowledge of musical phenomena through the
[alleged] degree of elementary state of the current system of musical notation . . ."
(Aretz 1984:39). For her, it is clear that sociocultural considerations of the music-
making process detract from the fundamental objective of ethnomusicology, that
is, the study of music as product.

Perhaps only a study of the sociology of the discipline's actual practitioners
could provide partial explanation of the reasons why such scholars have retained
these particular conceptual modes. Social and cultural constraints enter into the
explanation. For example, according to Latin American academic customs during her generation, Aretz could not have challenged and dismissed her mentor's
basic theories. And although she did not remain insulated from North American
or European scholarship, she felt strongly that the anthropology and sociology of
music as articulated since the 1960s addressed issues of importance but of little
immediate application in her studies.

The basic problem has been and continues to be a lack of conceptual distinction between "musical folklore" as thought and practiced throughout Latin
America and ethnomusicology. Musical folklore has had, unfortunately, little or
no theoretical and methodological formulation. Uses and functions, for example,
have hardly been mentioned in most studies of folk and popular music. The well-
known study of the late Brazilian folklorist Oneyda Alvarenga, *Música popular
brasileira* (1950), for example, does not show any concern at all in describing and
interpreting the social dimensions of a musical phenomenon. The great majority

of Latin American researchers of folk and traditional music worked until recently with the firm conviction that their level of understanding of the musical data of "their" country and of the culture of that country would be necessarily more refined than if they were studying some foreign musical culture. Since they consider themselves members of the popular/folk culture of their country, they never put in doubt the objectivity of their observations. The reality of such a presumption is, however, very doubtful if we consider that within the pronounced Latin American social stratification, folklorists and ethnomusicologists come from the dominant social groups, with, in general, a strong degree of Eurocentrism. Thus, the same cultural adjustment and consideration of *emic* thought-processes appear essential for a proper representation of the culture under study. As late as 1963, for example, the Mexican folklorist Mendoza chose to illustrate one of his lectures on traditional Mexican Indian music by singing himself various songs of the Huichol, Seri, and Tarascan Indian repertory, without the slightest doubt that his singing accurately represented that original repertory!

Neither musical folklore nor the incipient Latin American ethnomusicology of the last three decades has contributed in any substantial way to a general theory of ethnomusicology because of the descriptive emphasis previously mentioned. This does not mean, of course, that Latin American ethnomusicologists should follow blindly the lessons of European or American ethnomusicology. Rather, Latin American scholars ought to attempt to formulate and elaborate their own theoretical objectives, based on their own conceptualization of research problems and purposes and the problematics of research in their specific countries. In so doing, they would also arrive at a better personal sense of their own ideology or sociopolitical position as scholars. Such a positioning is especially critical for scholars from Third World cultural areas because these areas face numerous social, economic, and political issues that must be viewed as integral parts of the scholarly community as well. The current problems of cultural hegemony and prevailing cultural populism in some regions of Latin America must be faced by local scholars with the proper level of honesty. For example, the consideration of the internal market pressures of the multinational music industry that tend to alienate numerous folk communities—to precipitate changes or to require adaptive strategies—has become a fundamental necessity in the very scholarly study of these communities.

To illustrate further the significance and some of the shortcomings of Latin American ethnomusicology, I will now turn briefly to some examples of the contrasting treatment of Luso-Brazilian music, Afro-Brazilian traditional music, and Indian music in Brazil. With the necessary adjustment resulting from the assessment of the work of numerous personalities active in the study of musical folklore in specific countries, these examples suggest valid generalizations for the main issues confronting Latin American ethnomusicology.

In terms of the conceptualization of Brazilian ethnomusicology, the well-known poet and writer Mário de Andrade (1893–1945) was the real pioneer. Although unable to rely on a tradition of musicology or comparative musicology, as yet not established in Brazil, Andrade was forced to develop his own ideas and methods. Motivated by the *modernismo* movement of the 1920s, his essay *Ensaio sobre a música brasileira* (1928) represented not only a manifesto for musical nationalism for Brazilian art-music composers but also the first penetrating attempt to delineate and analyze the various sound-structural elements of Brazilian folk music. In the context of his country in the 1920s and 1930s, his concepts were modern indeed and "ethnomusicological" to a significant extent. In his studies of the dramatic dances and of "witchcraft music," for example, he gave attention to sociocultural as well as musical matters and considered the ethnographic basis and justification of musical-performance contexts. He conceived of musical dynamics as multidirectional in his studies of the three main Brazilian musical traditions. Andrade's only student, Oneyda Alvarenga, adhered, however, to the prevailing descriptive method of folklore studies in her survey of Brazilian folk and popular music (1950) and in her analyses of black influence on the music of Brazil (1946).

Luso-Brazilian folk music has been studied regularly by Tavares de Lima (1954, 1964, 1971a, 1971b, 1978) and by Andrade himself for the south-central folk cultural area (1941). Geraldo de Souza (1963) revealed analytically the influences of Gregorian chant (especially church modes), through missionary work, on Brazilian folk songs. Corrêa de Azevedo (1944) was among the first scholars to turn attention to the *cantoria* tradition (the narrative, ballad-like tradition of improvised singing) of the northeastern provinces. Carvalho (1975) provided specific musical analyses of songs of the same repertory. Dances and music associated with popular religious rituals, such as the Festa do Divino, the Folia de Reis, or the Bailes Pastoris, have also been studied by Corrêa de Azevedo (Universidade do Brasil 1953, 1956, 1959) and folklorists such as Maynard de Araújo (1964). The Portuguese tradition of the festivities of the Dança de São Gonçalo and the Dança de Santa Cruz, together with the whole complex of *romanceiro* (balladry), has been thoroughly documented in Brazil by folklorists and musicologists (Cascudo 1954, Souza 1966, Giffoni 1973). For the most part, however, their approach has been geared toward historical questions attempting to clarify various kinds of syncretism. In the area of organology, in spite of the supremacy of the *viola* (folk guitar of Portuguese origin) in Brazilian folk music in general, instruments of

African derivation have received more attention, particularly percussion instruments. Organological studies, such as Araújo (1953) and Tavares de Lima (1964, 1965), are, for the most part, direct physical descriptions of the instruments and do not explain much of their functions and potential symbolic meanings. Northeastern instrumental ensembles and festivals have been described by Guerra-Peixe (1956, 1970) and Dantas, among others. The Luso-Brazilian tradition has received more attention, probably because of the alleged superiority assigned to the culture of the colonizers and the fact that it is found more or less equally throughout the Brazilian territory. The study by Setti (1985) on the music of the fishermen-peasants of the coastal area of São Paulo state is a good model of what needs to be pursued in Brazilian ethnomusicology, namely, the specialized and comprehensive ethnographic study of a given musical community, its history, and dynamics in contemporary perspective, all based on careful and methodical field research.

Despite the existence of a substantial folkloric, anthropological, and sociological scholarly literature on black culture, little has been achieved in the area of Afro-Brazilian musical traditions. Andrade's study on the *samba* from São Paulo (1937) has no counterpart for the numerous regional varieties of the *samba*. Luciano Gallet (1934) provided the best general coverage of black music in Brazil for its time, but his analyses are conceived in strongly Eurocentric terms, and the information provided did not result from extensive field experience. Since then some good but sporadic studies have appeared, such as Carneiro's posthumous work (1974), which included a study on *batuque* and *samba*, and Waddey's study of the *samba de viola* from Bahia (1980–81). The Bahian group of anthropologists that brought up the first serious studies of the sociocultural significance of Afro-Brazilian popular religions (especially Nina Rodrigues, Artur Ramos, and Edison Carneiro) generally neglected the musical aspect of such religions, since music was probably the most esoteric discipline for them. The American Melville Herskovits (1944) recognized the importance of music and dance as integral parts of the ritual structures, but failed to treat that importance ethnomusicologically. His essay with Richard Waterman (1949) is quite informative but does not provide the much needed ethnographic and musical integration, most likely because of the absence of Latin American field experience in the case of Waterman. In-depth monographic study of *candomblé, Xangô* cult, *macumba,* and *umbanda* music repertories is still not available. Merriam's dissertation (1951) gave some pertinent analysis of Herskovits's material at the time, but failed to provide the desirable holistic approach to analysis. Much later, *candomblé* music was treated very competently by Binon-Cossard (1967) but in too general terms. Contexts of performance of Bahian *candomblé* music and the latter's relationship to other national trends in popular religious music were examined in Béhague (1975, 1984). Carvalho's doctoral thesis in anthropology (1984) represents the type of study desirable in this area, but questions dealing with codification of repertories, music's relationship to belief systems and practices, music as part of religious behavior and as performance understood in ethnographic terms—all are open for investigation in the numerous regional versions of cult music from the state of Pará to Rio Grande do Sul. Nonreligious music of predominantly black Brazilians has received more attention, particularly the *capoeira* of Bahia and the *frevo* and *passo* of Recife. It is quite significant in the 1970s to see two Africanist scholars, the Austrian Kubik (1979) and wa Mukuna from Zaire (1979), studying Afro-Brazilian music with different kinds of a priori expectations and cultural ethnocentrism, one searching for Angolan traits while the other stressing the Bantu contribution in Brazilian music. The Bahian carnival *afoxé* (carnival associations built around cults) still awaits a proper ethnomusicological treatment.

Until recently the most neglected branch of Brazilian musical studies was the area of traditional Indian music. That tradition has remained foreign to most Brazilian researchers despite a substantial social-scientific literature on Brazilian Indian cultures. Quite symptomatic in this respect is Helsa Cameu's Indian music survey (1977), which is a useful compendium but one undertaken by a dedicated musician with little or no awareness of ethnomusicological methods. Musical features and instruments are quite competently described, but the author's lack of field experience is especially felt in her failure to assess the whole ethnographic complex of Indian music and dance. Most relevant studies on Indian music have been undertaken by anthropologists. Bastos has studied in great detail Kamayurá music and culture (1978, 1986), with attention to such factors as native conceptualization and classifications and the interrelatedness of social, political, economic, and musical structures. The American anthropologist and ethnomusicologist Anthony Seeger taught for a number of years at the Museu Nacional in Rio de Janeiro and had a beneficial influence on young Brazilian scholars in anthropological and folkloristic studies. He himself worked among the Suyá Indians of the Upper Xingu and has produced some of the best studies on the subject (1979, 1980, 1987). One of his students, Elisabeth Travassos, has worked on music and shamanism among the Kayabi (1985, 1986).

*

Latin American and Caribbean ethnomusicology has suffered also from a serious lack of attention in institutions of higher learning. Schools of music, conservatories, and music departments in universities tend to recognize the need to provide at least an introduction to local musical traditions, but they do so in terms of "musical folklore" conceived as an exotic subject matter. Whenever it is recognized as a discipline in its own right, ethnomusicology tends to receive more regular attention from social scientists than musicians, although younger musicians trained either abroad or in anthropology are now beginning to embrace their field much more broadly.

The explosive and far-reaching growth of urban popular musics since the 1960s has had important ramifications for ethnomusicology throughout Latin America. Until then the study object of folklorists and ethnomusicologists had been primarily folk and primitive musical traditions. Gradually there has been a new awareness of the importance of treating urban popular music in scholarly terms. Few trained ethnomusicologists, however, have given it much attention. Well-informed studies have appeared during the 1970s and early 1980s but primarily from the standpoint of sociological, historical, or literary critical concerns. A review of this literature is provided in my chapter in the *Handbook of Latin American Popular Culture* (1985).

In retrospect, one must recognize that the ideological history of ethnomusicology in Latin America has had little time to develop its own cohesiveness, perhaps, not only because of the heavy domination of European scholarship in most Latin American countries, but also because of the relative isolation of individual efforts in various countries. The last fifteen to twenty years, however, have seen maturation through some qualitatively meritorious efforts in the broader conceptual approach to ethnomusicological studies. In Argentina, Chile, Brazil, and Mexico, especially, true musical ethnographies have been or are being written with very successful results, for fundamental questions of musical meaning can now be elucidated in terms of a particular cultural setting and of the relationship between ideology and meaning. While the present appears more positive than the past, the future looks ever so more promising.

Works Cited

Alvarenga,Oneyda
1946   "A influência negra na música brasileira," *Boletín Latino-Americano de Música* 6 (April):357–407.
1950   *Música popular brasileira.* Porto Alegre: Editora Globo.
Andrade, Mário de
1928   *Ensaio sobre a música brasileira.* São Paulo: Martins.

1937   "O samba rural paulista," *Revista do Arquivo Municipal* 41 (Ano 4):37–116.
1941   *Música do Brasil.* Curitiba: Editora Guaira.
1959   Danças dramáticas do Brasil. São Paulo: Martins.
1963   *Música de feitiçaria no Brasil.* São Paulo: Martins.
Araújo, Alceu Maynard de
1953   "Instrumentos musicais e implementos: achegas ao folclore paulista," *Revista do Arquivo Municipal* 57:147–217.
1964   *Folclore Nacional.* São Paulo: Edições Melhoramentos.
Aretz, Isabel
1984   *Síntesis de la etnomúsica en América Latina.* Caracas: Monte Avila.
Azevedo, Luiz Heitor Corrêa de
1944   "A arte da cantoria," *Cultura Política* (Rio de Janeiro) 42:183–87.
Bastos, Rafael José de Menezes
1978   *A musicológica Kamayurá: para uma antropologia da comunicação no Alto-Xingu.* Brasília: Fundação Nacional do Índio.
1986   "Música, cultura e sociedade no Alto-Xingu: a teoria musical dos índios Kamayurá," *Latin American Music Review* 7 (1):51–80.
Béhague, Gerard
1975   "Notes on Regional and National Trends in Afro-Brazilian Cult Music," in *Tradition and Renewal,* Merlin H. Forster, ed. (Urbana: University of Illinois Press), pp. 68–80.
1984   "Patterns of Candomblé Music Performance: An Afro-Brazilian Religious Setting," in *Performance Practice: Ethnomusicological Perspectives,* Gerard Béhague, ed. (Westport, Conn.: Greenwood Press), pp. 222–54.
1985   "Popular Music," in *Handbook of Latin American Popular Culture,* Harold E. Hinds, Jr., and Charles M. Tatum, eds. (Westport, Conn.: Greenwood Press), pp. 3–38.
Binon-Cossard, Gisèle
1967   "Musique dans le candomblé," in *La musique dans la vie,* Tolia Nikiprowetsky, ed. (Paris: Office de Cooperation Radiophonique).
Cameu, Helsa
1977   *Introdução ao estudo de música indígena brasileira.* Rio de Janeiro: Conselho Federal de Cultura e Dept. de Assuntos Culturais.
Carneiro, Edison
1974   *Folguedos tradicionais.* Rio de Janeiro: Edições Funarte/INF.
Carvalho, José Jorge de
1975   "Formas musicais narrativas do nordeste brasileiro," *Revista INIDEF* 1:33–68.
1984   "Ritual and Music of the Sango Cults of Recife." Ph.D. dissertation, The Queen's University of Belfast.
Cascudo, Luís da Câmara
1954   *Dicionário do folclore brasileiro.* Rio de Janeiro: Ministério da Edução e Cultura, Instituto Nacional do Livro.

Gallet, Luciano
1934   *Estudos de folclore.* Rio de Janeiro: Carlos Wehrs.
Giffoni, Maria Amálie Corrêa
1973   *Danças folclóricas e suas aplicações educativas.* 3d ed. São Paulo: Edições Melhoramentos.
Guerra-Peixe, César
1956   *Maracatus do Recife.* São Paulo.
1970   "Zabumba, orquestra nordestina," *Revista Brasileira de Folclore* 10:15–38.
Herskovits, Melville J.
1944   "Drums and Drummers in Afro-Brazilian Cult Life," *Musical Quarterly* 30:477–92.
Herskovits, Melville J., and Richard Waterman
1949   "Música de culto afrobahiana," *Revista de Estudios Musicales* 1(2): 65–127.
Kubik, Gerhard
1979   *Angolan Traits in Black Music, Games and Dances of Brazil.* Lisbon: Junta de Investigações Científicas do Ultramar.
Lima, Rossini Tavares de
1954   *Melodia e ritmo no folclore de São Paulo.* São Paulo: Ricordi.
1964   "Estudo sobre a viola," *Revista Brasileira de Folclore* 4 (8–10):29–38.
1965   "Música folclórica e instrumentos do Brasil," *Boletín Interamericano de Música* 49.
1971a   *Romanceiro folclórico do Brasil.* São Paulo: Irmãos Vitale.
1971b   *Folclore das festas cíclicas.* São Paulo: Irmãos Vitale.
1978   *A ciência do folclore.* São Paulo.
Mendoza, Vicente T.
1956   *Panorama de la música tradicional de México.* Mexico: Imprenta Universitaria.
Merriam, Alan P.
1951   "Songs of the Afro-Bahian Cults: An Ethnomusicological Analysis." Ph.D. dissertation, Northwestern University.
Mukuna, Kazadi wa
1979   *A contribuição bantu na música popular brasileira.* São Paulo: Globo.
Seeger, Anthony
1979   "What Can We Learn When They Sing? Vocal Genres of the Suyá Indians of Central Brazil," *Ethnomusicology* 23:373–94.
1980   "Sing for Your Sister: The Structure and Performance of Suyá Akia," in *The Ethnography of Musical Performance,* Norma McLeod and Marcia Herndon, eds. (Darby, Penn.: Norwood)
1987   *Why Suyá Sing: A Musical Anthropology of an Amazonian People.* Cambridge: Cambridge University Press.
Setti, Kilsa
1985   *Ubatuba nos Cantos das Praias (Estudo do Caiçara Paulista e de Sua Produção Musical).* São Paulo: Ática.

Souza, José Geraldo de
1963   "Contribuição rítmica modal do canto gregoriano para a música
          brasileira," *Revista CBM* (Conservatório Brasileiro de Música) 21–22.
1966   *Folcmúsica e liturgia*. Petrópolis: Editora Vozes.
Travassos, Elisabeth
1985   "Xamanismo, rituais terapêuticos e modalidades vocais de
          comunicação com o sobrenatural entre os Kayabi," *Revista Pesquisa e
          Música* (Rio de Janeiro), vol. 1 no. 1.
1986   "Die Musik der Kayabi: Schamanen- und Kriegslieder," in *Brasilien:
          Einführung in Musiktraditionen Brasiliens*, Tiago de Oliveira Pinto, ed.
          (Mainz: Schott), pp. 14–47.
Universidade do Brasil
1953   *Relação dos discos gravados no Estado do Ceará*. Rio de Janeiro.
1956   *Relação dos discos gravados no Estado de Minas Gerais*. Rio de
          Janeiro.
1959   *Relação dos discos gravados no Estado do Rio Grande do Sul*. Rio de
          Janeiro.
Vega, Carlos
1944   *Panorama de la música popular Argentina*. Buenos Aires: Losada.
Waddey, Ralph C.
1980–   "*Viola de Samba* and *Samba de Viola* in the Recôncavo of Bahia
   81   (Brasil)," *Latin American Music Review* 1 (2):196–212 and 2 (2):
          252–79.

Carol M. Babiracki

Tribal Music in the Study of Great and Little Traditions of Indian Music

S INCE THE EARLIEST written accounts in the midnineteenth century, the study of India's "little" music traditions—that is, the music of village castes and tribes—has taken a different course from the study of its classical or "great" music traditions. Scholars of classical music, continuing a centuries-old scholastic tradition, have concerned themselves with great individuals, the historical development of the tradition, and aspects of the musical sound such as theory, repertoire, performance practice, and aesthetics.

Those studying the little musical traditions, on the other hand, have tended to focus on the ethnographic present rather than the past and, until recently, on the texts and contexts of the musical expressions rather than their musical structure. Their studies are rich in descriptions of rituals, festivals, and dances; they often contain enumerations of genres and instruments; and they are dominated by the extensive collection, translation, and literary interpretation of song texts. The chroniclers of India's little musics have presented them as group rather than individual expressions, and they have sought to describe cultural norms rather than individual exceptions or exceptional individuals.

In general, approaches to the study of the little musical traditions have been in keeping with the text-centered literary approaches to European folk song in the late nineteenth and early twentieth centuries. On the other hand, scholars of the little traditions have not dealt with some of the common themes of more contemporary Euro-American folklore and folk-music study, such as processes of composition and transmission, individual performers and their repertoires, the geographic mapping of tunes and styles, tune typologies, or the study of music as performance and event. Most of these scholars, moreover, have not followed the contemporary approaches of Euro-American ethnomusicology. Analyses of musical change, musical style, or music and identity, for example, are relatively rare, as are comprehensive musical ethnographies. And the little traditions have not been analyzed as symbolic systems or reflections of deep cultural patterns and values.

Perhaps because they have been approached so differently by researchers, India's great and little traditions have also been studied in isolation from each other. Their historical connections have been little explored beyond superficial references to the possible folk or tribal origins of the names of *rāga*s and possible affinities between ancient Vedic and contemporary tribal scales. Likewise, until recently, their more contemporary interaction has been virtually ignored. Scholars in India, particularly, have been interested in either the great or little traditions, but seldom both. Those who study the great traditions are trained in performance and music theory and history. Those interested in the little traditions are generally either anthropologists or folklorists.

GREAT AND LITTLE TRADITIONS

The conception of Indian civilization as an interplay of great and little traditions was developed in the 1950s by Robert Redfield (1955, 1960), McKim Marriott (1955:171–222), and Milton Singer (1959:i–xvii, 141–82).[1] Their model is particularly relevant to the present discussion. It recognizes two basic social and cultural strata of Indian civilization. The great tradition, centered in geographically dispersed cities, palaces, schools, and temples, is maintained by a relatively small, educated elite. It is supported by doctrine that is recorded in Sanskrit and Persian texts, and it is identified with major religious systems, principally Hinduism and, to lesser extents, Islam and Buddhism. The many and diverse little traditions are localized in villages, maintained by a large, nonliterate or semiliterate peasant class, unstandardized, and orally transmitted. The little traditions contribute to the great tradition as well as draw upon it, reinterpreting its doctrine for local consumption.

Redfield's great-little dichotomy of Indian civilization corresponds to a similar two-part classification of music that is generally accepted in India today. Sudhibhushan Bhattacharya calls these two musical strata "cultivated" ("classical" music) and "uncultivated" ("folk-music" and "tribal music") (Bhattacharya 1968:15, 1970:68). Shyam Parmar's classification is similar. He considers tribal music to be one of three subcategories of folk music, the other two being devotional songs with a close link to classical styles and "countryside music," which includes ceremonial, seasonal, work, ritual, narrative, and love songs (Parmar 1977a:44–45). The common classification of tribal music as a type of folk music in India is also implied in titles such as "Folksongs of the Tribals of West Bengal" (Raha 1967) and *Folk-songs of the Bhils* (Bhuriya 1979).

The classification of the world of Indian music into two strata, *mārga sangīt* and *deśi sangīt,* dates back at least to the eighth- or ninth- century treatise *Bṛhad-deśi* by Matanga.[2] As Matanga used them, the two terms distinguished the divine ritual music of the Vedas *(mārga saṅgīt,* music of the Way) from secular, regional music *(deśi saṅgīt,* music of the country-side or province). Matanga and theorists who followed him considered *deśi saṅgīt* provincial music, "developed and cultivated by the thinking folk of the land" (Sambamoorthy 1952:68). "It was the art music of the land. This was different from the folk music which was current among the lower strata of society" (Sambamoorthy 1952:105; see also Ayyangar 1972:5, 152; Capwell 1986:38). The "folk music" of Sambamoorthy's "lower strata" was not discussed in Matanga's treatise. The *mārga deśi* dichotomy of the *Bṛhad-deśi* was reiterated as late as the thirteenth cen-tury in Sarngadvea's *Saṅgīta Ratnākaram.* According to R. Rangara-manuja Ayyangar, Sarngadvea's *deśi saṅgīt,* like that of Matanga, "could not be equated with folk or tribal music" (Ayyangar 1972:5).

Today, *mārga* and *deśi saṅgīt* are interpreted rather differently in common usage. *Mārga saṅgīt* is often taken to mean the major canonical, classical tra-ditions, and *deśi saṅgīt* has come to mean all regional, localized village little traditions (Capwell 1986:38; Vatsyayan 1980:159; Parmar 1977a:36). As they are used today, *mārga* and *deśi* are roughly equivalent to the more com-mon terms *śāstriya saṅgīt* (scientific, canonical music) and *lok saṅgīt* (folk music) and to Redfield and Singer's great and little traditions.

As Capwell has noted, *lok saṅgīt* is the semantic equivalent of the En-glish "folk music" (Capwell 1986:38), and the *śāstriya-lok* or great-little model of India's musical traditions does resemble the European concep-tion of classical and folk strata of music, with the exception that *lok* may also include certain types of urban "cultivated" folk music within its scope (Bhattacharya 1970). Whether the shift in the interpretation of *mārga* and *deśi* since the thirteenth century arose spontaneously or as a result of Western influence would be difficult to determine. There is no doubt, however, that Western scholarship has had a more considerable impact on the study of the little musical traditions than on the great traditions in In-dia and thus has contributed to the dichotomy of approaches to the study of India's musics. Before considering the nature of that scholarship in more detail, this discussion turns for a moment to the little musical tradi-tions themselves and the definition of tribal music in India.

"FOLK" AND "TRIBAL" MUSIC IN INDIA

The *śāstriya-lok,* or great-little, taxonomy of musics in India and the corre-sponding dichotomy in approaches to their study reflect certain characteristics of the musical cultures themselves. Little traditions, whether of peasant castes or tribes, share some common features, particularly in their extramusical aspects. They lack an articulated theory or doctrine and are transmitted orally, without the systematic instruction of the canonical traditions. Based in villages, their performance is often collective and connected to agricultural and seasonal rituals and festivals. Scholars generally consider the little musical traditions more functional than classical music, performed more for pragmatic needs than for aesthetic satisfaction (Parmar 1977a:13; Ranade 1985: 8–9, 12). The little traditions are also thought by some to have a timeless quality that "defies chronological placement in time"(Ranade 1985:12). Their histories are undocumented, and the complex patterns of changes in song texts, tunes, and rhythmic accompaniment as they pass from village to village and generation to generation make historical reconstruction extremely difficult. Although it is not always acknowledged by scholars, there is also a constant musical interaction among tribes and between them and castes, further frustrating the possibility of accurately reconstructing their musical histories. In my experience, participants in little musical traditions have a sense of their musical pedigrees, but pedigree is not necessarily required to gain status within the traditions and is not remembered or documented in any systematic way, as it is among classical musicians.

On the basis of such contextual similarities, Bonnie Wade has seen little significant difference between the musical traditions of tribal and nontribal villagers of India. In her article on Indian folk music in *The New Grove,* she writes: "In this article 'tribal music' is not considered categorically distinct from 'folk music' because the traditional uses of music appear to be similar among tribal and nontribal peoples. Also, in terms of music itself the divergences do not necessarily fall along tribal and nontribal lines" (Wade 1980:147).[3]

So we might ask, in what sense *is* it valid to speak of tribal music as a category of Indian music distinct from other village musical traditions? I might have begun this essay with that question and with the larger issue of the definition of tribe in India. The word "tribe" was first applied in India by the early British administrators to ethnic groups who were geographically and socioculturally isolated from the mainstream of Indian society. Since then, determining the similarities and differences between tribes and nontribal peasant castes has been a major issue among anthropologists studying village communities in India (see, for example, Ghurye 1943; Atal 1963; Mathur 1972).

The primitive, isolated tribal ideal type of Redfield (1955) probably does not exist in India today. The 427 distinct groups classified as tribes in the 1971 census actually represent a broad spectrum of societies, from those that are highly autonomous, culturally distinct, and isolated from caste society to those almost completely assimilated into it. Anthropologists have developed relatively clear, though debated, criteria for distinguishing tribal societies from peasant, caste societies and for plotting the movement of groups in one direction or the other (see, for example, S. Sinha 1965, 1973; Roy Burman 1968; Sachchidananda 1970). At one extreme of this tribe-caste continuum are tribal groups such as the Birhor, Juang, and Baiga, whose communities today remain relatively isolated, unstratified, occupationally unspecialized, and kinship-based. They maintain distinct languages, belief systems, and customs, and have rejected acculturation into the predominantly Hindu caste social order. Rural peasant castes, at the other extreme, are occupationally specialized and part of a larger hierarchical social order. Their linguistic and cultural orientation is regional, and they operate within the sphere of a still larger, urban-based, literate sociocultural system (the great tradition) with which they maintain economic, political, social, cultural, and religious ties. The majority of tribes in India fall somewhere between the tribe and caste extremes of the continuum.

A key consideration to emerge from studies of the complex relationships between tribes and peasant castes is a tribe's self-perception of its identity and status. As Surajit Sinha has noted, many tribes in India have moved closer to caste society in terms of their economy, social organization, customs, or festivals, but do not consider themselves subservient to a larger social, religious, or cultural system (Sinha 1965:61, 69, 75; Roy Burman 1968:88). A tribe's perception of itself as a separate social unit and its cultural self-sufficiency remain important indicators of tribal status in India today.

Tribal identity has become institutionalized in modern India through the government's classification of certain groups as Scheduled Tribes (ādivāsi, original inhabitant) under Article 342 of the constitution. The purpose of scheduling is to provide economic and educational opportunities to disadvantaged groups while safeguarding their way of life. However, the constitution does not offer any operative definition of tribe, and it is clear that the list was not compiled according to any uniform set of criteria. Nonetheless, official classification as a Scheduled Tribe does play a role today in the maintenance of a group's tribal identity.

In the anthropological literature, in government bureaucratic parlance, and in common usage, tribe (ādivāsi) is a meaningful classification of people in India today. In this sense, at least, "tribal music" may be taken as a meaningful category as well. The terms "tribal" and "folk," as categories of music, however, are far less well defined. As it is commonly used, the term "tribal music" simply means the music of a group considered to be a tribe. Folk music *(lok sangīt)* is much more difficult to circumscribe. For example, the term may be used to designate the music of various categories of people: villagers in general, which includes most tribal people; agricultural peasants, which includes some tribal people; or caste, Hindu peasants, which excludes most tribal people. A reader coming upon references to a "folk-culture" or the "village folk" cannot be sure whom the author means. As a designation of musical strata, the term "folk" is equally vague. It may denote a broad category that includes the music of both tribal and nontribal village communities (Parmar 1977a:44–45), or it may more specifically refer to only that of nontribal villagers (Bhattacharya 1968).

Ashok Ranade prefers to define "primitive" (tribal) and "folk" musics according to characteristics of the "products" themselves rather than the identities of the producers. Thus, he classes as folk those musics characterized by collectivity in performance and composition, oral transmission, emotional content, function, association with a particular geographic area, and close interaction with art music. He prefers the term primitive to tribal and defines this category of music by such characteristics as its close association with dance, functional and ritualistic qualities, greater emphasis on rhythm than on melody, lack of literary quality, and symbolic properties (Ranade 1985). Bhattacharya's classification of tribes and their music is similar. He subdivides tribal music into three categories, those of the primitive tribes, the semitribes, and the semicastes, on the basis of musical complexity and ritualistic function (Bhattacharya 1968:6). According to Ranade and Bhattacharya's taxonomies, the music of some of India's tribes would be classed as primitive, while that of others must be considered folk. Among some tribes, certain musical genres and performances would be primitive, while others would be folk.

Although tribal music tends to be designated by many as a type of uncultivated or folk music in India, it is frequently treated as separate and distinct from other types of little musical traditions. In his book *Ethnomusicology and India* (1968), Bhattacharya begins his taxonomy of Indian music with the overall two-part classification of cultivated and uncultivated (p. 15), but he later writes, "there are, therefore, three major types of Indian music, namely, classical music, tribal music (or primitive music) and folk-music" (p. 23). Ranade dispenses with the two-part classification altogether in favor of a four-part taxonomy: primitive (tribal), folk, classical (art), and popular (Ranade 1985). The association of tribal music with a particular category of people may account for this special treatment. But there are also important differences between tribal and nontribal village musical cultures, particularly in musical style and content, aspects that have received the least scholarly attention.

The music, or some portion thereof, of a tribe that has maintained a unique linguistic and cultural identity also tends to be unique, different from that of both its tribal and nontribal neighbors. Even linguistically related tribes living within the same geographical region appear to differ from each other more musically than they do linguistically (Bhattacharya 1970:66, 68; Parmar 1977a:47; Nag 1981:323). The multiethnic Chotanagpur plateau of southern Bihar provides a good example. There, some twenty-nine tribes and many more artisan and agricultural castes share common economies, material cultures, and belief systems. In performance and context, the musical cultures of the tribes and some artisan castes ("Scheduled Castes") are similar, and they all use similar drums as accompaniment. However, large geographically circumscribed tribes, like the Santal, Munda, Oraon, Ho, and Kharia, have maintained distinct languages and musics. That is, the individual tunes, song texts, drum patterns, and musical styles of each tribe are unique as are the steps and styles of their dances. And the songs and dances of each tribe are performed by and for the members of that tribe alone. In Chotanagpur, as in many other tribal areas of India, the divergences in musical sound do indeed fall along tribal lines. The maintenance of a distinct music may, in fact, be a marker of tribe in India.

By contrast, a nontribal, regional folk music unites castes of different occupations, statuses, customs, and beliefs (*jātis*). When tribal groups do choose to identify with the more widespread, regional, Hindu-based social and cultural system, they usually adopt the language and regional folk music of that system as well. Regional folk musics tend to unite diverse populations over a large geographic area, while indigenous tribal musics are confined to one linguistic and cultural group.[4] In any one area, a regional folk-music culture may also be more diverse than those of tribes in the same area. A single regional folk-song repertory may be performed by groups of nonspecialists and by semiprofessional soloists, with dance and without, in a courtyard festival or a stage performance (see Henry 1976, 1977). The musical expression of a single tribe, on the other hand, tends to be more homogeneous, typically nonspecialized, participatory, and often accompanied by collective dance. Furthermore, most tribes do not segregate musical performances by men and women as is typical of nontribal village musical performances, even among low-status artisan castes.

We are at a disadvantage in evaluating the differences in musical sound between tribal and nontribal folk musics because of the lack of recordings, transcriptions, and useful descriptions. However, the little that is available suggests that there may be musical characteristics that are unique to indig-

enous tribal musics in India. For example, singing in parallel harmonies
and bitonality in responsorial song performance are found among tribes
throughout India, including the Kuravan of Kerala and the Jaunsari of Uttar Pradesh (Wade 1980:153), the Gond (Knight 1983), the Santal (Parmar
1977b:23), and the Munda. Some scholars have noted a preference for
asymmetrical rythmic patterns in tribal musics across India (Bhattacharya
1970:67, 70), and Roderic Knight has observed other rhythmic features
that are also found in indigenous Mundari songs: the simultaneous performance of duple and triple meters (Knight 1987), and a characteristic "out-
of-phase" relationship between phrases or beats of a song and its accompanying drum pattern and dance (Knight 1983, 1987). Harold Powers has
noted that, although most South Asian melodic lines are characterized by
conjunct motion, those of the Sherpas of Nepal and the Gonds of Madhya
Pradesh—and, we might add, those of most tribes in the central plateau—
are characterized by gapped scales and skips of large intervals (Powers
1980:72). The sound characteristics of the vast majority of tribal musics
have yet to be analyzed, and recorded examples are rare. Comparative
study of tribal musics may reveal features that do distinguish indigenous
tribal music, or perhaps a strata of indigenous tribal music, from the nontribal little traditions.

   Tribal and nontribal folk musics differ most in their respective relationships to the great, classical music traditions. Indigenous tribal musics do
not stylistically resemble the classical traditions, and their song texts, when
in tribal languages, show little or no content related to the great tradition,
whether it be Hindu, Muslim, or Buddhist. It is on this basis that Parmar
and others consider tribal music a special category in spite of its functional
or contextual resemblence to other little traditions (Parmar 1977a:46–52,
1977b:23; Bhattacharya 1968:24; Ranade 1985:14). In my experience in
southern Bihar, tribal people do not recognize classical music as a cultivated or ideal form of their own music and do not aspire to emulate it in
content or performance style. In fact, many, perhaps most, tribal people
have little or no knowledge of its existence. What contact they have with
the great tradition is mediated through nontribal folk musicians with
whom they may come into contact.

   India's nontribal, regional folk musics developed under the patronage of
feudal rajas and landlords and in temples and other religious centers.
Through these institutions, nontribal, village musical specialists from
across India came into contact with each other and with classical musicians. It is a hallmark of the nontribal little musical traditions that they

have borrowed from and contributed to the great traditions. Powers notes several text-related musical features that are shared by classical music and devotional song traditions and, we should add, by the nontribal folk traditions as well. These include a cyclical leading back from stanza to refrain, musical and textual contrast between verse and refrain, and musical and textual end rhyme (Powers 1980:75). These characteristics are lacking in many, perhaps most, indigenous tribal musics. Nontribal village musicians typically aspire to emulate classical performance style, often introducing a drone and melodic support on harmonium or *sarangi* to their stage and media performances. Classical and nontribal folk musics may indeed be regarded as great and little expressions of the same tradition. This was Redfield and Singer's original understanding of the model. On the basis of their sound and textual structure, the tribal musical traditions would seem to demand a classification separate from the nontribal folk traditions.

The generalizations about India's tribal musics presented here are, of course, not true for all groups officially classified as tribe in India. Some groups classified as tribe no longer maintain distinct languages or musical systems. Others maintain their own musics, but participate to various degrees in the regional folk musical culture as well. The varieties of interaction between the indigenous tribal and regional folk musics are probably as diverse as the tribes themselves. The generalizations may be typical, however, of those tribes that exhibit relatively high degrees of "tribalness," those that fall closest to the tribal extreme of the theoretical tribe-caste continuum.

The scholarly and popular classification of both tribal and nontribal folk musics within a single category (folk, uncultivated, little, *lok*) has been based primarily on considerations of performance context and textual content rather than on sound characteristics or textual structure. Scholarly study of the little musical traditions was initiated by colonial administrators and missionaries from the West and shaped by their backgrounds and purposes. Their attention to tribal and folk rather than classical musics and to performance contexts and song texts rather than musical sound contributed to the view of tribal and folk musics as two aspects of the same nonclassical strata of Indian music.

THE COLONIAL LEGACY

The earliest chroniclers of tribal musical cultures in India were British colonial administrators, European travelers and missionaries, and the Indians they trained to assist them. These men were not skilled in musical analysis and were unfamiliar with and uninterested in India's classical music. As Powers has observed, although British interest, thought, and organization shaped disciplines in India from law to archaeology, anthropology, and folklore, the British "did nothing for music" because they were "unable to accept Indian art music" (Powers 1980:90). To put it another way, they were unable or unwilling to accept Indian music as art. Their interest in nonclassical village musical expression was not for its artistic value but as a source of information about the languages, beliefs, and customs of the land they governed. As foreign rulers, they had a pragmatic need to understand the people of India in order to carry out their missions, whether trading, governing, converting, or guiding social reform. While foreign scholars studied the texts and contexts of village songs, Indian scholars continued to apply indigenous models of analysis to the structure, aesthetics, and history of the classical traditions. This dichotomy in traditions of scholarship has continued to reflect and reinforce the *śāstriya-lok* division of the world of Indian music.

The colonial researchers of the rural tribes and castes drew their methods and models from both folklore and anthropology (specifically, ethnography and ethnology), two disciplines that were taking shape in the West, sustained by European colonial adventures abroad. Regardless of their national origin, these researchers wrote primarily in English, the official language of the colonial government. Articles and books in other languages were translated into English, often soon after their initial publication. The work of the European researchers of tribes would have been impossible without the often unheralded assistance of their Indian translators and collaborators.

The study of India's little musical traditions began in the late eighteenth century as the British East India Company began to take a territorial interest in the subcontinent. The earliest research efforts were initiated, not at the government level, but by part-time scholars, amateur enthusiasts, and travelers. They established India's first scholarly research societies and journals. The Asiatic Society of Bengal, for example, was founded in 1784, and the Bombay branch of the Royal Asiatic Society followed in 1804 (Sen Gupta 1967:68). The earliest reports of the cultures and lore of the rural tribes and castes appear in their proceedings and journals, in travel accounts, and in Company reports.

The folklorists' approaches to both tribal and nontribal village-song traditions were virtually identical. Collections of nontribal village songs appear somewhat éarlier, however, perhaps because they were more accessible both geographically and linguistically. Most folklore studies of tribal songs appeared after 1860. Folklore research in India grew out of Indic, Sanskritic textual studies, but its aims and methods were shaped by European folklore scholarship as well. As might be expected, colonial folklore enthusiasts in India were interested primarily in collecting and classifying verbal lore. Their interest in tribal and folk music was confined to song texts, which they approached as samples of oral literature. Texts were usually presented in free or metrical English translations, occasionally with Roman transliterations, and without any accompanying musical notations. Collections were typically organized by thematic content rather than by song genre, performance occasion, or musical characteristics. For most tribes, this arrangement reveals nothing about song performance, cultural significance, or *emic* song taxonomies.

The folkloristic approach to tribal song traditions remained popular throughout the colonial period, and that popularity continues today. The last decades of the colonial period saw the publication of more ambitious, comprehensive collections (see, for example, Elwin 1946; Elwin and Hivale 1944) and the emergence of Indian collectors, most of whom published their works in English translation (see, for example, S. C. Majumdar 1925; D. N. Majumdar 1947).

W. G. Archer was one of the most ambitious collectors of tribal songs. Between 1940 and 1948, he published collections in six books and at least a dozen articles (see, for example, Archer 1940). A seventh book, on Santal culture and folklore, was published in 1974 (Archer 1974). Archer's work had a considerable impact on folklore study in India and on the tribal communities themselves. Four of his books, collections in tribal languages, were collaborative efforts with teams of collectors from the tribes themselves. In his 1940 collection in English of Oraon verbal lore, he expanded the usual folkloristic presentation of texts to include his analysis of their cultural background as well. His folkloristic/ethnographic model was accepted as a new standard for folklore scholarship in India.

It was the ethnographic approach to tribal traditions, however, that eventually distinguished studies of tribal music from those of other musical traditions. During the colonial period, most references to tribal songs, instruments, dances, and musical occasions were embedded in ethnographic studies. Articles and reports describing tribal people and their life styles actually appeared somewhat earlier than the collections of their verbal lore. Ethnographic research at the government level was initiated in the 1870s by the colonial census authorities, and the census office and other government agencies continue that work today. Government interest in the customs, languages, and histories of the tribes was probably responsible for the sudden increase in articles and books about tribes and tribal lore beginning in the late 1860s. Administrator-researchers such as E. T. Dalton

(1872), W. W. Hunter (1881), and W. Crooke (1896) were encyclopedic in their approach to collecting and presenting information about the tribes. Their apparent aim was to document everything concerning tribal customs, beliefs, history, social organization, festivals, and the like. References to musical genres and events and occasional song texts in English translation were rather inconsistently included within discussions organized by caste, tribe, or geographic area.

In the early years of the twentieth century, researchers began to produce more systematic ethnographic studies of single tribes. W. H. R. River's study of the To-das (1967 [1906]) was one of the earliest of the large, systematic ethnographies and became a model of the genre for other scholars. S. C. Roy, a lawyer by trade, was one of the few Indian ethnographers of the early twentieth century, and his work has had a great impact on tribal studies in India (Roy 1912, 1915, 1935). The ethnographies of the early twentieth century remain the most-quoted sources of ethnographic information about tribes today. Their authors tended to treat each tribal group as a well-defined isolate, and so overlooked or dismissed their cultural interaction with other tribes and castes. Most of these later ethnographies are better sources of musical information than those of the nineteenth century, and they all cover similar topics: the classification of music and dance genres, the so-cial organization of music making, instruments, and festivals and other musi-cal occasions. Like the folklorists, Rivers, Roy, and others were interested in songs as textual sources of literary and cultural information. Notations of melodies were rare.

The ethnographers and ethnologists of the twentieth century were the teachers and models for the scholars, both Indian and Western, who fol-lowed them. There were remarkable contributions from many: Christoph von Fürer-Haimendorf, D. N. Majumdar, W. V. Grigson, J. P. Mills, and many others. The efforts of a few are worthy of mention as typical in ap-proach and exceptional in scope.

Father John Hoffmann, a Jesuit priest from Germany, devoted twenty years to the study and welfare of the Mundas in Bihar. Like many other missionaries, Hoffmann was also an accomplished linguist and published a definitive grammar of the Mundari language in 1903. His sixteen-volume, English-language *Encyclopaedia Mundarica,* written between 1930 and 1941 with the help of Arthur van Emelen and other Jesuits, is filled with transliterations and translations of song texts accompanied by contextual information about their performance (Hoffmann 1950).

Verrier Elwin is probably the best-known of the colonial ethnographers. Like Hoffmann, Elwin immersed himself in tribal language and culture. He lived among the Gond in Madhya Pradesh for over two decades and was assisted in his research by his Gond wife (Misra 1971). In the 1940s and 1950s, Elwin and his team of researchers compiled ethnographic monographs on four tribes of Madhya Pradesh and another two of Orissa. Although Elwin did not consider the collection of folklore to be his primary task, he also published large, annotated compendiums of oral texts, including song texts, in English translation.

The approaches of Elwin and Hoffmann to the study of tribal culture were similar despite their different missions in India. Hoffmann's first purpose clearly was to spread Catholicism and safeguard the interests of his flock. Although trained in Christian theology, Elwin was neither a missionary nor primarily an administrator. A student of Gandhian ideals, he settled among the Gonds initially as a social worker and not a social scientist. However, both he and Hoffmann eventually represented tribal interests to the British colonial government and mediated between official India and the tribes.

These two men differed from most administrator-ethnographers in that they each lived among one tribe for decades, and their work reflects that intimate familiarity. Still, they collected the same sort of ethnographic information and verbal lore (including song texts) as did the administrators. Both were most interested in recording and preserving the original, untainted traditions and lore of the tribes before they became unrecognizable or disappeared altogether. The irony, of course, is that they preserved this legacy in English, rendering it inaccessible to most tribal people. Their influence also undoubtedly hastened the pace of cultural change among the tribes.

Any mention of musical sound itself was extremely rare in colonial ethnographies and collections of lore. Hoffmann and Elwin, however, both recognized the importance of studying the sound component of tribal songs, and, lacking the necessary expertise themselves, they brought in others to notate and analyze the tunes. Father Peter Hipp's 1908 notations of Mundari songs and drum patterns, bound within the *Encyclopaedia Mundarica,* are some of the earliest examples we have of tribal music in Western notation. Hoffmann turned over Hipp's notations to a third person, Father Hugo Aman, who made analytical notes concerning their structure (Hipp and Aman 1950). Both Hipp and Aman described Mundari tunes in terms familiar to them, referring to their "major and minor modes (keys)," "appoggiaturas," motives and themes, and implicit triadic harmonies.

It was through Elwin that Walter Kaufmann was able to make a brief trip to Madhya Pradesh in 1941 to collect the information about Gond songs and instruments that he published in brief articles in American journals

(Kaufmann 1941, 1960, 1961). Kaufmann presented the melodies and drum patterns in Western notation without their texts and with no analysis, aside from brief comments contributed by Curt Sachs. His ethnographic notes were also sparse. It is interesting that, despite the value that Hoffmann and Elwin both placed on an intimate knowledge of tribal language and culture, the melodies and drum patterns of tribal songs were collected and analyzed quite apart from their texts and contexts and by people with extremely limited exposure to the tribes and their musical performance.

The studies of Toda musical culture by the linguist Murray B. Emeneau deserve special mention. Emeneau's *Toda Songs* (1971) is the most thoroughly annotated and analyzed collection of tribal song texts. In this work and in related articles, Emeneau included detailed discussions about Toda processes of song composition, their ideas about music, and individual Toda composers and singers. To my knowledge, there has been no other study like it, before or since. Emeneau repeatedly stated that he was unable to record Toda song performances, but the Indiana University Archives of Traditional Music contain approximately nineteen cylinders of Kota and Toda songs recorded by him in the late 1930s.

Throughout the colonial period, India's tribal musical cultures were studied from two scholarly perspectives, the folkloristic and the ethnographic. The text-centered folkloristic approach was applied not only to tribal songs but to the other little musical traditions as well, while the ethnographers were drawn more strongly to the geographically isolated and culturally well-defined tribes. In their monographs they included information about musical occasions as well as the genres and texts of songs, although textual and contextual information was not always presented together. By the 1930s and 1940s scholars in each camp were beginning to combine the two approaches. Archer and the folklorists who followed him added cultural and symbolic interpretation to their song-text collections, and anthropologists and linguists like Hoffmann, Elwin, and Emeneau drew on large collections of textual lore for historical and ethnographic insight. In those rare instances when musical sound itself was addressed, it was by men with special knowledge of music but little of India's tribes. Text, sound, dance, performance context, and cultural context were still considered quite apart from each other, in separate chapters, in separate books, and by separate scholars.

POST-COLONIAL SCHOLARSHIP

Indian scholars of tribes and their cultures came into their own almost immediately after India's independence. Still, most scholarship on lit-

tle musical traditions has continued to fall within the colonial ethnograph-
ic/folkloristic model, even while more integrated and comprehensive
approaches to the study of musical culture were being tested elsewhere in
the world, particularly in Africa and native North America. Even in the
last twenty years or so, when Indian scholars have embraced other approaches to the study of music, their focus has been selective, on texts
alone, texts and contexts, or musical sound, but rarely on all three.

There have been some notable departures from the colonial models of
scholarship. Collections of song texts published today are more likely to
include transcriptions of their melodies, although their inclusion is by no
means standard. And the customary forms of melodic transcription, staff
notation and *sargam* notation, are increasingly replaced or supplemented
by graphic notation which visually highlights melodic contour (see Deva
and Kuckertz 1978; Satpathy 1980; Prasad 1985). And, unlike many of
their colonial forerunners, postcolonial researchers have tended to collect
their information in short visits (days or weeks), often in collaboration
with teams of assistants and translators. Field research involving long im-
mersion in tribal life, language, and culture is a phenomenon of the colonial era.

Collections of tribal lore in Hindi, regional languages, and tribal languages began appearing in the 1930s and 1940s. The pioneering work of
Archer and his many collaborators has been noted. In the last forty years,
such efforts have flourished, and published collections of song texts are increasingly available to the tribal communities themselves. The impetus for
these efforts has come from educators, government agencies, language and
cultural organizations, church organizations, and tribal cultural leaders.
Many publications in tribal languages are no more than pamphlets, often
published by the poets and singers themselves. They find their way to villages where they are circulated as sources of new song texts and supplements to personal "songbooks."

The study of India's tribal musics by Western scholars has been limited
in the last twenty years or so by restrictions imposed by the government on
their movements in tribal villages, particularly in border regions and politically unstable areas. Those Western ethnomusicologists who have contributed to postindependence scholarship have continued to follow two broad
and typically Euro-American approaches: (1) descriptive collections of
texts with background information and perhaps melodic transcriptions
(Kuckertz 1982; Deva and Kuckertz 1978) or (2) more comprehensive musical ethnographies documenting many aspects of a musical culture, such
as sound, text, performance techniques, cultural context, and social orga-

nization, and relying on Western concepts of tune, phrase, interval, scale, and beat that are meaningful to Western ethnomusicologists, but foreign to most tribal conceptualizations of music (Deva and Kuckertz 1981; Knight 1983, 1985; Babiracki 1984, 1985, 1990).

Within the last twenty years, Indian scholars have begun to challenge the applicability of Western conceptual models, particularly those developed during the colonial period, to the study of little musical traditions. They are debating the very definitions of ethnomusicology and musicology in the Indian context. Many Western ethnomusicologists today are inclined to define their field less by its subject matter and more by its methods and approaches, particularly those that are believed to have some universal applicability.[5] A number of Indian scholars, on the other hand, have begun to seek definitions and approaches that are specific to music in India. I. E. N. Chauhan has argued that to include all of India's music within the scope of ethnomusicology is to disregard the differences between the "highly developed" classical music and that of the "primitive" tribes (Chauhan 1973:27–29). For Chauhan, ethnomusicology in India is the study of non-Vedic and nonclassical music. Likewise, Ashok Ranade would place the study of folk and tribal musics within the scope of folkloristics and ethnomusicology ("cultural musicology") and the theoretical studies of art music within the discipline of "comparative musicology" (Ranade 1986). Both Chauhan and Ranade's definitions of these fields, while different in terminology, reiterate the śāstriya-lok, great-little dichotomy of music and musical scholarships in India.

Addressing the study of little ("folk") performing art traditions, Ranade has sharply criticized the continued application of models of scholarship that were developed by the colonial researchers. He argues that the "nonselective, total-view models tried out by the ethnodisciplines," with their attempts to remain "valuationally neutral," do not have the same validity for an insider as they do for the outsider. Instead, Ranade advocates approaching folk traditions like other performing arts, with emphasis placed on their qualitative, nonverbal, and performing aspects (1983:39–40).

A small number of Indian scholars have recently turned their attention to another neglected aspect of tribal music, the musical sound itself. Instead of seeking approaches developed outside India, these scholars have drawn terminology, methods, and conceptual models from those developed within India for the study of the great musical traditions. For example, Bhattacharya (1968:64; 1970:69) and Sunil Satpathy (1980:15–18) have both sought the antecedents of India's Vedic and classical musical traditions in the contemporary songs of selected tribes, such as the Santal and Kinnara.[6] Tribal melodies and rhythms are frequently described in terms of classical rāgas, thāṭs, and tālas (Chauhan 1973:38; Nag 1981:312–16).

One of the most interesting applications of a great-tradition analytical model to the study of tribal music is Purnima Sinha's 1970 comparative study of tribal, folk, and classical music in a multiethnic district of West Bengal (P. Sinha 1970). Sinha seeks to establish an underlying connection between the pitch material of primitive (Santali), folk (Indo-Aryan, caste), and classical (Hindustani) musics through a method of quantified, mathematical analysis proposed by A. N. Sanyal (1959) for the analysis of Hindustani *rāga*s and *rāgini*s. We might question her application of Sanyal's methods. She postulates the latent presence of pitches in tribal scales based on their presence, both latent and real, in Hindustani *rāga*s.

Nevertheless, Sinha's study is significant for the new ground it breaks. It is problem-oriented and comparative and presents a rare examination of the interaction of musical strata within one cultural area in India. She also includes brief explanations of performance contexts and song genres, texts in transliteration and translation, and tunes in *sargam* and graph notation. Onkar Prasad has recently applied the same analytical method to a study of Santal songs to demonstrate their underlying continuity (Prasad 1985). Both studies show tribal music to be worthy of musical as well as folkloristic and ethnographic analysis.

The application of great-tradition models to the study of India's little musical traditions represents a blurring of the clear dichotomy of scholarly approaches to Indian music that is the legacy of the colonial period. It does not, however, represent a true merging of those approaches. Musical sound and text/context are still analyzed quite apart from each other and with models derived from different scholarly traditions. And while methods and approaches for describing and analyzing sound materials have been borrowed from the classical scholastic traditions, other approaches to the study of music have not. We still know little about learning and transmission of little musical traditions, about the aesthetic judgments of their performers, or about the role of individuals in their creation and performance.

*

The conceptual classification of the world of Indian music into two parts—great and little, *śāstriya* and *lok,* classical and nonclassical—has been shaped to some extent by the nature and contexts of the musical expressions themselves. The dichotomy has been supported, however, by a corresponding dichotomy of traditions of musical scholarship. While an indigenous tradition of scholarship developed within the great musical tradition, there were no indigenous models for the study of the little traditions. The study of nonclassical, village music was introduced by Europeans, who were interested in both tribal and folk musics for the same reasons, as sources of historical and ethnographic information and as specimens of poetry. The recent studies of Santal music by Sinha and Prasad may reflect a new search for indigenous analytical models that are applicable to the tribal musical traditions. Meanwhile, the great-little dichotomy of musical scholarship remains, and the unique characteristics of India's tribal musics remain largely unknown.

Notes

1. All three men, with other social anthropologists, were involved in Redfield's Project on Comparative Civilization at the University of Chicago. The project ran from 1953 to 1961. In the spring of 1956, a seminar held on the subject at the University of Chicago was conducted jointly by Redfield, Singer, and Surajit Sinha, who also contributed to the great-little conceptual model (Singer 1964:95, 1966:1; Sinha 1959:311).

2. The date of the *Bṛhad-deśi* given here is according to Powers (1980:78).

3. In the text that follows, Wade does make brief references to the music of specific tribes and points out some important differences between tribal and nontribal musics. It should be noted that there is still very little information about the music of India's diverse tribal groups, beyond samples of song texts and sketchy descriptions of musical occasions. Because scholars have been concerned primarily with the texts and contexts of the little musical traditions, tribal and nontribal village musics may appear more alike in the literature than they actually are.

4. This has been observed by Bhattacharya (1968:24; 1970:68) and Parmar (1977a:46−52) and has been confirmed by my own research in the southern-most districts of Bihar.

5. I will note only a few, by way of illustration: musical ethnography, including Alan Merriam's sound-concept-behavior model of musical culture; sociolinguistic interpretations of music and music making; and interpretations of musical change based on concepts of urbanization, modernization, and Westernization.

6. Certain tribal songs and Vedic chants were chosen for comparison by virtue of their simple or "primitive" structures rather than any demonstrated cultural or historical connections. Speculations about the connection between tribal and Vedic music would appear to be based on a colonial model of evolution and development whereby human culture progresses from the ancient and simple to the contemporary, advanced, and complex. Bhattacharya and Satpathy's speculations on the tribal-Vedic connection have been convincingly challenged by N. G. Nag (1981).

Works Cited

Archer, W. G.
1940   *The Blue Grove (The Poetry of the Oraons)*. London: George Allen and Unwin Brothers.
1974   *The Hill of Flutes: Life, Love, and Poetry in Tribal India*. Pittsburgh: University of Pittsburgh Press.

Atal, Yogesh
1963   "The Tribe-Caste Question," *Bulletin of the Bihar Tribal Research Institute,* 5 (1).
Ayyangar, R. Rangaramanuja
1972   *History of South Indian (Carnatic) Music from Vedic Times to the Present.* Madras: the author.
Babiracki, Carol M.
1984   Articles on the musical instruments of northeastern Central India, in *The New Grove Dictionary of Musical Instruments,* Stanley Sadie, ed., 2 vols. (London: Macmillan).
1985   "Indigenizers," in Bruno Nettl, *The Western Impact on World Music* (New York: Schirmer), pp. 93–96.
1990   "Music and the History of Mundari-Caste Interaction," in *Ethnomusicology and Modern Music History,* S. Blum, P. V. Bohlman, and D. M. Neuman, eds. (Urbana: University of Illinois Press).
Bhattacharya, Sudhibhushan
1968   *Ethnomusicology and India.* Calcutta: Indian Publications.
1970   "The Role of Music in Society and Culture," *Sangeet Natak* 16:65–72.
Bhuriya, Mahipal
1979   *Folk-songs of the Bhils.* Indore: Mahipal Publications.
Capwell, Charles
1986   *Music of the Bauls of Bengal.* Kent, Ohio: Kent State University Press.
Chauhan, I. E. N.
1973   "Ethnomusicology and Kinnaur: A Suggested Methodology," *Sangeet Natak* 27:27–48.
Crooke, W.
1896   *The Tribes and Castes of the North-Western Provinces and Oudh.* Calcutta.
Dalton, E. T.
1872   *Descriptive Ethnology of Bengal.* Calcutta: Superintendent of Government Printing.
Deva, B. C., and J. Kuckertz
1978   "Songs of the Todas of the Nilgiris," *Sangeet Natak* 50:5–26.
1981   *Brhadud Vaghyamurali and the Daff-gan of the Deccan: Studies in the Regional Folk Music of South India.* Munich: Katzbichler.
Elwin, Verrier
1946   *Folk Songs of Chhattisgarh.* Bombay: Oxford University Press.
Elwin, Verrier, and Shamrao Hivale
1944   *Folksongs of the Maikal Hills.* Bombay: Humphrey Milford.
Emeneau, Murray B.
1971   *Toda Songs.* London: Oxford University Press.
Ghurye, G. S.
1943   *The Aborigines—"So-Called"—and Their Future.* Poona: Gokhale Institute of Politics and Economics.
Henry, Edward O.
1976   "The Variety of Music in a North Indian Village: Reassessing Cantometrics," *Ethnomusicology* 20:49–66.

1977 "The Ethnographic Analysis of Four Types of Performance in Bhojpuri Speaking India," *Journal of the Indian Musicological Society* 8 (4):5–22.

Hipp, Peter, and Hugo Aman
1950 "Notation and Analysis of Mundari Music," in J. Hoffmann and A. van Emelen, *Encyclopaedia Mundarica* (Patna: Superintendent, Government Printing), vol. 4, pp. 1–38, insert at p. 1164.

Hoffmann, John, and Arthur van Emelen
1950 *Encyclopaedia Mundarica.* 16 vols. 2d ed. Patna: Superintendent, Government Printing. First printed 1930–41.

Hunter, William Wilson
1881 *Imperial Gazetteer of India.* 9 vols. London: Trubner.

Kaufmann, Walter
1941 "Folk-songs of the Gond and Baiga," *Musical Quarterly* 27 (3): 280–88.
1960 "The Songs of the Hill Maria, Jhoria Muria, and Bastar Muria Gond Tribes," *Ethnomusicology* 4 (3):115–28.
1961 "The Musical Instruments of the Hill Maria, Jhoria, and Baster Muria Gond Tribes," *Ethnomusicology* 5 (1):1–9.

Knight, Roderic
1983 "Tribal Music of India: The Muria and Maria Gonds of Madhya Pradesh," LP disc with notes (Folkways FE 4028).
1985 "The Harp in India Today," *Ethnomusicology* 29 (1):9–28.
1987 "The Drum, Dance, and Song Repertoire of the Baiga of Madhya Pradesh, India." Paper presented at the Twenty-Ninth Conference of the International Council for Traditional Music, East Berlin.

Kuckertz, Josef
1982 "Folk Songs of Central India," *Journal of the Madras Music Academy* 53:141–50.

Majumdar, D. N.
1947 *Field Songs of Chhatishgarh.* Lucknow: University Publications.

Majumdar, S. C.
1925 "Some Santal Songs," *Visva-Bharati* 3:67–69.

Marriott, McKim, ed.
1955 *Village India: Studies in the Little Community.* Chicago: University of Chicago Press.

Mathur, K. S.
1972 "Tribe in India: A Problem of Identification and Integration," in *Tribal Situation in India: Proceedings of a Seminar,* K. Suresh Singh, ed. (Simla: Indian Institute of Advanced Study), pp. 57–61.

Misra, Bhabagrahi
1971 "Verrier Elwin's Field Methods and Fieldwork in India: An Appraisal," *Asian Folklore Studies* 30:97–127.

Nag, Narendra Gopal
1981 "Some Aspects of Ethnomusicology of Kinnara with Special Reference to Issues Relating to Primitiveness," *Man in India* 61 (4):305–26.

Parmar, Shyam
1977a   *Folk Music and Mass Media.* New Delhi: Communication Publications.
1977b   "Utilising Folk Music in Mass Media," *Sangeet Natak* 46:22–31.
Powers, Harold S.
1980   "India, Subcontinent of," sections 1–2, in *The New Grove Dictionary of Music and Musicians,* Stanley Sadie, ed. (London: Macmillan), vol. 9, pp. 69–141.
Prasad, Onkar
1985   *Santal Music: A Study in Pattern and Process of Cultural Persistence.* New Delhi: Inter-India Publications.
Raha, Manis K.
1967   "Folksongs of the Tribals of West Bengal," in *Folkmusic and Folklore. An Anthology,* Hemango Biswas, ed., vol. 1 (Calcutta: Folkmusic and Folklore Research Institute).
Ranade, Ashok
1983   "Researches in Folk Performing Arts: Aims, Objectives, and Relevance," *Quarterly Journal of the National Centre for the Performing Arts* 12 (4):36–40.
1985   "Categories of Music," *Quarterly Journal of the National Centre for the Performing Arts* 14 (4):6–19.
1986   "Perspective Studies in Music," *Sangeet Natak* 80:14–19.
Redfield, Robert
1955   "The Social Organization of Tradition," *Far Eastern Quarterly* 15 (1): 13–21.
1960   *The Little Community and Peasant Society and Culture.* Chicago: University of Chicago Press. First published 1956.
Rivers, W. H. R.
1967   *The Todas.* The Netherlands: Anthropological Publications. First published 1906.
Roy, Sarat Chandra
1912   *The Mundas and their Country.* Calcutta: Kuntaline Press.
1915   *The Oraons of Chota Nagpur: Their History, Economic Life, and Social Organization.* Calcutta: Brahmo Mission Press.
1935   *The Hill Bhuivas of Orissa.* Ranchi: City Bar Library.
Roy Burman, B. K.
1968   "Some Dimensions of the Transformation of Tribal Societies in India," *Journal of Social Research* 11 (1):88–94.
Sachchidananda
1970   "Tribe-caste Continuum: A Case Study of Gond in Bihar," *Anthropos* 65 (5–6):973–97.
Sambamoorthy, P.
1952   *A Dictionary of South Indian Music and Musicians.* vol. 1. Madras: Indian Music Publishing House.
Sanyal, Amiya Nath
1959   *Ragas and Raginis.* Calcutta: Orient Longmans.

Satpathy, Sunil
1980   Part III of "Bakens: The Ritual Invocation Songs of the Santals, A
          Preliminary Statement," *Quarterly Journal of the National Centre for
          the Performing Arts.* 9 (1):1–18.
Sen Gupta, Sanka
1967   *A Survey of Folklore Study in Bengal.* Calcutta: Indian Publications.
Singer, Milton
1959   *Traditional India: Structure and Change.* Philadelphia: American
          Folklore Studies.
1964   "The Social Organization of Indian Civilization," *Diogenes* 45:84–119.
1966   "Social Anthropology and the Comparative Study of Civilizations," in *The
          Comparative Approach in Area Studies and the Disciplines,* Ward More-
          house, ed. (Albany: State University of New York Press), pp. 1–13.
Sinha, Purnima
1970   "Folk Classical Continuum in Indian Music," in *An Approach to the Study
          of Indian Music* (Calcutta: Indian Publications), pp. 59–116.
Sinha, Surajit
1959   "Tribal Cultures of Peninsular India as a Dimension of Little Tradition in
          the Study of Indian Civilization: A Preliminary Statement," in *Traditional
          India: Structure and Change,* Milton Singer, ed. (Philadelphia: American
          Folklore Society), (Bibliographic and Special Series, 10), pp. 298–312.
1965   "Tribe-Caste and Tribe-Peasant Continua in Central India," *Man in India*
          45 (1):57–83.
1973   "Rethinking about Tribes and Indian Civilization," *Journal of the Indian
          Anthropological Society* 8:94–108.
Vatsyayan, Kapila
1980   "India, Subcontinent of," section 7, in *The New Grove Dictionary of Music
          and Musicians,* Stanley Sadie, ed. (London: Macmillan), vol. 9, pp. 158–66.
Wade, Bonnie C.
1980   "India, Subcontinent of," section 6, in *The New Grove Dictionary of Music
          and Musicians,* Stanley Sadie, ed. (London: Macmillan), vol. 9, pp. 141–58.

Oskár Elschek

Ideas, Principles, Motivations, and Results in Eastern European Folk-Music Research

Periods of Development

I N THE SECOND HALF of the nineteenth century, comprehensive folk-music research in Eastern Europe began with fieldwork and the publication of folk songs (by such figures as O. Kolberg, F. Sušil, and F. Bartoš), organized by unions, societies, and laymen. In a search for ethnic and cultural identity, these investigations were strongly influenced by national movements, pan-Slavic ideas, and the desire for self-determination, all with the aim of creating new national arts on traditional folk arts and music.

The twentieth century, especially the period after World War I, can be characterized by new individual and institutional approaches, associated particularly with the names of B. Bartók, C. Brăiloiu, F. Kolessa, K. Kvitka, A. Chybiński, and V. Stoin, which integrated the principles of the "Berlin School" of comparative musicology and traditional folk-music research. Aside from collecting and recording folk music, these scholars gave attention to theoretical and methodological problems of fieldwork and outlined systems of documentation. Evolution of music, the origin of music, and the reconstruction of national and folk-music traditions were of great concern. The research projects were typically restricted to national limits. There was little international cooperation, and national points of view prevailed. Authenticity was claimed, and the peculiarities of various traditions were pointed out and directly connected with universals and common, basic music concepts. Comparative study was subordinated to research of national significance.

Since the 1950s, however, a number of professional research institutions have been established in Eastern Europe, while the existing ones widened the scope of their research and thus began to include, besides the conventional field- and archival work, the publication of special synthesizing editions and major monographic projects and the development and application of new procedures. Large-scale projects and international cooperation were initiated, as ethnomusicologists took on positions of importance in musicology and anthropology, beginning to take part in interdisciplinary investigations. Ethnomusicology became an independent field of specialization and entered into a manifold system of interdisciplinary relations. However, governmental, scientific, and cultural policies as well as ideology influenced and determined both the aims and the results of research.

Because Eastern Europe has a differentiated, manifold ethnic structure, and because there have been colonization and migration for centuries, cultural elements have moved over hundreds of miles. At the present time, in many of the relatively small countries, there are minorities maintaining their particular cultures. Contacts among ethnic groups have existed for decades and centuries. Thus we have in almost every country a set of subcultures with their own musical physiognomy. Research on minorities, therefore, has played an important role in the Eastern European conception of ethnomusicology. In particular, Hungarian scholars have carried out extensive research on their minorities in Slovakia and Romania. Slovak ethnomusicologists have for many years carried out fieldwork on the Slovak minorities in Hungary, Romania, and especially in northern Yugoslavia.

TOPICS, FIELDS, AND RESULTS OF RECENT AND CONTEMPORARY RESEARCH

During the last two decades, ethnomusicology and folk-music research in Eastern Europe as a whole and in the individual nations has changed significantly. It is possible to give an account of a characteristic set of problems, preferred themes, and results.

1) Folk Music and Its Cultural and Historical Context

A special interest in the cultural and historical aspects of folk music was brought about by the desire to reconstruct its history. In the nineteenth century, historical considerations had mostly been based on text analysis, but twentieth-century historical investigations searched for a model emphasizing autonomous musical features. The three styles—old, new, and mixed—proposed by B. Bartók are paradigmatic.[1] Of important influence here were the approaches of the German diffusionist school of anthropology as they were applied in German comparative musicology (Schneider 1976:66–100). In Eastern European ethnomusicological research, these ideas and theories were used in connection with three approaches: (1) attempts that followed the theories of the German diffusionist school of anthropology, particularly in Hungary; (2) attempts to reconstruct the evolution of music in general and that of individual cultures in particular (e.g., in the monographs by Geist 1970, Knepler 1977, and Szőke 1982); and (3) interpretations of historical music sources.[2]

The first of these, as a theory of the geographic distribution of music phenomena that continued to claim the allegiance of a few scholars even after it had been widely abandoned, appeared here and there in a residual form with little influence on research as a whole, but it was to serve as the starting point of historic-genetic reconstructions of individual folk-music cultures (as mentioned above under point 2). Possibly the most significant representative of this approach was J. Kresánek in his monograph on Slovak folk songs.[3] Kresánek developed a specific historic-genetic theory based on thorough evaluation of cultural and musical sources, applying a system of music theory that had been worked out by the music historian J. Hutter (1929, 1943). This approach is very different from the early work of others, such as B. Fabó (1908), for whom the verbal text was the starting point for historical considerations.[4] At that time, B. Bartók was trying to find a typological and classificatory procedure that would enable him to reconstruct the evolution of Hungarian folk songs, for he was also proposing theories of the development of Slovak[5] and Romanian folk music. Kresánek's genetic theory, having been mostly determined by historical and functional aspects, has recently been improved upon (Elscheková 1978). The foremost position in Hungarian scholarship remains based on geographic distribution, which is the basis of the studies in the series *Népzene és történelem*.[6] This strand of comparative research, it must be confessed, is somewhat old-fashioned in its methods and procedures.

In the fifties and sixties there arose a new historical understanding of folk music based on critical evaluation of the historical sources. Ethnomusicologists came to be aware of the inadequacy of separating historical musicology and ethnomusicology, based on written and oral sources, respectively, and claiming diachronic and synchronic spheres. This was a widespread tendency of which two early manifestations were important conferences: "Der volkskundliche und völkerkundliche Beitrag zur Musikgeschichte" (1953, organized by the Gesellschaft für Musikforschung in Bamberg); and "The Contribution of Ethnomusicology to Historical Musicology" (1961, part of the New York Congress of the IMS). Also relevant here were articles by B. Nettl (1958) and F. Bose (1966). Remarkable changes were further initiated by the Seventeenth Conference of the IFMC in Budapest in 1964, which included twenty-one papers on the theme of "Folk Music and History," published in *Studia Musicologica* 7

(1965). Organizational support for this topic continued to be provided, and it played a major role at the IMS Conference in Ljubljana in 1967, in which year a newly formed Study Group of the IFMC, "Historical Sources of Folk Music," began a research project in Freiburg i. Breisgau in the Federal Republic of Germany. A series of six meetings of this study group followed, all in Eastern Europe. Voluminous editions, published in Hungary, Poland, and Austria, have complemented these conferences. The abiding interest of Eastern European ethnomusicologists in this theme was demonstrated in a colloquium held in 1984 in Wiepersdorf (GDR) entitled "Historical Approaches to Orally Transmitted Music: Perspectives and Methodologies."[7]

Two more factors should be mentioned in evaluating the historical activities of Eastern European ethnomusicologists: (1) preference for the theory and methodology of historical materialism, which has played some role in the investigation of musical changes, and (2) integration of ethnomusicologists' activity within comprehensive national ethnological and anthropological projects, which have led to the elaboration of historical outlines of folk-music cultures, and to attempts to determine strands and periods of their inner development. One notes a preference for relative chronology defining periods of folk-music development in Eastern European music cultures.

2) Folk Music—Function and Genres

Attempts to overcome the limitations of interpreting individual elements of folk music have appeared in the last two decades as a reaction to the restrictive practice of separating research on text and tune by folklorists and ethnomusicologists. Better mutual understanding has come, and ethnomusicologists have thus come to concentrate their interests on functional, structural, and comparative analysis of melodies and musical elements, as well as song texts. The development of integrated genre studies as part of song editions followed. A comprehensive monograph of this type was provided by O. Demo and O. Hrabalová (1969), and closely connected was a series of disciplinarily integrated studies published by A. Elscheková on songs for driving out winter and bringing in summer (1976), lyric love and courtship songs (1981), lullabies and songs to entertain children (1987), and wedding songs (1989). This approach also dominated in the anthology *Slovenské l'udové piesne a nástrojová hudba* (Elscheková-Elschek 1980–82).

A model genre monograph, with a comprehensive methodological view, is the book about the lullaby by the Romanian scholar G. Suliţeanu (1986). In other folk-song editions as well, aspects of social function have played an important role: take, for example, the classic Hungarian series, *A magyar népzene tára,* whose volumes are devoted to children's games (1951), tunes of calendric customs (1955), wedding songs (1955, 1956), laments (1966), etc. Here, uses are the main criterion, but in the analysis the texts play a rather subordinate role.

The edition of Polish folk songs from Kujawy (1974–75) presents texts and melodies in separate volumes which are coordinated in their typological order and contents. The social functions of the song texts were analyzed and compared in cooperation with specialists. In the kinds of genre editions discussed here, epics and ballads have played a central role in Eastern Europe and elsewhere. Two other Eastern European examples may be cited. Slovene ethnomusicologists prepared a comprehensive collection *Slovenske ljudske pemsi* [Slovene Folk Songs], including a group of ballads and legends (Kumer and Vodušek 1970, 1981). The editors supplemented the edition with numerous special indices for both music and texts, in many respects using as a model the German ballad collection published in the classic *Deutsche Volkslieder mit ihren Melodien* (1935–). The edition of Russian musical epics, published under the editorial leadership of B. M. Dobrovolskij and V. V. Korguzalov (Moscow 1981), was developed along the same lines. In Eastern European folk-song research, the functional aspects of folk-song genres played a leading role. It is a viewpoint still of great importance, as indicated in recent volumes of *Musicologica Slovaca* (Elschek 1988 and 1989), which take into account syncretic forms and genres of folklore, especially those connected with music and dance.

Alan P. Merriam's *Anthropology of Music* (1964) provided a major stimulus to Eastern European musical scholarship. Consequently, Slovak ethnomusicologists developed related systems of comprehensive analysis of music, text, and context. In Czechoslovakia of the 1960s, Merriam's ideas were presented by T. Volek in the Czech journal *Hudební rozhledy* [Music Review]. In the Soviet Union, I. I. Zemcovskij (1972) followed some functional and semantic theories connected with Merriam's concepts. Those scholars in particular who visited the United States and its ethnomusicological institutions in the 1970s introduced new ideas of musical anthropology; among them are A. Czekanowska, L. Bielawski, M. Kahane, and R. Petrović as well as their students. The interrelationships of

American and Eastern European ethnomusicology in terms of subject matter, method, basic concepts, and basic research have been much greater than might have been expected. During the last two decades, Merriam's influence was more or less replaced by the theories and concepts of John Blacking who, developing ethnomusicological research in much the same direction, had particularly good contacts with Eastern European ethnomusicologists.

3) Folk-Music Instruments and Instrumental Music

Developments in the 1950s produced a widening of research interests from folk songs to other important areas of folk music, including instruments, instrumental music, and related areas of folk dances. Research began with the cataloging of instruments in museum collections and continued with intensive fieldwork, descriptions of instruments, and acoustical and typological investigations. Instrumental music was transcribed (one of the most difficult tasks) and analyzed differently from song. Folk dance, too, became the object of thorough investigation.

Encouraged throughout Europe and elsewhere, the development of these activities was, in Eastern Europe, accelerated by central ethnomusicological institutions established at national academies as well as by independent organizations which produced monographs of folk-music instruments and editions of instrumental music. The principal example is the large project entitled *Handbuch der europäischen Volksmusikinstrumente,* which was launched by E. Emsheimer and E. Stockmann in 1959, and which at first emphasized Eastern European material. It gave rise to a series of meetings, beginning with a conference of its authors in Berlin in 1962, who continued to meet during the ensuing decades, largely in Eastern European locations. At these conferences, the focal points were instrument typology, playing techniques, acoustics, history and historical sources of folk instruments, children's instruments, and the instruments of shepherds and other occupational groups, especially of the host countries or areas. Papers resulting from these activities were published in the series *Studia instrumentorum musicae popularis,* sponsored by the Swedish Academy and Museum (1969–88). Monographs on folk instruments appeared in participating countries: in Slovakia by L. Leng (1967), Bulgaria by V. Atanasov (1977), Slovenia by Z. Kumer (1972), and Poland by S. Oledzki (1978); and for countries outside Eastern Europe: Spain, Greece, Finland, and Norway. Synthetic and comprehensive national or regional studies on folk instruments are included in this reference work, with individual volumes devoted to Hungary by B. Sárosi (1967), Bohemia by L. Kunz (1974), Switzerland by B. Bachmann-Geiser (1981), and Slovakia by O. Elschek (1983). Besides descriptions of the instruments cited, these volumes provide characterization of ergological aspects, terminology, acoustical features, history, playing technique, repertory, and geographical distribution. In the Slovak volume, for example, 171 instrument types are characterized, and a more recent volume describes 103 types of folk aerophones.

Instrumental music has become an especially interesting area of research. For example, in the years 1954–55 the Hungarian musicologist and composer L. Lajtha published two volumes of scores of string-ensemble music entitled *Kőrispataki* and *Széki gyüjtés* [Collections of Kőrispatak and Szék] (1955 and 1954), with transcriptions of records from the 1930s. J. Markl in 1962 prepared scores of Czech bagpipe music. In the years 1966–73 three volumes with studies, transcriptions, and scores of traditional Slovak folk violinists were edited; these were reissued in 1984 (Vargyas 1984). D. Holý was the author of a study on East Moravian instrumental music (1969). One of the best studies presenting perfect multichannel recorded and transcribed scores as well as harmonic-melodic analysis using a new system of terms and categories for ornaments is that of Leng (1971). Solo forms of instrumental folk music were characterized in a study by Elschek (1985). A monograph of special interest was published in the Soviet Union by M. Beregovskij (1987) with documents for and transcriptions of Jewish Klezmer music. A comprehensive two-volume edition on folk-music instruments and instrumental music in the Soviet Union was prepared by E. V. Gippius and I. V. Maciejevskij (1987) with a selection of contributions by European scholars. Systematic, analytical, historical, and comparative approaches have been preferred by Soviet organologists. Worthy of special mention from the methodological point of view is the monograph of Romanian folk music by C. D. Georgescu (1984). It is a typology of instrumental tunes which contains excellent transcriptions, a history of instrumental music research in Romania, analysis of tunes, and typological characterizations of rhythm and meter, along with semantic interpretations. Ethno-organological research, it is clear, is one of the most developed fields in Eastern European research.

4) Analytical and Classificatory Work

The Polish scholar A. Czekanowska, commenting on the major contributions of postwar Eastern European ethnomusicologists, wrote: "They have developed a systematic activity of collection and documentation; they started to publish a number of series with source material; analysis and classification of folk melodies were initiated" (1971:49). The last point refers to a central issue of Eastern European ethnomusicology which has a tradition dating back to the beginning of this century. Its extensive history and the contemporary developments of this research can only be summarized here. Large and comprehensive publication projects required new methods of analysis and systematization. The early tradition, including the work of Bartók, F. Kolessa, K. Kvitka, and V. Žganec, was to be improved and enriched by new findings and procedures after World War II, particularly as its themes and problems entered into the working program of the IFMC. Again, face-to-face meetings played a major role. In 1956 a meeting preceding the regular conference in Freiburg (FRG) was devoted to typology and comparative methods. Later, special study groups were established. From 1960 to 1965 a "commission" on classification of folk songs organized a series of eight seminars on this topic in Czechoslovakia, focusing on a wide range of problems of general concern as well as on the details of analytical practice. More than 20,000 melodies have been analyzed and classified in various systems. "Methods of Classification and Lexicographic Arrangement of Tunes in Folk Music Collections" was a major topic at the Seventeenth Conference of the IFMC; and of the fifteen resulting papers, ten were by authors from Eastern Europe. The IFMC Study Group on Analysis and Systematization was established, and its first meeting was held in Bratislava in 1965. Half of its subsequent meetings took place in Eastern Europe, with Eastern European ethnomusicologists playing a leading role, and the majority of the papers therefore dealing with Eastern European folk music.

New approaches and devices came into use, particularly applying mathematical procedures and computers. In Czechoslovakia in 1970, a working group under the heading "Computer and Folk Song" was established, and, as of 1978, it had published four volumes with papers and programs including numerous specialized studies.[8] In the 1980s this working group split in two, pursuing separate topics, "Music and Computers" at large, and nonstandard methods in musicological research.[9] Thus, since the late 1970s, they have not frequently addressed ethnomusicological themes.

In 1975 international cooperation in the field of computer-oriented folkmusic research was initiated within the framework of a series of ethnomusicological seminars held in Slovakia (Elschek 1976). In the same year, at the Academy of Sciences of the Armenian SSR, the first All-Union Seminar on "Machine Aspects of Algorithmic Formalized Analysis of Musical

Texts" took place, giving a summary of related activities in the Soviet Union, especially in Yerevan (Goshovskij 1977). A project based on computerized factor analysis and carried out by R. Kluge and D. Stockmann in the GDR was oriented to folk music (Kluge 1974), while folk melodies and similar phenomena were the subject of a study applying mathematical methods and computer programs in analysis by L. Ballová (1982).

The following list summarizes the principal problems and approaches that were the subject of the various conferences and publications of the last two decades: (1) Procedures for archive cataloging and principles for lexicographic ordering and analytical purposes have been worked out; (2) Music-theoretical terms and categories, particularly in the areas of tonality, metric-rhythmic phenomena, tectonics, and multipart techniques have been defined in detail; and (3) Complete and complex multidimensional analytical and classification procedures were outlined in Hungary (by P. Járdányi, I. Olsvai, L. Dobszay, J. Szendrey), in Slovakia (A. Elscheková), in Moravia (K. Vetterl, J. Gelnár, O. Hrabalová), and in the Ukraine and Armenia (V. Goshovskij). In the course of this work, some hundreds of thousands of folk-music items were cataloged and entered in archival data-retrieval systems, becoming the subject of the numerous studies, monographs, and anthologies mentioned.

5) Interethnic and Interregional Projects

Most research activity in Eastern Europe took—and still takes—place within the borders of nations and cultures. The great diversity of folk music in Eastern Europe has led to national differentiation in method and to specific national purposes based on various research traditions influenced by leading personalities. For this reason there is in Eastern Europe an absence of comprehensive syntheses of European folk music, such as those presented by W. Danckert (1939, 1966), W. Wiora (1952), B. Nettl (1965), and A. Lomax's cantometrics project (1968, 1976), or, for that matter, *The New Grove*. There is thus no comprehensive textbook on Eastern European folk music. Actually, similar problems were faced by students of other geographical areas, the significant exception being Scandinavia, perhaps because of the excellent cooperation among its countries in the field of folklore and, in that context, in scholarly activities dealing with folk music. The European situation, of course, calls for methods of cooperation on interethnic, interregional, and international projects.

Béla Bartók was one of the first to attempt coverage of Central European folk music on the bais of extensive fieldwork and comparative analytic procedures. His work has particularly influenced research in postwar Hungary. Zoltán Kodály encouraged fieldwork among Finno-Ugric nationalities in central Russia, having in mind a comparison with Hungarian material. L. Vikár specialized in the area of Finno-Ugric relationships, but investigations have been carried out also by P. Szőke who pointed out the shortcomings of that kind of comparative approach (1959, 1982), in which L. Vargyas was to join later, taking into account musical styles and especially the repertory of ballads. Restrictive centralization and nationalistic points of view strongly influenced the comparative work of Hungarian scholars.

As already indicated, Eastern European ethnomusicology has found a valuable base for international cooperation in the Study Groups of the IFMC/ICTM, above all in the methodological aspects of tune systematization, musical instruments, historical sources, and dance. Aside from matters of theory, two international projects should be noted. The first, supported in Slavic countries, came from the desire to investigate common Slavic musical elements and styles. An idea dating back to the nineteenth century acquired new dimensions as archaic, ritual musical strata with narrow melodic ranges were identified. International working groups for this task have been established. Cooperation has not been restricted to folk music, as the foremost aim was the editing of sources of old Slavic music. But because of the close connections between different functional strata and styles in art and folk music, it seemed useful to deal with them together.

A few monographs investigating these matters should be mentioned. The edition entitled *Anfänge der slawischen Musik* (1966) was the result of an international symposium held in 1964 in Bratislava, and includes contributions on old folk-music strata by A. Elscheková, V. Karbusicky, and W. Kaminski. N. Kaufman was the author of a comparative monograph entitled *Njakoi obšči čerti meždu narodnata pesen na Blgarite i istočnite Slavjan* (1968). Some common features between Bulgarian and East Slavic folk songs were suggested by F. Rubcov (1962) in a study based in part on elements of intonation. Czekanowska (1972) has published a detailed special study of narrow-range folk melodies in Slavic countries, with a survey of source documentation and classification applying the so-called Wrocław method of taxonomy. In the same year, a collection of studies, written by twenty authors on Slavic folk music and directed in part to mutual relations between styles and stylistic elements (tonality, rhythm, multipart singing, musical instruments, etc.), was published (Zemcovskij 1972). A monograph by V. Goshovskij (1971, later enlarged in Czech, 1976), which discusses general methodological considerations, refers particularly to Central European phenomena of Slavic folk music, especially those of the Carpatho-Ukrainians in their interrelation to the Western and Eastern Slavs. In October 1978 an international musicological colloquium took place at Brno on music of the Slavic nations, covering the entire area of historical and contemporary music in this field. Unfortunately, only modest attention was given to folk music, but nevertheless, this colloquium served a useful function in taking a holistic view of Slavic music.

The study of Slavic folk music per se has received less attention than other musical and cultural studies. In the 1950s, however, an international project arose under the sponsorship of the International Commission for Investigating the Culture of the Carpathians and Balkans, centered in Bratislava. The undertaking involved the entire field of economic and social research, including ethnomusicology. At a meeting in 1961, the entire range of problems involving folk-music research was set forth, and this was followed by papers presented at the Carpathian-Balkan Conference in Cracow and then, in 1965, at the first ethnomusicological symposium organized in Bratislava. In 1975 the next specialized ethnomusicological seminar devoted to shepherds' musical culture in the Carpathians and Balkans took place. Two volumes of papers were published (Elscheková 1980, Gašpariková 1981). Epics, shepherd calls and songs, types of musical instruments, multipart singing, style stratigraphy, and many other special problems were the subject of the studies.

In the 1960s a new comprehensive project was suggested for the purpose of summarizing national and comparative ethnomusicological research; its basic concepts and methods were finally clarified and presented in volume 8 of the *Studia instrumentorum musicae popularis* (Elschek 1985). In the course of studies that are being carried out to complete this synthetic undertaking on Eastern and Southeastern European folk music, national borders are being crossed and new connections suggested. The project will be published in two-volume supplements with a series of documentary recordings. This is only one of many research projects that have given shape to Eastern European ethnomusicology. They include major bibliographical efforts and participation in national ethnographic atlases. It is worth noting that cooperation with anthropology and ethnology has been more successful than with historical musicology.

6) Synthetic-Comprehensive Work

Studies, monographs, and anthologies concentrating on problems of folk music within national borders are innumerable. Relatively few titles have had international impact because they were usually written and published by the authors in the languages of their own countries, which may have restricted their significance and also their opportunity to influence ethnomusicological research in Eastern Europe at large. In particular this is true of works of methodological relevance and perspectives concerning folk music and its history in the area.

Thus J. Maróthi published a monograph about the beginnings and roots of European folk songs (1960), which for a long time reached most readers only through short summaries published in foreign languages. This study emphasizes the roots of the songs of lower classes and their social and stylistic features in relationship to art music. A. Czekanowska is the author of the first introduction to ethnomusicology published in Eastern Europe. Entitled *Etnografia muzyczna: Metodologia i metodyka* (1971), this book, in its historical account of research, gives a central role to the development of ideas, methods, and working procedures of ethnomusicologists. The tradition of Polish folk-music research, ethnological issues, and especially the American approach to anthropology of music are its major points of departure. A similar publication by the Slovenian scholar Z. Kumer (1977) is of introductory character and content and directed mainly to students. It is organized in accordance with historical problems emphasizing Yugoslav research. Besides the chapters on folk song, instrumental music, dance, and contemporary ethnomusicology, the author has included short chapters on European folk music as well as on traditional and art music in the world's non-Western cultures. This book has an encyclopedic and data-oriented character.

The three above-mentioned books produced by Eastern European scholarship tended to remain restricted to the authors' spheres of activity, but they came to have considerable influence through the authors' educational work at their respective universities. There are, however, few works of this general sort in Eastern Europe, and, therefore, educational activity there cannot yet be carried out without the consistent use of the generally known books in English by Hood, Kunst, Merriam, and Nettl, or those coming from German comparative, systematic, and musical-anthropological scholarship by such authors as F. Bose, K. Reinhard, and W. Suppan.

CONTEMPORARY PROBLEMS

In discussing the practical problems in Eastern European folk-music research and ethnomusicology, I am not concerned only with temporary considerations. Some of them derive from issues that have maintained their influence over decades, and I would like to mention a few of these.

(1) The lack of a common language is a significant obstacle which restricts communication between schools of researchers, and inhibits the kind of exchange of information and results without which one can hardly speak of a cultural-geographical integration of research. The important editions and studies have of course been published in national languages, but foreign-language editions are rarely available. Summaries in foreign languages may help but are insufficient for serious scholarship.

(2) In Eastern Europe, there is a multitude of national folk-music cultures and style strata which make it virtually impossible to use unified procedures, methods, and research tools. These differences, pointed out in the course of many investigations, have not been mitigated by the development of common ideas and concepts. Progressive fragmentation is easier to find than growing unity.

(3) Old and established traditions of research have had to be renewed and supplemented by newly developed professional research techniques and institutional ethnomusicological facilities and projects. We can now identify a modern and mature scholarly field of ethnomusicology taking advantage of all kinds of methodological, technical, and conceptual improvements; but these improvements have not been applied consistently throughout Eastern Europe. On the contrary, as described above, a multitude of nationally differentiated approaches has been followed.

(4) Because of the emphasis on national aims, often in a nationalistically or chauvinistically narrow-minded vein, the striving for international scholarly conjunction has faced particular difficulties. Objectivity, subjectivity, and pragmatism appear in strange mixtures.

(5) In the context of this (brief and necessarily incomplete) report on Eastern European research, it must be pointed out that there are many scholarly approaches common to all of European and indeed worldwide research. Eastern Europe shares many basic viewpoints and purposes with the rest of the ethnomusicological world. A problem arises when similar working procedures are associated with different and often contradictory aims and goals, and thus scholars evaluate roles and positions of their musical traditions differently. International projects have, in part, consolidated working procedures in source interpretation, principles of fieldwork, editorial demands, choice of problems, and areas of preferred research.

Notes

1. The historical orientation was presented in almost all studies by Béla Bartók and presented particularly in his monograph on Hungarian folk music (1931; 1981:11).

2. In this connection I should mention the activities of the Study Group on Historical Sources of Folk Music of the International Council for Traditional Music (ICTM).

3. Kresánek's layout of the development of Slovak folk music (1951) was essentially the starting point of Slovak ethnomusicology.

4. At the beginning of the century, B. Fabó published a series of studies concerning the historical background of Hungarian folk and popular music (1906, 1908).

5. Bartók also proposed a hypothesis concerning Slovak folk music, basing it on certain concepts of Slovak folkloristics, particularly of M. Lichard and K. Medvecky. See Bartók's articles written in the late 1920s (e.g., Bartók 1924).

6. The great importance accorded to these historical problems was made evident in the special series of comparative character prepared by L. Vargyas, who served as editor.

7. The results have been summarized in papers published in *Beiträge zur Musikwissenschaft* 27 (21).

8. A series of publications appeared under the title *L'udová pieseň a samočinné počítače* [Folk Song and Computers], vols. 1 and 3, Brno, 1972 and 1976; vol. 2, Bratislava, 1978. See also Elschek (1976).

9. Special meetings were begun in 1980, and a series of publications appeared under the heading *Hudba a počítače* [Music and Computers]. Bratislava: Banska Bystrica 1981, 1985, 1987.

Works Cited

A magyar népzene tára
1951– [Collection of Hungarian Folk Music]. vols.1–5. Budapest: Akadémia
73 Kiadó.

Alexandru, Tiberiu
1956 *Instrumentele musical ale Poporului Romîn* [Folk Music Instruments of the Romanian People]. Bucharest: Editura de Stat Pentru Literatura si Arta.

Anfänge der slawischen Musik
1966 Bratislava: Slovak Academy of Sciences.

Atanasov, Vergilii
1977 *Sistematika na blgarskite narodni instrumenti* [Systematics of the Bulgarian Folk Music Instruments]. Sofia: Blgarskata akademiia na naukite.

Bachmann-Geiser, Brigitte
1981 *Die Volksmusikinstrumente der Schweiz*. Leipzig: Deutscher Verlag für Musik.

Ballová, L'uba
1982 *Totožnosť a podobnosť melódií* [Identity and Similarity of Melodies]. Bratislava: Opus.

Bartók, Béla
1924 "Slovak Folk Music," in *A Dictionary of Modern Music and Musicians* Arthur Eaglefield-Hull, ed. (London: J. M. Dent).

1931, *Hungarian Folk Music*. London: Oxford University Press.
1981

Beregovskij, M.
1987 *Jevrejskaja narodnaja instrumentalnaja muzyka* [Jewish Instrumental Folk Music]. Moscow: Vsesojuznoe izdatel'stvo Sovjetskij kompozitor.

Bezić, Jerko
1985   *Glazbeno stvaralaštvo narodnosti (narodnih manjina) i etničkih grupa:
        Traditional Music of Ethnic Groups—Minorities.* Zagreb: Zavod za
        Istraživanje Folklora.
Bose, Fritz
1966   "Musikgeschichtliche Aspekte der Musikethnologie," *Archiv für
        Musikwissenschaft* 24:239–51.
Czekanowska, Anna
1971   *Etnografia muzyczna: Metodologia i metodyka* [Musical Ethnography:
        Methods and Methodology]. Warsaw: Panstwowe Wydawnictwo
        Naukowe.
1972   *Ludowe melodie wąskiego zakresu w krajach Słowiańskich*
        [Narrow-Range Folk Melodies in Slavic Countries]. Cracow: Polskie
        Wydawnictwo Muzyczne.
Danckert, Werner
1939   *Das europäische Volkslied.* Berlin: Bernard Hahnfeld.
1966   *Das Volkslied im Abendland.* Bern: Francke.
Demo, Ondrej, and Olga Hrabalová
1969   *Žatevné a dožinkové piesne* [Harvest and Harvest Festival Songs].
        Bratislava: Vydavatel'stvo Slovenskej Akadémie Vied.
Deutsche Volkslieder mit ihren Melodien
1935–   Freiburg i. Br.: Deutsches Volksliedarchiv. Multi-volume, with volumes
        in preparation.
Dobrovolskij, B. M., and V. V. Korguzalov
1981   *Byliny: Russkij muzykalnij epos* [Byliny: The Russian Musical Epic].
        Moscow: Vsesojuznoe izdatel'stvo Sovjetskij kompozitor.
Elschek, Oskár
1959   "Objet et buts des recherches portant sur la musique populaire
        Carpatique," *Slovenský národopis* 9:663–65.
1976   *Musikklassifikation und EDV (Abstracts).* Bratislava: Umenovedný
(ed.)   ústav Slovenská Akadémia Vied.
1983   *Die slowakischen Volksmusikinstrumente.* Leipzig: Deutscher Verlag
        für Musik.
1985   "Volksmusik und Volksmusikinstrumente der Karpaten und des
        Balkans—Prinzipien eines interkulturellen Projektes," *Studia
        instrumentorum musicae popularis* 8:63–66.
1985   "Die ethnischen Besonderheiten der slowakischen instrumentalen
        Volksmusik," *Ethnologica Slavica* 14:13–56.
1988   "Hudobnofolklórne druhy a ich systémové suvzt᷉ ažnosti" [Genres of
(ed.)   Musical Folklore and Their System-Relations], *Musicologica Slovaca*
        13.
1989   "Hudobné a tanečné zvykoslovie" [The Music and Dance Customs],
(ed.)   *Musicologica Slovaca* 15.
Elscheková, Alica
1976   "Vynášanie zimy a prinesenie leta v Gemeri" [Sending Out Winter and
        Bringing in Summer in the Region of Gemer], *Gemer* 2:235–311.
        German summary.

1978 "Stilbegriff und Stilschichten in der slowakischen Volksmusik," *Studia Musicologica* 20:263–303.

1980 *Stratigraphische Probleme der Volksmusik in den Karpaten und auf*
(ed.) *dem Balkan*. Bratislava: Veda Verlag der Slowakischen Akademie der Wissenschaften.

1981 "Lúbostná lyrika v gemerskom l'udovom speve" [Love Lyrics in Folk Songs of the Region of Gemer], *Gemer* 4:245–330. German summary.

1986 "Uspávanky a detské zabávanky v Gemeri" [Lullabies and Children's Amusements in the Region of Gemer], *Vlastivedné štúdie Gemer* 5:88–151. German summary.

1987 "Svadobné piesne v slovenskej folklornej tradícii" [Wedding Songs in the Slovak Folklore Tradition], in *Lidová píseň, hudba a tanec*, Brno, pp. 87–110.

1989 "Svadba a svadobné piesne" [Wedding and Wedding Songs], *Musicologica Slovaca* 15:72–122.

Elscheková, Alica, and Oskár Elschek
1980– *Slovenské l'udové piesne a nástrojová hudba antológia* [Slovak Folk
82 Songs and Instrumental Music Anthology]. Bratislava: Osvetový ústav.

Emsheimer, Ernst, and Erich Stockmann
1959 "Vorbemerkungen zu einem Handbuch der europäischen Volksmusikinstrumente," *Deutsches Jahrbuch für Volkskunde* 5:412–16.

Fabó, Bertalan
1906 *A magyar népdal kormeghatározása* [The Time Determination of Hungarian Folk Songs]. *Ethnographia* 16 (4):239–43.

1908 *A magyar népdal zenei fejlődése* [The Musical Development of the Hungarian Folk Song]. Budapest: A Magyar Tudományos Akadémia Kiádása.

Gašpariková, Viera, ed.
1981 *Interetnické vzt'ahy vo folklóre karpatskej oblasti* [Interethnic Relations in the Folklore of the Carpathian Area]. Bratislava: Veda Verlag der Slowakischen Akademie der Wissenschaften.

Geist, Bohumil
1970 *Původ hudby* [The Origin of Music]. Prague and Bratislava: Editio Supraphon.

Georgescu, Corneliu Dan
1984 *Jocul Popular Romanesc* [Romanian Folk Dance Music]. Bucharest: Editura Muzicala.

Gippius, Evgenij V., and Igor Maciejevskij, eds.
1987 *Narodnye muzykalnye instrumenty i instrumentanaja muzyka* [Folk Music Instruments and Instrumental Music]. 2 vols. Moscow: Vsesojuznoe izdatel'stvo Sovjetskij kompozitor.

Goshovskij, Vladimir
1971 *U istokov narodnoj muzyki Slavjan* [The Roots of Folk Music of the Slavs]. Moscow: Vsesojuznoe izdatel'stvo Sovjetskij kompozitor.

1977 *Pervyj vsesojuznyj seminar po mašinnym aspektam algoritmičeskogo formali-*
(ed.) *zovannogo analiza muzykalnych tekstov* [The First All-Union Seminar on Machine Aspects of Algorithmic Formalized Analysis of Musical Texts]. Jerevan: Izdatel'stvo Academii nauk Armjanskoj SSR.

Gurvin, Olav
1958– *Norsk folkemusikk* [Norwegian Folk Music]. 5 vols. Oslo:
67   Universitetsforlaget.
Holý, Dušan
1969   *Probleme der Entwicklung und des Stils der Volksmusik.* Brno:
       Universita J. E. Purkyne.
Hudba a počitače
1981, [Music and Computers]. Bratislava: Banska Bystrica.
1985,
1987
Hutter, Jozef
1929   *Melodický princíp stupnicových řad* [The Melodic Principles of the
       Scales]. Prague: Česka Akademie.
1943   *Hudební myšlení* [Musical Thinking]. Prague: Vaclav Tomsa.
Kaufman, N.
1968 ⸱ *Njakoi obšči čerti meždu narodnata pesen na Blgarite i istočnite
       Slavjan.* Sofia.
Kluge, Reiner
1974   *Faktorenanalytische Typenbestimmung von Volksliedmelodien.* Leipzig:
       Deutscher Verlag für musikwissenschaftliche Forschung in der DDR.
Knepler, Georg
1977   *Geschichte als Weg zum Musikverständnis: Zur Theorie, Methode und
       Geschichte der Musikgeschichtsschreibung.* Leipzig: Reclam.
Kresánek, Jozef
1951   *Slovenské ľudové piesne zo stanoviska hudobného* [Slovak Folk Song
       from the Musical Point of View]. Bratislava: Slovenska Akademia Vied
       a Umení.
Kujawy
1974– *Kraków.* 2 vols. Cracow: Polskie Wydawnictwo Muzyczne.
75
Kumer, Zmaga
1972   *Slovenska ljudska glasbila in godci* [Slovene Folk Instruments and
       Village Musicians]. Maribor: Zalozba Obzorja.
1970   *Slovenske ljudske pesmi* [Slovene Folk Songs]. 2 vols. Llubjana:
       Slovenska matica 1981 (ed.)
1977   *Etnomuzikologia.* Ljubljana.
Kunz, Ludwig
1974   *Die Volksmusikinstrumente der Tschechoslowakei.* Leipzig: Deutscher
       Verlag für Musik.
Lajtha, László
1954   *Széki gyüjtés* [The Collection of Szék]. Budapest: Zenemükiadó
       vállalat.
1955   *Körispataki gyüjtés* [The Collection of Körispatak]. Budapest:
       Zenemükiadó vállalat.
Leng, Ladislav
1967   *Slovenské ľudové hudobné nástroje* [Slovak Folk Music Instruments].
       Bratislava: Vydavateľstvo Slovenskej Akademie Vied.

1971   "L'udovu hudba Zábajovcov" [The Folk Music Band of Zubajs],
          Musicologica Slovaca 10:25–40.
Lomax, Alan
1968   Folk Song Style and Culture. Washington: American Association for
          the Advancement of Science.
1976   Cantometrics: An Approach to the Anthropology of Music. Berkeley:
          University of California Extension Media Services.
Markl, Jaroslav
1962   Česká dudácka hudba [Czech Bagpipe Music]. Prague: Supraphon.
Maróthi, János
1960   Az európai népdal születése [The Birth of European Folk Song].
          Budapest: Akadémiai Kiadó.
Nettl, Bruno
1958   "Historical Aspects of Ethnomusicology," American Anthropologist
          60:518–32.
1965   Folk and Traditional Music of the Western Continents. Englewood
          Cliffs, N.J.: Prentice-Hall.
Oledzki, Stanislav
1978   Polske instrumenty ludowe [Polish Folk Instruments]. Cracow: Polskie
          Wydawnictwo Muzyczne.
Picken, Laurence
1975   Folk Musical Instruments of Turkey. London: Oxford University Press.
Rubcov, F.
1962   Intonacionnoje svjazi v pesennom tvorčestve slavjanskich narodov
          [Relations in the Intonation of the Folk Songs of the Slavs]. Leningrad:
          Izdatel'stvo Muzyka.
Sárosi, Bálint
1967   Die Volksmusikinstrumente Ungarns. Leipzig: Deutscher Verlag für
          Musik.
Schneider, Albrecht
1976   Musikwissenschaft und Kulturkreislehre: Zur Methodik und
          Geschichte der vergleichenden Musikwissenschaft. Bonn: Verlag für
          Systematische Musikwissenschaft..
Studia instrumentoram
1969   Studia instrumentorum musicae popularis 1–9 (1969–88). Stockholm:
          Swedish Academy and Museum.
Suliţeanu, Ghisele
1986   Cintecul de leagan [The Lullaby]. Bucharest: Editura Muzicala.
Szőke, Péter
1959   A melódia belső fejlődésének dialektikája, a nepzenének sokféleségének
          egysége [The Dialectic of the Inner Development of Melody: The
          Unity of Our Multifaceted Folk Music]. Budapest: Zenemükiadó
          vállalat.
1982   A zene eredete és három világa [The Origin of Music and its Three
          Worlds]. Budapest: Magvetö Könyvkiadó.

Vargyas, Lajos, ed.
1978– *Népzene es történelem* [Folk Music and History], vols. 2–4. Budapest:
82 Editio Musica.
1984 *Variačná technika predníkov v oblasti západného, stredného a*
východného Slovenska [The Technique of Variation of the First
Violinists in the Regions of West, Middle, and East Slovakia].
Bratislava: Osvetový ústav. First published 1966–73.
Wiora, Walter
1952 *Europäischer Volksgesang.* Cologne: Arno Volk-Verlag.
Zemcovskij, Isalij I.
1972 *Slavjanskij muzykalnyj folklor* [Musical Folklore of the Slavs].
Moscow: Vsesojuznoe izdatel'stvo Sovjetskij kompozitor.

II

Dominated by a Group of Abiding Issues

James Porter

Muddying the Crystal Spring: From Idealism and Realism to Marxism in the Study of English and American Folk Song

T HE FIRST PART of the title of this paper refers to the English traditional tune, "The Crystal Spring," which Cecil J. Sharp recovered (or at least cited) and Maud Karpeles, his collaborator and disciple, later used as the title of a folk-song collection (see Sharp 1907; Karpeles 1975). I introduce it here to signify the way in which later theorists have criticized the idealism of Sharp before and after World War I as he strove to portray traditional song as the pure and crystalline musical expression of an English "peasant class." The influential figure in the Folk-Song Society, founded in 1898, Sharp expressed his forceful views on the nature of folk song and folk music in his well-known study *English Folk Song: Some Conclusions* of 1907, which rapidly gained the status of a classic even though he himself regarded the book as incomplete. Nevertheless, Sharp's concepts and methods, however influential, were not universally accepted even in his own day, and I want to emphasize that the second part of my paper's title does not imply any kind of evolution of theories over the past eighty years or so but rather confirms the existence of several contrasting paradigms. Among these, Marxist or socialist interpretations of traditional song in England have continued to emerge as an alternative to Sharp's idealism on the one hand and the realism of, for example, Percy Grainger and Phillips Barry on the other.[1] But I also want to stress that I am using the terms *idealism* and *realism* here to refer to generalized attitudes arising from, or governing, approaches to the musical data rather than formalized intellectual or philosophical systems of analysis.

Cecil Sharp's idealism, which stemmed from his need to demonstrate the musicality of the English people and to educate their children by teaching them authentically traditional tunes rather than so-called "national" melodies, can be contrasted with the position of Percy Grainger, namely that singing style must be portrayed as it actually is, the transcriber working from cylinder-recorder playback to make a detailed description of the traditional singer's utterance. In contrast to Sharp's rejection of this technical aid to transcription and insistence on noting the singer's "idea" of the tune, Grainger made elegant and detailed transcriptions of his Lincolnshire songs which were published in the *Journal of the Folk Song Society* in 1908 (Grainger 1908; see also Yates 1982 and Blacking 1987). These undoubtedly influenced Bartók, causing him to write to Frederick Delius in 1908 and ask for an introduction to Grainger, whose work with folk song Bartók had come to admire. Although Bartók and Grainger never met, they shared a passion for accuracy in the transcription of traditional music, and Bartók was, of course, to take this passion for accuracy to astonishing lengths in his published collections (Porter 1983).

Grainger also influenced Phillips Barry, the American scholar whose emphasis on the personality of the traditional singer can be attributed directly to Grainger's two essays on the topic (Grainger 1908, 1915). The deep sympathy held by Grainger towards his informants should also be noted here, an attitude he conveyed openly and with some emotion when describing the poverty-ridden circumstances of the singers he encountered, and he dedicated his "Lincolnshire Posy" folk-song suite for wind band to them (1937). Barry, similarly, was interested in psychological factors and how these could shape the concepts of the individual singer. In a short article entitled "On the Psychopathology of Ballad-Singing" (1936), Barry noted how singers could, because of personal trauma in their lives, alter the words or style of a song and thus transform it on many levels. His most extended statement appeared posthumously in his "The Part of the Folk Singer in the Making of Folk Balladry" (1961), and this attention to the individual singer has resulted in productive studies in both Britain and America, influencing the work of A. L. Lloyd, Roger Abrahams, and Edward Ives among others.

While the stream that resulted from the work of Grainger and Barry has developed into the studies of anthropologists or folklorists such as Abrahams or Ives, few ethnomusicologists have pursued research of this kind in the Anglo-American world. The dominant tradition has stemmed, without doubt, from Sharp and his interest in analysis and classification. This is particularly evident in the work of Bertrand Bronson on the tunes of the Child ballads (1959–72), though problems of tune classification have been dealt with by others, notably Jan Schinhan in his treatment of the melodies from the Frank C. Brown Collection of North Carolina folk songs (1957), George Foss's attempt to fuse Sharp's and Bartók's systems of classification (Foss 1964), and Samuel Bayard's extensive studies of instrumental music (e.g., Bayard 1944, 1982), a genre Sharp largely ignored in his Appalachian field trips.

The concept of tune families as a typological device was largely developed by Bayard, and was adopted by Bronson for his grouping of tunes in the Child ballad volumes (Bayard 1950, 1954; cf. Powers 1980). Bronson's comprehensive statement on techniques of ballad-tune analysis, which he developed in the late 1940s using IBM cards, is contained in his *The Ballad as Song* (1969), and in his introduction to *The Singing Tradition of Child's Popular Ballads* (1976), where he reiterates his long-held view that the traditional tune acts with force in shaping the verbal component, a conclusion at variance with the accepted notion of literary scholars such as George Lyman Kittredge, who held that ballad singers simply adapt a tune to an existing text (Bronson 1976:xxii–xxiv).

It is not without significance that Bronson was attached to an English department rather than a music or anthropology department at the University of California, Berkeley. Steeped in the works of Chaucer and Samuel Johnson, on both of whom he was an authority, he undertook a lifetime's study of the ballad tunes in a way that refers back to the original goals of the Folk-Song Society. An admirer of Sharp and his methods, even though he could be critical in discussing Sharp's notion of *continuity, variation,* and *selection* as the decisive factors in the origin and transmission of folk song (concluding that the last of the three, *selection,* could be subsumed under the second, *variation*), Bronson marks the end of a long period of influence stemming ultimately from Sharp (Bronson 1969:144–61, 273–81).

Other scholars have been aware of Sharp, however, as a man with blind spots caused, in the main, by his idealization of "the folk" and his intense desire to return to the people its heritage of traditional music and song. George Foss, for example, has observed that "many of Sharp's techniques and methods have remained standard . . . however, some aspects . . . leave something to be desired in constructing a basis for the serious study of traditional music" (1964:45).

In recent years, a number of English scholars with socialist or Marxist leanings have increased their attacks on Sharp through articles published not only in the *Folk Music Journal,* the organ of the English Folk Dance and Song Society, but in periodicals such as *History Workshop: A Journal of Socialist Historians* (now *Journal of Socialist and Feminist Historians*). They have accused Sharp of distorting the repertoires of the singers from whom he collected by selecting only what he wanted to find. This "blinkered historical outlook" of Sharp is what most upsets his socialist critics.[2]

The Marxist influence upon these younger scholars, who themselves come from an urban working-class background, is from literary critics such as Raymond Williams, author of the classic *Culture and Society 1780–1950* (1958), and historians such as E. P. Thompson, whose *The Making of the English Working Classes* (1966) has had a powerful effect, or Eric Hobsbawm, coeditor of the more recent collection of essays *The Invention of Tradition* (1983) and his latest study *The Age of Empire* (1988). The ultimate influences are not only from Marx himself and Lenin, but also from Trotsky, whose ideas traditionally found favor among British communists not affiliated with the generally Stalinist Communist Party of Great Britain, and in recent times from the Sardinian Antonio Gramsci, whose prison notebooks, written during internment by Mussolini, were published in English in 1971.

One of these Marxist critics, Dave Harker, has characterized Sharp as "a product of metropolitan-oriented English bourgeois culture." A victim in part of his own and his sources' nostalgia, he writes, Sharp remained ignorant of "the broadsides and their printers, the history and development of social events such a fairs, merry-makings, races, weddings and dances, of church musicians, fit-up theaters, rogues, town waits, mobility, literacy, or the technology of workers' music-making"—ignorant, in other words, of the entire context of popular music and its performance (Harker 1982).

While these are harsh words, and not without their own ideological bias, the evolutionism of the period undoubtedly shaped Sharp's notion of the folk-music process. The emphasis he placed on the idealized peasant community is evident in his characterization of this process: *continuity, variation,* and *selection,* a theoretical trinity devised by Sharp, anointed by Maud Karpeles, and sanctified in 1955 by the organization she helped to found, the International Folk Music Council (now, since 1980, the International Council for Traditional Music; see IFMC 1955). This tripartite scheme is set forth in Sharp's book *English Folk Song: Some Conclusions,* where he elevates the idea of the song of "the common people," meaning by this expression "those whose mental development has been due not to any formal system of training or education, but solely to environment, communal association, and direct contact with the ups and downs of life. . . . The non-educated, or 'the common people,' are the unlettered, whose faculties have undergone no formal training, and who have never been brought into close enough contact with educated persons to be influenced by them" (1907:3–4).

This idea was actually challenged at the time by other English scholars such as Frank Kidson, who championed the historical role of the broadside tradition. The reviewer of Sharp's book in *The Times Literary Supplement* was also critical, noting the author's comparatively late arrival in the ranks of folk-song collectors, and suggesting that Sharp used expressions which imply that the most authoritative versions have become so "by the accident of being discovered by Mr. Sharp rather than by some other collector." What is more, the reviewer challenged Sharp's ability to recognize modal music, even in composed pieces, and Sharp had no phonographic record with which to rebut these accusations. Yet the modal theory was a central part of Sharp's musical concept of folk song.

Another socialist critic, Vic Gammon, writing in the *History Workshop Journal,* is thinking primarily of Sharp when he sums up the achievement of English folk-song collectors from the turn of the century: "Idealistically, they believed that folk song would act as a regenerating force in English musical and social life. In serious music they can be credited with some success as the work of Vaughan Williams, Holst and Grainger testifies. In social life their achievement is more difficult to assess. That they saved generations of children from the worst 'national songs' must count for something. [But] the cultural regeneration they hoped for was ultimately very limited in its scope" (Gammon 1980:84).

The reevaluation of Cecil Sharp by Gammon, Harker, and others followed in the wake of A. L. Lloyd's provocative study, *Folk Song in England* (1967). Lloyd had in fact been working on the industrial songs of Britain for some years, as his *Come All Ye Bold Miners* (1952) demonstrates, and this direction in scholarship was influenced in part by the research of George Korson in the United States. Korson had published his *Songs and Ballads of the Anthracite Miners* in 1927, and followed it with *Minstrels of the Mine Patch* (1938) and *Coal Dust on the Fiddle* (1943). For this last work he was assisted in his collecting through twenty states by the United Mine Workers of America, which offered contacts in some of the remoter camps. Lloyd's 1952 collection was also an outcome of the mining industry's desire to contribute to the postwar Festival of Britain in 1951 with the first national collection of miners' songs. Lloyd organized a competition through which miners were encouraged to submit songs relating to life in the pits; later, in partnership with the Workers Music Association, Ewan MacColl, and Topic Records, Lloyd introduced a new dimension, that of industrial folk song, to the folk revival in Britain (cf. Arthur 1979).

Yet Lloyd, who was openly Marxist in his interpretation of English folk song, did not go far enough in his relating of folk song to culture theory, in the eyes of the younger group of scholars, nor did he launch the full-scale attack on Sharp which they felt a thorough-going Marxist position demanded. With the death of Maud Karpeles in 1976, one of the last obstacles to an attack on Sharp's theories and methods was removed. Already in 1972, however, Dave Harker had published a withering assault on Sharp (Harker 1972), which provoked Leslie Shepard, author of a well-known study on broadside ballads, to a retort in the *Folk Music Journal* (Shepard 1973). Harker took the attack further in his books *One for the Money: Politics and Popular Song* (1980) and *Fakesong: The Manufacture of British 'Folksong,' 1700 to the Present Day* (1985), works which place the class struggle and its relationship to industrial song squarely at the center of his arguments.

In these studies Sharp and others are portrayed as "mediators of working class culture," and Sharp himself is depicted as a racist who would wheedle old men and women into parting with arbitrarily selected songs which were then cleaned up for bourgeois consumption, eliminating anything that might offend polite ears (e.g., Harker 1980:148). In his 1973 rebuttal of Harker's original attack on Sharp, Leslie Shepard asserts that Harker has grossly misrepresented Sharp's good taste, broadmindedness, and courage in an age of bourgeois values. His inevitable concessions to prim taste in printed versions, Shepard observes, is outbalanced by the preservation of his original notebooks for specialized study. Further, Sharp's book *English Folk Song* was written in ill-health and partial blindness, and Sharp had to publish it on his own account, referring to it modestly as "not much of a book, but it contains something that should be said; and although I realize that I have said it all very clumsily, yet on the whole I think it should be said so rather than not at all" (Fox-Strangways 1933:66).

Shepard continues,

> I cannot accept that it was "bourgeois" of Sharp to respond to the beauty of songs like "The Trees They Do Grow High," "The True Lover's Farewell," "The Seeds of Love," and "Geordie." . . . There was no condescension in Sharp's genuine appre-

ciation of working-class rural singers. . . . Mr. Harker's own terminology in calling country singers and musicians "small-timers and semi-professionals" is peculiarly insensitive. . . . The theory of communal folk song creation was not Sharp's invention, but the currently accepted view of the most esteemed scholars before and during Sharp's lifetime. The concept of broadsides as "corrupt" versions of traditional songs was also generally accepted. Today, students with relatively unlimited research facilities and access to a wealth of great collections are in a position to modify these views, but they should beware of creating new dogmas. . . . Of course, every generation of scholarship revises and modifies earlier pioneering work—this is itself something of a folk process. But before we pour scorn on the social idealists of the 19th and early 20th century we might ponder the modern mass media exploitation and shallow bourgeois politics that have superseded their efforts. . . . If there is some mythology involved in the vanishing rural ethos, at least one cannot deny its beauty, emotional maturity, good manners and tolerance, to which writers like Marson, Sharp, and others attested. (Shepard 1973:319)[3]

Similarly, the English folk-song scholar Bob Pegg (1976) has warned that criticizing Sharp from too extreme a standpoint can be a distortion in turn. Sharp, he comments, was more humane than many collectors would have been, and there is evidence that he treated his singers, and was treated by them, with affection. In choosing to portray Sharp as a butcher of texts but a relatively accurate transmitter of tunes, Harker has got the emphasis quite wrong. Sharp "amended the texts much less than some of his contemporaries, and it was the tunes that suffered, for they were squeezed into a tonal and metrical straitjacket by the demands and conventions of piano arrangement. They were drained of the vitality which is so striking in Percy Grainger's transcriptions, and the phonograph recordings from which these transcriptions were made" (ibid.:177).

In defence of Sharp and his North American collection, *English Folk Songs from the Southern Appalachians* (1932), Douglas Kennedy has pointed out that Sharp was invited to the United States by Olive Dame Campbell because of his reputation as a leading scholar of folk music, stressing that it was she who had given Sharp the picture of a mountain community "sheltered in a fortunate backwater where early forms of speech and music had been preserved" (Kennedy 1981:165). Vic Gammon, one of Sharp's socialist critics, has objected in turn that Kennedy is so much in tune with Sharp that his own romanticism is similarly lacking in historical perspective (Gammon 1982).

Citing clichés in Kennedy's defence of Sharp, such as the description of traditional singers as being mostly without the benefit of education and often unable to read or write, and that of mountain families having "a unique character, one which had remained unaffected for decades while so-called progress passed them by," Gammon however suggests that Kennedy fails to consider that our perceptions are shaped largely by our preconceptions, and that we often see what we expect to see. In any case, Kennedy readily admits that Sharp probably avoided singers who played for themselves on guitar and banjo, for Sharp had "found at an early stage in his quest that the music of such singers was not of good quality," a view that the singers would probably not have shared. This attitude, Gammon continues, denies that the singers were rational people making aesthetic choices; it also makes the claim that Sharp could make eternal distinctions between good and bad (ibid.:228).

From these exchanges one might reasonably assume that, while Harker and other socialist commentators have rightly criticized Cecil Sharp for his ideology and selectivity, they have been guilty of the same faults, and the truth about Sharp doubtless lies somewhere between the adulation of his peers in the Folk-Song Society and the denigration of the Marxists. It is difficult to avoid the conclusion, nevertheless, that Sharp's idealism prevented his developing a relatively objective (read "realistic") method of folk-song analysis.

One final point worth mentioning about Sharp concerns his political persuasion. A. H. Fox-Strangways, in his 1933 biography, mentions Sharp's socialist convictions, and his son later gave this account of his father's politics: "The salient points of his political beliefs were . . . 1) that untrammeled private enterprise was leading us nowhere, and that collectivism in some form or other was essential; 2) that any form of collectivist government must also be democratic if it is to function properly; 3) that it was grossly unfair that there should be such a thing as a privileged class, and that it was of doubtful utility in any case [though *Folk Songs from Somerset* was dedicated to The Princess of Wales]; 4) that the mob in the long run was nearly always right" (1933:23).

In fact Sharp, in his "conservative socialism," was only one of a line of folklorists in England who took a similar stance: the Rev. Sabine Baring-Gould became an ardent Tractarian, that is, a member of the Oxford

Movement, which sought in its move towards Catholicism within the Anglican Church to encourage the better-educated clergy to be more concerned with pastoral care of their church members. Baring-Gould in fact worked among the poor in London's Pimlico before inheriting the family estate at Lew Trenchard in Devon. Vaughan Williams too was attracted to socialism, influenced by the same Fabian tracts that Sharp had read. Grainger declared himself a socialist from an early age, and Gustav Holst was an active member of the Hammersmith Socialist Club. Sharp himself joined the Fabian Society (founded in 1883–84 in London) in 1900, a society whose goal was the establishment of a democratic socialist state in Great Britain, and Sharp's Morris Dancers made appearances at Fabian functions (cf. Gammon 1980:82–83).

The recent attack of the Marxists in England upon Cecil Sharp is based not only in a controversy over cultural history. It is colored by the traditional contempt felt by revolutionary socialists for gradualism, which is what the Fabians by their very name stood for. "For the Fabians," writes Ian Watson in his *Song and Democratic Culture in Great Britain,* "education was the key to a better society, which meant not the elimination of class division by a socialist revolution but, by means of a policy of 'permeation,' to achieve a just social order without altering the basic class structure. And in the concrete historical context of pre-Great War British imperialism, Sharp's attempt to propagate a *united* national culture became openly chauvinist and manipulative, instilling in children 'the subtle bond of blood and kinship' " (Watson 1983:31).

Thus the Marxists are not just attacking Sharp for his cultural attitudes; they are attacking him on the basis of his brand of socialism, which does not coincide with theirs. Poor Cecil Sharp: although he has cast a long shadow over the study of traditional music and song, both in Britain and North America, his strengths and weaknesses as a scholar seem small beer when set against the competing ideologies of the modern world, and perhaps on the whole he deserves our sympathy rather than our condemnation.

It is instructive to compare the situation in England with that in the United States, where after George Korson several scholars have continued his interest in industrial folk song, usually interpreting from a trade-union rather than an overtly Marxist standpoint. I am thinking here of works such as John Greenway's *American Folksongs of Protest* (1953) or Archie Green's *Only a Miner: Studies in Recorded Coal-Mining Songs* (1972). Greenway's work, in which he deals with the songs of miners and other

groups in industrial society, was singled out by the Soviet folklorist L. Zemljanova in an article in the journal *Sovetskaja Etnografia* in 1962, later translated in the *Journal of the Folklore Institute* (1964). There she praised the
studies of those whom she terms the "leading progressive folklorists of the
United States": Irwin Silber, Russell Ames, John Greenway, Peter Seeger, Alan
Lomax. These writers constantly emphasize the class nature of folklore and
the specific trait of folklore as an art form, namely collectiveness.

Quoting Silber as declaring that the process of the collective reworking
of songs is for folklore the vital basis of artistic creation, she welcomes his
opinion that "the folksong expressing social reality reflects the most important feelings and views of the masses of the people and therefore it is
usually the most progressive and democratic expression of its time" (Zemljanova 1964:141; Silber 1957:31). Zemljanova approves of Greenway's
book in particular, even though it is not explicitly Marxist, because it deals
with the songs of weavers and miners, songs which were "born in strikes
and which fix the most important moments in the history of the labor
movement in the United States" (ibid.:144). She also commends its portraits of outstanding folk performers such as Woody Guthrie and Joe
Glazer: it reveals "the connection between workers' folklore and the political struggle of the American proletariat" and affirms "the important role
of folksongs in the social-political life of the country" (ibid.). The problem
of the urban working class, however, who preferred the hits of Tin Pan Al-
ley to the music of rural workers, is neither addressed nor explained. The
special difficulty of deciding between the merits of a rural music that is
generally fatalistic or ironic, and those of a music that is progressive and
symbolic of the urban proletariat's struggle, is one which has faced Marxist cultural policy in countries other than the United States, as Tokaji's recent book on the situation in Hungary attests (1983; see also responses to
Zemljanova by Botkin 1965 and Espinosa 1965).

The story of Pete Seeger's upbringing, discovery of rural American musical idioms, and eventual clash with the House Committee on Un-American
Activities has been well documented both in his autobiography, *The Incompleat Folksinger* (1972), and in David Dunaway's biography, *How
Can I Keep From Singing: Pete Seeger* (1981), and there is no need to re-
peat the details here. But it is of course symptomatic of the close relationship between Pete and his father, Charles Seeger, that Pete was able to continue some of the social inroads in populist music making that his father
was unable to. Pete is quoted in Dunaway as saying, "My father was the
one person I really related to" (Dunaway 1981:39), and "the one person

that all my life I was able to talk and argue with" (ibid.:26). But Charles added in an interview (1976, published in Dunaway 1980) that Pete took hold in 1941 with the Almanac Singers and "did what we ought to have done" in the Composers' Collective, to which Charles belonged with others such as Henry Cowell, Marc Blitzstein, Elie Siegmeister, Herbert Haufrecht, Henry Leland Clarke, Earl Robinson, and Norman Cazden from 1931 (1980:159). The collective was an ideological but not a formal adjunct of the Communist Party (cf. Reuss 1979:227; also Green 1979:393).

Charles's colleagues had disliked traditional folk music because it was to them defeatist, and he himself referred to it at that time as "dead relics." But Charles's own attempts to write protest songs were too highbrow to succeed; it was Pete who was to adopt his father's New England radicalism and realize the potential in the native music of the period, when Western music was blossoming with Bob Wills in Tulsa and Bill Monroe's Bluegrass Boys in Kentucky. It was just at this time, in the mid-1930's, that a handful of folklorists were attempting to widen the audience for traditional Anglo-American music: Robert Gordon, Ben Botkin, John and Alan Lomax, and Charles Seeger. The period of the Popular Front led to the Communist Left and its intellectuals uniting behind President Franklin Roosevelt and turning to traditional music and song as an expression of patriotism.

This was the beginning of the Folk Song Revival, when the Seegers and the Lomaxes exerted a powerful influence under Roosevelt's New Deal policy: Charles administered programs for the Resettlement (later Farm Security) Administration while Pete, excited by the recordings made available to him through Charles's access to the Library of Congress, learned banjo picking from Bascom Lunsford in North Carolina, and absorbed the tonal and rhythmic elements of style from Dock Boggs, Uncle Dave Macon, Buell Kazee, and others. Alan Lomax introduced Pete to Woody Guthrie, the greatest single influence upon him, and a result was the well-known anthology *Hard Hitting Songs for Hard Hit People*, assembled in 1940 but not published until 1967. In this collaboration Lomax was responsible for compiling the songs, Guthrie for the notes to these, and Seeger for the music transcription and editing. The central position of Alan Lomax as a stimulus to such populist publications must duly be noted; in his position at the Library of Congress he was in a position to effect considerable influence on the course of events in the Revival, and one should also note the presence of his sister, Bess Lomax Hawes (a fellow member of the former Almanac Singers), as current Director of the Folk Arts Section in the National Endowment for the Arts.

Pete Seeger, of course, was and is a performer and songwriter rather than a scholar, but apart from composing over one hundred songs he contributed over two hundred pieces to *People's Songs Bulletin, Broadside,* and *Sing Out!* He also edited half-a-dozen songbooks and tutors. But it is *The Incompleat Folksinger* that remains his most important statement, in which he denigrates his own achievement and expresses an aversion to the cult of personality. Although he joined the Young Communist League and the Party itself in 1941, he later left it in 1950, dissatisfied with its ideological rigidity just as his father in turn had become dissatisfied with conventional ideology. It is evident that he viewed the Party as an organization worthy of support, but only out of duty (Dunaway 1981:94). Perhaps the real place of Pete Seeger in the ideological development of the study, and practice, of Anglo-American traditional song is his stature as a music educator. In the 1950s, as he was under siege for his political beliefs, he was reaching a generation of children through progressive social clubs, summer camps, and unions (ibid.:172). This generation was the one to populate and popularize the Folk Song Revival that began in the 1930s with the Seegers, Lomaxes, and Woody Guthrie. Charles Seeger, in his note on British-American folk music in *The New Grove,* has summarized the contribution of his son's generation to the field: "The singing of folk- and near-folksongs by trained singers and other city people [in the 1930s] presaged genuine recapture by the country at large of the transformed remnants of the folk music traditions of its dominant English-speaking majority" (C. Seeger 1980:440).

With Pete Seeger's essentially populist idealism the wheel comes full circle, only this time the idealism is translated into creative action and performance rather than academic reasoning. Ideology alone, as with his father, did not hold his interest; the puritan instinct to preach, to embrace moral purity, to maintain a certain emotional aloofness, and, despite his protestations of anti-individualism, a Yankee idiosyncrasy and stubbornness have all been a marked part of the Seeger character. Possibly this reluctant individualism is the key to a New England, and by extension an American, resistance to rigid systems that overwhelm and minimize the human figure; the individualism is balanced, on the other hand, by a need for collectivity in social and cultural relationships.

Antonio Gramsci, in his prison notebooks, comments that "the Anglo-Saxon immigrants [of America] are themselves an intellectual, but more especially a moral, elite. . . . They import into America, apart from moral energy and energy of will, a certain level of civilization, a certain stage of

European historical evolution which, when transplanted by such men into the virgin soil of America, continues to develop the forces implicit in its nature" (Gramsci 1971:21-22). More particularly, the New England radical or southwestern populist might recognize himself in E. P. Thompson's picture of the Methodist political rebel in England, who "carried through into his radical or revolutionary activity a profound moral earnestness, a sense of righteousness and of 'calling,' a 'Methodist' capacity for sustained organizational dedication and (at its best) a high degree of personal responsibility" (Thompson 1964:394). Clearly, some of this applies to the Seegers in their life and work.

Marxism has not made the long-term impact on folk-song and folk-music scholarship in the United States that it has in Western Europe, largely because Marxism has not taken hold in the country at large despite vigorous interest in events in the Soviet Union after 1917. This is not the place to analyze the social reasons for such a situation, although they are dealt with by, for instance, Irving Howe in his *Socialism and America* (1985) and by Paul Buhle in *Marxism in the United States* (1987). But the serious consideration given to it by the Seegers and others deserves the attention of students of American music; Serge Denisoff has dealt with it to some extent in his *Great Day Coming: Folk Music and the American Left* (1971), as has Richard Reuss in his dissertation "American Folklore and Left-Wing Politics: 1927–37" (1971).

While Marxism has fueled the attacks of English scholars upon cultural idols such as Cecil Sharp, American critics have taken a more moderate stance, regarding both the limitations of past achievement and the place of traditional music among the industrial enclaves of Britain and America. The study of indigenous folk music in these countries, however, has not yet developed a powerful theory that can tie together the contexts, performers, materials, and musical style in a convincing way, taking into consideration urban and rural forms, men's, women's, and children's music and their various significations. In North America, the increasing emphasis on cognitive and epistemological questions, especially in relationship to the individual tradition-bearer, contrasts markedly with the predominantly sociological concerns of scholars in England (Ireland, Scotland, and Wales manifest more traditional attitudes to folk song, being less markedly affected by industrial and urban mass culture).

But it would be altogether too simple to imagine that, in the study of Anglo-American music, British scholars are following either traditional empiricist paradigms (the realism of Grainger and Barry) or sociocultural models of music drawn up by Lenin, Trotsky, or Gramsci (the anti-idealist model of dialectical materialism), while Americans are moving towards more idealist or rationalist models of understanding as it relates to music. The picture is more complicated, especially since, in the wake of such classics as Marcuse's *Eros and Civilization* (1955), his rereading of Freud, alternative approaches such as feminism have again come to the forefront. At the other end of the idealist scale there is the computer classification of Anglo-American folk tunes, given fresh impetus in the work of such scholars as Ann Dhu Shapiro (1975) and Jerome Wenker (1978). It will be interesting to see whether, in the next phase, empiricism or Marxism will give way before a variety of new idealistic approaches. Awaking to the challenge of alternative paradigms, the study of British and American traditional music and song seems to be abandoning its often blinkered and amateurish past and to be moving closer to the intellectual mainstream of ethnomusicology.

Notes

1. I am dealing specifically with England here, not Scotland, Wales, or Ireland, although Marxist and socialist interpretations of folk song can also be found in recent Scottish writing (e.g., the "Gramsci" number of *New Edinburgh Review,* August 1980). It is also pertinent to note that the great collection of Gavin Greig and the Rev. J. B. Duncan in Northeast Scotland just after the turn of the century, amounting to 3,500 texts and 3,300 tunes, was made with rather less idealistic preconceptions than those of Sharp, even though they acknowledged his influence. While Greig, a schoolmaster, and Duncan, a Presbyterian minister, neglected the rich Traveller tradition of the area (no doubt for practical as well as social reasons), Greig explicitly stated that folk song could contribute to the study of the psychology, emotions, social life, and speech of the people, and advocated what amounts to an ethnological approach in understanding it (see Shuldham-Shaw and Lyle 1981:xiii).

2. That is not to say that these critics blandly agree with one another. Watson, for example, attacks Harker as "fuelled by a sometimes twee [arch], sometimes creepily pathological anti-communism" and maligns his "jaundiced view and bitchy presentation of the second [folk song] revival so far" (1983:41). Gammon (1986) criticizes Harker's stance on the relationship between politics and popular song as well as Lloyd's interpretation of erotic song (Gammon 1982).

3. Shepard also comes from a working-class background (Shepard 1986:125).

Works Cited

Arthur, Dave
1979   Review of A. L. Lloyd, *Come All Ye Bold Miners, Folk Music Journal*
         3 (5):88-90.

Barry, Phillips
1936   "On the Psychopathology of Ballad-Singing," *Bulletin of the Folk-Song Society of the Northeast* 11:16–18.
1961   "The Part of the Folk Singer in the Making of Folk Balladry," in *The Critics and the Ballad,* MacEdward Leach and Tristram P. Coffin, eds. (Carbondale: Southern Illinois University Press), pp. 59–76.
Bayard, Samuel P.
1944   *Hill Country Tunes.* Memoirs of the American Folklore Society, no. 39. Philadelphia: American Folklore Society.
1950   "Prolegomena to a Study of the Principal Melodic Families of British-American Folksong," *Journal of American Folklore* 63:1–44.
1954   "Two Representative Tune Families of British Tradition," *Midwest Folklore* 4:18–33.
1982   *Dance to the Fiddle, March to the Fife: Instrumental Folk Tunes in Pennsylvania.* University Park: The Pennsylvania State University Press.
Blacking, John
1987   *A Commonsense View of All Music: Reflections on Percy Grainger's Contribution to Ethnomusicology and Music Education.* Cambridge: Cambridge University Press.
Botkin, Ben
1965   "Zemljanova on Folklore and Democracy" (Comment), *Journal of the Folklore Institute* 2:225–26.
Bronson, Bertrand H.
1959–   *The Traditional Tunes of the Child Ballads.* 4 vols. Princeton:
72   Princeton University Press.
1969   *The Ballad as Song.* Berkeley and Los Angeles: University of California Press.
1976   *The Singing Tradition of Child's Popular Ballads.* Princeton: Princeton University Press.
Buhle, Paul
1987   *Marxism in the United States: Remapping the History of the American Left.* London: Verso.
Denisoff, R. Serge
1971   *Great Day Coming: Folk Music and the American Left.* Urbana: University of Illinois Press.
Dunaway, David K.
1980   "Charles Seeger and Carl Sands: The Composers' Collective Years," *Ethnomusicology* 24:159–68.
1981   *How Can I Keep from Singing: Pete Seeger.* New York: McGraw-Hill.
Espinosa, Aurelio M., Jr.
1965   "Zemljanova on Folklore and Democracy" (Comment), *Journal of the Folklore Institute* 2:226–27.
Foss, George
1964   "The Transcription and Analysis of Folk Music," in *Folksong and Folksong Scholarship: Changing Approaches and Attitudes* (Dallas: Southern Methodist University Press), pp. 39–71.

Fox-Strangways, A. H.
1933   *Cecil Sharp*. London: Oxford University Press.
Gammon, Vic
1980   "Folk Song Collecting in Sussex and Surrey, 1843–1914," *History Workshop Journal* 10:61–89.
1982   "Song, Sex and Society in England, 1600–1850," *Folk Music Journal* 4:208–45.
1986   "Two for the Show: David Harker, Politics and Popular Song, 1600–1850," *History Workshop Journal* 21:147–56.
Grainger, Percy
1908   "Collecting with the Phonograph," *Journal of the Folk Song Society* III/iii (12):147–69.
1915   "The Impress of Personality in Unwritten Music," *The Musical Quarterly* 1:416–35.
Gramsci, Antonio
1971   *Selections from the Prison Notebooks*. New York: International Publishers.
Green, Archie
1972   *Only a Miner: Studies in Recorded Coal-Mining Songs*. Urbana: University of Illinois Press.
1979   "Charles Louis Seeger (1886–1979)," *Journal of American Folklore* 92:391–99.
Greenway, John
1953   *American Folksongs of Protest*. Philadelphia: University of Pennsylvania Press.
Harker, Dave
1972   "Cecil Sharp in Somerset: Some Conclusions," *Folk Music Journal* 2 (3): 220–40.
1980   *One for the Money: Politics and Popular Song*. London: Hutchinson.
1982   "May Cecil Sharp Be Praised?" *History Workshop Journal* 14:44–62.
1985   *Fakesong: The Manufacture of British 'Folksong,' 1700 to the Present Day*. Milton Keynes: Open University Press.
Hobsbawn, Eric, and Terence Ranger, eds.
1983   *The Invention of Tradition*. Cambridge: Cambridge University Press.
Howe, Irving
1985   *Socialism and America*. San Diego: Harcourt Brace Jovanovich.
IFMC (International Folk Music Council)
1955   [Definition of Folk Music], *Journal of the International Folk Music Council* 7:33.
Karpeles, Maud
1975   *The Crystal Spring: English Folk Songs Collected By Cecil Sharp*. London: Oxford University Press.
Kennedy, Douglas
1981   "Correspondence," *Folk Music Journal* 4 (2):165–67.
Korson, George
1927   *Songs and Ballads of the Anthracite Miners*. Philadelphia: University of Pennsylvania Press.

1938   *Minstrels of the Mine Patch*. Philadelphia: University of Pennsylvania Press.

1943   *Coal Dust on the Fiddle*. Philadelphia: University of Pennsylvania Press.

Lloyd, A. L.

1952   *Come All Ye Bold Miners*. London: Lawrence & Wishart. Reprint ed. 1978.

1967   *Folk Song in England*. London: Lawrence & Wishart.

Lomax, Alan, Woody Guthrie, and Pete Seeger

1967   *Hard Hitting Songs for Hard Hit People*. New York: Oak Publications.

Marcuse, Herbert

1955   *Eros and Civilization*. New York: Vintage Books.

Pegg, Bob

1976   *Folk: A Portrait of English Traditional Music, Musicians, and Customs*. London: Wildwood House.

Porter, James

1983   "Bartók and Grainger: Some Correspondences and a Hypothesis," *Studia Musicologica* 25:221–28.

Powers, Harold

1980   "[Mode] IV. Modal scales and folksong melodies," in *The New Grove Dictionary of Music and Musicians*, Stanley Sadie, ed. (London: Macmillan), vol. 12, pp. 418–22.

Reuss, Richard

1971   "American Folklore and Left-Wing Politics: 1927–1937." Ph.D. dissertation, Indiana University.

1979   "Folk Music and Social Conscience: The Musical Odyssey of Charles Seeger," *Western Folklore* 38:221–38.

Schinhan, Jan

1957   *The Music of the Ballads*. (*The Frank C. Brown Collection of North Carolina Folklore*, 4). Durham, N.C.: Duke University Press.

Seeger, Charles

1980   "United States of America. Folk Music," in *The New Grove Dictionary of Music and Musicians*, Stanley Sadie, ed. (London: MacMillan), vol. 19, pp. 426–47.

Seeger, Pete

1972   *The Incompleat Folksinger*. Edited by Jo Metcalf Schwartz. New York: Simon & Schuster.

Shapiro, Ann Dhu

1975   "The Tune-Family Concept in British-American Folk-Song Scholarship." Ph.D. dissertation, Harvard University.

Sharp, Cecil J.

1907   *English Folk Song: Some Conclusions*. London: Simpkin, Novello. 4th rev. ed. prepared by Maud Karpeles. Belmont, Calif.: Wadsworth Publishing, 1965.

1932   *English Folk Songs from the Southern Appalachians*. 2 vols. London: Oxford University Press.

Shepard, Leslie
1973   "Correspondence," *Folk Music Journal* 2 (4):318–19.
1986   "A. L. Lloyd—A Personal View," in *Singer, Song and Scholar,* Ian Russell, ed. (Sheffield: Sheffield Academic Press), pp. 125–32.
Shuldham-Shaw, Patrick, and Emily B. Lyle, eds.
1981   *The Greig-Duncan Folk Song Collection.* Vol. 1. Abderdeen: Aberdeen University Press.
Silber, Irwin
1957   "They Are Still Writing Folksongs," *Sing Out!* 7:30–31.
Thompson, Edward Palmer
1966   *The Making of the English Working Classes.* New York: Vintage.
Tokaji, András
1983   *Mozgalom és Hivatal. Tömegdal Magyarországon 1945–1956.* Budapest: Zenemükiadó.
Watson, Ian
1983   *Song and Democratic Culture in Britain: An Approach to Popular Culture in Social Movement.* New York: St. Martin's Press.
Wenker, Jerome
1978   "A Computer-Aided Analysis of Anglo-Canadian Folksongs." Ph.D. dissertation, Indiana University.
Williams, Raymond
1958   *Culture and Society 1780–1950.* London: Chatto and Windus.
Yates, Michael
1982   "Percy Grainger and the Impact of the Phonograph," *Folk Music Journal* 4 (3):265–75.
Zemljamova, L.
1964   "The Struggle between the Reactionary and the Progressive Forces in Contemporary American Folkloristics," *Journal of the Folklore Institute* 1:130–44.

Philip V. Bohlman

Representation and Cultural Critique in the History of Ethnomusicology

INITIAL IMAGES: OF MISSIONARIES AND MONTAIGNE

L EAVE IT TO Montaigne to pen one of the first ethnomusicological passages in modern European letters! In his 1580 essay, "Des cannibales," the French essayist, that marvelous and obsessed portraitist of the Other, commented on the music of Native South Americans living on an island in the Bay of Rio de Janeiro with the following lines, which he based on the observations of the Calvinist missionary Jean de Léry who had recently published an account of his 1557–58 sojourn at a French settlement in Brazil (1578):

> I have a song composed by a prisoner who addresses a challenge to his captors with the song. He invites them all to approach and begin their meal of his flesh because they will also be eating the flesh of their own fathers and grandfathers, who had earlier provided him with nourishment. . . . Truly here are real savages according to our standards; either they must be completely savage, or we must be; there is an amazing distance between their character and ours. . . . In order that you not imagine that these acts result from slavery to tradition or from their complete bondage to ancient customs, a bondage that witnesses a lack of reason or judgment, and because they are so simple-minded that they have no other choices available to them, I must cite some examples of their full capacity for expression. Besides this warlike song, I have another, a love song, which begins in this vein: "Adder, stay; stay, Adder, that from the pattern of your coloring my sister may fashion a rich girdle that I may give to my love." . . . Now I am familiar enough with poesy to make the following judgment: not only is there nothing barbarous about this song, but it is completely Anacreontic. The language of these people, moreover, is a soft lan-

guage, quite agreeable, somewhat like Greek in its endings. (1952:242–44; for excerpts from Jean de Léry's account of the musical activities he observed, see Harrison 1973: 6–24).

If Montaigne's reputation for producing trenchant images of the Other and for drawing the world beyond the self closer did not give us pause (de Certeau 1986:67–79), we might quickly dismiss this account as just another observation by titillated travelers of marvelous musical monsters occupying the earth's uncivilized realms and producing a music that was equally uncivilized, its seductive allure for the observer notwithstanding. That non-Western and folk music have long piqued the curiosity of sundry observers confronting the unfamiliar is well known to all of us (Harrison 1973 and Bohlman 1988a). The ascription of foreign characteristics to modes, climatic differences to musical style (Ibn Khaldūn 1958 1:434), or myriad labels like *carmen barbarum* or *Gassenhawerlin* to folk songs (Danckert 1966:5–8) indicates a level of description that clearly transcends common curiosity. Instead, these earlier writings are frequently concerned with the perception of meanings not immediately apparent to the interloping European, with the classification of musical instruments, or with the rendering of strange musical sounds in European notation (see, e.g., Bor 1988). That such acts of reformulating the exotic served to some degree as a means of extending the colonizer's power goes without saying. But they also tendered new means of representing the music of the Other, forging a place for it in European thinking, and empowering it to subvert the unquestioned supremacy of a musical culture that knew of nothing else. However inchoate, these early attempts bore witness to the compelling presence of nascent ethnomusicological practices and the emerging poesis that would establish a place for non-European music in the European discourse on music.

Let us turn again to those images of non-Western musicians and music making with which we are familiar from our too-often fleeting glimpses at an earlier ethnomusicological literature. What responses have they traditionally triggered? How often have they made us laugh? How have we dismissed them as simply naive or ethnocentric, unworthy of the rigorous objectivity of modern ethnomusicology? How are they products not of our ethnomusicological worldview, but of that to which another generation clung? And finally we are wont to ask: How can such images belong to *our* ethnomusicology?

In this article I investigate several ways of answering these implicitly historical questions. I do not base this consideration of the history of ethno-

FIGURE 1. Frontispiece from Athanasius Kircher, *Musurgia universalis, sive ars magna consoni et dissoni* (Rome: Francesco Corbelletti, 1650).

FIGURE 2. Frontispiece from Joseph-François Lafitau, *Moeurs des sauvages amé-*
riquains, comparées aux moeurs des premiers temps, vol. 1 (Paris: Saugrain et
Hochereau, 1724).

Figure 3. From photo gallery between pp. 32 and 33 of Ethel Rosenthal, *The Story of Indian Music and Its Instruments* (London: William Reeves, 1929).

FIGURE 4. Frances Densmore, ethnomusicologist, with Mountain Chief, a Blackfoot Indian, who is interpreting in sign language a song being played on a phonograph. By Harris and Ewing, Washington, D.C., 1916. Courtesy Smithsonian Office of Anthropology.

musicology on historiographic models that insist that the field has been engaged in the ongoing attempt to define its object more accurately or to understand another music "in terms of itself." Such models presume that the refinement of analytical techniques will someday reveal an objective and unassailable reality, the "true" understanding of non-Western music. I posit instead that sufficient response to the historical questions above lies not so much in the objects of early observations as in the processes of presenting them—or, more accurately, *re*presenting them. These processes of representation have formed the literature constituting the history of our field, a literature whose ethnographic richness we are only now, in the present moment of historical reflection in ethnomusicology, beginning to plumb.

There were many motivations for these diverse modes of representation, but there were several that have proved distinctly paradigmatic, which is to say they have historically served to transform observations into meaningful data, theories, and ideas shared by a community of ethnomusicologists; they constitute a body of ethnomusicological texts that allows all the scholars in the present volume to construct the history of our field (cf. Bohlman 1988b). I have begun with Montaigne and the small gallery of images accompanying this article not to suggest historiographic beginnings or boundaries, but because the concern these images demonstrate for representing non-Western music partakes of many of the ethnomusicological practices that we also find in the field's canonic texts: narrowing the distance between the music of one culture and another; searching for meaningful comparisons; experimenting with representational modes and innovative approaches to musical ethnography; understanding another music by first examining that music's own internal criteria and structures (cf. Marcus and Fischer 1986:24–25).

Montaigne, for example, bases his observations on an exegesis of song texts, concluding that the music of cannibals proves them to be fundamentally no different from us. He does not stop at observing the rational intent of the singer, but valorizes that intent by his "Anacreontic" allusion and his remarks about a possible sonorous parallel with classical Antiquity, surely a deliberate choice in Renaissance Europe. Ritual dance depicted in the frontispiece of Athanasius Kircher's *Musurgia universalis* anchors the Native American performers to the earth, to nature, to the human origins of all music. For the cleric Kircher this image is an objectifying gesture, one that bears visual witness to the revelation that all musics are not rooted in the biblical soils of cultural creationism. Joseph-François Lafitau's cherubs bring the symbols of Native American ritual to the scribe poised to give them historical meaning in the frontispiece of his ethnography of Native American customs. Indeed, Lafitau was a remarkable experimenter with musical ethnography, publishing, for example, comparative diagrams of musical instruments used by different North and South American Indians, thereby demonstrating that such instruments possessed no less rational functions than similar instruments of the Greeks, also placed in the diagram (Lafitau 1724 1:opposite p. 212; see also Hodgen 1964:347 and Bohlman 1988a). The piano and piano stool framing the uncomfortably perched vina player are intended, nonetheless, to diminish the distance between him and us. He, in effect, enters a liminal arena in this representation, an arena specified for closer observation and the persuasive assurance of musical kinship. And finally, we see a bit of ourselves in Frances Densmore, honing ethnomusicological practices by scientifically capturing an accurate musical text and insisting on the appropriate cultural context, if indeed the traditional Blackfoot clothing seems out of context against the backdrop of a stiff-backed chair and the Smithsonian's drab walls in Washington, D.C. In their different ways, all these cases of representation seem engaged in similar ethnomusicological practices. During the course of the field's earlier history, each representation and the larger ethnomusicological project of which it was a part added something new to the larger understanding of music and its role as an expressive phenomenon within human society, a task not unlike that of many ethnomusicologists in the late twentieth century.

THE NATURE OF CULTURAL CRITIQUE AND REPRESENTATION IN ETHNOMUSICOLOGY

The framework for the history of ethnomusicology that this essay employs takes as its unifying factor the field's historical concern for cultural critique. In other words, I approach ethnomusicology's history here not by looking primarily at *what* its scholars studied, but at *how* they represented it. I do not presume to deny that this process of representation often accompanied larger projects impelled by colonialism or aesthetic exoticism. But even if we take these as givens, as the hidden agenda in the cultural missions established by Christian churches and the Ford Foundation alike, we accept also the very fundamental nature and persistent presence of cultural critique whenever one culture is studied by someone from another. It is the cultural critique that inevitably results from turning beyond one's familiar world to learn something about oneself by observing another.

Clearly, the concern here is less with the commonly construed subject matters of ethnomusicology—non-Western music, folk music, even music in or as culture—than with traditions of writing about these subjects: musical ethnography. The historiographic relationship evident in the development of ethnomusicological writing is considerably more far-reaching and consistent than historical connections one could find by concentrating on the rightness or wrongness in descriptions of different musics over time. Indeed, despite the claims of one scholar or another that he or she was embarking on a program to "get the music right this time" or "fill in the gaps of our knowledge," the history of ethnomusicology does not contain an abundance of claims that such programs were actually achieved, that the book on a particular repertory or musical culture was actually closed. Few ethnomusicologists need to be told that musical ethnography is an endeavor concerned with the representation of "partial truths" (Clifford

1986a). It is in the particular historiographic domain of this essay, perhaps best called the history of musical ethnography, that the interaction of specific and persistent ethnomusicological practices is particularly striking. As they were engaged in representing other musics in musical ethnography, so too were our ethnomusicological forebears writing the history of their and our field.

Ethnomusicology has always relied on a variety of media and techniques to represent other musics and musical cultures. The visual, verbal, and sonorous all interact in musical ethnographies, producing a history characterized by multivalent forms of texts and the concomitantly polysemous representation of meaning. Transcription and meticulous field notes, melograph studies and tune-family charts, all share in this polysemy, all tell us more about music while simultaneously revealing what we still do not know. And so, the attempt to find a more meaningful musical ethnography is ongoing. Experimentation and innovation in musical ethnography receive their constant impetus from a need to represent something only partially explained by previous approaches. Just as early musical ethnographies used visual images to supplement explanation in their texts (e.g., Amiot 1779), recent experimental approaches might include cassette recordings or employ the structure of ritual as a framework for their texts (e.g., Seeger 1987). The constant search for new means of representation and new ways of shaping these to create a meaningful and effective text has been one of the most characteristic features of ethnomusicology's history.

The four components of a larger, historical ethnomusicological praxis discussed in this essay unquestionably encompass many other practices that most ethnomusicologists would consider essential to their field. While concentrating my remarks on these paradigmatic practices, it is not my intent to exclude one research approach or to valorize another. Rather, I am especially interested in these broad categories because of their interaction when ethnomusicologists write or otherwise convey a concept of music to others through a medium of representation. This interaction, moreover, has changed and continues to change during the course of the field's history, and by extension it may become feasible to look at patterns of change in the interaction of ethnomusicological practices as a means of reconstructing the intellectual history addressed by all of the essays in this volume.

Scientific observation. The first paradigmatic practice is subsumed under the incredibly general rubric, scientific observation. I mean something, however, that is rather more specific, both historically and culturally. My concern here is with isolating and specifying data analyzable within a science of ethnomusicology. Scientific observation assumes many forms in the history of ethnomusicology, not least because of the different ways the field has participated in the scientific endeavors of the social sciences. Athanasius Kircher, assembling the individual pieces for his mid-seventeenth-century tomes on universal music, sought to display an assortment of specimens for his readers (Allen 1962:19–20). Père Lafitau compared instruments related by structure (hand-held percussion instruments) and presumably by ritual function, for example in Figure 2 above, where several of the same instruments acquire specific iconographic meaning (Lafitau 1724 and Bohlman 1988a:6, 8, and 15). Jesse Walter Fewkes, while leading the Hemenway Expedition in the American Southwest, judiciously chose which ceremonies and songs he would record, making the observational decisions ahead of time for the readers of his reports regularly published by the Bureau of American Ethnology (Hinsley 1983:65–66). Alexander Ellis sought more precise ways of describing the datum of the pitch, and Charles Seeger sought to employ the melograph as a revolutionary scientific tool fashioned for ethnomusicology. Whether working in the eighteenth or twentieth century, the ethnomusicologist often undertakes and adapts observation according to the prevailing percepts of scientific method, hence linking the field also to the histories of other sciences.

Scientific observation is also essential to the field because it yields specific approaches to representation and frequently new techniques of representation. Ellis's division of the octave into cents constituted such a technique (e.g., 1885); so, too, did Densmore's volumes of transcription, which sought to represent the music of entire tribal peoples by dint of an unassailable quantity of data. Anthropologists and philologists studying music are no less concerned about the role of appropriate data than are musicologists or folklorists, and it is precisely for such reasons that ethnomusicology—as a science characterized by particular observational practices—has such a uniquely interdisciplinary history.

Experimentation. Proper scientific observations necessarily lend themselves to a second ethnomusicological practice, experimentation. Experimentation as a component of ethnomusicology entails the investigation of quantifiable data to discover some form of objective meaning. It therefore relies on forms of representation that a community of scholars shares, that the community employs as a standard currency for the exchange of meaningful data. In some cases experimentation may mean no more than the positivistic belief that the facts can tell us something. As a component of disciplinary praxis, experimentation may also prescribe scientific method, especially the ability to examine repeatedly the same data in the same ways in order to produce the same results. The attribution of meaning to a cent led directly to experimentation at the end of the nineteenth century, as one witnesses in the articles assembled for the first volume of the *Sammelbände für vergeleichende Musikwissenschaft* (1922), which hardly by chance contains a German translation of Ellis's "On the Musical Scales of Various Nations" (Stumpf and von Hornbostel: 1–75).

Ethnomusicologists have consistently turned recording technology to the task of identifying the most reliable techniques of experimentation (see Schneider and Shelemay in this volume). The ethnomusicology archive in consequence emerged as a venue for experimentation. At the beginning of the twentieth century Stumpf and Hornbostel recognized the potential for experimentation promised by the recordings assembled in the Berlin Phonogrammarchiv (ibid.:v–vi), and today the ethnomusicology archive has emerged as the venue for experimentation, whether within the university or the academy of science. The eighteenth-century concern with taking the visible and then subjecting it to clarification (*lumière*) so that facts spoke more vividly provided yet another practice of experimentation for eighteenth-century writers on non-Western music, such as William Jones (1964) and Joseph-Marie Amiot (de Certeau 1980). The central concern in experimentation, therefore, is how it goes about representing the data on which it relies; ideally, experimentation leads to forms of representation that at least aspire to the universal expression of meaning.

It is hardly surprising that the modes of musical ethnography have been polysemous, given the historically polymorphous forms of ethnomusicological experiment. The different disciplines that have contributed to and been a part of ethnomusicology ipso facto employ different types of experimentation. The intellectual history of the field thus yields abundant cases of philological, psychological, and sociological experimentation, studies based on mathematical testing and religious speculation, biological models for music history, and acoustical studies rooted in physics. Examined in relation to this area of ethnomusicological praxis, transcription and classification are clearly examples of scientific experimentation and the ordering of knowledge based on the repetition and refinement of experimental models. What is most striking, however, is the way this diversity has historically produced unity in the field. It may well be that one of the most distinctive features of ethnomusicological experimentation is its ability to draw techniques from many different scientific domains, but to focus those techniques on the common problem of interpreting and representing music.

Fieldwork. If I reach fieldwork only as the third component in a broader ethnomusicological praxis, it is not because its importance is somehow less than the components addressed previously. Quite the contrary, it is only through the introduction of fieldwork that one can distinguish ethnomusicology from other types of musical scholarship. Field studies are perhaps the clearest evidence for the underlying assertion of this paper that ethnomusicology's history does not depend on what is studied, but how the study is carried out. Most recently, ethnomusicologists have engaged in the study of Western art music in incisive ways, not to learn more about the music itself, but to reveal more about the concepts and meaning attending all musical phenomena (Kingsbury 1988; Koskoff 1988; Nettl 1989). Obversely, one must also recognize that the study of a non-Western music by one of its practitioners does not immediately become ethnomusicology, a realization that is apparent to anyone who has made the mistake of addressing an Indian scholar of Indian music as an ethnomusicologist. From this standpoint the most obvious case of medieval Arabic ethnomusicologist would be Ibn Khaldūn, an inveterate fieldworker and ethnographer, rather than Arabic musical scholars largely concerned with the digestion of music theory from treatises; when Ibn Khaldūn turns to musical ethnography in the *Muqaddimah* (1377), the real innovation in his thinking and in the experimentation in his methodology emerges from passages devoted to non-Arabic and non-Islamic peoples, not in the chapters tempered by Islamic orthodoxy (cf. 1958 2:360–61, 395–405). Just as travel to lands outside of Europe during the Age of Discovery brought about the inception of modern anthropology, however attenuated its development may have been (Hodgen 1964:78–107), it was only when fieldwork became a practice in the study of non-Western and folk music that the history of ethnomusicology began to form from the confluence of each of the practices dicussed in this essay. Fieldwork in ethnomusicology seems particularly concerned with the abrogation of geographical and cultural distance, hence its distinguishing characteristic of representing the music of the Other with a verifiable level of scientific observations and in the contexts of the society where it is found.

Seeing ourselves in the Other and the Other in ourselves. Although it might seem on first glance to be a practice that effectively undermines the objectivity gained by fieldwork, the final component of ethnomusicological praxis embodies the appeal and practice of drawing the music of the Other closer to one's own culture to dispel its foreignness. George Marcus and Michael Fischer regard this "promise" as one of the primary motivations of anthropology, which, though frequently neglected, expresses nevertheless a pervasive desire to empower the field "to serve as a form of cultural critique for ourselves. In using portraits of other cultural patterns to reflect self-critically on our own ways, anthropology disrupts common sense and makes us reexamine our taken-for-granted assumptions" (1986:1). Cultural critique at some moments in ethnomusicology's history may have been an even more compelling promise than it has been for anthropology because of the explicit aesthetic availability of another music. At least as early as Guillaume Villoteau, who served as the ethnomusicologist in the team of French savants accompanying the Napoleonic incursion into Egypt, understanding another music involved some practice of internalizing that music through the assistance of a musician with "native" fluency (Villoteau 1826). This mode of ethnography emphasizes the sometimes stark contrast between similarities and differences. Another musical culture may be extolled because it has all the levels and degrees of sophistication of Western music (e.g., Amiot 1779), or its integrity may rest on its distinctiveness, the enchantment with diversity that produces a "poetics of displacement" (cf. Clifford 1988). The rhetorical modes and ethnographic motivations of ethnomusicological cultural critique are multifarious, but historically reflective of the changing ways in which the music of the Other is engaged and appropriated.

Of all the ethnomusicological practices, therefore, cultural critique is most dependent on the choices made during the processes of representation. Clearly, it is a practice that privileges writing and the perspective gained from multiple forms of representation and therefore seems most unlike the first two practices discussed in this section. Comparative approaches, searches for musical universals, and such recent historical directions as the role of ethnomusicology in music-education systems all depend to a large degree on the exercise of different forms of cultural critique in ethnomusicology. Some might disdain its presence in the study of other musics, holding that only objective study truly respects the integrity of musicians unlike ourselves, but this desire to conflate self and Other is rarely absent from ethnographic motivations. After all, most ethnomusicologists think there is something important about liking the music they study.

The practices of cultural critique further illustrate the multitude of issues beyond a putatively truthful and objective description of the music that are essential to a full treatment of the intellectual history of the field. Colonial power and the subversion thereof, cultural salvaging and the forging of new musical genres by movements of political resistance, the roles of gender and class in the interpretation of musical meaning, all these concerns have historically formed part of the ethnomusicological canon because of the persistent presence of a compelling cultural critique. I do not pretend to claim that the field as a whole has handled such issues well or poorly, has better served colonial power or its subversion, but rather that ethnomusicological praxis, with its willingness to include multiple forms of representation, has historically given voice to such issues. It has not been lost upon ethnomusicologists that a bit of themselves resided with the powerless and repressed of the world.

In different ways these four ethnomusicological practices have come to constitute the processes of representation fundamental to the history of musical ethnography. They form an essential tension between internal sensitivity to another culture and its music, and the dispassionate external analysis of the culture. Throughout the history of the field they have yielded new modes of representation, new ethnomusicological vocabularies, new symbols, and new images. But only together do they lay the foundations of musical ethnography, the way we write about other musics. Only together do they require the development of vocabularies that capture the meanings of musical data, place them within both a social scientific and humanistic framework, and then reformulate their meanings for another culture. These vocabularies are as various as the different images illustrating this essay, as the unending attempts to determine the best way to transcribe music, or as the complex of rhetorical gestures and jargon that enter a hopelessly interdisciplinary field. What stands above all else as remarkable is that these diverse practices have so often functioned in a concerted fashion to lend historical unity to ethnomusicology's past.

Three Historical Moments, Three Processes of Ethnomusicological Representation

The ways our disciplinary ancestors wrote about music were, of course, very different from the ways we go about musical ethnography. Many early studies that provide us with observations and data about non-Western music do so without full integration of any consciously ethnomusicological practices, either like those suggested in this essay or any other kind. One of the first musical scholars to begin the process of representation by integrating distinctly different practices was Athanasius Kircher, whose encyclopedic output in the mid-seventeenth century aimed at assembling a universe of musical activities replete with musical menageries and mysticism. Kircher was a collector, an antiquarian who put the curiosities he assembled on display, both in the museums he established in Rome and on the pages of his books. Reading the tomes published by Kircher, one encounters a great deal that, at least on the surface, would appear to establish him as the first European ethnomusicologist. He approaches the essence of tone and intervallic structure systematically and from a number of different perspectives, not least the analysis of Jewish notational systems and what data he could muster about non-Western theoretical systems (1650:43–79). He writes at great length about the origins of music in nature, incorporating long passsages about the music of Native Americans, or rather, music in the Americas, even that of some of the zoological curiosities abundant in the New World (ibid.:26–27). His museum-in-a-book method of ethnography seems even to be on the verge of taking off in the direction of more recent ethnomusicological approaches, for example when he attempts to flesh out the conceptualization of music by offering lists of "Definitions in Music" and "Axioms and Postulates about Music" (ibid.:81). Engravings of instruments, tables of intervals, extensive melodic transcriptions, and mathematical designs of interlocking scale structures all contribute different representational modes to the sixth book of the *Musurgia universalis,* revealing an ethnographic approach overflowing with a fantasy and universalizing intent.

But is it ethnomusicology? Are these elements of ethnomusicological praxis? There can be no question that Kircher explicitly tries to bring the music of the Other closer to a European readership. His overt motivation is, therefore, a type of musical ethnography. There is, of course, an ethnomusicological practice absent from his method, namely fieldwork, which in turn would necessarily postpone scientific experimentation and render inchoate any true narrowing of the distance between the Other and the seventeenth-century European. His museological approach to musical ethnography may depend on the fieldwork of others, but only insofar as that facilitated collecting artifacts. The music of non-European cultures held a place in Kircher's larger universal scheme, but he stopped far short of any reflexive recognition of the European, much less himself, in any aspect of non-European music.

That fieldwork has the potential to transform other components of ethnomusicological praxis, that it empowers these to cohere as ethnomusicological cultural critique, becomes axiomatic in the discipline only during the eighteenth century. Indeed, one can say that fieldwork was the essential catalyst that reformulated Enlightenment attitudes toward the music of other cultures into a systematic way of writing about that music. Charles

Fonton, a French diplomat and translator, used his direct experience in the Middle East, especially youthful years of study in Turkey, to write a treatise in which he compared Turkish music and European music (1751; see Neubauer 1985 and 1986). His experience in the field empowers Fonton to use his *Essai sur la musique orientale comparée à la musique européene* not just as an account of Turkish music, but as a critique of European attitudes toward music, a bold, if not unprecedented, rhetorical gesture. The major musical ethnographies of the late eighteenth century, William Jones's essays on Indian music (e.g., 1784) and Amiot's *Mémoire sur la musique des chinois* (1779) resulted from considerable time in the field. It was during his long career as a Jesuit missionary in Beijing that Amiot studied Chinese music and discovered it to be no different from other musics in its complexity; indeed, its history exceeded anything in the West, so Amiot asserted, and on the basis of this criterion alone Amiot tacitly suggested that any culture capable of producing such a music was superior to Europe, at least when considered as a whole and over the course of its entire history (1779:1–21).

Fieldwork at this time, of course, had institutional motivations that were colonialist in one form or another, but it was almost in spite of these that studies like Guillaume Villoteau's two volumes on music in Egypt came to distinguish the importance of meticulous observation in the field itself (1823 and 1826). Villoteau may have been an official agent of the French government, but his early experiences in the field taught him the necessity of finding new ways of preparing his eventual account of the musics of Egypt. Moreover, one cannot discount the importance of institutional connections in the establishment of a community of scholars with ethnomusicological interests; Villoteau's writings, the final two volumes in the eventually encyclopedic output of the French expedition, were read throughout the nineteenth century and served as a major source for the study of music in the Islamic world well into the present century (Bohlman 1987).

Just a century later, at the turn of the present century, it was the institution that provided the environment for the ethnomusicological practice which had until that time lagged in its development within the field: scientific experimentation. Not only did the institution bring about new approaches to fieldwork and experimentation, but its intermediary role meant that new modes of ethnography and representation were possible. For the Central Europeans experimentation became a distinguishing practice because of the growing role played by the Phonogrammarchiv, not by chance as a department within the academy of science. Experimentation made it conceivable to examine data in what were surely understood as radical new ways, whether through the reconstruction of entire non-Western tonal systems of the use of techniques from linguistic and psychological analysis. Experimentation turned existing technologies to new uses and caused revolutionary innovation in traditional endeavors, for example transcription (e.g., Gilman 1891).

Musical ethnographies presented such studies as a whole, and in the major publications in the early decades of the century, the *Sammelbände für vergleichende Musikwissenschaft,* for example, ethnomusicologists such as Stumpf and Hornbostel moved from recorded collection to recorded collection, whether Japanese, Native American, or German, running their systematic experiments and tabulating their results in diverse forms of ethnography (see Schneider in this volume). The American institutions, in contrast, were emphasizing fieldwork by organizing expeditions and charging scholars such as Jesse Walter Fewkes and Benjamin Ives Gilman with the task of documenting musical traditions in situ. The field, too, became a venue for experimentation. Rather striking in this phase of ethnomusicological history is the extent to which one scholar's field studies provided the source for another's experimentation (e.g., Stumpf 1886 and 1892), clearly indicating an institutionalization of scientific observation and the forms of data it employed. Concern for dividing the labors associated with different paradigmatic practices and then linking them again in the new texts of the field thereby became normative and systematic, by the 1920s imparting to the diverse practices the power to unify an entire field and to give a concerted voice to its representation of the music of the Other.

TOWARD AN INTELLECTUAL HISTORY OF ETHNOMUSICOLOGICAL PRAXIS

More and more over the course of the past few years, our growing reflection about our intellectual history has exhibited a decidedly positive tone. This positive tone may be due, in part, to the initial glow that attends discovery: the awareness that the history of the field is far more extensive than many had assumed or admitted, and that early ethnomusicological writings offer a richness from which the field can benefit today. The present volume, which partakes of the positive reflection of recent years and is surely a product of it, emphasizes the multitude of approaches that ethnomusicology has historically embraced. Clearly, all of these essays are interested in establishing an expanded concept of ethnomusicology's history as the sum resulting from many different, but reflected, parts.

This essay, in many ways, consciously pushes the reflective efforts to still greater extremes, whose limits we may not yet be prepared to set and define. I am suggesting here that we consider as ethnomusicological genres of scholarship and writing that we might never before have seen from the perspective of disciplinary kinship. Accordingly, we might begin to take seriously some of the accounts and images of other musics and musicians that heretofore may have served only as sources for a good laugh. Reasoned deductively, the history of the field has a remarkable wholeness comprising an abundance of individual parts. The multitude of cultural meanings it sets out to discover and the diverse forms of musical ethnography with which it attempts to express those meanings seem to bear witness to a disciplinary postmodernism that predates the fashionable invention of that concept in our own times. These individual practices and representational forms of ethnomusicology cohere in ways we are only now beginning to understand as we more actively seek to construct the intellectual history of the field. To a large degree it is because of the persistence of these diverse ethnomusicological practices, those proposed in this essay and others that I might have proposed but chose not to because of their exclusivity, that this remarkable degree of historical cohesion has been possible. Looking at the impact and interaction of these practices and the changing forms of musical ethnography they have shaped into the encompassing discipline of ethnomusicology stands not only to unify the field's long and rich history, but to reveal that the musical menageries and mysteries of earlier ethnographies were not the mere curiosities that many had imagined them to be; rather, they were reasoned endeavors by our own intellectual forebears to narrow the distance between themselves and the societies whose music and musical life they so passionately wished to render as meaningful.

Works Cited

Allen, Warren Dwight
1962   *Philosophies of Music History: A Study of General Histories of Music, 1600–1960*. New York: Dover. First published in 1939.
Amiot, Joseph-Marie
1779   *Mémoire sur la musique des chinois, tant anciens et modernes*. Paris: Nyon.
Bohlman, Philip V.
1986   "R. G. Kiesewetter's 'Die Musik der Araber': A Pioneering Ethnomusicological Study of Arabic Writings on Music," *Asian Music* 18 (1):164–96.

1987 "The European Discovery of Music in the Islamic World and the 'Non-Western' in 19th-Century Music History," *The Journal of Musicology* 5 (2):147–63.
1988a "Missionaries, Magical Muses, and Magnificent Menageries: Image and Imagination in the Early History of Ethnomusicology," *The World of Music* 33 (3):5–27.
1988b "Traditional Music and Cultural Identity: Persistent Paradigm in the History of Ethnomusicology," *Yearbook for Traditional Music* 20:26–42.

Bor, Joep
1988 "The Rise of Ethnomusicology: Sources on Indian Music 1780–c. 1890," *Yearbook for Traditional Music* 20:51–73.

de Certeau, Michel
1980 "Writing vs. Time: History and Anthropology in the Works of Lafitau," *Yale French Studies* 59:37–64.
1986 *Heterologies: Discourse on the Other.* Translated by Brian Massumi. Minneapolis: University of Minnesota Press.

Clifford, James
1986a "Introduction: Partial Truths," in Clifford and Marcus 1986:1–26.
1986b "On Ethnographic Allergory," in Clifford and Marcus 1986:98–121.
1988 "A Poetics of Displacement: Victor Segalen," in James Clifford, *The Predicament of Culture: Twentieth-Century Ethnography, Literature, and Art* (Cambridge: Harvard University Press), pp. 152–63.

Clifford, James, and George E. Marcus, eds.
1986 *Writing Culture: The Poetics and Politics of Ethnography.* Berkeley and Los Angeles: University of California Press.

Danckert, Werner
1966 *Das Volkslied im Abendland.* Bern: Francke.

Ellis, Alexander J.
1885 "On the Musical Scales of Various Nations," *Journal of the Royal Society of Arts* 33:485–527.

Fonton, Charles
1751 *Essai sur la musique orientale comparée à la musique européene.* For locations of extant manuscripts see Neubauer 1986.

Gilman, Benjamin Ives
1891 "Zuñi Melodies," *A Journal of American Archaeology and Ethnology* 1:63–91.

Harrison, Frank
1973 *Time, Place and Music: An Anthology of Ethnomusicological Observation c. 1550 to c. 1800.* Amsterdam: Frits Knuf.

Hinsley, Curtis
1983 "Ethnographic Charisma and Scientific Routine: Cushing and Fewkes in the American Southwest, 1879–1893," in *Observers Observed: Essays on Ethnographic Fieldwork,* George W. Stocking, Jr., ed. (Madison: University of Wisconsin Press), pp. 53–69.

Hodgen, Margaret T.
1964   *Early Anthropology in the Sixteenth and Seventeeth Centuries.*
         Philadelphia: University of Pennsylvania Press.
Ibn Khaldūn
1958   [1377] *The Muqaddimah: An Introduction to History.* Translated by
         Franz Rosenthal. 3 vols. New York: Pantheon.
Jones, William
1964   [1784] *On the Modes of the Hindoos,* in Sourindro Mohun Tagore,
         Hindu Music from Various Authors (Varansi: Chowkhamba Sanskrit
         Series), pp. 88–112. Originally Published in *Asiatick Researches.*
Kingsbury, Henry
1988   *Music, Talent, and Performance: A Conservatory Cultural System.*
         Philadelphia: Temple University Press.
Kircher, Athanasius
1650   *Musurgia universalis, sive ars magna consoni et dissoni.* Rome:
         Francesco Corbelletti.
Koskoff, Ellen
1988   "Cognitive Stategies in Rehearsal," *Selected Reports in
         Ethnomusicology* 7:59–68.
Lafitau, Joseph-François
1724   *Moeurs des sauvages amériquains, comparées aux moeurs des premiers
         temps.* 2 vols. Paris: Saugrain et Hochereau.
de Léry, Jean
1578   *Histoire d'un voyage faict en la terre du Bresil.* La Rochelle: Antoine
         Chuppin.
Marcus, George E., and Michael M. J. Fischer
1986   *Anthropology as Cultural Critique: An Experimental Moment in the
         Human Sciences.* Chicago: University of Chicago Press.
Montaigne
1952   *Essais.* Paris: Editions Garnier Frères.
Nettl, Bruno
1989   "Mozart and the Ethnomusicological Study of Western Culture,"
         Yearbook for Traditional Music 21:1–16.
Neubauer, Eckhard
1986   "Der *Essai sur la musique orientale* von Charles Fonton mit
         Zeichnungen von Adanson," *Zeitschrift für Geschichte der
         arabisch-islamischen Wissenschaften* 3:335–76.
Neubauer, Eckhard, ed.
1985   *"Essai sur la musique orientale comparée à la musique européene,"*
         Zeitschrift für Geschichte der arabisch-islamischen Wissenschaften
         2:225–324.
Rosenthal, Ethel
1929   *The Story of Indian Music and Its Instruments.* London: William Reeves.
Seeger, Anthony
1987   *Why Suyá Sing: A Musical Anthropology of an Amazonian People.*
         Cambridge: Cambridge University Press.

Stumpf, Carl
1886 "Lieder der Bellakula-Indianer," *Vierteljahrsschrift für Musikwissenschaft* 2:405–26. Reprinted in *Sammelbände für vergleichende Musikwissenschaft* 1:87–103.
1892 "Phonographierte Indianermelodien," *Vierteljahrsschrift für Musikwissenschaft* 8:127–44. Reprinted in *Sammelbände für vergleichende Musikwissenschaft* 1:113–26.
Stumpf, Carl, and Erich M. von Hornbostel, eds.
1922 *Sammelbände für vergleichende Musikwissenschaft*, vol.1. Munich: Drei Masken Verlag.
Villoteau, Guillaume
1823 [1809] *Déscription historique, technique et littéraire, des instruments de musique des orientaux*. Paris: C. L. F. Pancroucke.
1826 [1809] *De l'état actuel de l'art musical en Egypte, ou relation historique et descriptive des recherches et observations faites sur la musique en ce pays*. Paris: C. L. F. Pancroucke.

Regula Burckhardt Qureshi
Whose Music? Sources and Contexts in Indic Musicology

H INDUSTANI ART MUSIC[1] has a rich, documentable history, and at some level its writers have laid the foundation for what may be termed educated musical consciousness and its communicative norms. It is through these norms that the outsider normally gains access to the music in the first place, and they are likely to remain his or her frame of reference for any consideration of historical materials—a frame of reference much like the one shared by students of Western music history.

The a priori nature of this frame of reference first became strikingly illuminated for me eighteen years ago, when I clashed with an important American scholar of Indic music over fundamental notions of musical substance and terminology. We had each returned after a year's study of Hindustani music, he from Benares Hindu University, I from Karachi and Lucknow, both Muslim centres. I came away somewhat devastated that I had learned deviant material from illiterate Muslim practitioners ignorant of the Sanskritic norms of music history elucidated by learned Brahmins.

This confrontation—by two North American proxies—had caused the surfacing of three disharmonies between our respective musical sources. The first and most obvious disharmony pertains to their religious-communal matrix—Hindu versus Muslim—and the second, to their social class identity—educated middle class versus service professional. The third disharmony is a corollary emanating from this combination and pertains to the sources themselves—musical authority founded in written texts as against mere oral tradition. Not surprisingly, I found that the standard literature on music, too, represented my "side" rather poorly. For embodied in this literature is an Indian consensus supporting a unitary system of art music with a standard theory, ideology, and history.[2] This system is supported by a network of institutions for study, teaching, and performance, and buttressed by governmental support. Indeed, a strong sense of the normative pervades the entire Indian enterprise of Hindustani classical music, supported, as it is, by an upper-and middle-class elite of patrons who are linked together by a sense of responsibility for shaping national culture.[3]

Across the border, in Pakistan,[4] the present-day vantage point is very different, although here too an elite is shaping national culture in a newly independent nation, but one in which music occupies an entirely insignificant place. Two radically different sociopolitical environments have evolved around what is essentially the same musical "language" of Hindustani art music. Accordingly, two kinds of music history have been generated for this music in India and Pakistan. One, the Indian one, quite multifarious, is fueled with two strong regional traditions in Bengali and Marathi but primarily comprising an array of general histories, all in English, the shared elite language.[5] Several music journals provide a wide forum for a nationally based musicological discourse, and a number of universities have active research programs producing historical scholarship in music, all within the paradigm emanating from that normative framework.

Music history in Pakistan lacks just such a paradigm. Groping for norms apart from those across the border in India, Pakistan can boast only a trickle of music writing in Urdu and English, little of it truly historical in orientation, and only one incipient music journal. Consensus among the small elite of music lovers is based on a shared concern for the very survival of art music, and norms about music exist rather by implication than in any concretely articulated form. Some effort is made to assert the centrality of the local hereditary tradition of Hindustani music; on the other hand, reference is also made to the norms of the central tradition in India, including bibliographic sources drawn from Indian writings.[6]

The political division of the Hindustani music area thus highlights something of the cultural-historical heterogeneity which had been a reality in Hindustani music long before. But one has to look beyond what are essentially two unitary views of music—the Indian one of incomparably greater veracity—to a reality of greater historical complexity which needs to be accounted for if historiography is to be more than a servant of the normative. This paper is an attempt to bring some clarity of perspective to the vast canvas of historical sources for Hindustani music, by a scrutiny of its complex palette of data, criteria, and motivations. The specific motivation comes from an inquiry into the historical antecedents of a specific performance tradition—bowed string playing—and the obvious need for an expanded focus on sources that includes both the musical idiom and its human agent, a shift from product to process.

A great variety of source materials is actually available for the historical study of Hindustani music; what makes their use problematic is their diversity not only in kind but in character and context. The only reasonable procedure for relating data contained in different sources to each other is to be able to place the sources within their particular societal-functional contexts, so that contiguities and contrasts between them can suggest a historically valid basis for establishing such relationships. The quality of historiography resulting from this procedure is directly related to the degree of coherence that can be established between different source types pertaining to the same topic or theme.

Assuming that historiography cannot be neutral and that, in Collingwood's terms, the "common-sense" theory of history does not yield "facts" (Collingwood 1956:234), the historian in pursuit of the Rankean ideal of historiographic truth[7] must thus begin by identifying the contexts of social function and motivation which are relevant to the source material at hand—in Kuhnian terms, to view his sources within their appropriate paradigmatic framework (Kuhn 1970). Taking a cue from the general historiography of India which is well-established, yet pluralistic in orientation, can help provide the historical sophistication that as yet eludes the literature on Indic music.[8]

What complicates the historiographer's task for the Hindustani music area is "paradigmatic overlay." Focusing on the period historians term "modern," that is, from 1556 (*Mughal* emperor Akbar's accession) to the present,[9] reveals the existence of three "paradigms" which are embedded in their respective intellectual-cultural traditions and contain their own perspective on music and on the past. Broadly termed Hindu, Muslim, and British/Western, they are linked with the three dominant civilizations that succeeded each other, resulting in a complex historical overlay which is reflected variously in the historicism of subsequent periods. At base, these "views" or paradigms are really representative of the successive power elites, each guided by its particular ideology, as has been well articulated by historians of their respective domains.

It is in the nature of art music to be identified with elite establishments, hence the term "canonical" is appropriate for Hindustani music, denoting a system articulated by, or rather for, ruling elites in accordance with their ideologies and hence very immediately associated with them. Given its elite patronage, the documentation of "canonical" music, too, reflects elite ideology and purposes; indeed, music history is ultimately written by and for these elites. Thus another way of identifying the three paradigms of music is as representations of three successive kinds of rules in North India: Hindu,[10] Muslim,[11] and British—or rather, British-Hindu and British-Muslim,[12] which become transformed into the independent nation-states of India and Pakistan.

THE SOURCES AND THEIR CONTEXTS

A perusal of Powers's comprehensive historical survey in the *New Grove Dictionary of Music and Musicians* (Powers 1980) presents a graphic view of the diversity of sources in type and content, comprising treatises, iconographic evidence, and what Powers terms "traditions," in which he includes chronicles and narratives and, indirectly speaking, oral tradition. By implication the term covers sources not primarily or explicitly documenting music; indeed, this source picture dominates the period under consideration here. In pragmatic terms, the music historian needs to enter the domain of the historian of art and literature, the court historian, and the social anthropologist. In addition, he or she confronts written sources in Sanskrit and Persian as well as in modern Indic and European languages, which also means dealing with both Devanagari and Persian scripts. Indeed the role of the two vastly different scripts needs to be acknowledged in keeping these texts in two different intellectual worlds—despite the fact that the two language groups are related. Not surprisingly, all-round historians of Hindustani music are hard to come by! Those who bridged those worlds in the past were Hindus acculturated to the Muslim courts.[13] What may initially be attempted here is a consideration of relevant source categories. Grouping these according to their respective paradigmatic contexts yields the following clusters of written, iconographic, and oral sources.

HINDU SOURCES (SANSKRIT TEXTS, RELATED VERNACULARS, IN DEVANAGARI SCRIPT)

First and most authentically Indian are the sources generated by the Hindu musical paradigm. Works on music are part of a scholarly discourse in traditional Hindu epistemologies of literature, aesthetics, other representational arts, and related or analogous symbolic systems, embedded more or less explicitly in Hindu cosmology. Their frame of reference is essentially mythological, not historical. In V. Savarkar's words, "the Hindu counts his years not by centuries but by cycles—the Yug and the Kalpa—and amazed asks, 'O Lord Rama, where has the kingdom of Ayodhya gone? O Lord Krishna, where has Mathura gone!'" (quoted in Hay

1958:883). The Hindu view of the past thus is one of an ever-present norm, founded in the beginning-less (and endless) nature of primal matter and spirit. Theories of causation are founded in truth or basic reality, becoming manifest—really or apparently—in the phenomenal universe. Articulated in the *Vedanta*, this basic duality is articulated between the absolute and the relative, or higher and lower knowledge; temporality is thus irrelevant or at least secondary.

Treatises, even in a period and region dominated by Muslim rule, continue to articulate this duality. Their authors are brahminical scholars,[14] contributing to a general literary-mythological-aesthetic enterprise of articulating norms and precepts, linking them with an authentic prototype. Thus most Sanskrit treatises reflect the model of the thirteenth-century *Sangita-Ratnakara* (Sarangdeva 1978) in organization and in content through paraphrase or commentary; even contemporary musical information is presented in reference to the same model (cf. Powers 1980:81). The aim, whether through imitation or innovation, is normative; the method is classification,[15] and chronological reference is notably absent, for music is ultimately identified with the Divine: "Adoring sound means adoring the Trinity" (Sarangdeva: *Sangita Ratnakara* 1.3.1–2; quoted in Raghavan and Dandekar 1958:275); and according to the *Skanda Purana Suta Samhita* (4.2.3.114–6; quoted in Raghavan and Dandekar 1958:274), music is "an effective means of attaining oneness with Shiva."

At the concrete level, treatises were composed for and commissioned by a feudal or religious patron to articulate his cultural/religious heritage and his patronage of experts and expertise. But their normative-ideological character means that functional content and historical assignability pose a special challenge for the historian.

Another type of source relevant to music making are collections of devotional poetry in Hindi and other vernacular languages[16] containing reference to musical settings for performance.

MUSLIM SOURCES (PERSIAN, ALSO URDU, IN ARABIC SCRIPT)

The Muslim view of the past is a chronological one, connecting the present age with Islamic norms as lived by the Prophet (Hardy 1958:520f), and creating a record for future judgment. According to Ziauddin Barni, author of *Tarikh-e-Firoz Shahi* (Calcutta: Bibliotheca Indica 1860–62:9–17; reprinted in Hardy 1958:522ff), history is the deeds of the past of great examples, hence it authenticates tradition, for it is inseparable from truth. Its writing is a great obligation, as a record for judgment day. Dates, places, and names form part of that record, and indeed a linear conception of time-permeates this tradition.

Directly emanating from this vision are the chronicles written for, and even by, Muslim rulers, mainly of political events, but also of court establishments including information *about* music, musicians, patrons, and performance establishments.[17] Court records, also in Persian, provide similar information but more concretely so, including information on musicians and their duties; hence they also provide definitions of musical categories. Such courts included Hindu rulers like the Maharaja of Jaipur (Erdman 1985:28–115), who were inspired by the *karkhana* organization of Akbar the Great. Music itself, in this view, is entirely secular, a prominent part of the "fine arts" (*funun-i-latifa*) and of traditional Muslim high culture, notwithstanding the negative religious valuation of music in Islam.[18] This freedom from religious ideology results in artistic eclecticism but also in a lack of an important motivation for patronage.

Eclecticism is clearly manifested in the Persian treatises on music which are almost invariably fashioned after, commenting upon, or translated from Sanskrit treatises, so as to make the brahminical tradition of music available to the Muslim elites. They also, but not consistently, aim at synthesizing Persian theory or materials into the Indic system, and at including compilations about contemporary practice. In addition, literary narratives both in epic poetry[19] and later in prose (Urdu)[20] provide valuable sources for musical practice.

British Sources (English)

A Western view of history and chronology in India excluded music from its orbit because access to the Indian idiom was found impossible, while canonical Western music was both impractical and not important enough to import. It was the seminal British concept of orientalism (to be discussed below) which affected Hindustani music indirectly, by marginal inclusion in its enterprise, such as through the publication of Sanskrit treatises as well as a few British treatments of music that mostly lack cultural appropriateness. Vastly more important was the prestige lent to the study of ancient sources through the medium of English.

Unlike that of the Muslims, British rule remained quintessentially foreign to India, hence its vantage point on India was fundamentally Eurocentric. At an immediate level, this resulted in the continuous production of reports destined for European consumption, both for entertainment and for better colonial administration. The sources generated thereby include travelers' accounts—including those by non-British Europeans—and diaries as well as the more focused accounts of "customs and manners" (e.g., Crooke 1926) and of social structure, especially caste studies (e.g., Blunt 1931). These latter focus on hereditary communities and their professions, and ambulatory groups like musicians are often singled out as "vagrant," even "criminal," clearly reflecting the perspective of the colonial administrator. This, and the lack of interest in the relations between classes, reduces the utility of such reports. Administrative reports, district gazetteers, and census reports provide useful population data, but much of it is decontextualized. What is important beyond the factual content of these sources is the impact of such objectification, mainly of lower classes, reinforcing for the Anglicized Indian a sense of negativity and dissociation from these groups, including professional musicians. The use of "native" collaborators for gathering data (for example, Jafar and Herklots 1921) further helped spread the paradigm and contributed generally toward the self-definition of the new Westernized elite.

ICONOGRAPHY (PAINTING, PHOTOGRAPHY)

Iconographic sources provide the most easily accessible information about musical performance, but they are not always easy to identify and interpret, especially because of a long tradition by Western collectors of separating pictures from the texts they often serve to illustrate. This has made iconographic research less immediately fruitful than it could be.[21]

The tradition of court paintings is a strong one for Muslim as well as Hindu—and Sikh—feudal establishments, all of which also patronized hereditary "schools" of painting. In fact, they are often indistinguishable from each other, an illustration of the ease of exchange and adaptation in the nonverbal arts. The religion of the patron is reflected in the prevalence of specifically Hindu or Muslim scenes—Holi celebrations or dancing Sufis—whereas typical court and romantic scenes around the ruler cut across the religious community.

In the sense of the Muslim chronicle, the tradition of court painting is also a record of court activity, but a representational one. It includes, very prominently, classical musical entertainment—not per se, but as enhancing the noble patron who is seen enjoying it. While the accuracy of detail provides excellent musical performance data, accurate historical placement is often problematic, due to a traditional tendency in these paintings to antiquate the settings painted. Contextualization is crucial but difficult, for it requires textual as well as art-historical resources. The court paintings show best and most graphically the common socioeconomic basis of the Hindu and Muslim feudal establishments in which music is patron-initiated and executed by hereditary servant groups. Much like in Renaissance Italy or in eighteenth-century Germany, music is here essential as a tool for sociocultural enhancement.

The British also took on the patronage of hereditary painters, but mainly for painting for "home" consumption, imposing European stylization on both the subjects painted and the paintings themselves. Good subject examples are the many series of "professions," including musicians, all appearing as a man and a wife and often sporting European facial features. No doubt, the painters' forebears had earlier learned Muslim pictorial styles in the same way!

A special repertoire is the many photographs taken in the decades around 1900 of musicians entertaining officials on their visits to various indigenous establishments. Highly representational, poses and subject selection need to be scrutinized and contextualized as carefully as in paintings, especially since the photographic medium gives the illusion of providing naturally accurate documentation.

In iconographic, as in written sources, the British sociocultural orbit, like that of the Muslims, extends to indigenous—or non-Muslim—collaborators; a ruling elite always finds its servants.

INDOLOGY AND INDIAN MUSICAL NATIONALISM

The Western view of history, together with the European orientalist embrace of the Hindu scriptural/mythological past, served as a foundation for contemporary Hindu identity, starting from cultural and culminating in political nationalism, initially through a filter of Anglicized criteria embodied in the reformist movements (such as the *Brahmo Samaj* or *Arya Samaj*). This led to the increasing assertion of Hindu ideals and traditions, but in a frame of reference that was Western, or at least Westernized. This frame of reference included the sociopolitical domain, locus of the Westernized elites' self-assertion vis-à-vis their English models and masters. Their self-definition through this new vision of Hinduism thus became enshrined in the nascent idea of Hindu nationalism which has been defined as "created through a unison of religious and political ideals" (Hay 1958:707).

Solidification of the sense of collective identity with the authentic Hindu past was achieved in two ways. One was through an intense historical focus, to generate a rich image of authentic, classical Hindu culture. The second was to reify this ideal, giving it a concrete shape compatible with modern life. This meant re-creating authentic Hindu culture—as enshrined in the Hindu scriptural records of the past—in a portable form compatible with modern, Westernized, Indian urban life.

Music was an ideal target for this goal in two respects. First and foremost, music has had a significant place in religion since the Upanishads, considered there "an effective means of attaining oneness with Shiva" (*Skanda Purana Suta Samhita* 4.2.3.114–16; quoted in Raghavan and Dandekar 1958:274). Its ancient roots and links with Hindu ideology endowed it with an unassailable status of spiritual significance. Second, music—unlike literature and other arts—had been consistently neglected, if not denigrated by the British elite. Thus music, newly re-Hinduized, symbolized self-assertion vis-à-vis the British as well as the Muslims who during their centuries of rule had appropriated and secularized it. At the same time, despite all political implications, music was politically neutral, and though religiously imbued, it could take its place in modern secular life. British models for its dissemination were available: the conference and concert, the college and later the media.

Somewhat ironically, it was British Indology which showed the way to reclaiming the spiritual status of music, through its paradigm originating in European alienation and today debunked by Indian Marxist historians (Thapar 1977): the Hindu Golden Age of Spirituality, whose ideation and historical reality is enshrined in Sanskrit texts. Modern music history thus begins as an effort to rediscover "the ages when music breathed solemn and sacred numbers" (Willard 1962:63), unsullied by "the muddy rivulets" of Mohammedan, that is, foreign, secularizing influence, to paraphrase Jones (1962:95). Accordingly, the study of Sanskrit treatises became the primary goal of music historians, for it provided important ammunition for establishing norms of music theory along with terminology, so that music could be brought into the realm of literacy.

The visionary who set out to achieve the new goal in a comprehensive way is V. N. Bhatkhande.[22] He directly embodies this "engaged" pursuit of historical scholarship as a pivotal figure in the entire enterprise of musical revival and of redefining Hindustani music. Pandit Bhatkhande was "the father of music conferences"; as the life and soul of the first five such events,[23] he engaged nationalists and their noble patrons to support socially acceptable teaching and performing venues. At the same time he inspired or directed Western-style colleges of musical learning in Baroda and Lucknow. Most important, he interpreted and synthesized historical data in the service of creating standard texts for music instruction in these colleges.

But there was a major shift required to realize this musical transformation: that of personnel. Initiated and articulated very clearly by Bhatkhande, it became the agenda for middle-class Hindu music lovers for a generation: to take music out of the hands of the Muslim hereditary professionals and win it for the Hindu elite through discipleship and devotion. This was a formidable task demanding personal sacrifice, for in G. N. Joshi's words, "(these) musicians were considered to be almost untouchables by the elite of society" (Joshi 1984:2)—and its members were largely Brahmins![24] This, then, is not only a communal shift from Hindu to Muslim: it is as much a shift in class, from the service professional to the bourgeois elite. The most crucial consequence of this shift is the abolition of the social gulf between patron and performer, since they now share the same milieu—a truly remarkable sociomusical development. Not by accident, it is in the most Westernized and urban centers with the longest tradition of Westernization, Bombay and Calcutta, where this process has been carried out most thoroughly.

The fact is that living musical knowledge and performing competence had been in the hands of hereditary professionals as part of the feudal, class-caste management of the division of labor. During the Muslim hegemony, their hereditary servants were naturally Muslim. Even after the dispersal of the central artistic establishment from Delhi to many non-Muslim provincial courts, Muslim musicians retained their position under the same patron-client arrangement and in accordance with the same secular, competitive ideology and aesthetic that characterizes feudal patronage of music.[25] Indeed, the strictly endogamous social organization of these music professionals enabled them to control access to their art reinforced by an ideology of secretiveness toward outsiders and excessive emphasis on student loyalty. Only in the holy city of Benares did the religious requirements for music, along with the presence of a Hindu Maharaja, create conditions for the rise of a Hindu community of hereditary professionals. Significantly, these Hindu hereditary, professional musicians are quite akin to their Muslim counterparts in background and attitudes, and even in aspects of social organization.[26] But their shared religion with the new music elite has given them better access to patronage and upward social mobility, helped also by the fact that they are Brahmins, though of a relatively lower status.

It has been said that in independent India there is a national historiography which "stands in the service of national self-understanding" (Kulke 1982:3). Certainly, that has been the major and declared motivation for the enterprise of musical historicism in the Indian subcontinent, for it became a salient part

of the nationalist agenda to define indigenous cultural identity for British India's Anglicized elites. The entire effort led to a remarkable renaissance of music in India, as a renewed, modernized canonical system, with patronage from
state and national elite; today it is an important component of the new "public culture" of India.[27]

The encounter of British orientalism and Muslim Westernization could
not result in a similar fusion. For one, British orientalism of Islamic civilizations targeted cultures outside of India—notably Iran—and was therefore not immediately accessible to Indian Muslims. For another, Indian
Muslims were only marginal participants in the English educational enterprise in India and hence hardly Westernized. Most important, no spark
could arise from Muslim ideation given the absence of a place for music in
Islam; hence no process parallel to the Hindu musical revival could take
place, and Muslim participation in that revival was minimal as well. Art
music therefore continued to survive essentially through the oral tradition.

In independent Pakistan, too, urbanization and Westernization have
since generated a new middle class whose search for a modern sociocultural identity includes artistic self-expression, but the sources tapped
hardly include Hindustani music, given a continuing need to deny what is
Indian. Still, Hindustani art music continues to live in the oral tradition of
the numerous Muslim hereditary professionals, many of them migrants
from India. But they are locked into the feudal-type patronage that lingers
on, along with very limited institutional support for a tradition which is so
strongly identified with India.

The reality of this situation makes it clear that Hindustani music has
flourished historically when its musician class has had a compatible patron
class to constitute an ongoing music-making tradition. A change in patron
class—and this really means, a change in political dominance, given the
"canonical" character of this art music—must of necessity lead to a change
in the music-making class. Such a change is of course gradual, so that music makers can be "left over," as is the case today with Muslim hereditary
professionals in India. The stark reality is that within a generation most of
these musicians, along with their oral musical heritage, can be fully expected to fade away, a process which can be solidly documented already.
For different reasons, but due to similar underlying factors, this is as true
for India as it is for Pakistan.[28]

The implication for the historian of Hindustani music is clear: Rather
than dismissing its evidence because it does not accord with the new canonical norms, the oral musical heritage of the Muslim—and Hindu—

hereditary professional needs to be recognized as a valuable historical resource, especially where it does not "fit" those norms! In other words, I am
today no more ashamed of the "non-standard versions" of ragas or performance practice which I learned from unlettered teachers knowing neither
Sanskrit nor English.

What is called for is a systematic inquiry into the nature and content of
this highly perishable oral source and to integrate it with other sources of
Hindustani music history. Starting with an assessment of its authors and
their vantage point and its function within the larger sociomusical context
that generated it, what emerges foremost is that this oral tradition is both
self-contained and dependent. A review of its content, gleaned from my
prolonged and close association,[29] shows first and foremost a body of
knowledge by and for musicians, about their exclusive professional domain of musical composition and performance. Closely interwoven are an-
cillary domains of knowledge related to the transmission and control of
this domain: teaching and learning processes, acquisition and maintenance
of competence ("quality control"), as well as reinforcement and legitima-
tion through an aesthetic and ideology derived primarily from Greco-Arab
and Islamic ideation.[30]

Of course, the idea structure of music arises ultimately from the Muslim
context of patronage which is even more directly reflected in what is perhaps
historically the most salient facet of the Muslim hereditary oral tradition: notions regarding the context of performance, especially notions linking the musical and contextual domain. This idea structure of music, however, is hardly
self-generated; performers depend on the educational and cultural resources
of the patron class for the meaning system and symbolism expressed in the
ideology and in the performance of the music itself. A fine musical example is
the *tan* passages handed down in the musical lineage of Mamman Khan
(Delhi *gharana*) which are named for, and audibly represent moves in, chess,
kite flying, animal racing, and wrestling, all courtly games of Muslim aristo-
cratic provenance.

Today the patrons of those games are gone; clearly, the Muslim oral tradition is at present a truncated one, lacking its proper elite of patrons in
both India and Pakistan. Thus, studying this tradition in its own terms is in
a real sense studying recent music history, but "from below," requiring it to
be complemented with information "from above," about the nature of its
feudal patronage. Such information can be gleaned from documentary
sources and, to a limited extent, in live form in Pakistan and also in some
traditional areas of Uttar Pradesh and Bihar. At the same time, even these

live contexts are subject to change, and musicians are ever adapting to changing conditions. As an example, many Muslim hereditary musicians in India are today adopting their new Hindu patrons' ideology and symbols.[31] In Pakistan, on the other hand, there are no new patrons in sight, so that there is essentially nothing to adapt to; the danger there is rather one of attrition.[32]

For the scholar focusing on either country, not to acknowledge noncanonical traditions, be it for reasons of positive or negative cultural nationalism, is both unproductive and historically inappropriate, as has been convincingly argued for general history in India (Thapar 1977, Devahuti 1979). Indian musicologists, especially performer-scholars, are in fact beginning to focus on the oral dimension, now that they can do so from their own secure musical-ideological base (e.g., Ranade: 1984:23–49). May it be our colleagues there who will help realize for the historiography of Hindustani music what the Islamicist von Grunebaum terms the ideal of *Kulturfähigkeit* (quoted in Gordon 1971:184)—the capacity for cultural pluralism—by admitting into the historiographic enterprise the diversity of oral tradition.

Notes

1. The term Hindustani here denotes the system of classical music common to the northern part of the Indian subcontinent, including the regions of North India, Pakistan, and, more peripherally, Bangladesh, as against the Southern or Karnatak system of classical music.

2. A fine and concise example is Mutatkar (1964).

3. In effect, this parallels rather closely the societal situation of art music in nineteenth-century nationalist Europe.

4. Because of a paucity of data and to avoid a duplication of the argument, given its membership in Pakistan until 1972, Bangladesh is not dealt with separately in this discussion.

5. For an early review of the latter see Powers (1965).

6. For an example see Malik (1983) and Haque (1982).

7. "Wie es eigentlich gewesen ist" (quoted in Gordon 1971:3).

8. For the seminal role of Marxist historians in generating a historiographic debate see Lütt (1982).

9. This time frame seems appropriate, given the historical scope of antecedents for contemporary Hindustani music.

10. By the period under consideration only local rulers remained who, however, gained in importance under British rule.

11. Mughal as well as local rulers.

12. The British never established an indigenous rule.

13. Perhaps the best-known such scholar was Acharya Brhaspati who had been associated with the Rampur court (e.g., 1975). An exceptional Muslim counterpart is music historian Shahab Sarmadee (e.g., 1978).

14. For a review see Bhatkhande (1972) and Powers (1980, 9:76ff).

15. Historical works are notably absent, with one significant eleventh-century exception.

16. Notable examples are the seventeenth-century Sikh scripture *Guru Granth Sahib* in Panjabi (Mansukhani 1982:107ff) and the eighteenth-century Islamic mystic Shah Abdul Latif's *Risalo* in Sindhi (Sorley 1966:220ff). The *Kitab-i-Nauras* by the seventeenth-century king Ibrahim Adil Shah in Farsi clearly follows the same tradition (Nazir Ahmad 1956).

17. Probably best-known and most important is the *Ain-i-Akbari* by Akbar's courtier Abual-Fazl Allami (1927).

18. Religious musical expression is conceptually set off from music; see Nelson (1985) and Qureshi (1972).

19. A remarkable example is the early nineteenth-century Persian narrative of Jahandar Shah.

20. The late nineteenth-century masterpiece *Umrao Jan Ada* (Ruswa n.d.) is the most obvious example.

21. A case in point is the rich iconographic documentation, accessible in standard collections but often lacking clear historical and local identification, as can be seen in Bor (1986).

22. This is not to ignore the important contributions toward the same goal by other pioneers, notably Vishnu Digambar Paluskar (Misra 1981:70–77) and S. M. Tagore.

23. Held between 1916 and 1925, these conferences were patronized by the rulers of Baroda, Rampur, and Benares and supported by nationalist leaders of Gwalior, Lucknow, Bombay, and Nagpur (Misra 1985:15).

24. Compare also Nikhil Banerjee's telling statement in Landgarten (1987:11–12).

25. Evidence from seventeenth-eighteenth-century Europe is quite comparable.

26. They marry rather more closely within their group than is standard for North Indian Brahmin practice.

27. As logically as one may be able to explain this development, it still continues to amaze that music could assume such an important function in the development of a modern nation-state.

28. Just one example is the musician community of Banda, locus of Augustus Willard's musical expertise (Willard (1834) 1962:80, n51), who decided collectively to stop training their sons as musicians.

29. Musical training in 1965, 1968–69, 1975–76, 1983, and 1984.

30. Neuman has presented important aspects of this tradition, albeit without clearly identifying their Muslim roots (Neuman 1990).

31. Umrao Bundu Khan (1969). For instance, some musicians now remember their family's earlier conversion from Hinduism and the retention of Hindu worship practices. As for repertoire adaptation, already Abdul Karim Khan responded to his urban Hindu patrons by regularly performing *bhajans*. Another strategy is to change to a name that does not sound Muslim (often used is the surname *Bharati*).

32. In the words of one senior broadcasting official, "in twenty years archaeologists will be needed to research music in Pakistan" (Interview, Karachi, July 1987).

Works Cited

Allami, Abual-Fazl
1927   *A'in-i-Akbari*. Translated by H. S. Jarrett and H. F. Blochmann. 3 vols.
        Calcutta: Asiatic Society of Bengal.

Bhatkhande, V. N.
1972   "A Comparative Study of Some of the Leading Music Systems of the
        15th, 16th, 17th, and 18th Centuries,"*Journal of the Indian
        Musicological Society* 3 (2):1–61 and 3 (3):1–52.

Blunt, E. A. H.
1931   *The Caste System of Northern India With Special Reference to the
        United Provinces of Agra and Oudh*. London: Oxford University Press.

Bor, Joep
1986   *The Sarangi*. Bombay: National Center for Performing Arts.

Brhaspati, Acharya
1975   "Mussalmans and Indian Music," *Journal of the Indian Musicological
        Society* 6:27–49.

Collingwood, R. G.
1956   *The Idea of History*. London: Oxford University Press.

Crooke, William
1926   *Religion and Folklore of Northern India*. London: Oxford University
        Press.

Devahuti, ed.
1979   *Problems in Indian Historiography*. Delhi: D. K. Publications.

Erdman, Joan L.
1985   *Patrons and Performers in Rajasthan*. Delhi: Chanakya Publications.

Gordon, David C.
1971   *Self-Determination and History in the Third World*. Princeton:
        Princeton University Press.

Haque, Qazi Zahoorul
1982   *Mu'allam-al-Naghmat*. Islamabad: Idara Saqafat-i-Pakistan.

Hardy, Peter
1958   "Islam in Medieval India," in *Sources of Indian Tradition*, W. T. de
        Bary et al., comp. (New York: Columbia University Press), vol. 1, pp.
        367–528.

Hay, S. N.
1958   "Islam in Medieval India," *Sources of Indian Tradition*, W. T. de Bary
        et al., comp. (New York: Columbia University Press), vol. 1, pp.
        551–932.

Jafar, Sharif, and G. A. Herklots
1921   *Islam in India or the Qanun-i-Islam*. New ed., rev. London: Oxford
        University Press.

Jones, Sir William
1962   "On the Musical Modes of the Hindus," in William Jones and
        N. Augustus Willard, *Music of India* (Calcutta: Susil Gupta),
        pp. 89–112. First printed 1793.

Joshi, G. N.
1984   *Down Melody Lane.* Bombay: Orient Longman.
Khan, Umrau Bundu
1969   *Lesson.* Karachi: Marachi.
Kuhn, Thomas
1970   *The Structure of Scientific Revolution.* 2d ed., rev. Chicago: University
        of Chicago Press.
Kulke, Hermann, et al.
1982   *Indische Geschichte vom Altertum bis zur Gegenwart.* Munich:
        R. Oldenbourg. Special issue of *Historische Zeitschrift.*
Landgarten, Ira
1987   "First My Music Then Everything Else: An Interview with Nikhil
        Banerjee," *Bansuri* 4:8–26.
Lütt, Jürgen
1982   "Historiographie," in Hermann Kulke, et al., *Indische Geschichte vom
        Altertum bis zur Gegenwart* (Munich: R. Oldenbourg), pp. 110–
        114.
Malik, M. Sayeed
1983   *The Musical Heritage of Pakistan.* Islamabad: Idara Saqafat-e-Pakistan.
Mansukhani, G. S.
1982   *Indian Classical Music and Sikh Kirtan.* New Delhi: Oxford University
        Press.
Misra, Susheela
1981   *Great Masters of Hindustani Music.* New Delhi: Hem Publishers.
1985   *Music Makers of the Bhatkhande College of Hindustani Music.*
        Calcutta: Sangeet Research Academy.
Mutatkar, Sumati
1964   "The Evolution of Indian Music," in *Music East and West.* Delhi.
Nazir Ahmad
1956   *Kitab-i-Nauras.* Introduction and translation. New Delhi: Bharatiya
        Kala Kendra.
Nelson, Kristina
1985   *The Art of Reciting the Qur'an.* Austin: University of Texas Press.
Neuman, Daniel M.
1990   *The Life of Music in North India.: The Organization of an Artistic
        Tradition.* Chicago: University of Chicago Press. First published 1980.
Powers, Harold
1965   "Indian Music and the English Language," *Ethnomusicology* 9 (1):
        1–12.
1980   "India, Subcontinent of," in *The New Grove Dictionary of Music and
        Musicians,* Stanley Sadie, ed. (London: Macmillan).
Qureshi, Regula Burckhardt
1972   "Indo-Muslim Religious Music: An Overview," *Asian Music* 3:15–22.
Raghavan, V. and R. Dandekar
1958   "Hinduism," in *Sources of Indian Tradition,* W. T. de Bary et al., comp.
        (New York: Columbia University Press) vol. 1, pp. 203–366.

Ranade, Ashok
1984   *On Music and Musicians of Hindoostan.* New Delhi: Promilla.
Ruswa, Mirza M. Hadi
n.d.   *Umrao Jan Ada* ["The Courtesan of Lucknow"]. Translated by
           Khushwant Singh and M. A. Husaini. Delhi: Hind Pocket Books.
Sarangdeva
1978   *Sangita Ratnakara.* Edited and translated by R. K. Shringy and P. L.
           Sharma. Varanasi.
Sarmadee, Shahab, ed.
1978   *Ghunyat-ul-Munya.* Bombay: Asia Publishing House.
Sorley, H. T.
1960   *Shah Abdul Latif of Bhit, His Poetry, Life and Times.* Lahore: Oxford
           University Press. First published 1940.
Tagore, S. M.
1965   *Hindu Music from Various Authors.* 3d. ed. Calcutta. First published
           1875.
Thapar, Romila, et al.
1977   *Communalism and the Writing of History.* New Delhi: People's
           Publishing House.
Willard, N. Augustus
1962   "A Treatise on the Music of India," in William Jones and N. Augustus
           Willard, *Music of India* (Calcutta: Susil Gupta), pp. 1–88, 113–14.
           First printed 1834.

Christopher A. Waterman

The Uneven Development of Africanist Ethnomusicology: Three Issues and a Critique

I "African Music, One or Many?"

AFRICANIST ETHNOMUSICOLOGY may be said to have begun in 1902–3, eighteen years after the Berlin Conference dividing Africa among the European powers, when Erich M. von Hornbostel and Otto Abraham joined the linguists Carl Meinhof and Dietrich Westermann in analyzing the relationship of lexemic tone and melody in a group of Ewe songs, collected in the then-German colony of Togo.[1] However, the field and its core concerns were not systematically defined until a quarter of a century later in Hornbostel's 1928 article, "African Negro Music," published in the first issue of the ethnological journal *Africa* (Hornbostel 1928). Much has changed in the succeeding six decades: the political, if not economic, independence of Africa north of the Limpopo; an increase in the number of African scholars and the total population of specialists in African music; and the emergence of various schools of theory and method. However, scholarly discourse about Africans and their music continues to be shaped by what Nettl identifies as "an underlying and frequently frustrating issue" (Nettl 1983:118) in the history of ethnomusicology: the interpretation of similarity and difference.

The literature presents a fundamental dual image: on the one hand, a relatively compact musical area characterized by a high degree of stylistic similarity (Lomax 1970, Nettl 1986:17); and, on the other hand, a "vast area within which substantial diversity occurs" (Merriam 1977:244). The notion that African music, from Cape Town to Nairobi and across to Dakar, forms "an indivisible whole" (Jones 1959:200) has proved tenacious despite mounting evidence of variation within and between local traditions. This concept is historically grounded as much in tenacious Eurocentric conceptions of Black Africa as a geographic and ethnological unit, and of Africans as a "people" or "race," as it is in principled comparative analysis of musical styles. The involvement, particularly after World War

169

II, of Americanists who viewed Africa through the lens of the Atlantic Slave Trade and the influence of *Négritude* and pan-African ideologies, which stressed cultural unities among peoples of color, reinforced the dominant notion that sub-Saharan African music is homogeneous.

It is interesting to note, in the light of Edward Said's critique of the ideology of orientalism (Said 1978), that any contemporary scholar who wrote an analysis of Hmong, Balinese, Tibetan, Tungus, Persian, or Turkish music and titled it "A Study of Oriental Music" would likely be hooted out of the profession. In contrast, one could point to numerous books and articles that focus upon the music of one or at most several ethno-linguistic groups, and nonetheless present themselves as studies of "African Music."

In the last two decades, however, Africanists have become increasingly loath to generalize. In 1969 Klaus Wachsmann wrote that: "Observations like that of A. M. Jones, 'the music of the Western Sudanic-speaking Ewe people is one and the same music as that of the Bantu-speaking Lala tribe,' are correct in their context but may mislead because they are based principally on only a few parameters. One could argue with equal justification that African Negro music and Persian music are one and the same because hemiolas occur frequently in both" (1969:134). By the late 1970s Wachsmann had concluded that the difficulty of identifying common features might rest as much in the varying rigor and orientation of field research as in any objective differences among musical styles (1980:144). J. H. Kwabena Nketia adopted a statesmanlike approach in his 1974 book *The Music of Africa,* characterizing its subject matter as "a network of distinct yet related traditions which overlap in certain aspects of style, practice, or usage" (1974:4). Gerhard Kubik has recently gone so far as to assert that "there is no African music, rather many kinds of African music" (1983:27, tr. by C. W.). This gradual shift has been conditioned by the accumulation of data about particular traditions, and by ideological patterns typifying African Studies as a whole in the post-Independence period, particularly the perceived need to counteract stereotypes by highlighting the diversity of African cultural production.

II "MOTOR ACCENT" AND "METRONOME SENSE": PSYCHO-MOTOR THEORIES OF AFRICAN RHYTHM

Perceptions of similarity and difference have played an important role in the formulation of hypotheses about African musical practice, including psychomotor theories of rhythm. The initial questions raised by European comparative musicologists working with cylinder recordings of

African music must surely have been: first, "Where's *one* !?" and second, "How do *they* know!?" In the absence of data concerning performance practice, these scholars framed general hypotheses which, it was presumed, could be tested as the information base expanded. Hornbostel's influential article "African Negro Music" begins with the following statement of purpose and conclusions:

> The purport of this article is to provide an answer to the following questions:
> 1. What is African music like as compared to our own?
> 2. How can it be made use of in Church and School?
> The answer might be as brief as the questions:
> 1. African and (modern) European music are constructed on entirely different principles, and therefore
> 2. they cannot be fused into one, but only the one or the other can be used without compromise. (1928:30)

Hornbostel posited a wide and unbridgeable "gulf" between African and modern European music. In support of this view he cited the difference between the "pure polyphony" of Africa and European functional harmony; the close relationship in Africa, but not in modern Europe, of language and music, speech and song; and finally, "an essential contrast between our rhythmic conception and the Africans'; we proceed from hearing, they from motion" (1928:53).

Hornbostel's theory of African rhythm grew in part from the axiom that rhythmic patterns "present themselves to the mind as unities," that is, that rhythmic experience is rooted in the perception of whole shapes, rather than atomistic stimuli.[2] This principle, applied in the laboratory analysis of sound recordings, yielded a psychomotor inference concerning African musical experience and practice. African rhythm was, Hornbostel argued, fundamentally modeled upon drumming, and grounded in a twofold "acting of beating." The lifting of the hand tensed the muscles, creating a "motor accent," while the sudden lowering of the hand relaxed them. From this premise Hornbostel reasoned that upbeats—what Europeans would regard as *weak* beats—were unknown to Africans, and, more fundamentally, that African musical rhythm was grounded in motion and muscular sensation (1928:53).

A moment's reflection suggests that the lift-and-drop hypothesis is based neither upon close observation of African performance practice nor personal experience with drums. But, setting aside for the moment the problem of its empirical validity, it seems clear that Hornbostel's argument discloses a leap of logic, an internal gap that invites external explanation. Even if we grant, first, that all aspects of African rhythmic practice (e.g., stamping, clapping, beating a xylophone or bell) are based upon the prototype of drumming, and second, that drumming involves lifting one's arm and then dropping it, it still does not follow that African rhythm is grounded in motor sensation *rather than* hearing. Why did Hornbostel formulate the hypothesis in either/or terms, positing an opposition between hearing and bodily motion? This is particularly intriguing given his earlier observations concerning a fundamental "unity of the senses" (Hornbostel 1927), including relationships between haptic and auditory sensation.

It does not detract from Hornbostel's brilliance to recognize that his work was produced under certain historical circumstances and toward certain practical ends. In order to understand Hornbostel's radical distinction between a rhythmic practice grounded in hearing and another grounded in bodily motion, we must inquire into his views concerning the practical consequences of musical interaction between Europeans and Africans. Reporting that the descendants of African slaves in the New World had abandoned their own music wholesale and adopted European styles, Hornbostel asserted that "this process is already at work in Africa. . . . Every musical instrument and every gramophone, every folk-song or sacred song that we import into Africa will accelerate it. It is therefore to be feared that the modern efforts to protect culture are coming too late. As yet we hardly know what African music is. If we do not hasten to collect systematically and to record by means of the phonograph, we will not even learn what it was" (1928:60). The pragmatics of preservation ideally dictated that African music be segregated from European music. This, Hornbostel saw, was impossible. The next best strategy was to emphasize *differences* between the two musical macrosystems. His conclusion that "the mixture of 'white' and 'black' music, with a kind of musical pidgin as result, would be, if not impossible, yet most undesirable" (1928:61) is in fact an axiom of his analysis of rhythm, and flows at least in part from the practical goals of encouraging field recording, and convincing missionaries and colonial administrators that they should not infect Africans with oompah functional harmony.

Although criticism of Hornbostel's explanation of African rhythm appeared in print as early as 1934 (Jones 1934), an alternative psychomotor theory—also embedded within a larger argument concerning similarities and differences between European and African musics—was not published until 1952. In "African Influence on the Music of the Americas," Richard Waterman provided a psychological basis for concepts first adumbrated in

1943 in a paper given to the American Musicological Society (Waterman 1948). This theory of African rhythm centered on the *metronome sense*, a learned, subjective, equal-pulse framework "assumed without question or consideration to be part of the perceptual equipment of both musicians and listeners." African music, Waterman suggested, is generally music for the dance, although "the dance involved may be entirely a mental one" consisting of inhibited motor responses (1952:211). His answer to the questions "Where's *one*?" and "How do *they* know?" rested on the notion that: "The assumption by an African musician that his audience is supplying these fundamental beats permits him to elaborate his rhythms with these as a base, whereas the European tradition requires such close attention to their concrete expression that rhythmic elaboration is limited for the most part to mere ornament" (ibid.:211–12). The link between theory and the exigencies of analysis is clear in this case, for Waterman explicitly stated that metronome sense was a skill that had to be developed in order properly to analyze African music.

Waterman's work falls within the tradition of American or Boasian cultural anthropology. Franz Boas, a student of physics, psychology, and philosophy, played a role in the critique of psychophysics during the 1880s. His first publications dealt with the notion that the perception of stimuli was conditioned not only by the objective interval between them, but also by situational factors, including the mental state of the observer.[3] By the time he taught Melville Herskovits at Columbia University in the 1920s, Boas had been influenced by both behaviorist and Gestalt theory. Herskovits's hypotheses of syncretism and reinterpretation, rooted in the neo-Kantian axiom that new sensations are inescapably perceived and evaluated in terms of preestablished subjective patterns, played a crucial role in Waterman's work on Afro-American and African music:

> The maintenance of a subjective meter . . . requires effort and, more particularly, a series of efforts regularly spaced in time. The regular recurrence of these "rhythmic awarenesses" involves the expectancy, at the moment of any beat, that the next beat will occur precisely at some succeeding moment determined by the tempo. . . . The off-beat phrasing of accents . . . must threaten, but never quite destroy, the orientation of the listener's subjective metronome. In practice, this means that a sufficient number of notes of varying degrees of importance . . . must coincide with the auditor's rhythmic set to validate the gestalt through reinforcement of key points. (ibid.:213–14)

The notion that expectation conditions perception comes, via Boas and Herskovits, from the critique of psychophysics; the idea that perception is an active process, and that mental experience is organized in structures which possess an immanent tendency toward completion or equilibrium, from Gestalt theory; and the emphasis on overt and inhibited motor response, from behaviorist psychology.

In his 1959 article "African Music," Merriam suggested that "If Waterman's theory of the metronome sense is to be questioned, it is on grounds similar to those involved with Hornbostel's theory. Again, a psychological process is involved which is not easily proved, and Waterman offers no empiric documentation save from the logic of the proposition itself" (1959:81). Some West Africanists have indeed amended or rejected the metronome-sense hypothesis. James Koetting, for example, asserted that timing in Anlo Ewe drumming depends upon the perception of a "fastest pulse" or "density referent" resulting from the cumulative interaction of individual patterns. "A person oriented toward the basic metrical system of Western music might easily underestimate the importance of the relatively unstructured African fastest pulse by considering the African gross beats, ·which can be associated with the prescribed regular beats of more highly structured metrical measures, as the level of precise timing" (1970:123). Koetting's analysis disputed the importance, though not the existence, of an internalized framework of "gross beats," such as suggested by the metronome-sense hypothesis. Ethnomusicological hypotheses are inevitably grounded in scholars' experience with particular musics in particular social settings. Koetting studied Ashanti and Anlo Ewe drumming at UCLA. His analysis of West African drum-ensemble music was shaped by his encounter with these particular traditions, and by the practical goal of applying the Time Unit Box notation system, which posited the density referent as a minimal structural unit.

Waterman's notion of the metronome sense was, on the other hand, strongly conditioned by years of experience as a string-bass player. In the types of music that he most often played—New Orleans jazz and swing music—the bassist's livelihood and reputation is founded on his ability to establish a steady two- or four-beat pulse, a framework of regular rhythmic awarenesses in relation to which other players (and dancers) orient their patterned behavior. In this instance, we can clearly see the impact of the internalized musical norms of the scholar on his analysis. According to Waterman:

> Jazz depends, for its effect, largely on the metronome sense of
> its listeners and players. Jazz terminology makes constant refer-

ence to this metronome sense. Musical terms like "rock" and "swing" . . . stem from African concepts, as does the extremely basic idea of the application of the word "hot" to musical rhythms. The development of a "feeling for the beat," so important in jazz musicianship, is neither more nor less than the development of the metronome sense. (1952:217)

These deep-seated norms, shaped by musical practice, provided the experiential basis for a psychomotor theory of rhythm. This was, in fact, recognized by Hewitt Pantaleoni, who wrote that the metronome-sense concept "seems to be based on American jazz. [Waterman] suggested that a single, subjective beat permeates the music. . . . Had Waterman applied his hypothesis to specific Anlo examples he surely would have modified it" (1972:56).

Hornbostel's and Waterman's models of African musical practice differed in at least one fundamental respect: while the former viewed African rhythm as based fundamentally in motion *rather than* hearing, the latter grounded his explanation in the *interaction* of aural perception and motor behavior.[4] It is interesting to note, however, that both arguments flow from the same intellectual wellspring, a German psychological tradition linking the Berlin School and Boasian cultural anthropology. In addition, both Hornbostel and Waterman based their hypotheses about African rhythm on inferences from Afro-American as well as African data. Although both worked with African informants, neither did fieldwork in Africa.[5]

At a more general level, both arguments were consonant with pervasive ideological patterns concerning the relationship of peoples of African and European descent. There is, it must be emphasized, no evidence of nineteenth-century racist thought in Hornbostel's work. It is fair to note, however, that his "separate development" approach to African and European musics, couched in the language of scientific common sense, is embedded within a more inclusive culture pattern: that is, the anti-Creolization ideology evident in much scientific writing, art, and literature of Western Europe in the late nineteenth and early twentieth centuries, grounded in a fundamental ambivalence concerning Western-educated people of color (see, for example, Asad 1973, Collins and Richards 1982:121, Killam 1968).

If Hornbostel's "wide and unbridgeable gulf" had ideological and practical implications, so, too, did its refutation. Waterman's metronome-sense hypothesis was one aspect of a larger argument concerning the tenacity of African culture patterns, outlined in Herskovits's book *The Myth of the*

Negro Past (1941). Waterman's work was, in a sense, the musical portion of Herskovits's program, a comparative overview of African cultural continuities in the Americas aimed in part at refuting the notion, dominant in much sociological research of the time, that slavery and subsequent oppression had left Blacks in the United States a people with no history.

III SOME AFRICANIST CONTRIBUTIONS TO THE ETHNOGRAPHY OF MUSIC

The adoption of ethnography as the means and model of research has been the most profound force in the development of ethnomusicology since World War II. Africanists, like Americanists, played a major role in this development. As early as 1934, for example, Percival Kirby asserted that participant-observation provided the only way "for a European observer to learn and understand the principles underlying native music" (1934:vii). There have, however, been surprisingly few attempts to construct a holistic overview of the musical life of an African people (Blacking 1965, Ames and King 1971, Zemp 1971). Ethnomusicologists have sometimes adopted indigenous sociomusical institutions as units of description and analysis (for example, age-grade-initiation "schools" (Blacking 1969, Kubik 1971), cults (Besmer 1983), royalty (Brown 1984)). Other accounts have focused primarily upon specific aspects of musical thought or behavior in a given society, for example, the cultural role and symbolism of instruments and ensembles (e.g., Tracey 1948, Nketia 1963, Wachsmann 1965, Berliner 1978), communication in performance events (Stone 1982), praise singing (Smith 1957, Erlmann 1980), and relationships between style, philosophy, and power (Chernoff 1979, Keil 1979).

There are many interesting variations in the focus and flavor of ethnographies of music produced by scholars trained in various anthropological "schools." Merriam's minutely detailed field notes on the construction of a Basongye drum (1969) are reminiscent of the ethnographic texts of Franz Boas, Merriam's anthropological progenitor one generation removed. This seemingly mundane article engendered—and was likely intended to engender—"a small furor" (1982:191) concerning the proper scope of the journal *Ethnomusicology,* and by implication the epistemology of the field as a whole. Ames and King's (1971) glossary of Hausa sociomusical terminology, described by the authors as a "shorthand ethnography," is one of the first examples of the influence of ethnosemantics on ethnomusicology. It is a book often discussed and infrequently emulated.

Major streams of European anthropology have also shaped Africanist ethnomusicology. Hugo Zemp's (1971) *Musique Dan* falls within a Francophone, West Africanist tradition that produced such classics as Griaule's *Conversations with Ogotemmeli* (1965) and Calame-Griaule's *Ethnologie et langage: la parole chez les Dogon* (1965). Like these other scholars, Zemp emphasizes indigenous ideas and depicts the relationship of Dan musical concepts to the cosmology that invests them with vitality and significance. John Blacking, the most notable representative of British social anthropology in ethnomusicology, may in some regards be seen as a parallel to Sir Edmund Leach. Both men were trained first in structural-functional anthropology—Blacking by Meyer Fortes at Cambridge—and later strongly influenced by contact with French colleagues, a shift evident in their adoption of aspects of structuralist theory. Blacking's concern with motor patterning and, later, with establishing an "anthropology of the body," may be traced to the influence of Hornbostel's ideas about African rhythm, discussed above (see Blacking 1955a).

The prevalence of anthropologically sophisticated scholars in Africanist ethnomusicology has produced some important insights into music as a species of culture pattern. Africanists have, for example, made vital contributions to the comparative study of aesthetics. Extensive vocabularies for the metaphoric description of music, dance, and other forms of expression have been documented among the Kpelle and Vai of Liberia, the Dan of the Ivory Coast, the Dagbamba of northern Ghana, the Yoruba and Tiv of Nigeria, the Baganda of Uganda, the Basotho of southern Africa, and other peoples. However, a survey of the literature reveals a great deal of variation among societies in regard to verbalization and systemicity of aesthetic norms. In his last published statement on the subject, Merriam (1982:322–23) noted that societies with clear cognitive parallels to Western notions of "art" and "aesthetics" have attracted disproportionate attention from scholars:

> What of societies like the Bala-Basongye . . . in which the basic categories simply do not fit, the outsider is forced to puzzle over the very nature of the phenomena he hopes to study, and transference of concepts will not work? These are potentially the most fruitful cases and the societies in which the problems of cross-cultural applicability must be solved. It would be foolish, even unthinkable, to suggest that the Yoruba of Nigeria do not have clear concepts of "art" and "aesthetics" which are structural parallels to our own, but it would be equally foolish to suggest that the Bala-Basongye do. (1982:322–23)

Few scholars of African music, dance, verbal performance, or visual arts would accept the early, strong version of Merriam's argument vis-à-vis cross-cultural viability of the term aesthetic: that is, that if people do not have Western bourgeois aesthetic values, then they have none at all.[6] Africanists—led by such pioneers as Robert Farris Thompson (1974)— have generally developed an inclusive approach to aesthetics that includes the full range of social, ethical, and philosophical values that guide musical performance and interpretation.

Some research has focused upon parallels between social and musical values. Thus, Blacking suggests that Venda musical order is linked to social order at a number of levels—"tone/companion tone, tonic/counter-tonic, call/response, individual/community, theme/variation, chief/subjects, etc." (1971:104)—while Thompson characterizes the high-intensity interlocking patterns typical of Yoruba music, dance, and visual arts as "a communal expression of percussive individuality" (1966:91). Nicholas England has suggested that the contrapuntal structures of !Kung music reflect "the Bushman desire to remain independent . . . at the same time that he is contributing vitally to the community life" (1967:60). These hypotheses are persuasive because they derive from careful observation of social interaction, rather than from the search for homologies between reified musical and social structures.

Other scholars have developed the notion of music as a medium of social communication. A clear link has begun to emerge between the role of music in symbolic and economic transaction (Wachsmann 1980:148–49) and the position of musicians in many African societies as mediators between social groups, or between the human and supernatural realms. Recent work emphasizes various aspects of this theme. For example, Veit Erlmann, in his 1980 monograph *Die Macht des Wortes,* analyses Fulbe praise singing as a mode of exchange grounded in the "quasi-magical" functions of speech and song. Michels-Gebler provides a broad overview of relationships between musicians and blacksmiths, both widely associated with social deviance and supernatural power (1984). Ruth Stone's analysis of Kpelle musical events emphasizes the role of performance in the reproduction and transformation of social relationships (1982), while David Coplan views African urban musicians as cultural brokers, mobile individuals skilled at manipulating multiple expressive codes in heterogeneous environments (1982).

IV CONCLUSION: THE UNEVEN DEVELOPMENT

Any field of study is characterized by gaps or absences as well as by positive achievements. To understand the growth of a discipline we need to know what has gone unsaid. Many of us, in teaching music survey courses, search for vivid examples of the inseparability of music from the whole cloth of human life. However, the notion that ethnomusicology is the study of music "in context"—a phrase often invoked but rarely defined—has implicitly encouraged the reification of musical sound and the epistemological disjunction of music from the social and historical grounds of its existence. This has by and large allowed ethnomusicological discourse to bracket itself outside the very real world of colonialism, power relations, and the social production of knowledge.

I would suggest that our understanding of sub-Saharan African music has been conditioned by factors infrequently discussed in the literature: for example, the varied training and practical goals of investigators; the portrayal of similarity and differences between peoples of African and European descent; the invention of "traditional" or "tribal" musics under colonialism and since independence; and the variable, though always unequal, relationship of the scholarly subject to the human objects of his or her study. Africanist ethnomusicology has, with a few notable exceptions, lagged behind other branches of African studies in critically examining its own ideological "context."

Some progress has been made in the last twenty years. For example, Africanists have played a role in introducing the philosophical and methodological notion of reflexivity to ethnomusicology. In 1979 John Miller Chernoff noted that "the most important gap for the participant-observer . . . is not between what he sees and what is there, but between his experience and how he is going to communicate it. . . . Finding the proper level of abstraction to portray with fidelity both the relativity of his own viewpoint and the reality of the world he has witnessed necessarily involves an act of interpretation" (1979:11).

This suggests that every scholar of African music—the American anthropologist in Zaïre, the Ghanaian ethnomusicologist in Tanzania, and the Anlo Ewe drummer in his natal community—is involved in an interpretive project conditioned by his or her personal experience and sociohistorical horizons. Although a bipartite distinction between *emic* and *etic* perspectives is thereby rendered problematic, the principle of reflexivity reaffirms the methodological importance of participant-observation and musical performance, and explicitly relates ethnomusicological knowledge to the interaction of scholar and informant.

This interaction, the heart of fieldwork, has been conditioned by the transformation of indigenous economic and political structures, the emergence of urban centers and socioeconomic classes, and the development, within and without Africa, of centers for the "preservation" of culture. Kenneth Gourlay has pointed to the constraints imposed on African scholarship by colonial languages, citing a study in which *nkwa*, an Igbo term denoting singing, playing instruments, and dancing, is uncomfortably glossed as "music": "By forcing the Igbo concept into the Procrustean bed of western conceptualization, she is in effect surrendering to the dominance of western ideas—or at least to the dominance of the English language! How different things would have been if the Igbo tongue had achieved the same "universality" as English! We should then have been seeking for universals in *nkwa* and regarding the whole process of western "serious" music as an aberration because it excluded dance" (1984:35).

The relationship of ethnomusicology to neocolonialism has been addressed by only a few scholars. Klaus Wachsmann, always the pioneer, optimistically suggested in 1966 that the era when "African performers and listeners alike were cast into a passive role" (1966:65) as objects of scholarly attention had come to an end. In *Tiv Song* Charles Keil predicted that the political pressure on scholars would "increase and accelerate over the coming years as more people resist arrest and refuse to be packaged as 'ethnographic presents' (1979:5). In 1984 Nketia and DjeDje (1984:xiii) issued a call for the "decolonization" of fieldwork, though they did not define it or suggest how it might be achieved.

It is to be hoped that African musical values and concepts will contribute to ethnomusicology, not just as empirical grist for an academic mill, but as potential elements of theoretical dialogue (see, for example, Agawu 1987). This is, I think, the fundamental unease underlying Kerman's critique of ethnomusicology: the fear that the people who make African and other "less developed musics" (1985:13) might actually respond in ways that will affect *"us"* (in Hornbostel's sense), *ideologically as well as musically; that what ethnomusicologists learn about human musicality may in the long run challenge institutionalized patterns of academic analysis and authority.*

I have attempted in this paper to point out some factors that have shaped ethnomusicological understanding of and discourse about sub-Saharan Africa. It seems clear that the future of ethnomusicology, and the role of ethnomusicologists in Africa's future, will depend not only upon increasing theoretical and methodological sophistication, but also upon a critical awareness of the social and cultural patterns that ineluctably condition scholarly perception and interpretation. From this perspective, Carl Stumpf's famous dictum—"What we need most in this field are monographs that will give us a conscientious description of the facts, free of theoretical premises" (1886:405)—might better be rephrased: what we need are monographs that give us a conscientious interpretation of the relationship of facts to theoretical premises and cultural values.

Notes

1. This paper was written while I was a Junior Fellow of the Society for the Humanities at Cornell University (1987–88), on leave from the Ethnomusicology Division of the School of Music, University of Washington. I am indebted to both of these institutions, and to Philip Yampolsky, Steven Clingman, and V. Kofi Agawu, who commented on previous versions.

2. Hornbostel was trained in what might be termed proto-Gestalt psychology, a movement of the early 1880s united around a critique of the field of psychophysics, established by Gustav Fechner in the 1860s. A number of figures involved in the founding of ethnomusicology as a comparative science participated in this critique, including Carl Stumpf (1848–1936), who trained Hornbostel at the Berlin Psychological Institute. Stumpf had continued the work of his teacher, Hermann Helmholtz (1821–94), shifting emphasis from the structure of the ear as a sensory organ to the study of aural experience, its functions and patterns. This concern with the nature of auditory patterns provided Hornbostel with a set of basic conceptual tools and questions, reflected in his work on African music.

3. George Stocking has documented the importance of these ideas in the epistemological formation of modern anthropology (1968).

4. It may be that each of the hypotheses mentioned in this discussion—the "motor accent," the "metronome sense," and the "density referent"—fits certain musical traditions better than others. Among the Yoruba of southwestern Nigeria, for example, it seems likely that social dance-music rhythms are most often grounded in a gross pulse implied in the movements of dancers and musicians (the metronome-sense concept), while bàtá drumming—a fast, virtuoso style, associated with the thundergod Sàngó—depends upon an emergent fastest pulse created by interlocking patterns at a higher level of activity (the density referent).

5. The hypothesis that adequate explanations of African musical rhythm should deal with the dynamics of motor behavior and pattern perception has also influenced research in eastern and southern Africa, where the development of multipart choral and ensemble textures is a focal aesthetic value. Thus, scholars of Kiganda instrumental music have described the perception of "inherent rhythms" (Kubik 1962) or "resultant musical structures" (Anderson 1984), produced by the cumulative interaction of individual patterns. In 1962 Gerhard Kubik introduced the notion of *motor images,* suggesting that in some instrumental musics "the musicians playing together (or in the case of a soloist, his left and right hands or fingers) produce rhythmic patterns, which are not perceived by the listener as they are actually played by the musicians. . . . *The image as it is heard and the image as it is played are often different from each other in African instrumental music*"

(1962:33). This concern with psychomotor processes has been important in Kubik's subsequent work: in a 1972 discussion of transcription from silent films, for example, he suggested that African musicians rely upon "a tendency inherent in human perception to hear 'gestalts'" (1972:29) more than musicians elsewhere in the world, and that motor images are in fact the deep structures guiding the production of African music.

Hornbostel's ideas concerning African rhythm have also been a formative element in the work of John Blacking. As early as 1955 Blacking suggested that "a 'physical' analysis of the instrumental music of Africa may often prove more enlightening than a purely musical analysis" (1955b:52). In "Deep and Surface Structures in Venda Music" (1971), Blacking asserted that "Venda music is not founded on melody but a rhythmical stirring of the whole body, of which singing is but one extension. Therefore, when we seem to hear a rest between two drum beats, we must realize that for the player it is not a rest: each drum beat is part of a total body movement in which the hand or a stick strikes the drum skin" (1971:98).

6. An interesting parallel is presented by the Boasian redefinition of the term "culture," from a bourgeois concept emphasizing relative refinement as measured by ethnocentric criteria, to a more universal, and necessarily abstract, concept useful for comparative purposes.

Works Cited

Agawu, V. Kofi
1987   "The Rhythmic Structure of West African Music," *Journal of Musicology* 5 (3):400–418.
Ames, David W. and Anthony V. King
1971   *Glossary of Hausa Music and Its Social Contexts*. Evanston: Northwestern University Press.
Anderson, Lois
1984   "Multipart Relationships in Xylophone and Tuned Drum Traditions in Buganda," *Selected Reports in Ethnomusicology* 5:121–44.
Asad, Talal, ed.
1973   *Anthropology and the Colonial Encounter*. New York: Humanities Press.
Berliner, Paul
1978   *The Soul of Mbira*. Berkeley and Los Angeles: University of California Press.
Besmer, Fremont
1983   *Horses, Musicians and Gods: The Hausa Cult of Possession-Trance*. South Hadley, Mass.: Bergin and Garvey.
Blacking, John
          "Some Notes on a Theory of African Rhythm Advanced by Erich von Hornbostel," *African Music* 1 (2):12–20.
1955b   "Eight Flute Tunes from Butembo, E. Belgian Congo," *African Music* 1 (2):24–52.
1965   "The Role of Music in the Culture of the Venda of the Northern Transvaal," *Studies in Ethnomusicology* (New York) 2:20–53.

1969   "Songs, Dances, Mimes, and Symbolism of Venda Girls' Initiation Schools," *African Studies* 28:215–66.

1971   "Deep and Surface Structures in Venda Music," *Yearbook of the International Folk Music Council* 3:91–108.

Brown, Ernest D.
1984   "Drums of Life: Royal Music and Social Life in Western Zambia." Ph.D. dissertation, University of Washington.

Calame-Griaule, Geneviève
1965   *Ethnologie et langage: la parole chez les Dogon.* Paris: Gallimard.

Chernoff, John Miller
1979   *African Rhythm and African Sensibility.* Chicago: University of Chicago Press.

Collins, John, and Paul Richards
1982   "Popular Music in West Africa: Suggestions for an Interpretive Framework," in *Popular Music Perspectives,* D. Horn and P. Tagg, eds. (Göteborg and Exeter: International Association for the Study of Popular Music), pp. 111–41.

Coplan, David B.
1982   "The Urbanization of African Music: Some Theoretical Observations," *Popular Music* 2:113–29.

DjeDje, Jacqueline C., and William G. Carter
1989   "African Musicology: An Assessment of the Field," in *African Musicology: Current Trends,* J. C. DjeDje and W. G. Carter, eds. (Los Angeles: UCLA African Studies Center), pp. 39–44.

England, Nicholas
1967   "Bushmen Counterpoint," *Journal of the International Folk Music Council* 19:58–66.

Erlmann, Veit
1980   *Die Macht des Wortes: Preisgesang und Berufsmusiker bei den Fulbe des Diamaré (Nordkamerun).* Hohenschäftlarn: Klaus Renner Verlag.

Gourlay, Kenneth A.
1984   "The Non-universality of Music and the Universality of Non-music," *The World of Music* 26 (2):25–36.

Griaule, Marcel
1965   *Conversations with Ogotemmeli: An Introduction to Dogon Religious Ideas.* London: Oxford University Press.

Herskovits, Melville J.
1941   *The Myth of the Negro Past.* Boston: Beacon Press.

Hornbostel, Erich M. von
1927   "The Unity of the Senses," *Psyche* 7 (28):83–89.
1928   "African Negro Music," *Africa* 1:30–62.

Jones, Arthur M.
1934   "African Drumming," *Bantu Studies* 8 (1).
1959   *Studies in African Music.* London: Oxford University Press.

Keil, Charles
1979   *Tiv Song.* Chicago: University of Chicago Press.
Kerman, Joseph
1985   *Contemplating Music: Challenges to Musicology.* Cambridge: Harvard
        University Press.
Killam, G. D.
1968   *Africa in English Fiction, 1874–1939.* Ibadan: University of Ibadan
        Press.
Kirby, Percival
1934   *The Musical Instruments of the Native Races of South Africa.* London:
        Oxford University Press.
Koetting, James
1970   "Analysis and Notation of West African Drum Ensemble Music," *Selected
        Reports in Ethnomusicology* 1 (3):116–46.
Kubik, Gerhard
1962   "The Phenomenon of Inherent Rhythms in East and Central African
        Instrumental Music," *African Music* 3 (1):33–42.
1971   "Die Institution mukanda and assozierte Einrichtungen bei den
        Vambwela/Vankangela und verwandten Ethnien in Südostangola." Ph.D.
        dissertation, University of Vienna.
1972   "Transcription of African Music from Silent Film: Theory and Methods,"
        African Music 5 (2):28–39.
1983   "Musikgestaltung in Afrika," in *Musik in Afrika,* A. Simon, ed. (Berlin:
        Museum für Völkerkunde), pp. 27–40.
Lomax, Alan
1970   "The Homogeneity of African-Afro-American Musical Style," in
        Afro-American Anthropology, N. Whitten and J. Szwed, eds. (New York:
        Free Press), pp. 181–201.
Merriam, Alan P.
1959   "African Music," in *Continuity and Change in African Cultures,* W.
        Bascom and M. Herskovits, eds. (Chicago: University of Chicago Press),
        pp. 49–86.
1969   "The Ethnographic Experience: Drum-Making Among the Bala
        (Basongye)," *Ethnomusicology* 13:74–100.
1974   Review of J. H. K. Nketia, *The Music of Africa, Yearbook of the
        International Folk Music Council* 6:136–38.
1977   "Traditional Music of Black Africa," in *Africa,* P. Martin and
        P. O'Meara, eds. (Bloomington: Indiana University Press),
        pp. 243–58.
1982   *African Music in Perspective.* New York: Garland Press.
Michels-Gebler, Ruth
1984   *Schmied und Musik.* Bonn: Verlag für systematische Musikwissenschaft.
Nettl, Bruno
1983   *The Study of Ethnomusicology: Twenty-nine Issues and Concepts.*
        Urbana: University of Illinois Press.

1986   "Africa," in *The New Harvard Dictionary of Music*, D. Randel, ed.
        (Cambridge: Harvard University Press), pp. 16–24.
Nketia, J. H. Kwabena
1963   *Drumming in Akan Communities of Ghana*. London: Nelson.
1974   *The Music of Africa*. New York: W. W. Norton.
Nketia, J. H. Kwabena, and Jacqueline C. DjeDje
1984   "Trends in African Musicology," *Selected Reports in Ethnomusicology* 5:
        ix–xviii.
Pantaleoni, Hewitt
1972   "Three Principles of Timing in Anlo Dance Drumming," *African Music* 5
        (2):50–63.
Said, Edward
1978   *Orientalism*. New York: Pantheon.
Smith, Michael G.
1957   "The Social Functions and Meaning of Hausa Praise Singing," *Africa* 27
        (1):26–44.
Stocking, George W., Jr.
1968   *Race, Culture, and Evolution: Essays in the History of Anthropology*.
        Chicago: University of Chicago Press.
Stone, Ruth
1982   *Let the Inside Be Sweet*. Bloomington: Indiana University Press.
Stumpf, Carl
1886   "Lieder der Bellakula-Indianer," *Vierteljahrsschrift für Musikwissenschaft*
        2:405–26.
Thompson, Robert Farris
1966   "An Aesthetic of the Cool: West African Dance," *African Forum* 2 (2):
        85–102.
1974   *African Art in Motion*. Berkeley and Los Angeles: University of California
        Press.
Tracey, Hugh
1948   *Chopi Musicians: Their Music, Poetry, and Instruments*. London: Oxford
        University Press.
Wachsmann, Klaus
1965   "Some Speculations Concerning a Drum Chime in Buganda," *Man* (n.s.)
        1:1–18.
1966   "The Trend of Musicology in Africa," *Selected Reports in
        Ethnomusicology* 1:61–65.
1969   "Ethnomusicology in African Studies: The Next Twenty Years," in
        Expanding Horizons, G. Carter and A. Paden, eds. (Evanston:
        Northwestern University Press), pp. 131–42.
1980   "Africa," in *The New Grove Dictionary of Music and Musicians*, Stanley
        Sadie, ed. (London: Macmillan), vol. 1, pp. 144–53.
Waterman, Richard A.
1948   "'Hot' Rhythm in Negro Music," *Journal of the American Musicological
        Society* 1:24–37.

1952   "African Influence on the Music of the Americas," in *Acculturation in the Americas*, S. Tax, ed. (Proceedings of the 29th International Congress of Americanists 2) (Chicago: University of Chicago Press), pp. 207–18.

Zemp, Hugo
1971   *Musique Dan: la musique dans la pensée et la vie sociale d'une société africaine.* Paris: Mouton.

Alexander L. Ringer
One World or None?
Untimely Reflections on a Timely
Musicological Question

M ORE THAN a hundred and twenty years have passed since that universal musical mind, François Fétis, published his "new method of classifying the human races according to their musical systems." Though virtually forgotten today, it was this pioneering essay which, in the long run, spawned the scientific discipline known in Central Europe, where it grew its strongest roots, as *Vergleichende Musikwissenschaft* (Schneider 1976:67). The decisive impetus had come in 1885 from Alexander Ellis who upset the quiet world of musical philology with a brilliantly executed study of "the musical scales of various nations" and in the process laid the solid empirical foundations of comparative musicology as practiced by generations thereafter. The fact that the legitimate father of comparative musicology had focused on musical systems rather than musical artifacts left its inevitable imprint on many a subsequent investigation, in striking contrast to the stress on music as a cultural phenomenon which became the hallmark of ethnomusicology with its strong anthropological bias, especially in the wake of World War II, when the word "race" had come to be identified with man's inhumanity to his fellow man at its unspeakable worst. Meanwhile, the racial policies of the Third Reich had caused a dramatic shift of the center of musicological activity from Germany to the United States, and young Americans were anxious to contribute to mutual understanding at home and abroad on the "self-evident" premise that "all men are created equal." In so doing, they not only tended at times to confuse equality with sameness but looked askance upon any and all hierarchical value systems, in the aesthetic realm no less than in the social.

Fétis, needless to say, had used the term "race" without prejudice in the manner of the Darwinian era he represented. It was a time when Americans called blacks "negroes," lest "persons of color" feel offended. Today, the opposite pertains, and "ethnicity" implies positive cultural values. In the Soviet orbit, where comparative thinking governs a good deal of musicological research to this day, the strictly musical term "intonation" con-

187

tinues to be favored. Inevitably, scientific terminology reflects changing historical as well as relatively stable ideological contexts. But whatever the intellectual and/or semantic conventions of the moment or the particular situation, the truism remains that social entities differ musically even more, and often more subtly, than in other forms of collective behavior, if only because by and large song and dance tend to mirror the deepest layers of the individual experience as well. And yet, it seems that the more we plunge into music as an intrinsic aspect of culture, and the more we learn about specific cultures in this respect, the less investigators care to analyze their data in ways that might help us understand what it is that makes a given culture musically unique in the extended family of musical cultures, which members are its close relatives, which, if any, mere distant cousins, etc. In short, lacking the necessary comparative base, we are at a loss in trying to assess the distinctive as opposed to more or less widely shared characteristics.

As a result, while the neutrality of the research product may satisfy current psychological or social fixations, scholarship fails to be enriched by insights of the sort that justified the humanistic claims of musicology throughout its youth and early maturity. The traumatic events of the Nazi era and the Second World War changed all that. Egalitarianism and, eventually, affirmative action in various guises set the tone not only for the postwar generation but also those who had witnessed the evils of racial and cultural prejudice firsthand. By 1959 even Curt Sachs felt constrained to preface the revision of his prewar outline of *Vergleichende Musikwissenschaft* with the disclaimer that the term itself was liable to lead to confusion and had, therefore, been generally abandoned (Sachs 1959:5). Sachs, however, was not one to deny that all science is comparative virtually by definition. What he wished to convey was rather that insofar as comparative musicology was prone to reveal in musical terms relatively early stages of human evolution, it should be considered a branch of musical history.

In Germany, the original home of comparative musicology as an academic discipline, the intrinsic logic of comparative musicology continued to be taken for granted: "No culture—including one's own—can be understood in isolation only by itself. We must confront it with other cultures, if we are to grasp its specific nature more precisely and want to be in a position to distinguish properly between what is uniquely its own and what is universal" (Dittmer 1957:66). Recalling Erich von Hornbostel, one of the founders of the discipline, these words had lost little of their validity when the Sachs pupil Walter Wiora quoted them as late as 1975 in his expert summary of the past achievements and future tasks of a field of inquiry which, in his estimation, ought to cover all musics, whenever and wherever practiced and irrespective of the means employed to maintain a given tradition (Wiora 1975:11). Wiora, needless to say, had experienced in the flesh what ideological and/or historical circumstances will do to scientific research, all protestations of *Wertfreiheit* notwithstanding. Comparative studies promised to ensure at least a modicum of "objective" control and thus tangible results relatively unaffected by extraneous considerations. As an historian of musicology, moreover, Wiora was well aware of the often oddly worded descriptions of what early visitors to faraway places regarded at best as musical curiosities, intriguing aspects of *couleur locale,* and at worst sonorous evidence of the alleged savagery of the alien creatures in question. Still, for us to dismiss any and all such reports as unacceptably "eurocentric" and hopelessly impressionistic would surely amount to a form of methodological totalitarianism worse in essence than the historical attitudes that provoked it.

Unpopular though the view may be right now, ethnomusicology, as widely understood today, would seem to owe a considerable debt to those dedicated men and women who pioneered comparative musicology, unquestionably in many instances in hopes of proving the uniqueness, if not outright superiority, of the European written tradition. Clearly, no discipline claiming the academically respectable "ology" ending is likely to be anything but "eurocentric" in origin and early orientation. The scientific method itself was, after all, a product of that peculiarly Western stress on rational behavior and intellectual rigor exemplified in the writings of Aristotle and kindred representatives of the great classical tradition. Medieval Arab scholarship may have been instrumental in handing that tradition down to European Christianity; the effects proved momentous for Europe, not the Middle East. Be this as it may, though, attitudes toward human knowledge and creativity and concomitant modes of thought developed in ancient Greece over two thousand years ago underlie all modern research, including that of non-Westerners who have gone to great pains to acquire the Western methodologies needed to identify and evaluate the peculiarities of their indigenous musics in their own cultural setting. Indeed, whether actually raised in an educational environment governed by written tradition or introduced to it gradually through intensive study and, possibly, some form of cultural osmosis, only an individual steeped in rational procedures and their manifold ramifications is likely to be properly equipped and motivated for the scientific challenges that any systematic investigation of musical phenomena entails. Hence, even the best of local musicians rarely meet the requisite standards of meaningful scholarly work; yet with expert guidance, far from serving as mere passive respondents, they are apt to contribute substantially to the musicological merits of the work in progress. To recall but one famous case in point: the Cairo Congress of 1932 was instigated and organized for the most part by Western scholars, but it was the carefully planned role of judiciously selected master musicians from the Arab world which turned that unprecedented event into a milestone for the study of Middle Eastern music, while affording the musicians involved a unique opportunity to regain some of the self-respect and broad recognition as outstanding representatives of an old civilization saddled, unfortunately, with a modern elite ready to embrace every supposed blessing emanating from the West.

That interest in non-Western music was always closely tied to strictly material and/or ideological concerns should come as no surprise, since Western art and scholarship, while contributing by no means insignificantly to change, also inevitably reflect shifting trends in the realms of religion, politics, and economics. The explorers of a more remote past, to whom we owe those fragmentary yet valuable reports of music from so many strange lands, rarely embarked on their strenuous and dangerous undertakings just for the sake of disinterested knowledge. Pious missionaries determined to bring the blessings of Christianity to the pagan multitudes may not have thought of it in those terms, but their devoted labors did produce various forms of Christological imperialism. Indeed, the very roots of what we like to think of as a strictly scholarly discipline were inextricably intertwined with the aspirations of the powers-that-be in search of information concerning those they sought to convert, subject, and/or exploit. By the same token, colonizing missionaries as far back as the days of Pope Gregory the Great recognized measured compromise with local customs and habits as an absolute must, if their Christianizing effort was to have any realistic chance of success, which rather complicates the task of musicologists trying to demonstrate pure traditions where such could not possibly exist.

The Earl of Macartney's Embassy reports from China during the last decade of the eighteenth century might be cited as an instructive, anything but unique, instance of musical information collected and disseminated for strictly extramusical reasons. Eager to learn as much as possible about that mysterious empire, which had become the center of the lucrative opium trade, the British government requested not only economic and political information "but also military, intellectual, cultural and social" (Harrison 1973:167). By then, Père Amiot, the French missionary who spent nearly his entire active life in China, had gathered a host of factual data as well as anecdotal material concerning Chinese music, which he proved willing to share with Macartney's agents, no doubt in exchange for an appropriate consideration. Macartney and/or his men, in turn, passed some of this on to John Barrow whose "Travels in China" contains not only descriptive accounts but several tunes in musical notation (see Harrison 1973:171–73). One of these was subsequently picked up by Carl Maria von Weber and then, in our own century, became the principal source of Paul Hindemith's *Symphonic Metamorphosis on Themes by Weber.*

Colonialism contributed mightily to the broadening interest in non-Western musics and sparked many a serious study. Indonesian music is a particularly striking example, since most of what was known about the music of Java until quite recently had been explored and analyzed by a single individual, the late Jaap Kunst, who did his fieldwork as a Dutch government official in the Netherlands East Indies. As for military campaigns, it was the Turkish penetration of much of Eastern Europe which sparked the Western fascination with "exotic" musical elements. And, had it not been for one Napoleon Bonaparte and his North African campaign, surely Villoteau's admirable study of "the present state of musical art in Egypt" would have remained unwritten as part of that monumental *Description de l'Égypte* commissioned by the victorious general. Nor, for that matter, could Georg Schünemann or Robert Lach have done their musicological work with German minorities in Russia on the one hand and, on the other, Russian prisoners in German camps, had their political masters opted for peace instead of the First World War.

In this country, early concerns with native music, exemplified by Theodore Baker's pioneering thesis (1976), were direct consequences of the American Indian wars. And until the United States saved democracy in Korea under the United Nations label, few Americans displayed any interest in the music of Seoul. It is hardly necessary to cite additional instances in support of the contention that international violence has benefitted not only science and industry, the suppliers of its material wherewithal, but inevitably, and if you will ironically, knowledge and a better understanding of alien cultures as well. At the very least, there are always soldiers singing—and not only on command—as Walter Wiora pointed out at the height of the German triumphs of 1940, when the Nazi conquest of much of Europe offered the Freiburg Folksong Archive by which he was employed rare opportunities to broaden its collections in a hurry (Wiora 1940:20).

Needless to say, historical musicology, too, has labored under extraneous pressures from the very outset and, at the same time, benefited from its extramusicological motivations. The rather sudden prominence of history as a central academic discipline on the European academic scene was in itself an intrinsic aspect of the rise of bourgeois nationalism, exemplified by Michelet in France and Ranke in Germany. Nor was it sheer accident that some of the first academically sponsored monumental publications of older music were devoted to the musical heritages of Germany, Austria, and, indeed, forever separatist Bavaria. But musicology was equally responsive to prevailing romantic illusions about the then and far away as viable alternatives to a rather foreboding here and now. The growing fascination with some of the more exotic dimensions of music and musical life reflected thus, at least up to a point, a perhaps involuntary reaction to cultural nationalism and its inherent dangers of parochialism, if not outright chauvinism. No doubt, something of this sort contributed substantially to the amazing growth of ethnomusicology in the wake of the McCarthy era in this country. Be this as it may, however, universalistic notions and aspirations certainly have been and continue to be fundamental aspects of romanticism. Friedrich Schiller was anxious to embrace the entire world, and the Beethoven who endorsed that symbolic gesture so incomparably was the same who doted over Abt Vogler's improvisations on Eskimo tunes and other exotic musical matter, while producing an amazing "Dance of the Dervishes" of his own.

Given human nature and the nature of history, objectivity, the presumed sine qua non of all science worthy of that designation, remains at best elusive when it comes to human affairs. At worst, whether with respect to an alien culture or one's own, it is but a figment of the student's imagination conditioned by a social science so-called that has been anxious to establish and maintain its academic legitimacy. The outside observer is hardly ever sufficiently privy to events on the inside to rise to the level of objectivity several steps above mere mindlessness. Participant observers, on the other hand, are handicapped by their inescapably subjective involvement in the very events and/or processes they are supposed to observe and analyze "objectively." In short, bias is built into research among humans of and by any color, religion, or historical vintage. To deny its existence is not merely unrealistic; it also tends to obviate the kind of conscious control that can be its saving grace. Meaningfully controlled, bias has a positive role to play *but what of that on evaluation?*

?

in scientific research, since at the very least the investigator is likely to try and bolster his or her a priori position with every possible bit of factual evidence and/or idea, including some long known but neglected due to different biases, possibly even some entirely new and valid well beyond the occasion at hand. By contrast, uncontrolled bias is always in danger of deteriorating into prejudice, an intrinsically negative stance which, all moral considerations aside, deters from the path of truth, because it favors exclusive, rather than inclusive, patterns of thought and action. Unlike racial prejudice in Nazi Germany, the nationalistic bias of a good deal of early German musicology generated materials, theories, and insights, which in a number of cases have lost very little of their "objective" value. That comparative musicology was greatly indebted to the prevailing Darwinian bias goes without saying. And yet, the methodology it engendered vouchsafed a considerably higher degree of "objectivity" than the quantitative approaches which have taken its place.

Since the scientific concepts and procedures at its disposal were Western in origin and had been tested almost exclusively in Western contexts, nineteenth-century musicology seemed well advised when it set out for unknown shores determined to rely as long as possible on the familiar navigational lights provided by its native culture. Inevitably and quite predictably, these indispensable initial orientation marks grew dimmer and dimmer as the adventure proceeded and others, previously unknown, became visible and after some trial and error proved their considerable usefulness. Still, comparative methods never lost any of their inherent worth. Properly developed and employed, they have continued to yield more "objective" information as well as subjective understanding than some of the "tightest" of purely descriptive procedures, precisely because of the unavoidable liabilities of prejudice and to a lesser degree entrenched bias, not to speak of widespread insensitivity and lack of empathy, let alone sheer ignorance.

The potential results of comparison depend, of course, on both the quality and quantity of the available units. If for no other reason, comparative musicology has a vested interest in first-rate analytical studies of specific musics and individual musical cultures. None would, therefore, wish to denigrate what has been accomplished along these lines in recent decades, especially in the United States. The fact remains, nevertheless, that one may study, say, the great raga tradition with true devotion and intensity yet miss in the end what is altogether unique in raga as a concept, unless one has a solid understanding of maqam and other modal devices. Similarly, in view of the incidence of instrumental preludes, interludes, and/or postludes in any number of cultural contexts, only an acute awareness of this pervasive phenomenon in conjunction with a comprehensive grasp of its manifold manifestations is apt to ensure its adequate appraisal in the particular culture or cultural situation under study. Discussions of the musical traditions of the Maghreb without appropriate references to the musical practices of medieval Europe are likely, for their part, to produce questionable conclusions in matters of cause and effect, considering the intricate relationships between the Muslim and Christian worlds in Spain, Sicily and Provence, and, of course, the Latin Kingdom of Jerusalem. Nor does it seem reasonable to try and explain early jazz without due attention to European harmonic conventions as practiced in the southern United States around the turn of the century. But then, "objectivity" might well be served best in this instance, if jazz as a peculiarly American phenomenon were approached free of any Afro-American bias in terms of an Afro-European art bred in Louisiana and raised in the American Midwest.

Because it regarded melody, rhythm, vocal prowess, and the fashioning of musical instruments as human universals, nineteenth-century musical scholarship favored their systematic study on the largest possible scale in hopes of arriving eventually at meaningful distinctions between general laws and culture-bound specifics. Men like Carl Stumpf, Otto Abraham, and Erich von Hornbostel, trained as lawyers in some instances, as natural scientists in others, fully understood, moreover, that no field of inquiry can very well claim scientific standing, unless it has produced a basic set of generalizations adequately supported by empirical evidence. By 1905, when Hornbostel published his fervent plea for comparative musical research, he was in a position to refer for the first time to significant data obtained with the help of that crucial invention, the phonograph, something Alexander Ellis could hardly have dreamed of twenty years earlier (Hornbostel 1975:249–70). Before long, Thomas Edison's magic box became the ethnologist's portable equivalent of the historian's immutable archive, placing nonwritten traditions within reach of investigators virtually on a par with their written counterparts. But, as Hornbostel took care to point out, musicology was by no means the only, let alone the first, discipline in need of comparative procedures. Philology, for one, "initially examined the individual languages separately, until comparative linguistics began to tie connecting threads" (Hornbostel 1975:250). Suddenly, there were "new paths" and "new groupings." Languages of so-called primitive peoples, relatively unheeded until then, acquired unprecedented interest: "the dialects

within the known language areas of the civilized world were more carefully studied and increasingly abundant material became available for
comparison." Now that musicology had the requisite tools at its disposal,
he argued, it must follow suit, if only because comparison is the basic,
"the principal means by which the quest for knowledge is pursued." In the
end, all "systematization and theory depend on comparison," which is "a
general and not a specific method." And unless we find ways and means of
evaluating the totality of the world's highly diverse musical practices, how
can we ever hope to find an answer to the "initial problem . . . what is
music?"

More than eighty years later, Hornbostel's fundamental concerns about
"the complex of problems which comparative musicology will have to face
in the future" may sound rather old-fashioned. One wonders, though,
whether in the light of subsequent events, they are really that outdated.
While pointing to comparative linguistics as a convenient model for musicologists, Hornbostel did not fail to stress that in the field of philology
comparative studies presented a relatively late development. In the case of
musicology, on the other hand, the historical development has been in the
opposite direction. Initially convinced of the need for comparative research, it finds itself after some three generations caught in the very pattern
that spelled the doom of nineteenth-century philology. Nor do we bother
much, at least in this country, with what Hornbostel saw as musicology's
"initial problem." How many today consider the question "what is music"
germane to their particular research interests? Such fundamental issues
hardly arouse the passions of young scholars trained, rather than educated,
in our positivistic academic atmosphere.

Erich von Hornbostel made his thoughtful speech in Vienna at a time
when Arnold Schoenberg seemed in the very process of transvaluating all
established musical values, in particular the myth of functional tonality as
a mandate of nature. A few years later Ferruccio Busoni, in his sketch for
a New Aesthetic of Music, advocated the infinite "gradation of the
octave" (Busoni 1962:93). Then, Henry Cowell visited Hornbostel's
Phonogramm-Archiv in Berlin, and the rest, as they say, is history. "New
musical resources" are now taken for granted by musicologists, composers, and performers alike (Cowell 1930). By the same token, Hornbostel's
"initial problem" is still, indeed more urgently than ever, with us, thanks in
part to a one-time Cowell disciple named John Cage, not to speak of musical electronics. Current relevance aside, however, in the unlikely event that
the intrinsic worth of comparative work should once again find recog-

nition beyond facile labels like "The World of Music," "Man and His Music," "Music of the World's Peoples," etc., who, given the information explosion of the last decades, the data banks, and, above all, the academically driven commitment to specialization, could possibly assume such superhuman tasks? There is so much to know, after all, far more than even the most gifted may hope to acquire in a lifetime, though surely no more so in musicology than most areas of human inquiry. But that is precisely why we have National Institutes of Health or, at the university level, coordinated research laboratories. The answer obviously lies in cooperation as opposed to the short-range gains of all-out competition. Even industry—most recently the American Textile Association—is beginning to have second thoughts about the American Credo that competition alone ensures quality. Competition rather encourages short cuts at the behest of quick results—the sort of thing that looks good on an academic report or *curriculum vitae* but does little, if anything, to further the cause of knowledge, let alone understanding. What it does promote is self-delusion and the permanent retention of scholarly blinders.

As for the technological wherewithal, if Alexander Ellis knew nothing as yet of the phonograph when he did his pioneering work on scales, Hornbostel, for his part, could not have dreamed of the melograph, and microchips were not even a concept when in 1935 after two years of exile he passed away in Britain. Today, soundly conceived computer applications should go far in enabling properly educated and trained teams of musicologists to map entire geographic regions in terms of musical languages and dialects, the sort of thing no series of field observations and recordings as such can possibly convey. This, mind you, is by no means intended to denigrate the achievements and potential of anthropological approaches. Rather, without a true *musicology* of music, even the best of anthropology will remain as hidebound as a *Rezeptionsforschung* attempting to replace the study of historical sources and musical artifacts.

When all is said and done, I would submit, any "understanding musicology," after the model of Max Weber's "understanding sociology," must needs be predicated on the unity of all music and hence all musicology, not merely that particular segment which, for largely extraneous professional and/or purely academic reasons, has come to be known as "ethnomusicology." Historical, sociological, anthropological, psychological, philosophical, and various systematic analytical approaches struck the founding fathers of our discipline as but so many complementary ways of skinning the musical cat, whether male, female, or neutered, black, red, or tabby. Much of what they had every reason to take for granted, we may well have to re-learn, including the pertinent fact that what ultimately accounts for the rel-ative reliability of research in any area of human behavior—indeed not only there—is the quality, rather than the sheer quantity, of the data col-lected and invoked as evidence. Quality, however, presents itself as a com-plex of relative notions rooted in prior experiences and their comparative evaluations.

Even though comparative procedures are apt to ensure a higher degree of "objectivity" than most other methodological tools at our disposal, young musicologists in recent times have all too often been tempted, and encouraged by their elders, to cross the scholarly Styx to narrow special-ization, only to vanish ingloriously in the Hades of mindless parochialism that lies beyond its enticing banks. While none may legitimately claim certainty as to where salvation ultimately lies, we surely owe it to the unitary world of musical creativity to give comparative musicology in the best and broadest sense of the term a renewed fighting chance. Perhaps, with luck, we will thus in the long run reach those Elysian fields, which, if they do not offer eternal bliss, promise at last a more objective environ-ment in which to play our games with some confidence, aware of our limitations, to be sure, but also in justified hopes of promoting a somewhat better understanding of humankind in all its many-splendored musical variety.

Works Cited

Baker, Theodore
1976   *On the Music of the North American Indians.* Translated by Ann Buckley. Buren, Netherlands: Knuf. First published 1882.
Busoni, Ferrucio
1962   "Sketch of a New Aesthetic of Music," in *Three Classics of Music* (New York: Dover), pp. 75–102.
Cowell, Henry
1930   *New Musical Resources.* New York: Alfred A. Knopf.
Dittmer, Kunz
1957   "Ethnologie und Musikethnologie," in *Bericht über den internationalen musikwissenschaftlichen Kongress, Hamburg 1956,* (Kassel and Berlin: Bärenreiter), pp. 66–72.
Harrison, Frank
1973   *Time, Place and Music: An Anthology of Ethnomusicological Observation c. 1550 to c. 1800.* Amsterdam: Frits Knuf.

Hornbostel, Erich M. von
1975   "The Problems of Comparative Musicology," in *Hornbostel Opera Omnia,* Klaus Wachsmann, et al., eds. and trans. (The Hague: Martinus Nijhoff), pp. 249–70.
Sachs, Curt
1959   *Vergleichende Musikwissenschaft, 2. neu bearbeitete Auflage.* Heidelberg: Quelle und Meyer.
Schneider, Albrecht
1976   *Musikwissenschaft und Kulturkreislehre.* Bonn: Verlag für systematische Musikwissenschaft.
Wiora, Walter
1940   "Aufruf zur Sammlung von Soldatenliedern für das Volksliedarchiv," *Das Reich* (11 August 1940).
1975   *Ergebnisse und Aufgaben vergleichender Musikforschung.* Darmstadt: Wissenschaftliche Buchgesellschaft.

III
Inspired by Great Leaders

Dieter Christensen

Erich M. von Hornbostel, Carl Stumpf, and the Institutionalization of Comparative Musicology

E THNOMUSICOLOGY is giving increasing attention to the individual as the creator, performer, transmitter, consumer of music. The individual is seen as a member of various groupings, as center or part of multifarious and complex relationships, not any more as the representative of that hypothetical homogeneous entity, "culture," whose members would share one set of beliefs, knowledge, a way of life, and a musical style. A similarly ethnomusicological approach to the history of ethnomusicology and its antecedent, comparative musicology, appears indicated. A history of ethnomusicology has to proceed beyond the notion of "schools" to the individuals who, through their ideas and actions, contributed to the shaping of the discipline.

Erich Moritz von Hornbostel (1877–1935) shares with Carl Stumpf (1841–1936) the reputation of having fathered the "Berlin School of Comparative Musicology." When in 1952 I first learned about comparative musicology in the Berlin Phonogramm-Archiv, the gloss "Berlin School" had not yet been coined. As one of a small group of students around a solitary teacher, the Privat-Dozent Dr. Kurt Reinhard, I constructed an image of our academic identity populated with intellectual heroes—Hornbostel, Sachs, Stumpf—listening into the distant past of humankind through Edison phonograph horns, debating their findings and thoughts loftily, and far removed from all earthly troubles. I imagined them sharing their insights with other scholars in sessions of (multidisciplinary) scholarly societies, and I saw them penning letters to the likes of Béla Bartók, Jaap Kunst, Franz Boas, and even Frances Densmore.

From my work with the collections and tools Hornbostel left behind in the Berlin Phonogramm-Archiv, from my reading of letters and the literature, I formed the vision of the 1920s and early thirties as the Golden Age of comparative musicology, with the Berlin Phonogramm-Archiv as the center of a worldwide network of scholarly discourse, of gatherers of information and recordings, a fountainhead of ideas. A naive, idealized image, no doubt. One, I submit, that is not very far from what our more current, more erudite texts have to say about the "Berlin School." How did contemporaries see what we now call the "Berlin School"?

The *Zeitschrift für Musikwissenschaft* for 1934 carried an article, "Neue Aufgaben der vergleichenden Musikwissenchaft."[1] It appeared only one year after the first periodical for comparative musicology, the *Zeitschrift für vergleichende Musikwissenschaft,* had been launched, three years after the monumental record series *Musik des Orients* had appeared on the market, four after the Gesellschaft für die Musik des Orients, soon renamed Gesellschaft für vergleichende Musikwissenschaft, had formed— all enterprises initiated or carried out by Hornbostel or his close associates, a group of people of whom Fritz Bose, the author of the article, was one. Bose's article also appeared the year after Erich von Hornbostel had fled the country.

Bose appeals to the readers of the *Zeitschrift* to awaken comparative musicology from its "Dornröschenschlaf," its enchanted slumber. He calls for a renewal of comparative musicology as a *musicological* enterprise after long years during which it had been nothing more than a sleepy handmaiden to ethnology. He complains that "comparative musicology, thirty years ago a promising new field of topical interest, vividly discussed, with worldwide goals, [had] in recent years faded more and more into the background" (Bose 1934:229), and he made it clear that he meant the academic world as well as the general public to whom comparative musicology had lost its attraction.

Bose, one of the few students of Hornbostel's, was hardly launching a veiled attack at the new regime that had forced his mentor out of the country. There is no indication that he wished to attack Hornbostel, his teacher for whom he always expressed respect and admiration, nor are there polemics against Marius Schneider who had assumed the directorship of the Berlin Phonogramm-Archiv upon Hornbostel's departure. We can treat Bose's description as the perception of a participant who measures the standing of *his* chosen discipline against that of related ones—within academia as well as in the public eye.

Had comparative musicology in Germany indeed declined, fallen into enchanted slumber after the First World War, turned into a handmaiden of culture-historical ethnology, and lost its appeal to neighboring disciplines as well as to the general public? Or were both Bose and I victims of the Golden Age syndrome, and was it perhaps true that as a discipline, comparative musicology had never amounted to much? There are, of course, those who see the Berlin School as a well-established academic discipline in its own right, respected and secure among other disciplines that form the pantheon of Western learning. But how well established was comparative musicology? Is it not rather the case that it was fragile and insecurely placed? Why did it not take a more prominent place among the disciplines? What place, indeed, did it take? And what can account for the course of events?

These issues, I believe, are important for our understanding of the achievements and failures of comparative musicology, and their study can raise some questions about more recent, even current developments in what we now call ethnomusicology. But before we can address them, it will be necessary to clarify my use of some of the key concepts in our deliberations.

An issue has been made whether ethnomusicology—and by extension, comparative musicology—is a discipline, or a field or area of studies.[2] I do not intend to resume that discussion here. Suffice it to say that it is not difficult to find writings that treat these words as synonyms.[3] Yet these are, to me, different concepts. *Field* refers to a subject matter; *discipline,* short for academic discipline, connotes an organized, institutionalized process of inquiry, teaching, and learning in which disciples as a group of individuals carry a tradition of asking questions and seeking answers in an academic setting.

Another concept on which I wish to comment also appears in the title of this essay: "Berlin School." This stands, of course, for the Berlin School of Comparative Musicology, and while the ideas and scholarly practices developed in Berlin have certainly spread beyond that city—it is sufficient to mention George Herzog, Jaap Kunst, Mieczyslaw Kolinski—I shall take the term literally and concentrate on Berlin.

My considerations concern some aspects of the *history* of comparative musicology. Histories can be constructed as histories of thought—as *Geistesgeschichten,* as histories of ideas or of paradigms. Ideas, however, even paradigms, exist not by and of themselves, but rather because people have thought them, have expressed them, or have otherwise acted on or with them—in words or in their works, in what they did or did not do. Ideas underlie the perception and choice of options, and they are affected by their social environment and by the consequences of those choices. Since we are dealing with the history of comparative musicology as a discipline, then, the behavior and its products have to be studied as well.

How do academic disciplines as I define them come into existence? I propose that several conditions have to be met for a new academic discipline to become established. There have to be a theoretical basis for intellectual order; methods and techniques that permit dealing with specific questions in a systematic fashion; social need for the particular knowledge and insights; and individuals and institutions to carry on research and to provide continuity. In the case of the Berlin School of Comparative Musicology, much has been written about theoretical bases for intellectual order, and the roles of the phonograph and the cents system of measuring as specific methods and techniques that brought musical sound into the realm of positivistic investigations, but very little attention has been given to the social needs or uses for the knowledge and insights that comparative musicology would have to offer, or to the role of individuals and institutions in its development. These institutions include those of neighboring disciplines.

I propose that it is in the domain of people, institutions, and social needs that we may find some answers to the question of what place the Berlin School took among the disciplines, and why it developed the way it did. An understanding of the domain of social environment and needs—the transition from the colonialist-imperialist late nineteenth century through the disaster of World War I to the National Socialist era—is very important for a history of comparative musicology. For the present purpose, however, I shall concentrate on the role of individuals and institutions between 1900, the year that Carl Stumpf and Otto Abraham recorded and analyzed music of a Thai theater troupe in Berlin, and 1933, when Hornbostel fled Germany, two months after the National-Socialist takeover.

Stumpf and Hornbostel are, no doubt, the towering figures of the Berlin School. They affected the course of comparative musicology in quite different ways, yet it is difficult to imagine how one could have succeeded without the other. Stumpf, the psychologist and philosopher, student of Brentano and Lotze, assumed a rationalist position and believed in the unity of the human mind. For his psychological interest in the sensual experience of tones and intervals and their ordering into tone systems, and for the testing of his hypothesis of perceived fusion of tones (*Verschmelzungstheorie*), he needed data ideally from all cultures. His famous Bellakula essay (Stumpf 1886) and his "Tonsystem und Musik der Siamesen" (Stumpf 1901) were two of his own attempts to broaden the empirical basis for his psychological studies. As director of the Psychological Institute of Berlin University,[4] he was in a position to assign assistants to a task of his choice, and to seek funding for it. In 1901 he commissioned Otto Abraham, a medical doctor, and the newly arrived twenty-four-year-old Hornbostel, whose training was in philosophy and the sciences, especially chemistry, to build a collection of phonograph recordings in the Psychological Institute that should serve the purposes of psychological research.

Stumpf's great contribution to comparative musicology is that he made this assignment, that he provided an institutional basis and stability over two decades, and that he did not resist when young Hornbostel, still his assistant, took the project far beyond its original goals and scope to develop a new mode of scholarly inquiry that soon transcended the bounds of psychology. When Stumpf retired from the university in 1921, the Phonogramm-Archiv came under the administration of the Berlin State Conservatory[5] but remained physically at the Psychological Institute.

Stumpf made yet other important organizational contributions to music research. Above all, he attained for systematic musicology the recognition as an academic *Fach* by the University of Berlin. It is in this context, as part of systematic musicology, that comparative musicology came to be taught in the University of Berlin and could attract disciples, students in the proper sense.

Hornbostel addressed Stumpf on his eighty-fifth birthday as the *"Altmeister"* of comparative musicology and as the fatherly friend,[6] surely also of the discipline. Hornbostel himself adopted Stumpf's assignment—to develop the archive—as his life task,[7] and one could view his systematic and theoretical thought as a by-product, resulting from the inevitable striving of a trained and passionate intellectual for order and deeper insight. Hornbostel did not depend on an earned income, at least not until the inflation of 1922–23 diminished his independent means. Jaap Kunst describes Hornbostel in an obituary (Kunst 1937) as a genius of intuition and, at the same time, of childlike innocence,[8] someone who was loftily oblivious to the material aspects of daily life, not interested in politics, whose life-style was extremely simple, but whose daily schedule had little in common with that of people around him. In this respect, Kunst wrote, "he did not concern himself with others" (Kunst 1937:244).

This loftiness extended also to his professional life. Apart from the directorship of the Phonogramm-Archiv (which he apparently supported in part out of his own pocket), Hornbostel shunned institutional responsibilities.[9] He did not accept a teaching position until 1923 when, after much persuading, he took his *Habilitation* and began to teach two courses per semester, a lecture course *(Vorlesung)* and a seminar *(Übung)*, in the capacity of a nontenured, part-time university teacher.[10] His announced courses covered music psychology, comparative musicology, and music ethnology (*Musikalische Völkerkunde, Musikethnologie*) almost evenly—since 1906 he had carefully distinguished also in his terminology between the musicological-psychological and the anthropological perspectives.[11] Beginning in 1928, his courses were announced to be held at the Psychological Institute, always in the late afternoon and evening, and it has been reported that they were not very popular. Only two students of comparative musicology earned their doctorates under Hornbostel: Mieczyslaw Kolinski in 1930 and Fritz Bose in 1934, when Hornbostel was already officially "on leave"[12] and de facto in exile.

In a very strict sense, then, the lineage of the Berlin School of Comparative Musicology extends from Carl Stumpf through Hornbostel to Kolinski and Bose; but we must surely include the influential George Herzog, who worked closely under Hornbostel from 1923 until 1925, when Herzog went to Columbia University to study anthropology with Franz Boas; and there are several others who claim Hornbostel as their teacher, with more or less justification: Klaus Wachsmann, Walter Wiora, Hans-Heinz Dräger, Marius Schneider. But what about the other prominent names that are often mentioned in conjunction with the Berlin School? What about Curt Sachs, Georg Schünemann, Robert Lachmann? All three were certainly Berliners, but none of them received a formal training in comparative musicology, and none followed the theoretical and methodological orientations of Stumpf and Hornbostel.[13] In his essay for Stumpf's eighty-fifth birthday in 1933, Hornbostel offered congratulations on behalf of the "still small circle of *friends* of our branch of learning that is so remote from the turn of daily life."[14] The circle of practitioners was even smaller, and the personal disposition and preferences of each of the few individuals had therefore a powerful effect on the course of events.

Under the intellectual stimulation and institutional shelter offered by Carl Stumpf's Psychological Institute, Hornbostel had almost single-handedly designed and exemplified the scope and method of a scholarly discipline between psychology, anthropology, and historical musicology, but he had failed to place it firmly into the institutional network of academia and to provide early enough for its continuity. The broadness of his intellect that bridged the established disciplines—psychology, anthropology, musicology—had gained his recognition in all three, and a home for comparative musicology in none.

On 8 November 1933, the Prussian Minister for Science and Popular Education issued an Executive Order appointing Dr. Marius Schneider as director of the Phonogramm-Archiv and incorporating the archive into the Ethnographic Museum.[15] Hornbostel's Phonogramm-Archiv was moved from the Psychological Institute of the university to the museum's storage facilities in Dahlem, away from the academic setting and intellectual climate in which it had grown. No one succeeded him in his teaching position at Berlin University.

Hornbostel shares with Charles Seeger the distinction that his name is invoked probably much more often then his works are read and his thoughts and actions are understood. There are still lessons to be learned from the achievements as well as from the failures of the "Berlin School."

Notes

1. Bose 1934. Quotes translated from the original German by the author.
2. See Merriam 1977.
3. See for instance Nettl 1964:vii.
4. Psychologisches Institut der Friedrich-Wilhelms-Universität.
5. The Staatliche Hochschule für Musik Berlin assumed administrative responsibility in 1922.
6. Hornbostel 1933a:25.
7. "*Lebensaufgabe*"—Hornbostel 1933b:41.
8. "Mischung von genialer Intuition und kindlicher Arglosigkeit." Kunst 1937:244.
9. Hornbostel took no active role in the Gesellschaft für die Erforschung der Musik des Orients (1930), subsequently renamed Gesellschaft für vergleichende Musikwissenschaft, or in editing the *Zeitschrift für vergleichende Musikwissenschaft*. He does appear as coeditor with Stumpf of the short-lived *Sammelbände für vergleichende Musikwissenschaft* (1922–23), and as editor of a commercial enterprise, the record series *Musik des Orients* (1930).
10. Since 1923 Privat-Dozent, 1925 "Nicht-beamteter Außerordentlicher Professor," that is, nontenured Associate Professor; see bulletins of Berlin University 1923–33.
11. See Hornbostel and Abraham 1906:452, where the term *musikethnologisch* first occurs. Cf. also Hornbostel 1909, 1910:66, 1912:495, 1934:60.
12. "Als Gastprofessor nach New York beurlaubt bis Ende September 1935" (Bulletin of Friedrich-Wilhelms-Universität zu Berlin, Winter Semester 1933–34).
13. The art and music historian Curt Sachs contributed his encyclopedic knowledge of musical instruments to the famous classification (Hornbostel and Sachs 1914), but his unilinear-evolutionistic stance placed him far apart from Hornbostel's comparative musicology. Georg Schünemann's studies were primarily in music history, his interests in pedagogy and administration. During the First World War he participated in a project to record songs in prisoner-of-war camps. His collection of some four hundred German-Russian songs appears in the *Sammelbände für vergleichende Musikwissenschaft*. As Deputy Director of the Berlin State Conservatory (1920–32, Director 1932–33), he may have been supportive of the Phonogramm-Archiv, but his scholarly activities in the Berlin School were limited. Robert Lachmann, whom Bruno Nettl considers "a typical member of the Berlin School of Comparative Musicology" (Nettl 1960:29), discovered his love for non-Western and folk music also in a German prisoner-of-war camp. Encouraged by Stumpf and Hornbostel, he studied musicology under Johannes Wolf and Stumpf (Ph.D. 1922) and pursued a library career, continuing his interest in non-Western

music as a serious hobby. While his attention to scales is more in the style of Horn-bostel than in his spirit, and while he lacked the scientific-psychological founda-tion, he was certainly a member of the inner circle. Hornbostel's personal copy of Lachmann's book, *Musik des Orients* (1929), is inscribed "Herrn Prof. Dr. v. Hornbostel mit der Bitte, Nichtpassendes durchzustreichen" [To Prof. Dr. v. Horn-bostel with the request to cross out whatever is inappropriate].

14. Hornbostel 1933a:25. Italics are mine.

15. *Erlaß des Ministers für Wissenschaft und Volksbildung*, V I Nr. 54804 II/8. November 1933. "Dr. Marius Schneider zum Leiter des Phonogramm-Archivs und dessen Übernahme durch Museum für Völkerkunde." It is curious that Marius Schneider himself claims appointment only in 1934.

Works Cited

Bose, Fritz
1934   "Neue Aufgaben der vergleichenden Musikwissenschaft," *Zeitschrift für Musikwissenschaft* 16:229–31.

Hornbostel, Erich M. von
1909   "Phonographierte Melodien aus Madagaskar und Indonesien," in *Forschungsreise SMS Planet 1906/07, Anthropologie und Ethnographie*, A. Krämer, ed. (Berlin: Sigismund), 5:139–52.
1910   "U.S.A. National Music," *Zeitschrift der Internationalen Musikgesellschaft* 12 (3):64–68.
1912   "Musik auf den nordwestlichen Salomoinseln," in *Forschungen auf dem Salomo-Inseln und dem Bismarck-Archipel*, Richard Thurnwald, ed. Appendix. (Berlin: Reimer), 1:461–504.
1933a   "Carl Stumpf und die vergleichende Musikwissenschaft," *Zeitschrift für vergleichende Musikwissenschaft* 1:22–28.
1933b   "Das Berliner Phonogrammarchiv," *Zeitschrift für vergleichende Musikwissenschaft* 1:40–45.
1934   Review of H. H. Roberts, *Form in Primitive Music*, *Zeitschrift für vergleichende Musikwissenschaft* 2:60–64.

Hornbostel, Erich M. von, and Otto Abraham
1906   "Phonographierte Indianermelodien aus British-Columbia," in *Boas Anniversary Volume* (New York: J. J. Augustin), pp. 447–74.

Hornbostel, Erich M. von, and Curt Sachs
1914   "Systematik der Musikinstrumente: Ein Versuch," *Zeitschrift für Ethnologie* 46:553–98.

Kunst, Jaap
1937   "Zum Tode Erich von Hornbostels," *Anthropos* 32:239–46.

Lachmann, Robert
1929   *Die Musik des Orients*. Breslau: Jedermanns Bücherei.

Merriam, Alan P.
1977   "Definitions of Comparative Musicology and Ethnomusicology: An Historical-Theoretical Perspective." *Ethnomusicology* 21:189–204.

Nettl, Bruno
1960   "Lachmann, Robert," in *Die Musik in Geschichte und Gegenwart,* F.
        Blume, ed. (Kassel: Bärenreiter), vol. 8, pp. 28–29.
1964   *Theory and Method in Ethnomusicology.* New York: Free Press.
Stumpf, Carl
1886   "Lieder der Bellakula-Indianer," *Vierteljahrsschrift für
        Musikwissenschaft* 2:405–26.
1901   "Tonsystem und Musik der Siamesen," *Beiträge zur Akustik und
        Musikwissenschaft* 3:69–138.

Nazir Ali Jairazbhoy
The First Restudy of Arnold Bake's Fieldwork in India

Arnold Adriaan Bake (1899–1963), accompanied by his wife, Cornelia (Corry), spent nearly twenty years in south Asia studying music and language and conducting ethnomusicological field research on many tribal and folk traditions, as well as those of the court, the temple, and the urban world.

Arnold's involvement with music went back to his childhood, when he displayed a remarkable musical memory[1] and took lessons on the pianoforte and in singing. He entered the University of Leiden in 1918, under a government scholarship which, in a seven-year course including the study of Arabic, Sanskrit, and several Indonesian languages, would lead to a position in the Linguistic Survey of Indonesia.[2] A government budget retrenchment, however, forced him to discontinue this course, and in 1923 he entered the University of Utrecht for graduate studies in Sanskrit under the supervision of Professor W. Caland, who advised him to combine his interests in music and Sanskrit. This decision was influenced by Arnold's attraction to Rabindranath Tagore, whom he had met in Leiden during the poet's visit to Holland a few years earlier. For his thesis Arnold chose to translate the Sanskrit musical treatise *Sangita darpana*, and having made up his mind to complete this in Shantiniketan in Bengal, he studied Bengali and ensured that Cornelia Timmers, then his fiancée, also studied the language at the School of Oriental and African Studies in London. They were married in 1925 and shortly afterwards left for the first of their several visits to India.

In addition to his thesis research, Arnold studied classical music with Pandit Bhimrao Shastri and worked with Dinendranath Tagore, grandnephew of the Nobel laureate, Rabindranath (with whom he had considerable contact), transcribing many of the latter's songs.[3] As Rabindranath had been fascinated by folk and tribal music, particularly that of the Bauls, Santals, and even fishermen's songs, performers of these communities were frequently brought to Shantiniketan to perform.[4] Thus Arnold was exposed to a great variety of music which shaped his future research. It is noteworthy that during this period the Bakes traveled to archaeological sites in India, and also to Indonesia in 1927 where Arnold, in communication with the Dutch authorities, organized the program for Rabindranath Tagore's visit to Java and Bali a few weeks later.

The Bakes returned to Holland in 1929 where Arnold completed his dissertation,[5] receiving his doctorate in 1930. After a brief stay in Europe during which Arnold gave lectures on Indian music, illustrating them by singing Indian songs, especially those of Tagore, he was tempted by Sylvain Lévy's invitation to participate in his project of filming and recording Buddhist mantras in Nepal and thus returned to India to continue his research, this time under the auspices of the Kern Institute in Leiden. Mention must also be made of Arnold's professor of Sanskrit in Leiden, J. P. Vogel, the founder of the Kern Institute, who went to great trouble to find funding for Arnold's research from private sources.

On this occasion in 1931 he took with him, in addition to a still camera, a silent 16mm camera and a wax-cylinder recorder.[6] During this trip the Bakes traveled extensively, by train, bus, private car, and on foot, visiting Nepal, Ladakh, and parts of South India. One of Arnold's major achievements was his recording of *Samavedic* chant, which Brough (1964:250; see note 1) refers to as a "remarkable feat."[7] The grant from the Kern Institute was discontinued well before the completion of this field trip, and the Bakes sustained themselves by giving recitals, mostly in schools and colleges, with Arnold singing both Western and Indian songs, and Corry accompanying him on the piano. The Bakes returned to Europe in 1934 and stayed in London for the next few years, apart from a seven-month lecture tour in North America.[8] In London Arnold worked extensively with A. H. Fox-Strangways, translating parts of several Sanskrit musical treatises for him.[9] The Bakes rented a flat in Fox-Strangway's house for a period and undoubtedly shared with him a great deal about Indian music.

Arnold's third field trip to India (and Ceylon), in 1937–46, initially supported by a Senior Research Fellowship from Brasenose College, Oxford, was evidently, at least in part, a return to some of the sites of his earlier trip in 1931–34, but with more sophisticated recording equipment. On this occasion he took with him not only a still camera and a silent 16mm film camera, but a rather unique recorder, called a Teficord, which cut grooves in the gelatin along the length of an endless loop of 35mm film. With the "Tefi" recorder it was possible to make continuous recordings of as long as one-hour duration using the longest films (20 meters), which were, however, difficult to handle.[10] In 1938–39 the Bakes carried out a survey field trip, touring extensively through South Asia in their station wagon, a converted Ford V-8. This field trip began in Colombo, Ceylon (now Sri Lanka), where they acquired the station wagon,[11] then continued in Madurai, now in Tamilnadu, where they evidently acquired another station wagon, then proceeded south to Cape Comorin, and then north (with a diversion to Madras and another to Hyderabad), mainly through the western regions of India, through Kerala, Karnataka, Maharashtra, and Gujarat, and into Sind, now a part of Pakistan, where the trip was summarily interrupted by circumstances. I have reconstructed the following map of their route,[12] assisted by Amy Catlin-Jairazbhoy, from the notes on the Tefi recordings.

The Tefi broke down while they were in Sind and was sent back to Germany to be repaired, but during its return journey to India, war broke out in 1939, and the machine never reached its destination. Fortunately, however, the Tefi had a separate playback unit which was preserved. The details of the rest of the trip are hazy.[13] We know that they went north to Ladakh, and to Ley about three months later, visiting Tibetan monasteries in Hemis, Leh, and Phyang, recording (on a wax-cylinder recorder)[14] and filming Buddhist rituals, as well as folk music and songs, often traveling on foot and on mules and finally going on to Srinagar, where Arnold was forced to convalesce for several months after a serious illness.

The Tefi playback unit was thoroughly overhauled in 1967 with a grant I received from the University of London, and although a few of the films were damaged beyond repair, most of the recordings (786 separate items) were transferred to tape by Alastair Dick with the help of a second grant from UCLA. Three sets of copies of these recordings are now extant, one at the School of Oriental and African Studies in London (SOAS) (where Arnold Bake taught for the last fifteen years of his life), a second at UCLA, and a third at the Archives and Research Centre for Ethnomusicology in New Delhi. The quality of the recordings was initially remarkably good, except for the occasional speed fluctuation caused by variations of electric current from the portable generator used by Bake. This generator was evidently rather noisy and was therefore connected to the Tefi by a long cable. It was the chauffeur's responsibility to sit by the generator to make adjustments in order to prevent the needle from straying beyond acceptable limits, while Bake made the recordings some distance away. Evidently the chauffeur's concentration lapsed periodically, causing pitch changes on a number of the recordings. By the time the Tefi films were copied in 1967,

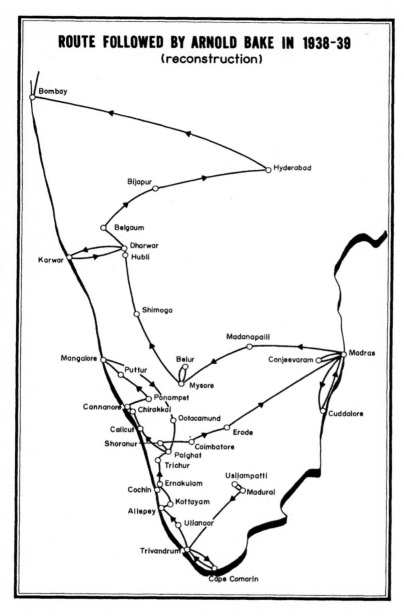

ROUTE FOLLOWED BY ARNOLD BAKE IN 1938-39
(reconstruction)

FIGURE 1. Reconstruction of route followed by Arnold Bake in 1938–39.

the film stock itself had become brittle and grooves often damaged so that tracking was not always consistent, some grooves repeating, others being skipped. Nevertheless, these recordings, with the many hours of 16mm film, which have only recently been copied (1987), and thousands of still photographs[15] provide a unique resource for the study of the more recent history of Indian music.

Although the Brasenose College Fellowship was extended until 1944, transfer of funds to India during the war years was irregular, and the amounts generally insufficient to support research. Arnold thus found employment working for a time for All-India Radio as Music Advisor in Delhi and in Calcutta, where he was Director of European Music Broadcasting in 1940. In addition the Bakes continued to give recitals as before.[16] During the war years, however, field expeditions must have been extremely difficult, and Arnold concentrated on studying, in depth, the Bengali *kirtan* tradition, actually singing with *kirtan* groups and occasionally leading them. The Bakes returned to Europe in 1946, and in 1948 Arnold was appointed Lecturer in Sanskrit at SOAS in London, with special reference to Indian Music.[17] In 1948 he was advanced to Reader.

The Bakes carried out one final field trip in 1955–56 to South Asia; this time the focus was on Nepal. On this occasion, they were part of a team of scholars from SOAS which included J. Brough. Arnold took with him a portable, full-track, E.M.I. tape recorder, a Bolex (silent) 16mm film camera, and a still camera. The recordings from this field trip, fifty hours (as stated by Brough),[18] about 3,000 feet of color and black-and-white films, and hundreds of photographs were taken in the Kathmandu valley, but include recordings of some of the tribes that had come to the valley on the occasion of the coronation of King Mahendra in 1956, at which the Bakes were present. These materials are housed in SOAS and have been studied by Carol Tingey.[19]

In 1958 Arnold and Corry were struck by a tram in Leiden, and for the last five years of his life, Arnold was severely handicapped with a broken thigh which had to be supported by a metal pin. The bone never healed, and he was in constant pain but nevertheless continued to teach at SOAS.[20]

Arnold Bake passed away in October 1963 while I was carrying out field research in India in connection with a book which he had been commissioned to write by Oxford University Press. This was to have been a comprehensive work on Indian music involving, on the one hand, historical Sanskrit treatises, and on the other, the practice of music in India ranging from the classical to the folk and tribal. Bake had undertaken this monumental work in collaboration with J. R. Marr and myself, Marr for his knowledge of South Indian classical music and Tamil sources, myself for recent North Indian classical music, Hindi, and Urdu sources, as well as some of the Muslim music traditions. My 1963–64 field trip[21] had been planned with him, and we had chosen a focus on parts of Central and Eastern India where he had not had the opportunity to carry out fieldwork. This would have been Arnold's major life work and one that only he could have completed effectively, with his vast experience of contemporary Indian performing traditions and knowledge of Sanskrit sources.

Arnold was an ethnomusicologist, who in terms of Indian studies was far ahead of his time. As a scholar, he recognized the importance of historical studies based on literary and archeological sources, but as a humanist, he was fully aware that these sources expressed the values and practices of the elite—as represented by the temple and the royal courts—not those of the populace. To understand the music of India in depth, he realized that elements of both the "greater" and "lesser" traditions needed to be taken into account. This is reflected in relatively few of his publications[22] which, apart from articles of encyclopedic scope, range from interpretations of Sanskrit musical treatises to contemporary folk performance practices of "hobby horse" and "stick" dances. One may feel inclined to diminish his importance to the scholarly world on the paucity of his publications, but it must be remembered that he was nearly fifty when he joined SOAS, his first academic appointment. In addition, he was a perfectionist and was never fully satisfied by any of his own writings. As his student and assistant, I was privileged to attend his lectures on Indian music[23] regularly for at least six years and can vouch for the fact that, although every lecture was meticulously typed and read in class, they were never exactly repeated. There was always something new that he had never said before. In fact, Arnold used to play games with me in the later part of my assistantship. I would be told the title of his next lecture and the examples (audio and film)[24] that he wanted me to assemble for it; but when I asked him about the connection between the examples, he would merely say, "Ah-ha, you'll see." And I would have to wait for the lecture. Often, I recall, he would look for my reaction when he sprang something quite unexpected during his lectures.[25]

The fun element was part of Arnold's character. In spite of his impressive size and demeanor, not to mention his awe-inspiring scholarly reputation, he loved to toy with words (especially "Spoonerisms") and to make jokes. Once, he told us, he had arrived in India and had been held up by the customs officials—they had no objection to his bringing in, what was then, sophisticated recording equipment, but found objection to the description which stated that the equipment was for 50 cycles (now more commonly known as hertz). Arnold would say, with a'smirk, that the equipment was approved, but that the cycles (i.e., bicycles) were refused entry. One of the most amusing and slightly shocking episodes I recall was when Arnold was visited by an elderly lady of about seventy. It happened to be teatime and Arnold, with a perfectly straight face, asked her if she would like a tot of pee. To her credit, she never batted an eyelid, and I was sent off to make the pot, as was my customary duty in those days.

It was always a pleasure to be and work with Bake. He was not demanding but inspired me to greater efforts than would have been the case otherwise. He never discouraged initiative on my part, and although he did not always agree with my views, he tolerated them with a hint of amusement and some kind of a joke. He was always considerate, and when he noticed that I was either tired or under a strain he would say, with a funny Indian accent, "You no good. You no good. You go home. You go home," evidently quoting from one of his memories in India. These personal reminiscences are included here to convey my attachment to Arnold and his work—one of the important reasons underlying my undertaking the Bake Restudy project.

THE BAKE FIELD TRIP OF 1938–39

It is clear that the Bakes' field trip of 1938–39 was intended as a survey of the music and performing traditions of the southern, western, and northwestern parts of South Asia to complement his research in eastern India. As is characteristic of surveys, the amount of documentation that can be collected in the short period available is inevitably limited. But, to provide justification for his approach, one should keep in mind India's half million villages and cities, not to mention innumerable languages and dialects. It is impossible for a single individual to conduct enough detailed studies to give the kind of overall view with which Arnold was concerned.

The primary source of information which was available to us for our Restudy in 1984 of the 1938–39 field trip was Arnold's catalog of the Tefi recordings. These, unfortunately, provide the barest minimum of information,[26] just the Tefi film number and item on the film, the place it was recorded, the date of the recording, a brief description or title of the item (generally without translation), and sometimes the name of the performer(s) or the name of the community to which the performer(s) belonged, as in the following examples of four of his 150 Tefi films, randomly chosen:[27]

[Tefi film no.] 20	Madura Minakshi Temple [19 February 19]38
Film 10 meters	Mr. Westlake's House [20 February] [21 February 19]38
9 items	a. tole nembi, śile nembi
	b. Tauriai Muthu
	c. Konjam karune puire
	d. Parvataraja Kumari (Minakshi) Raga Mayamalava-gaula
	e. Madavane
	f. Shivalingastotra (Raga Gaudaramakriya)
[20 February 19]38	g. Gotuvadyam (vina without frets) Raga Vijaya-Śri
[21 February 19]38	h. Raga Shankarabhara
	i. Tamil metres

21	Mr. Westlake's House [21 February 19]38 [23 February 19]38
Film 10 meters	a. Sanskrit Ramastotra—by Ramaswamy
17 items	x. idem Krishna stotra—same singer
	x. idem Subramanya stotra idem
	b. idem sandhya mantra, closing position idem
	c. 4 Tamil stotras
[23 February 19]38	d. Ganapati stotra
	e. marriage chants
	f. Purusha sukta
	g. Yajur (attempts). Bhagavan stotra
	h. Sāmaveda; Imam stomam arhate Agnaī ayāhi
	i. agnaī ayāhi
	j. hau (three times) bhraja uvāha

22. Trivandrum.	Mrs. Lakshmi Nair's songs [2 March 19]38 [12 March 19]38
Film 10 meters	a. demonstration of 34 out of the 35
7 items	classical S. Indian talas and Jhampa tala separately
	b. Vasanta Raga
	c. Kalyana Raga
	d. four lullabies, two Malayalam two Tamil

23. Cape Comorin	[5 March 19]38
Film 2 meters	a. Subhamangala (Mario Sylva & chorus of 8 men)

    b. Kapalpatu (About St. Francis Xavier by same singers)
    c. Ratnai Manakunda
    d. Kaninananagalama (?)

To illustrate some of the problems we faced, no performers' names are given for the songs in Tefi film 20, nor is there a mention of the genre of the songs, the only real clue being that it was recorded in Minakshi temple. By extraordinary good fortune we found a bhajan group in Minakshi temple, played the recordings back to them, and discovered that the present leader of the group, Tirrupati ÅcÅrya, a blind singer over sixty, was one of the singers recorded by Arnold and actually remembered the event! The group then proceeded to sing many of the same songs.

Long after the Restudy was concluded, in 1987 and 1988, copies of Arnold's 16mm silent films and his papers on microfilms were received at UCLA.[28] The latter include texts and translations of many songs from this trip prepared by many different Indian scholars. Evidently he kept no detailed records during his journey, nor any ethnographic notes, as none have been found among his papers. Instead, he sent letters to his relatives in Holland describing his experiences, keeping carbon copies for himself.[29] Arnold was also an excellent photographer and took thousands of photographs on his field trips. The original negatives are in Holland with the Voorhoeves, and some prints at SOAS. With a few exceptions these too were not available for our Restudy.[30]

In spite of the paucity of factual information available on the recordings from this trip,[31] it was possible to deduce many aspects of the Bakes' journey and Arnold's methodology. Based on the Tefi catalog which gives the places he visited and the dates of these visits, we were able to reconstruct their approximate route (see map p. 213).

On some occasions Arnold's catalog gave the venue of some of the recordings, for example, "Mr. Westlake's Garden, Madura." What was important about this information was not so much who Mr. Westlake was,[32] but the fact that Bake made many different recordings at certain locations.[33] This indicated that, in some cases at least, performers had gathered to be recorded. Arnold, through his connections with Brasenose College and other official sources, had impressive credentials and thus received a great deal of assistance from British administrators, District Commissioners and Collectors, police officers, and the like, who, through their subordinates, located performers and arranged for them to assemble at the appropriate venues.[34] Mr. Westlake was just one such person. There are several other instances of this; for example, in Cape Comorin Arnold Bake recorded *Villupâttu* [Singing to the bow] by musicians from the village Kotara, which is about ten kilometers away, and in Belgaum recorded musicians from Bail Hongal, more than thirty kilometers away.

The Bakes were also highly regarded by Indian scholars and influential people, including royalty, as is indicated by the fact that they were guests of the Maharaja of Mysore for at least three days. They were thus able to record the Maharaja's court musicians who, interestingly enough, included some from both the Karnatak and Hindustani classical traditions. The senior instrumentalist there was the vīṇā player, Venkatagiriappa, who performed for the Bakes, along with his young student, Mysore Doraiswamy Iyengar, then just seventeen. We were extremely fortunate to find Mysore Doraiswamy in Bangalore and to play back Arnold's recordings. He was thrilled to hear his guru's performance and told us that no other recordings of Venkatagiriappa had ever been made.[35]

Among the scholars who assisted them was Dr. Shivram Karanth,[36] now a well-known dramatist, who arranged two of their excursions, one in South Kanara, the other around Hyderabad, Deccan. It was he, in fact, who had arranged for Bhuta dancers, hobby-horse dancers, and other performers to assemble in a school compound in Mangalore for Arnold to film and record.

There were, of course, some occasions when the Bakes traveled to villages and documented events in their natural contexts; but it is clear that for most of Arnold's recordings on this trip, performers were generally brought together to be documented. For example, in the villages of Senpati and Ussilampatti, near Madurai,[37] Arnold Bake recorded in just two days twenty-one items, including instrumental *nagaswaram* music, stick and handkerchief dance music, hobby-horse music, devotional Hindu and Christian songs, as well as Kallar and Pallar community songs of transplanting, burial, devotion, and exorcism.

This discussion of Arnold's methodology is not intended to diminish the extraordinary achievements of the Bakes. Even with all the assistance he evidently received, a continuous and long travel period of fifteen months over such a large area of India by station wagon in 1938–39 is a daunting thought and would be grueling under the best of conditions even today. What were the roads like then, where did they stay overnight,[38] and what did they eat and drink? There could have been only a few "safe" restaurants—how did they avoid becoming ill?[39] Their work was unquestionably one of dedication, in which physical comfort could never have been a dominant consideration. On a previous trip, Dr. Karanth reported, they had trekked into Ladakh with a wax-cylinder recorder![40] This 1938–39 expedition must have seemed, at times, an endless sojourn, which was forcibly concluded, not by the weakness of their determination, but by the failure of the Teficord, problems with Arnold's health, and, undoubtedly, limited financial support after the beginning of World War II.

THE FIRST BAKE RESTUDY[41]

It is primarily in connection with the recordings Bake made on his 1938–39 trip that our Restudy was undertaken in January–May 1984. The project was funded by the American Institute of Indian Studies and was conducted with the collaboration of the Archives and Research Centre for Ethnomusicology (ARCE). The expedition, under the direction of the present author with the collaboration of Amy Catlin-Jairazbhoy, a specialist in South Indian classical music, and, at various times for short periods, joined by three members of the ARCE staff—Umashankar, Saraswati Swaminathan, and Kalpana Bandiwdekar—was carried out in the closed Mahendra jeep owned by ARCE and driven by their versatile chauffeur, Ram Gaekwad. The primary purpose of the expedition was to retrace Bake's steps in order to determine the kind and degree of musical change that had taken place in South India during the past forty-six years by attempting to rerecord the same items as in the Bake collection. Two other purposes were to acquire more information about Arnold's recordings and his field trip, and to give copies of his recordings to the original performers, their families, or their communities and to leave a copy in ARCE for those interested in further research.

Practical considerations limited our actual Restudy fieldwork period to about three months. Before this, however, over a year was spent at UCLA familiarizing ourselves with Arnold's field materials, carrying out library research on the various communities he had encountered,[42] planning the details of the trip, acquiring fieldwork equipment, reconstructing the route of the Bake trip, and, finally, writing thirty letters to scholars in various places en route, informing them of the Bakes' original fieldwork as well as our Restudy, and requesting their assistance in locating musicians relevant to it. Our requests were undoubtedly much more specific then Arnold's Bake's had been, and not being the period of the British Raj, our letters evoked little response—as we discovered when we arrived at each new venue. Very few of those contacted had made the kind of advance preparations that must have been fairly characteristic of Arnold's research. Nevertheless, we did receive a great deal of help from several Indian scholars after we arrived; indeed, without them, there would have been no Restudy.[43] But because performers had not been located in advance of our arrival, much time was lost, and on more than one occasion we were unable to follow up leads in order to stay close to our itinerary. It was, however, a most rewarding experience, not only because we encountered so many performing traditions virtually unknown to us, but because we met so many wonderful people, including a few who recalled the Bakes and their visit.

Right from the beginning, the Restudy challenged our powers of detection, even in connection with the route the Bakes had followed. But when the Restudy actually began, the problems mushroomed. Since their original trip, India had progressed from a British colony to an independent nation that wished to shake off the evidence of two hundred years of subjugation. Political boundaries had been changed, and new names (often Sanskritized or reverted to their older form) were given to many cities and towns, the classic examples being the city of Benares, whose name was changed back to Varanasi, and Cape Comorin to Kanya Kumari. Bake's approximate transcriptions of the names of small towns and villages he visited further enhanced our difficulties in locating places, many of which were not, in any case, to be found on the maps available to us.

Some of Bake's recordings had been made in what were then referred to as Criminal Tribe Settlements, in fact, policed reservations in which particular tribes and castes had been placed because their practices were contrary to the British concepts of law and justice. Soon after independence had been achieved in 1947, the barbed wire surrounding these settlements was removed, and the inmates were free to move as they wished (see note 37). Forty-six years later, when we carried out the Restudy, few remembered the location of these "criminal tribe settlements," which had long since been given respectable names, such as Gangadhar Nagar in Hubli, and it was presumed that the residents had dissipated into the broader community. Incredibly, this proved not to be the case when we located Gangadhar Nagar. The Haranshikaris, Bhats, and Banjaras who had been interred there still continued to live there after the barbed wire had been cut, even though in utterly depressed conditions—with the freedom to walk away from that world, but nowhere to go.

We also faced other problems in detection during the Restudy. Cities had, in the intervening period, grown to encompass a number of neighboring villages, some of which had been mentioned in the Bake catalog. Locating these often became a serious problem. Some had truly been absorbed into the world of the city with high-rise apartments and business premises, while others, such as the Bake-period village of Mutatara (now incorporated into Trivandrum), were merely surrounded by high-rises, the village remaining virtually intact, but out of sight of the casual viewer. Locating some of the villages in the Bake catalog was also problematic because, as we discovered, more than one village in the area evidently bore the same name. An example of this is the name Senpati, which is evidently used for three villages in the vicinity of Madurai, two of which we visited (unfortunately the wrong two, and we had no time to go to the third).

In view of the drastic political and social changes that had taken place since Arnold's original field trip, it is not surprising that we found many changes both in the music and in the context of performance and its patronage. This is not the time or place to discuss the details, which will be presented in a video-monograph format in due course.[44] On a more general level, there was much to learn. We had embarked on the Restudy with a rather naive view and approach, that we could have a fairly clear idea of continuity and change by analyzing our rerecordings of the Bake items in a kind of etic manner, not realizing that we had to deal first with the emic view. When we played a Bake recording to musicians and asked them, "Do you know this song?" and "Can you sing it?" the answers were often ambiguous. Sometimes when the answer was in the affirmative, the song they sang seemed to differ in terms of melody, rhythm, and/or structure. But on the other hand, on at least one occasion the song they sang was, in our perception, virtually identical, yet the musicians were diffident about equating their version with that recorded by Bake because one word in the initial stanza differed.

On reexamining these experiences, it became evident that the outsider's so-called "objective" views of identity and change did not necessarily coincide with those of the individual or the community concerned. From the insider's view, it is evident that the identification of one song with another was not necessarily based on *all* of its physical properties, but only those which were considered meaningful by the group concerned. This suggests the possibility that some forms of change might be endemic in all societies—and thus accepted as nonchange—whereas others (which may to us seem insignificant) may violate accepted patterns of stability within the society and are clearly recognized as change. This would then mean that change is regarded by the community concerned as the disruption of an understood evolutionary pattern, rather than as we perceive it in terms of the comparative analysis of the various components of the "then and now" phenomena. If this is the case, a comparison of the emic interpretations offered by the members of the culture with the etic perceptions of the outside researcher derived from such a Restudy may have much to contribute to the understanding of the society and its values.

Notes

1. Much of the information in this article is derived from Bake's obituary by J. Brough (Chair of the Department of India, Pakistan, Nepal, and Ceylon at the School of Oriental and African Studies in London (SOAS) published in the *Bulletin* of the School (1964 (27):245–64), as well as that of C. S. Mundy in *Folklore* (Autumn 1963 (74):498–501). This is supplemented by my own experiences as Arnold's Bake's student and assistant at SOAS from 1956–62, when I was appointed Lecturer in Indian Music, and by comments received from Dr. P. Voorhoeve, Mrs. Bake's brother-in-law.

2. This is in accordance with Dr. Voorhoeve's letter of 14 December 1988, which corrects the information provided by Brough in his obituary.

3. *Twenty-Six Songs of Rabindranath Tagore, Noted Down by Arnold A. Bake, with an Introduction by Arnold A. Bake and Philippe Stern, together with a literal Translation from the Bengali Poems and the free Translation of the same by Rabindranath Tagore.* Paris: Bibliothèque Musicale du Musée Guimet (First series, vol. 2).

4. Arnold's early photographs and films show some of these performers in Shantiniketan, but it is not known whether they were taken during this trip or the succeeding one.

5. Damodara's *Sangita darpana,* ch. i–ii, Sanskrit text with English translation, published as *Bydrage tot de kennis der Voor-Indische muziek, Proefscrift ter verkryging van den graad van Doctor in de Letteren en Wysbegeerte aan de Ryks Universiteit to Utrecht.* Paris: Paul Geuthner, 1930.

6. Two sets of the wax cylinders from this period are housed in the National Sound Archive in London and in the Berlin Phonogramm-Archiv. Tape copies of these have been made by both institutions, and a copy is with the present author. Neither of these copies is very satisfactory, but the National Sound Archive has indicated that it intends to try to improve on them at a future date. Copies of Arnold's 16mm films, recently made possible by a generous subvention from Dr. P. Voorhoeve, are now in several places, including SOAS and UCLA.

7. Actually Samavedic chant had been recorded earlier, for example, by Fox-Strangways, whose cylinders, not yet transferred to magnetic tape, are housed in the National Sound Archive in London. Arnold, however, was the first to record the Samaveda of the very conservative Nambudiri Brahmin community in Kerala. Brough (see note 1) acknowledges that Arnold told him little about the preliminary negotiations, but presumes that "the Brahmans were impressed by the warmth and charm of his personality" and thus consented to sing for him. I recall, however, Ar-

nold's telling me that the community had been opposed to the recordings, and that he had found an excommunicated member who was willing to be recorded.

8. Charlotte Frisbie has informed me that some letters with Arnold in connection with this visit are in Helen Robert's collection. There are also letters pertinent to this visit in Barchem.

9. Verbal communication from Arnold Bake.

10. Thus Arnold more often used shorter films of two, five, and ten meters.

11. Dr. Voorhoeve writes (personal communication, 14 December 1988): The station wagon "was adapted to the transport of the equipment by extra spring blades and an extension of the cabin at the back. The driver, called Francis, had to pass an extra examination for driving it, so at first a driver from the Ford garage drove them around Ceylon. After the trip through South India the first station wagon broke down, and Bake acquired a larger one, specially built for the purpose, driven by Ain Din, who was from Lahore, a great friend of my mother-in-law when she came to Kashmir in order to nurse Arnold during another illness. They used to call their station car, I think the first one, 'the elephant.' " Incidentally, I recall Arnold's mentioning Ain' Din more than once, not so much as a driver, but as a singer of Punjabi epics, such as Hir Ranjha, and I also recall Arnold's recordings of his songs.

12. This map was published previously in *Samvadi*, Newsletter of the Archives and Research Centre for Ethnomusicology (1:1 (1984)).

13. The Tefi catalog concludes at the end of March 1939. The other primary source of information is the letters Arnold wrote to his mother and sisters. Unfortunately there is a gap of nearly a year between 24 July 1938 and 28 June 1939, when the letters resume from a small Tibetan village near Leh.

14. According to Brough (1964:252; see note 1), Arnold rented, then bought, a Swedish disc recorder for this trip. In a letter dated 28 June 1939, Arnold states that he made recordings on a wax-cylinder machine and says that he also made recordings on his old phonograph, presumably this Swedish disc recorder. Of considerable interest for fieldwork is Arnold's comment in his following letter of 15 July that wherever possible he made two recordings of the same event, one for analysis, the other for purposes of preservation.

15. Some enlargements of these, which were part of an exhibit of Arnold's photographs, entitled "Masks and Faces," are still at SOAS; the major part of the photographs with negatives are, however, with Dr. Voorhoeve in Barchem, Holland. Frances Shepherd of Dartington College of Arts in Devon examined them in detail in 1988, and the present author, with Amy Catlin-Jairazbhoy, copied more than a thousand relevant photographs onto video-tape format in July 1989.

16. By a strange coincidence, the Bakes performed at my school (Doon School) in Dehra Dun, probably in 1942 or 1943. I cannot recall the details of their program, but clearly remember that Arnold sang not only Western songs, but also Tagore songs and Bengali folk songs. Our music teacher, Mr. Shirodkar, had already taught us some of the Bengali songs Arnold sang. I also remember being astonished at his size.

17. Brough (1964:256; see note 1) gives Arnold's title as Lecturer in Sanskrit and Indian Music, which, from my recollection, was not quite accurate.

18. I recall, however, that there were fifty-six five-inch reels, each of fifteen or twenty minutes duration, since they were full-track recordings.

19. Ms. Tingey's M. Mus. thesis from Goldsmith College, London, is entitled *"The Nepalese Field Work of Dr. Arnold A. Bake: A Guide to the Sound Recordings"* (1985). In 1987 she conducted in Nepal a Restudy of the Bake Nepalese materials from both the 1931 and 1955–56 trips, and she has made a catalog of Arnold's still photographs from these two trips.

20. Arnold spent the rest of his life using crutches, and on many occasions I transported him to SOAS in my Austin Mini from his house in Lansdowne Road. Getting in and out of the vehicle was a major and painful operation for him.

21. Materials from the trip have just been published by the UCLA Ethnomusicology Program (1988). They are in the form of ten talks which I originally gave for the BBC Third Programme in 1969, on three cassette tapes accompanied by a monograph.

22. A nearly complete list is given in the bibliography prepared by John Marr and Wendy Marr appended to Brough's obituary.

23. Just one hour a week during the academic nine-month year. These were the only lectures he gave regularly; otherwise he worked with students individually and carried on his research. I was privileged to be one of those students, and we worked together on the translation and interpretation of several Sanskrit musical treatises, including *Natyasastra, Sangita Ratnakara, Brhaddesi,* and others.

24. It is now horrifying to recall that the film edits I prepared for his lectures were from his original film footage—evidently he could never afford to have copies made.

25. Many of these lectures have been preserved at SOAS.

26. Arnold, of course, had a phenomenal memory and seldom had difficulty locating specific items.

27. We plan to publish the complete catalog of the Tefi recordings and Arnold's other field materials at a future date.

28. Thanks to Richard Widdess, now Lecturer in Indian Music at SOAS, who coordinated the copying of Arnold's films.

29. Dr. Voorhoeve reports that Arnold generally wrote one "work" letter per week, first to his mother, and after her decease to his sister Bertha. All letters are typewritten in Dutch, and copies are now in the India Office collection in London, the originals in Barchem with Dr. Voorhoeve. In all, the India Office has 378 letters written by Arnold—undoubtedly of great importance for the Restudy—but, unfortunately, it was not possible to examine them before the first Restudy was conducted. The Bakes, in addition, wrote personal letters, some of which might contain information relevant to future restudy projects. We visited Barchem in July 1989 to make copies of many photographs and were able to get rough translations of pertinent sections of numerous Bake letters from both Dr. Voorhoeve and Dr. Felix van Lamsweerde.

30. I had some prints made of Arnold's photographs of musical instruments, while his assistant, for one of my projects. For purposes of the Restudy, we needed photographs of the musicians so that they could be identified, but, unfortunately, had very few.

31. Much more is known of Arnold's field trip of 1931–33, as Arnold published a report of it entitled "Dr. A. Bake's Researches in Indian Music and Folklore" (*Indian Arts and Letters* 7(1)).

32. Since examining the microfilms of Arnold's papers, it is clear that Mr. Westlake was the District Commissioner in Madurai.

33. From Arnold's films, we also found other examples of this, such as, several different performers filmed in the same school compound.

34. This is confirmed by the microfilms which contain copies of official letters from "The Secretary to His Excellency the Crown Representative" to "The Hon'ble the Resident at . . . " (the places listed are Hyderabad, Mysore, Rajputana, States of Western India, Punjab States) and to "The Resident for . . . " (Baroda and the Gujarat States, Madras States, and Kashmir), "kindly" inviting them to afford all possible facilities to "Dr. Arnold Bake, Member of the Council of the India Society, during his visit to the State(s)." Also included are copies of affirmative responses.

35. Evidently, Venkatagiriappa had been approached by His Master's Voice, but "they didn't hit it off," according to Mysore Doraiswamy.

36. We were fortunate to find and interview Dr. Karanth in 1984 living in the small town of Shaligram in Southern Kanara. At 82, he was still sprightly and active professionally. In his two autobiographies, written in Kannada, he devotes several pages to his contact with the Bakes, not only in India, but also in London and Amsterdam. Among his recollections were the size of the Bakes (Arnold was about six foot three, Corry also tall by South Indian standards), their absence of concern for their health (they drank local water without any means of purification), and their fearlessness, courage, and dedication (trekking to Ladakh with all their equipment).

37. The British had interned a number of "anti-social" castes and tribes in settlements of this kind surrounded by barbed wire and guarded by policemen, with access restrictions, inmates only being allowed to venture outside under special conditions and required to register at police stations on arrival elsewhere. These settlements were located in many parts of India, and Arnold recorded and filmed in at least two of these, one in Hubli, the other in Ussilampatti.

38. There were, of course, Dak Bungalows and Circuit Houses that had been located by the British all over India, equipped with cooks and other facilities for traveling officials. The sometimes hectic pace of parts of their field trip must surely have forced them to other living arrangements and to accept the hospitality of Indian homes.

39. In fact, Arnold had long periods of illness in India, but not from eating unsafe food, according to Dr. Voorhoeve; Dr. Shivram Karanth confirms that the Bakes had completely adjusted to India's food, ate in their home, and drank unboiled water.

40. The Bakes did this again in 1939.

41. As mentioned above, note 19, a second Bake Restudy, based on Arnold's Nepalese materials, was undertaken by Carol Tingey in 1987. We plan, for a future date, another restudy, this time with better preparation, including copies of Arnold's films and photographs.

42. We could find no reference to some of the communities he recorded, for example, the Haranshikaris.

43. Among the many who assisted us, mention should be made of T. S. Parthasarathy, Chumar Choondal, and L. S. Rajagopalan, as well as the musician Mysore Doraiswamy Iyengar, who were particularly helpful.

44. A preliminary, incomplete edit of this video tape was shown at Bruno Nettl's conference on the history of ethnomusicology in Urbana, Illinois, in April 1988.

Charles Capwell

Marginality and Musicology in Nineteenth-Century Calcutta: The Case of Sourindro Mohun Tagore

IN RECENT YEARS I have been interested in matters pertaining to music in nineteenth-century Calcutta. More particularly, I have been interested in the involvement of one man—Sourindro Mohun Tagore—in the musical matters of that time and place. Because Bengal is out of the mainstream of the development of Hindustani music, and Sourindro Mohun is now nearly forgotten, this interest may seem an idle occupation rather than a scholarly endeavor, but as I have suggested elsewhere in reference to the writing of history, it is the richness of the historical record that illuminates and signifies rather than its consequences.

In this regard, the historian Eugen Weber, in reviewing a colleague's book, observed that "Historians like to bet on horses that have won, which means that also-rans are often lost from sight and winners tend to be idealized. But society . . . consists of individual people who live in groups; and one cannot know the whole if one ignores the part, or misplaces it. . . . To see society clear we must approach it through its members" (Weber 1988:52). Weber praises Michel Bruguière for doing the latter in his book *Gestionnaires et profiteurs de la révolution* through the use of prosopography[1]—the delineation of individuals in groups—a method Bruguière defends with the rhetorical question "Is it not very natural, then, to accord to the men who figure [in archival records] a certain coefficient of importance and to admit that in every case nothing that concerns them is indifferent to General History?" (Bruguière 1986:20). A teleological interpretation of the past—not unknown in the field of musical scholarship—may reveal much about what is important to the present, but we cannot determine who and what had significance to the past by selecting only the people and events that have connections to the currently significant.

Among the citations given in the *Oxford English Dictionary* to illustrate the original meaning of prosopography—which, incidentally, was the physical description of a single individual—is one that pairs it with ethopea, or the description of the mind and manners of an historic character,[2]

FIGURE 1. Sourindro Mohun Tagore. Photograph courtesy R. P. Gupta, Calcutta.

and it is through a kind of ethopea of Sourindro Mohun Tagore that I wish, in this article, to demonstrate my conviction of his importance to a full understanding of our field despite his not really having been one of the "horses that have won," in the words of Eugen Weber, or even one of the sires of winning horses.

In my title I have referred to the concept of "marginality," and I should say why. The Marginal Man, introduced by Robert Park in *The American Journal of Sociology* in 1928, was described in a book of that name by

Everett Stonequist in 1937. In the decades since then there has been much wrangling over the precise nature of the marginal man's personality and his social environment and over what exact relation, if any, exists between them. For my purposes, the marginal man or woman is one who straddles two groups. H. F. Dickie-Clark in his book on the Coloured Population of Durban, South Africa, refers to a similar idea of the marginal man in his discussion of Stonequist's doctoral dissertation; according to Dickie-Clark, Stonequist "says that anybody in transition from one group to another has [and now the quote continues with Stonequist's words] 'something—however mild and evanescent—of the marginal man's character'" (Dickie-Clark 1966:9). Transition, however, is not basically part of marginality, I think, since it implies change of position from one group to another, the case in liminal situations such as progress from one age grade to another; but as Stonequist points out in his book, the marginal person begins in childhood with no awareness of conflict, progresses in adolescence to awareness of his ambivalent position, and then achieves some adult accommodation with is permanent situation between two groups (Stonequist 1937:121–23). And Stonequist further suggests that "a certain degree of personal maladjustment is inherent in the marginal situation" (ibid.:201).

A slightly more positive aspect of marginality is found in the special case of the intelligentsia.[3] In their classic essay on "The Cultural Role of Cities," Redfield and Singer associate the marginal class with the intelligentsia whom they locate in secondary urban centers defined as the locus for the colonial contract between an indigenous, established culture and a newly dominant foreign one (Redfield and Singer 1962). Primary urbanization, in contrast, arises in transition from folk to peasant societies with their associated urban centers in which the class of "literati" elaborates and canonizes indigenous tradition. Associated with the idea of primary and secondary urbanization are ortho- and heterogenesis. "What makes the orthogenetic aspect of a city," Redfield and Singer say, "is the integration and uniform interpretation of preceding culture, whether its origins be one or several" (ibid.:335). In contrast, they say, "in cities of predominantly heterogenetic cultural influence there is a disposition to see the future as different from the past. It is this aspect of the city that gives rise to reform movements, forward looking myths, and planning, revolutionary or melioristic" (ibid.:340). Having developed their ideas largely on an understanding of the Indian situation, Redfield and Singer, not surprisingly, have projected in their concept of the secondary, heterogenetic urban center a fine description of colonial Calcutta.

It was in this city, in 1840, that Sourindro Mohun Tagore was born into one of the wealthiest and most influential Bengali families. Claiming descent from one of the eminent Brahmins brought from central India to Bengal in the tenth century by King Adisura, the Tagore family had more recently suffered a loss of caste prestige when one of its members married the daughter of a man who had once accidentally smelled the odor of polluting food.[4] From that time on, one might argue, the Tagores had been marginal persons since their culture was identical with that of the most elevated and revered segment of society, yet they were prevented from full social participation in it by an insuperable barrier.

Sourindro Mohun's great-great-grandfather Jayram established the Tagore family in Calcutta in the mid-eighteenth century, undoubtedly attracted there by the possibility of financial advancement through service to the East India Company. When it became necessary for the British to rebuild the fortifications of their factory after an attack by the Nawab of Bengal, they turned to Jayram for assistance and secured the use of his land for the erecting of Fort William. The money Jayram gained from the sale of the land, and possibly from help in construction of the fort, established the family fortune, the division of which by his two surviving sons resulted in a permanent alienation among their descendants. The elder son, Darpanarayan, was the great-grandfather of Sourindro Mohun, and the younger son, Nilmoni, was the great-grandfather of Rabindranath, the Nobel Laureate.

Fort William, built on the original Tagore property in Calcutta, became in 1800 the site of a new college where Company servants were trained in the vernaculars of the country. Bengali, Hindi, and Urdu all received an impetus to their modern development through the interests of foreign and native scholars employed in the College, and there was an interest in Persian, Sanskrit, Telegu, Marathi, and Kannada as well. In the view of the American historian David Kopf, this institution was the official arm of British orientalism which had begun on a more personal and amateur level in the eighteenth century. The aim of the founders and supporters of the college, according to Kopf, was to enable the British to achieve real competence in and understanding of the culture of India (Kopf 1969). The Bengali historian Sisir Kumar Das agrees with this but disputes the motive:

> The British Orientalists, even when they were protagonists of British colonialism, succeeded in keeping their scholarly persuasion free from their official duties and colonial interests. The Fort William College, on the other hand, was established primarily to help the British civil servants . . . and was but a means

to meet the demands of the administrative necessities of the
British rulers in India. . . . The kind of exercise the College encouraged very clearly indicates its interest in the living languages of India and of the adjoining countries, as opposed to
the Asiatic Society's which was primarily in the Indian past.
(Das 1978:xi–xii)

The Asiatic Society of Bengal had been inaugurated in 1784 by Sir
William Jones, a man whose learning and competence are truly astonishing
and included the realm of Indian music. In a discussion of Jones in his
book *Orientalism*, Edward W. Said makes an observation that effectively
links the attitudes of the Asiatic Society and of Fort William College as outlined by Das. "Proper knowledge of the Orient," Said says in reference to
Jones,

proceeded from a thorough study of the classical texts, and
only after that to an application of those texts to the modern
Orient. Faced with the obvious decrepitude of the modern Oriental, the European Orientalist found it his duty to rescue some
portion of a lost, past classical Oriental grandeur in order to fa-
cilitate ameliorations in the present Orient. What the European
took from the classical Oriental past was a vision (and thousands of facts and artifacts) which only he could employ to the
best advantage; to the modern Oriental he gave facilitation and
amelioration—and, too, the benefit of his judgment as to what
was best for the modern Orient. (Said 1978:79)

The rediscovery of a glorious Hindu past and the corollary desire of the
new Calcutta intelligentsia for its rehabilitation paradoxically led in 1816
to the foundation of the Hindu College, an institution for the imparting of
European education to Bengali youth. Among the founders was Gopi Mohun Tagore, the grandfather of Sourindro Mohun, and other prominent
Bengalis such as the Maharaja of Burdwan, who along with Gopi Mohun
was a lifetime governor of the institution (Furrell 1892:72; Kopf
1969:180). Although meant to convey European culture to its students,
this college was the locus of a serious crisis in 1831 when Henry Derozio, a
twenty-two-year-old instructor of mixed European and Indian parentage,
had to be dismissed for encouraging a group of admiring students to reject
everything Indian in favor of a total Westernization (Kopf 1969:259).
Derozio's attitudes were spawned in a new colonial atmosphere which had
started with the arrival in 1828 of Governor General William Bentinck.

Bentinck saw his mission as doing away with the habit of training up Company servants to be versed in the ways of the East and instead, as Thomas Babington Macaulay proposed to Parliament in 1835, to impart to Indians the incomparable benefits of a modern European education (ibid.:240–43).

Progressive in educational matters and himself fluent in several European as well as Indian languages, Gopi Mohun was nevertheless a staunchly conservative Hindu who resisted the monotheistic reform of Hinduism that was virtually to become the family religion of the junior branch of the Tagore family. Through his son Haro Kumar, Gopi Mohun passed on to his grandson Sourindro this taste for European culture and learning combined with a conservative religious belief and also a desire to raise the status of Indian music.

After receiving private instruction from European or Anglo-Indian tutors as a child, like his grandfather and father before him, Sourindro Mohun entered the Hindu College at age nine and continued his studies there for nine years. But he was also taught Sanskrit in order to continue a family tradition that had produced notable Sanskrit pundits in the past. As the family had retained the services of professional Hindustani musicians at least since the time of Gopi Mohun, Sourindro, after leaving Hindu College, and his elder brother Jotindro naturally received instruction in music, too. European music was also learned at home from an unidentified German professor (Tagore 1899:II). While Jotindro composed Bengali songs on the household organ and harmonium, it was his younger brother who was credited with having popularized the latter instrument in Indian music (gaṅgōpādhyāy 1979:20, 31).

Given the time and place of Sourindro Mohun's birth and his educational and cultural background, it is not surprising that his first musical publication, coming out in 1870, was an extended lecture having to do with the contact of musical cultures and the need for the uplift and improvement of the now decayed, yet once flourishing art of music in India. The title of this publication, which was originally a lecture, is *jātīyasaṅgītaviṣayakaprastāva*, which could be translated as *A Proposal Concerning National Music*; but I think the title is itself a translation of Carl Engel's work *An Introduction to the Study of National Music* (1866), to which Sourindro Mohun's lecture is indebted for some of its information and examples. This Carl Engel is, of course, the immigrant Englishman and not the later immigrant American. As his book on national music was published in London in 1866, only four years earlier than Sourindro Mohun's lecture, we can take it that the latter made every effort to keep up with current European musical literature and that these words of his from 1899 merit credibility: "With a view to collect all available information on the Science and Art of Music [I have] procured rare works from England, and old Sanskrit manuscripts from Benares, Cashmere, Nepaul, and other distant places, and have therewith established a musical library in my house which is the most valuable of any to be found in this country" (Tagore 1899:II).

In his 1870 lecture Sourindro Mohun explains the motivation for his interest in music in a way that will certainly be readily understood by his colleagues today.

> There is such a connection between music and Man's nature that how far there are differences and in what particular subjects there is unity regarding the quality and character of different races, these questions, too, could be determined if one were to know about national music quite thoroughly. Therefore, it is no less essential for ethnologists than for musicologists to investigate through the study of music what connections exist among the various natures of men.[5] (ṭhākura [1870]:39–40)

A more personal motivation was perhaps the immediate impetus to Sourindro Mohun's musical activism. In the beginning remarks of his lecture he notes the need to accept improvement from foreign music cultures when they have something to offer. Then taking an illustration of musical borrowing from Engel to show the circumstances when this is possible, he concludes with this rhetorical question: "India has been under British rule a long time and has learned many things from her, but does her music yet satisfy us?"[6] (ibid.:11). The implication here, stated quite plainly elsewhere in the lecture, is that India has a national music sufficient for its own needs; but attached to this belief in his own cultural heritage, in Sourindro Mohun's mind, is the colonial conviction that his heritage is a decayed and degraded one in need of rehabilitation and restitution to its past greatness. His frustration and impatience are evident when he exclaims: "O, Mother India!!! It is a sad fact that in this year of 1870, while many arts and sciences are being discussed indicating the advancement of civilization, we still see none of your offspring attempting to improve the national music"[7] (ibid.:30). Of course, he was being disingenuous as he certainly saw himself as fulfilling this role—one which arose naturally from the circumstances of Calcutta that gave "rise to reform movements, forward looking myths, and planning, revolutionary or melioristic," as Redfield and Singer said of heterogenetic, secondary cities (1962:340).

The melioristic impetus behind Sourindro Mohun's musical activity stemmed from a particularly colonial and marginal frame of mind, one which is closely examined by the Bengali psychological historian Ashis Nandy in his book *The Intimate Enemy: Loss and Recovery of Self under Colonialism*. In Nandy's view, the process of colonialism "alters cultural priorities on both sides and brings to the centre of the colonial culture sub-cultures previously recessive or subordinate in the two confronting cultures" (Nandy 1983:2).

The traditional balance in Indian culture among *puruṣatva*, the essence of masculinity, *nārītva*, the essence of femininity, and *klībatva*, the essence of hermaphroditism (ibid.:8), was altered in line with British cultural change in the nineteenth century that delegitimized women and children, as well as the aged, in opposition to the ideal of youthful masculine virility, vigor, and productiveness (ibid.:4–17, passim). The glory of ancient India came to be seen by the colonials of both sides as the glory of the martial and princely caste of *kṣatrīyas*: "Many nineteenth-century Indian movements of social, religious and political reform, and many literary and art movements as well—tried to make Ksatriyahood the 'true' interface between the rulers and ruled as a new, nearly exclusive indicator of authentic Indianness" (ibid.:7).

The success of British colonialism in India rested on the acceptance by the British and the Indians of this description of things—the British were adult, vigorous, and masculine; the Indians were childlike, effeminate, and weak but could be helped to recover their ancient virtue. Opposition to the British was on the same terms—it had to be martial and macho, but, of course, would remain ineffectual. As Nandy observes, the astonishing and foolhardy bravery of young Bengali terrorists in the late nineteenth and early twentieth centuries had little effect; it took Gandhi to turn the tables by ignoring the colonial game rules with his childlike simplicity and feminine passivity.

How does Sourindro Mohun fit in with this picture? We have already seen his acceptance of the European orientalist view that Indian culture was degraded and needed rehabilitation. Then how did he set about this rehabilitation? First through patronage. While it was most likely his elder brother Jotindro who first brought the musician Ksetro Mohun Goswami into the household, Sourindro was his particular patron and student.

Ksetro Mohun was a prominent member of what was considered the one legitimate link to the Hindustani music tradition in Bengal and which was associated with the courtly city Visnupur, then a part of the Tagore family properties.[8] In 1869 Ksetro Mohun published, with the patronage and help of his student Sourindro Mohun, a book on music called *saṅgītasāra* or *The Essence of Music* ([gosvāmi] 1879). A year later, when Sourindro Mohun delivered the lecture mentioned above, he introduced this, the first modern Bengali book of its kind, to his audience with this rhetorical statement: "As in times past with the establishment of various governments, Indians will not try to improve their musical science according to the cultivation of a canon—Is this how we will be mocked and ridiculed by European and other cultivated societies?"[9] (ṭhākura 1870:66). And then he asks what book exists in Bengali for the improvement of music other than that of his teacher.

A salient feature of his teacher's work is the use of a newly devised Bengali notation, the inspiration for which is clear from these words of the author: "What intelligent person would deny that the root cause of the prosperity of European music is notation?"[10] ([gosvāmi] 1879:80). After reference to Burney's discussion of the development of notation in the West, and references to the history of Greek contacts with India in the *Encyclopaedia Britannica*, the *Encyclopedia Americana*, and Pocock's *India in Greece*, Ksetro Mohun comes to the conclusion that the idea of notation was originally borrowed from India by the Greeks (ibid.:84; ṭhākura [1870]:65).

Much of Sourindro Mohun's later musical activity was devoted to promoting the utility of notation, and it became a subject for heated confrontation between him and an English critic named Charles Baron Clarke (sometimes spelled Clark). The latter grew up in a district of England apparently well known for its musical activity, and he retained an amateur interest in music throughout his life. He had been trained as a mathematician at Cambridge where he was bracketed third wrangler in the math tripos; but despite this he pursued a botanical career and was for a while Director of the Botanical Garden in Calcutta (Boulger 1912). While in Bengal he was also from time to time Inspector of Schools, and in this position he was enjoined in 1874 to review a number of music books which had recently appeared; among these were works by Ksetro Mohun and Sourindro Mohun. Clarke vehemently attacked the use of Bengali notation in their books and declared that European notation, used by one of the authors, was much to be preferred (Clark 1874). Sourindro Mohun thereupon wrote a rebuttal that appeared in the newspaper *Hindu Patriot*; this he later published as an independent essay and still later included it in his most widely known publication *Hindu Music from Various Authors* (Tagore 1965), an anthology of articles, mostly by Europeans, and mostly on Indian music. In defense of an Indian notation, Sourindro Mohun expresses himself in a way that could be thought appropriate to a more contemporary ethnomusicologist:

> Every nation that has a music of its own has also its own system of notation for writing it. Whether that system be an advanced one or not [the music] cannot be correctly expressed in the notation of another nation, however improved and scientific it may be. . . . Every civilized nation that has a music of its own has also a system of notation adapted to the peculiarities of that music. (ibid.:366, 380)

These words echo those of his teacher who said, "We deny absolutely the universal suitability of European notation"[11]([gosvāmi] 1879:87). To support his point, Sourindro Mohun makes passing reference to, among others, Chinese notation discussed by de Guignes and by E. W. Style, Japanese notation mentioned by Howard Malcolm—who also discusses that of Burma and Thailand—Tibetan notation mentioned by Capt. Turner, Egyptian notation in Villoteau's work on Egypt, and finally, Turkish notation as discussed in an article in the *Harmonicon*, an English music journal.

Insisting on his own notation, Sourindro Mohun employed it for the rehabilitation of native music by adopting it for use in the music schools he was the first to found on the European model. These schools Clarke grudgingly approved although he would naturally have preferred the use of Western notation in them rather than the new Bengali system (Capwell 1986:154–55). The latter he derisively referred to as "Nationalist," thereby openly recognizing the implicit political component in its creation.

Nationalist, Sourindro Mohun undoubtedly was, in this one vigorous—could one say *kṣatrīya*-like?—manifestation of opposition to British hegemony; but his action recalls to mind Ashis Nandy's dictum that "colonialism creates a culture in which the ruled are constantly tempted to fight their rulers within the psychological limits set by the latter. It is not an accident that the specific variants of the concepts with which many anti-colonial movements in our times have worked have often been the products of the imperial culture itself and, even in opposition, these movements have paid homage to their respective cultural origins" (Nandy 1983:3).

In other matters, Sourindro Mohun was a fervent and conservative loyalist. Indeed, many of the books he published that are of musical interest were encomia to the Empress or the Prince of Wales couched in terms that are apt to seem fulsome to us, yet his monograph entitled *Hindu Loyalty* (Tagore 1883), in which he documents the traditional Hindu reverence for monarchs and its contemporary validity, leaves no doubt about his sincerity. It was always as a Hindu, naturally, that he expressed his fealty to his monarch; somewhat less naturally, he always championed the restitution of Indian music as "Hindu" music, and six hundred years of the cultural contributions of the Muslims were pretty much ignored in his view, except when the decay of Hindu music was attributed to their influence. As his teacher expressed it:

> If the practice of notation is so old, then how did we come to lose it? To this we may answer that as India, through time and chance, came into the hands of *yavana*s, acquaintance with various of our treatises was lost, and by the neglect of Sanskrit treatises, canonic music was also neglected; but the very *yavana* kings, who bore such malice toward Hindu learning, were so far attracted by the excellence of our music that though they abandoned its other parts, they could in no way relinquish its practice, and they initiated the custom of the oral transmission of music. Therefore, on account of its prevalence, over the course of time this also became the custom for Hindus . . . [12]
> ([gosvāmi] 1879:85)

The word *yavana*, with a connotation of "outsider barbarian," was originally used in reference to Alexander's Greeks and was later used, as it still is, by Hindus to refer to Muslims. The persistent reference to "Hindu Music" in the work of Sourindro Mohun, and the implication that its present decrepitude could be attributed to Muslim hegemony, once again recalls to mind Ashis Nandy's penetrating insights into Indian colonialism. "The anti-Muslim stance of much Hindu nationalism can be construed as partly a displaced hostility against the colonial power which could not be expressed directly because of the new legitimacy created within Hinduism for this power" (Nandy 1983:267, n35). As I have just pointed out, much of Sourindro Mohun's musical activity contributed to the construction of that new legitimacy within Hinduism of the imperial power, and the corollary idea of a hostility displaced toward Muslim culture is a compelling one.

For all his activity on behalf of the betterment of Hindu music, as he thought of it, and on behalf of increasing its prestige in foreign eyes, Sourindro Mohun has had little attention from musical scholars after his death. During his lifetime, he was a corresponding or honorary member of literally dozens of musical and other learned societies in Europe and elsewhere, and he sent collections of books and instruments to various places around the world where, in some cases, they may still be examined. As a conservative Hindu, however, he never ventured across the sea since this would have caused a loss of caste.

Although *Grove's Dictionary of Music and Musicians* was published during his lifetime, he is not mentioned there; perhaps his time has come, however, as he is to be found in *The New Grove*. The prosopography of him that I have presented here is more in the nature of a cartoon for a full portrait than the completed portrait itself. I hope this sketch has been detailed enough, nevertheless, to suggest that Sourindro Mohun Tagore deserves a place in the intellectual history of our discipline. Even his marginality is pertinent to us since, as Stonequist says of the marginal man, "he combines the knowledge and insight of the insider with the critical attitude of the outsider. . . . If it is true that [quoting John Dewey's *How We Think*] 'the origin of thinking is some perplexity, confusion, or doubt,' then the marginal man is likely to do more reflecting than the ordinary person" (Stonequist 1937:155). In this regard, all of us, as ethnomusicologists seeking to comprehend the emic as well as the etic view, are marginal men and women like Sourindro Mohun Tagore.

Notes

1. See Stone 1972:107–40 for a discussion of the term. I am indebted for this reference to Professor Blair Kling, my colleague in history at the University of Illinois, Urbana-Champaign.

2. "1813 *Monthly Magazine* XXXVI.330 'An Historic character, says a German professor, should consist of two parts, the *proso[po]graphy*, or description of the person, and the *ethopea*, or description of the mind and manners.' "

3. Arnold Toynbee's discussion of this term is of particular interest to students of Bengal: "In any community that is attempting to solve the problem of adapting its life to the rhythm of an exotic civilization to which it has been either forcibly annexed or freely converted, there is need of a special social class . . . and the class which is called into existence—often quite abruptly and artificially—in response to this demand has come to be known generically, from the special Russian name for it, as the intelligentsia (a word whose meaning is expressed in its very formation, in which a Latin root and a Western idea are acclimatized in Russian by being given a Slavonic termination). The intelligentsia is a class of liaison-officers who have

learnt the tricks of an intrusive civilization's trade so far as may be necessary to enable their own community, through their agency, just to hold its own in a social environment in which life is ceasing to be lived in accordance with the local tradition and is coming more and more to be lived in the style that is imposed by the intrusive civilization upon the aliens who fall under its domination. . . . This liaison class suffers from the congenital unhappiness of the bastard and the hybrid. . . . An intelligentsia is hated and despised by its own people. . . . Through its awkward presence in their midst it is a living reminder of the hateful but inescapable alien civilization. . . . The intelligentsia's unpardonable offence in the eyes of its own kith and kin is the very indispensability of the social services which the intelligentsia performs. . . . And, while the intelligentsia thus has no love lost upon it at home, it also has no honour paid to it in the country whose manners and customs and tricks and turns it has so laboriously and ingeniously mastered. In the earlier days of the historic association between India and England a Hindu intelligentsia which the British Raj had fostered for its own administrative convenience was sometimes ridiculed by English philistines who dishonoured their own nation in insulting their Indian fellow subjects. . . . The intelligentsia is at the philistine's mercy because the essence of the intelligentsia's profession is, after all, mimesis; its art consists in a *tour de force*. . . . It will be seen that the intelligentsia complies in double measure with our fundamental definition of a proletariat by being 'in' but not 'of' two societies and not merely one; and while it may console itself in the first chapter of its history with the ironical reflection that it is an indispensable organ of both these bodies social, and that this very indispensability is the head and front of its offending, it is robbed of even this consolation as time goes on. . . . A Peter the Great wants so many Russian chinovniks or an East India Company so many Bengali clerks . . . [but] The process of manufacturing an intelligentsia is still more difficult to stop than it is to start; for the contempt in which the liaison class is apt to be held by those who profit by its services is more than offset by its prestige in the eyes of those who are eligible for enrolment in it; and the competition becomes so keen that the number of candidates rapidly increases out of all proportion to the number of opportunities for employing them. When this stage is reached, the original nucleus of an intelligentsia . . . becomes swamped by the adventitious mass of an 'intellectual proletariat' which is idle and destitute as well as outcast" (Toynbee 1939:154–57, passim).

4. This information and the biographical data that follow on various members of the Tagore family is based on Furrell.

5. "ābār soṅgīter sahito mānob prokṛitir ēto sombandho ýe bhinno bhinno jātir parosparer bhāb ebaṅ caritrer katodūr bibhinnotā ebaṅ kōn kōn biṣayer ēktā āche, jātīýo soṅgīt uttom rupe jānā thākile, ihāō abodhāroṇ karā ýāite pāre/ atoebo jātīýo soṅgīt śikṣā dvārā bhinno bhinno monuṣýer prokṛitir parospor kirup sambandho tāhā onusandhān karā soṅgītbitdiger pakṣe ýēmon prayōjonīýo ethnalojiṣṭ (*Ethnologist*) arthāt nṛitattvobitdiger pakṣe tāhā apekṣā kōno matei alpo nahe/"

6. "bhārotbarṣbāsirā ēto dīrghokāl parýanto susabhýo briṭis jātir adhīne āchen ebaṅ kathito susabhýo jāti hoite nānābidh darśonādi śāstrośikṣā koritechen ekathā satýo baṭe kintu sabhýo mohāśayrā bolun dekhi? ihāder soṅgīter prokṛitir 'abicolitattvo ēkhon parýanto bilakṣoṇ rohiýāche ki nā?"

7. "he mātoḥo bhārotbhūmi!!! ākṣeper biṣay, 1792 śokābdī gato hay, sabhyotā bṛiddhi sucok bhinno bhinno śāstrādi āndōlito hoiteche, kintu tōmār kōno susantānke ājiō jātīyo soṅgīt samunnotir ceṣṭā korite dekhite pāi nā/"

8. "He owns extensive landed property in several districts of Bengal and among the estates [is] . . . Bishenpur, at one time the principality of a historical house and the seat of musical learning" (Tagore 1899:10). On Visnupur as a musical center see Owens 1969, mukhopādhyāya 1980, and Capwell 1990.

9. "bhinno śāson somāgomer pūrbbābosthār nyāy bhārotbāsirā soṅgīt bidyār śāstrānuyāyik carccā bā tāhār unnoti ceṣṭā karen nā ei boliyā iurōpīyo ō anyānyo sabhyojon samāje ki āmrā dhikkṛito ō upohosito hoibo?"

10. "iurōpīyo soṅgīter śribṛiddhir [obscured word] kāroṇ ye, likhanproṇālī, ihā kōn buddhimān byákti svīkār nā koriben?"

11. ". . . iuropīyo svarolipir biśvoprocolitatvosaṁbandhe āmrā ēkebārei asvīkār kori. . ."

12. "svarolipiprothā yodi purāton, tobe tāhār lōp hoilo kēno? tāhār ei uttor ye, kāl ō adṛiṣṭokrome bhārote yabonhastogato hōyāte āmādiger anyānyo śāstrer ālōconār biluptābasthā hoiyā poṛe eban saṅskṛit śāstro hatādṛto haōyāy śāstrānugato soṅgīterō hatādor hay, parantu hinduśāstro bidbeṣī yabonrājārā hinudiger soṅgīter utkarṣe ētodūr ākṛiṣṭo hoiyā poṛiyāchilen ye, dveṣbhābe uhār anyānyo aṅśo porityág koriyāō kriyāsiddhāṅṣoṭī kōnomatei tyāg korite pāren nāi, tāhārā mowkhikrupei soṅgīter śikṣār prothā probarttito karen/ tajjātir probaltā hetu kālkrome hinudiger pakṣeō prothā procolito hoiyā poṛiyāche. . . ."

Works Cited

Boulger, George Simonds
1912   "Clarke, Charles Baron," in *The Dictionary of National Biography, Supplement Jan. 1901–Dec. 1911*, Sir Sydney Lee, ed. (London: Oxford University Press), vol. 1, pp. 366–67.

Bruguière, Michel
1986   *Gestionnaires et profiteurs de la révolution, l'adminstration des finances françaises de Louis XVI à Bonaparte*. Paris: Olivier Orban.

Capwell, Charles
1986   "Musical Life in Nineteenth-Century Calcutta as a Component in the History of a Secondary Urban Center," *Asian Music* 18 (1):139–63.
1990   "The Interpretation of History and the Foundations of Authority in the Visnupur *Ghārāna* of Bengal, " in *Ethnomusicology and Modern Music History*, Stephen Blum, Philip V. Bohlman, and Daniel M. Neuman, eds. (Urbana: University of Illinois Press).

Clark, C. B.
1874   "Bengali Music," *Calcutta Review* 58 (116):243–66.

Das, Sisir Kumar
1978   *Sahibs and Munshis, An Account of the College of Fort William*. New Delhi: Orion Publications.

Dickie-Clark, H. F.
1966   *The Marginal Situation, A Sociological Study of a Coloured Group.*
        Edited by W. J. H. Sprott. International Library of Sociology and Social
        Reconstruction. London: Routledge & Kegan Paul (New York: The
        Humanities Press).

Engel, Carl
1866   *An Introduction to the Study of National Music.* London: Longmans,
        Green.

Furrell, James W.
1892   *The Tagore Family.* 2d ed. Calcutta: Private circulation, printed by
        Thacker, Spink & Co.

gaṅgōpādhyāy, sowmyendro
1979   *saṅgītakalāvida śaurīndramohana ṭhākura* [Sourindro Mohun Tagore,
        Musicologist]. Calcutta: maṇi prakāśanī.

[gosvāmi], kṣetramohana śarmmā
1879   *saṅgītasāra.* 2d ed. Calcutta.

Kopf, David
1969   *British Orientalism and the Bengal Renaissance: The Dynamics of
        Indian Modernization 1773–1835.* Berkeley and Los Angeles:
        University of California Press.

mukhopādhyāya, dilīpakumāra
1980   *viṣṇupura gharāṇā* [The Visnupur Gharānā]. Calcutta: Bookland.
        Reprint of 1963 edition [?].

Nandy, Ashis
1983   *The Intimate Enemy: Loss and Recovery of Self under Colonialism.*
        Delhi: Oxford University Press.

Owens, Naomi
1969   "Two North Indian Musical Gharanas." M. A. Thesis, University of
        Chicago.

Park, Robert E.
1928   "Human Migration and the Marginal Man," *The American Journal of
        Sociology* 33 (6) (May 1928):881–93.

Redfield, Robert, and Milton Singer
1962   "The Cultural Role of Cities," *Economic Development and Cultural
        Change* 3 (Oct. 1954–July 1955):53–73. Reprinted in *Human Nature
        and the Study of Society: The Papers of Robert Redfield,* Margaret
        Park Redfield, ed. (Chicago: University of Chicago Press), vol. 1, pp.
        326–50.

Said, Edward W.
1978   *Orientalism.* New York: Pantheon.

Stone, Lawrence
1972   "Prosopography," in *Historical Studies Today,* Felix Gilbert and
        Stephen R. Graubard, eds. (New York: W. W. Norton), pp. 107–40.

Stonequist, Everett V.
1937   *The Marginal Man, A Study in Personality and Culture Conflict.* New
        York: Charles Scribner's Sons.

Tagore, Sourindro Mohun
1883   *Hindu Loyalty: A Presentation of the Views and Opinions of the Sanskrit Authorities on the Subject of Loyalty.* Calcutta: S. M. Tagore.
1899   *A Short Account of Raja Sir Sourindro Mohun Tagore with a List of His Titles, Distinctions and Works.* Calcutta.
1965   "Hindu Music," in *Hindu Music from Various Authors.* 3d ed. (The Chowkhamba Sanskrit Studies 49) (Varanasi: Chowkhamba Sanskrit Series Office), pp. 337–412.

ṭhākura, śaurīndramohana
[1870]   *jātīyasaṅgītaviṣayakaprastāva* [A Proposal Concerning National Music]. [Calcutta].

Toynbee, Arnold J.
1939   *A Study of History.* Vol. 5. London: Oxford University Press.

Weber, Eugen
1988   "A New Order of Loss and Profit," review of René Sédillot, *Le coût de la révolution française;* and of Michel Bruguière, *Gestionnaires et profiteurs de la révolution,* in *The Times Literary Supplement,* no. 4 (424) (January 15–21):51–52.

Charlotte J. Frisbie

Women and the Society for Ethnomusicology: Roles and Contributions from Formation through Incorporation (1952/53–1961)[1]

T HIS ESSAY EXAMINES women's roles in and contributions to the Society for Ethnomusicology from the formative years (1952–53) through legal incorporation in the State of New York (1961). It was stimulated by dual, personal concerns: contributing to gender-balanced studies in ethnomusicology (see Koskoff 1987 and the program of the 1987 annual meeting of SEM), and recognizing the need to include multiple voices when writing histories. When setting parameters for this essay, I chose *not* to assess the important intellectual contributions made to the discipline by the numerous female scholars of the period and *not* to review the activities of earlier individuals and groups in both Europe and America which led to the emergence of the Society itself. In the former case, I believed that basic bibliographic information was available, in Kunst (1959) and elsewhere; in the latter, I was certain that other contributors to the present volume would examine the matter of "roots." Suffice it to say, therefore, that the roots have many branches, and before the women on whom I am focusing appeared, a number of contributions had already been made, by both women and men. Among these individuals were Alice Fletcher, Natalie Curtis Burlin, Frances Densmore, Maud Karpeles, Curt Sachs, Jaap Kunst, Theodore Baker, Erich von Hornbostel, Benjamin Ives Gilman, Otto Abraham, Carl Stumpf, Robert Lachmann, Johannes Wolf, Marius Schneider, and John Comfort Fillmore.

Although numerous women have contributed regularly to the intellectual development of ethnomusicology as a field of inquiry, when I decided to restrict the topical focus to questions about women's roles in SEM and the temporal focus to 1952–61, the numbers shrank. Despite the activities of women such as Edith Gerson-Kiwi, Eta Harich-Schneider, Maud Karpeles, and Claudie Marcel-DuBois as well as many of their predecessors, they were not among those identified during a review of SEM publications when I asked which women were initially invited and/or agreed to assume worker/leadership roles in the Society for Ethnomusicology. Instead, ten other women emerged as the early worker counterparts to the four "founding fathers"; they are: Frances Densmore, Helen Roberts, Rose Brandel, Roxane McCollester (now Carlisle), Gertrude Kurath, Nadia Chilkovsky (now Chilkovsky-Nahumck), Barbara Krader, Johanna Spector, Rae Korson, and Barbara Smith. All, except Roberts, agreed to leadership positions on the Executive Board and/or Council during this period, and most made significant contributions.

The historical reconstruction that follows is based on SEM publications and Executive Board minutes, archival work,[2] and direct input (by phone, correspondence, and/or face-to-face conversations) from Kurath, Spector, Krader, Chilkovsky-Nahumck, Smith, Helen Roberts's niece, Jane Broman Brown (see Frisbie 1989), and one founding father, David P. McAllester. Other colleagues, including Judith Gray, Adrienne Kaeppler, Joe Hickerson, Ruth Stone, Ted Frisbie, Joann Kealiinohomoku, Bruno Nettl, Kay Shelemay, David Burrows, and Barbara Hampton, have also provided assistance, for which I am grateful. The multiplicity of sources as well as the opportunity to juxtapose them and, thus, cross-check data has made it possible to clarify some of the problems which became apparent early in the research.

In view of spatial restrictions, this essay highlights only two women before turning to generalizations about selected issues which have emerged from the data currently available on all ten. Frances Densmore and Helen H. Roberts have been selected for attention because of both their pioneer status and the fact that at present they are the only members of the group of ten who are deceased. Among the broader issues which receive comment are questions about how these ten women became involved in the Society for Ethnomusicology and the significance of their early service. At the present writing, data collection is in its final phase and analysis only begun for the larger project (Frisbie n.d.); thus, it is possible that interpretations presented here may be revised in the future.

FORMATIVE YEARS

Certain aspects of the formative years need to be examined before turning to other matters, if only to expand and correct the historical record. As is known from published descriptions of this period (McAllester 1963; Rhodes 1963), David P. McAllester, Alan P. Merriam, and Willard Rhodes met during the 51st Annual Meeting of the American Anthropological Association in Philadelphia in December 1952, and decided to try to reestablish "communication among students and scholars in the field" which had been interrupted by World War II (Rhodes 1963:178). A few days later, these three attended the American Musicological Society meeting in New Haven where they discussed their ideas with Charles Seeger. The latter willingly joined forces with them, contributing "invaluable information and counsel from his vast experience" and serving "as a unifying and continuing link between two generations of scholars" (ibid.).

According to McAllester (p.c. 6/29/87), the group then set out to construct a mailing list, pooling names of interested individuals, and Merriam, Rhodes, and Seeger wrote to various people to ask that they sign the letter which would constitute the first mailing and assess interest in forming a new professional society. After discussion of several drafts, the letter went out on 11 May 1953 to sixty-six people.[3] It was signed by ten individuals—one woman, Frances Densmore, and nine men: Manfred Bukofzer, Mieczyslaw Kolinski, David McAllester, Alan Merriam, Willard Rhodes, Curt Sachs, Charles Seeger, Harold Spivacke, and Richard Waterman. According to McAllester (p.c. 6/29/87), Helen Roberts had been included on this list and had agreed to sign, but was "out of the country when authorized signatures were collected."[4] The Herzog papers show that George Herzog was also asked to sign, by Merriam and Seeger, but did not respond to the request, although he had contributed names to the initial mailing list.

On 13 May Merriam began working on the first *Newsletter;* contents and format were discussed by the four founders both through correspondence and during an October meeting in New York which all but Seeger attended. The first *Ethno-Musicology Newsletter* appeared in mimeographed, stapled format in December 1953, and was followed by #2 in August of 1954 and #3 in December, with Merriam acting as Editor and Secretary pro tem, the other three helping to gather and edit materials, and McAllester taking charge of duplication and mailing. The four founders shared printing and mailing costs through the first five issues. Number 3 included the first attempt at a Curricula Survey; no women were shown teaching anything resembling ethnomusicology at the institutions included in the survey (cf. pp. 5–6). Number 4, published in April 1955, was devoted almost entirely to the publication of the mailing list which identified 472 individuals and institutions "with a serious interest in ethnomusicology." Of importance to the present work is the fact that the list included six of the ten women: Densmore, Krader, Kurath, McCollester, Roberts, and Spector.

Ethno-Musicology Newsletter 6 (January 1956), the first to use pamphlet-size format and to be published by Wesleyan University Press, included an account (pp. 3–5) of the organizational meeting held on 18 November 1955 in Boston during the 54th Annual Meeting of the American Anthropological Association. Therein is a list of twenty-four attendees; among the seven women reportedly present were Kurath, Krader, and McCollester. Krader (p.c. 9/20/87), however, noted that she did not attend an SEM meeting until 1956. At the organizational meeting, E. G. Burrows presented a panel of officers which, according to McAllester (p.c. 6/29/87), had been previously decided upon by the four founders. Parliamentary procedure moved rapidly with a second and move to close discussions also prearranged, and the proposed panel was quickly approved. McAllester (p.c. 6/29/87) recalled, "Charlie did not want anything left to chance. There was no discussion of different initial leaders. Burrows was all cued." Thus, the following were charged with serving the Society until the second annual meeting: Rhodes, President; Kolinski, Vice-President; McAllester, Secretary-Treasurer; and Merriam, Editor.

The last event to be mentioned in the brief examination of the formative years is the first annual meeting. Held on 5 September 1956 in Philadelphia during the 5th International Congress of Anthropological and Ethnological Sciences, this meeting was the first SEM meeting for Krader, Spector, and Chilkovsky. Krader (p.c. 9/20/87) was there because her husband, Lawrence, spoke at the Congress, and Chilkovsky (p.c. 10/18/87) was there to read Kurath's paper "and to add one of [her] own." About forty people participated in adopting the draft constitution, prepared by Seeger, and in other SEM business, including removing the hyphen from "ethnomusicology" and electing more officers. Nominations, once again, were preplanned. McAllester (p.c. 6/29/87) described them as "whizzing by, to the surprise of some in attendance. Conklin and Sturtevant were all primed to second and move nominations be closed." Voting was evidently done by printed ballot, according to provisions in the draft constitution (Society for Ethnomusicology 1956a), although to date I have not located a sample ballot. Frances Densmore became 2d Vice-President, moving Kolinski to 1st. Merriam, Herzog, and Kurath became Members at Large, and Sachs was named Honorary President. The first Executive Board meeting, held fifteen minutes later, was attended by Rhodes, Kolinski, Herzog, and McAllester, and by invitation, Seeger and Nettl. Minutes (Society for Ethnomusicology 1956b) show nine agenda items, the last of which directed the Secretary to write to both Jaap Kunst and Helen Roberts "expressing regret that they were not able to be at the meetings and appreciation for their work in ethnomusicology."

FRANCES THERESA DENSMORE (21 MAY 1867–5 JUNE 1957)

Frances Densmore, a pioneer American ethnomusicologist, is known especially for preservationist goals, energetic collecting, and prolific publications on North American Indian music. A native of Red Wing, Minnesota, Densmore came from a musical family and was trained in music theory and in piano and organ at Oberlin Conservatory of Music (1884–86). In 1889, after working as a music teacher and church organist, she went to Boston for further study of piano and counterpoint. It was there that her early interest in American Indians became a professional one, thanks to discussions with John Comfort Fillmore and supportive encouragement and training from her major mentor, Alice Cunningham Fletcher.

1901 brought Densmore's first publication, 1905, her first field trip, and 1907, her first phonograph recordings of Indian songs as well as the start of her fifty-year association with the Bureau of American Ethnology. Although initially interested in Fillmore's ideas, Densmore soon moved away from theoretical considerations, preferring to work in isolation and remaining relatively unaffected by contemporary European and American discussions about world musics. While the Densmore papers housed at the Goodhue County Historical Society in Red Wing, Minnesota, reveal much about her sister Margaret's importance in her fieldwork, Frances's austere existence, and some local impressions of her as a stereotypic Victorian woman except for her frequent travels and habit of smoking cigarettes, they make no mention of SEM or ethnomusicologists (Frisbie 1988). Holdings at other archives, however, suggest that she maintained correspondence with Hornbostel, Merriam, Rhodes, Seeger, and Herzog among others.

According to McAllester (p.c. 6/29/87), who never met Densmore, each of the founding fathers was responsible for staying in touch with specific people, and Rhodes was the contact person for Densmore. Thus, it was Rhodes who by 8 May 1953 secured her signature on the 1953 letter. At that time, Densmore had finished her work with Michigan Indians, had begun her fieldwork with the Seminoles, and was in the midst of producing more LPs with the Music Division of the Library of Congress. From then on, Densmore contributed news to the *Newsletter* and from 1953 to 1956 helped others assemble her bibliography which appeared in *Ethno-*

Musicology Newsletter 7 (April 1956), with additions in *Ethnomusicology Newsletter* 10 (May 1957) and the second issue of the journal *Ethnomusicology* (1958).

When the Executive Board of the Society was expanded during the first annual meeting in September 1956 to include an Honorary President, a 2d Vice-President, and three Members at Large, Densmore became SEM's first 2d Vice-President at the age of eighty-nine. McAllester (p.c. 5/4/87) recalled, "At the organizational meeting in, Boston in 1955, Willard called her to ask her to be 2nd Vice-President. 'She told me,' she said, 'Well, I can't travel anymore, but you can use my name.' I remember Will imitating a sweet little old lady's voice when he reported the conversation to us. She was pleased but said she couldn't come to meetings. I guess she was asked because of her age and prestige. . . . She never came to any Board meetings or Annual meetings." Executive Board minutes for 3/22/57 (Society for Ethnomusicology 1957a) show Densmore among the first group nominated by the Board for Council membership. In a letter to Willard Rhodes on 18 April, she (Densmore 1957) declined the nomination on the basis of advanced age, limited strength, and eyesight problems. She died a month and a half later, while serving as 2d Vice-President, on 5 June, after a short illness and fifteen days after her ninetieth birthday.

HELEN HEFFRON ROBERTS (12 JUNE 1888–26 MARCH 1985)

Helen H. Roberts, a Chicago native, was another illustrious pioneer in American ethnomusicology whose fieldwork was done by utilizing boats and other watercraft, "derelict cars," or by riding horseback astride, with a portable Edison phonograph in one hand, and the cylinders in a basket (Roberts 1979). Trained in music and piano performance at Chicago Musical College (1907–09) and the American Conservatory of Music (1910–11), Roberts taught music for several years before going to Columbia University in 1916, the year of her first publication, to pursue an earlier interest in Indians and to train in anthropology under Franz Boas. After receiving an M.A. in 1919, Roberts did her first fieldwork in Jamaica in 1920–21 and then turned to transcription and analysis projects for Jesse Walter Fewkes in collaboration with Clark Wissler, and for Edward Sapir and the National Museum of Canada in collaboration with Diamond Jenness. Work in California with Harrington followed, as did a year of collecting ancient music and *meles* in Hawaii. In 1924 Roberts went to the Institute of Psychology at Yale University, where she remained until 1936, surviving the enlargement of the Institute and its renaming as the Institute of Human Relations in 1929. At Yale her work focused on rerecording wax cylinders onto aluminum discs for many institutions and individuals, doing transcriptions and analyses for herself and others, lecturing in New York and New Haven, doing further fieldwork, and publishing. When she left Yale, she considered herself to be "retired" from ethnomusicology, even though her correspondence and publications suggested otherwise (Frisbie 1989).

Roberts, as noted above, was asked and agreed to sign the initial letter sent in 1953 to assess interest in forming a Society for Ethnomusicology, but was ultimately not included because she was in Europe when signatures were actually collected. However, unlike Densmore, she was never considered for the Executive Board, and when the Board nominated her as an "Honorary Member" of the Council at its 12/28/59 meeting, she declined (Society for Ethnomusicology 1959c).[5] Given Roberts's prodigious research, collecting, transcription/analysis, and publications on American Indian, Eskimo, Hawaiian, and Jamaican musics, let alone her pioneer status, such events raise questions. Pursuit of them with McAllester (p.c. 7/16/87), who was her "official contact person," resulted in the following: "Helen was never asked to serve on the Executive Board because of a blow-up she had with both Seeger and Herzog." In 1933 Roberts along with Seeger, Herzog, Henry Cowell, and Dorothy Lawton constituted the organizing committee that founded the American Society for Comparative Musicology. After the first year, Roberts replaced Seeger as Treasurer-Secretary for a year and then became Secretary in 1935, when Herzog became Treasurer and Seeger, President, jobs they all held until the Society went out of existence in October of 1937.[6] According to McAllester (p.c. 7/16/87),

> [Roberts] was left doing all the secretarial and other work of this Society when Charlie, George, and others got busy during the War. She had considerable independent means and probably supported the whole thing financially, too, until it got to be too much. She finally got indignant and quit, and that Society came to an end. While she never said a word about this to me, Charlie did tell me he had a bad conscience about her, for dumping the whole burden on her . . . and George told me the same.[7]
>
> George was also on her wrong side for having 'lost' her Nootka music manuscript when it went to him as a reader before publication.[8] He often did that, or took ages to read manuscripts, perhaps as a way of discouraging rivals.[9] Helen had to

do the whole thing over, which was great strain on her poor eyesight. And she was not one to suffer such treatment silently. So I suspect she gave both George and Charlie a piece of her mind when she quit.

Roberts's "retirement" from ethnomusicology was influenced by the 1936 withdrawal of support for her research job, obtained with Clark Wissler's help, at Yale's Institute of Human Relations. As Krader (p.c. 7/19/87; p.c. 4/2/88) said,

Helen was just simply let go from her job at the very same time she was being honored for what she was doing in Germany. She was very proud of her relation with the scholars in Berlin. She had an article in the first issue [1933] of *Zeitschrift für vergleichende Musikwissenschaft,* and she showed me the letter the editor wrote to her, saying that it was excellent and he would welcome any further writings by her and would publish them. . . . When she was let go [at Yale], she abandoned her music career and became an excellent botanist.

McAllester (p.c. 8/11/87) reported that when Roberts was asked to serve on the SEM Council in 1959, "she was adamant about being retired from ethnomusicology. We tried hard to involve her, but she'd already given her books to Ted Burrows, and turned her interests to the New Haven Symphony, a museum . . . in Guatemala where a niece was living, her orchids, and other things." That she had not totally retired, however, is clear in her correspondence with McAllester and others, her 1955 publication with Morris Swadesh, and her 1969 work *A History of the New Haven Symphony Orchestra Celebrating its Seventy-Fifth Season, 1894–1969* (Roberts and Cousins 1969; cf. also Frisbie 1989). Krader (p.c. 9/20/87) noted that Roberts *was* pleased when the Society paid homage to her later by publishing her bibliography in *Ethnomusicology* 11 (1967). Roberts assisted with its preparation, and in 1967, when the meetings were in New Haven, was escorted to the banquet by Alan Merriam and Frank Gillis.

SYNTHESIS

Having now highlighted the two pioneer women who were involved with the Society for Ethnomusicology in its formative years, it is time to turn to selected summary comments based on the data currently available on all ten of the women who had roles of one kind or another in the period from 1952–53 to 1961. The synthesis that follows is preliminary in the sense that my understandings continue to change as data analysis proceeds.

When I started this project, I did not know what would emerge during my attempt to learn more about women's roles in and contributions to the formative years of SEM. Certain things, however, now strike me as worth mentioning:

1) Networking was the basis for the new group's formation, as might be expected. However, unlike the early years of anthropological organizations in the United States, the networking, as initially started with lists constructed by the founding fathers, included *both* women and men. Before 1953 the one event that was mentioned by several women as important in establishing their professional connections with others who had similar interests was the International Folk Music Council meeting at Indiana University during the summer of 1950. At that time, for example, Krader met Kurath, Seeger, and Nettl, and Kurath met Nettl and Krader.

2) As others, including Nettl (1983:333), have noted, the climate for women in ethnomusicology was supportive and encouraging. Women interested in the discipline, both in the United States and abroad, sent news to the newsletters and journals and gave papers at meetings. Some eventually dropped out, but most of the more professionally oriented ones did not.

3) In the period under consideration, the Executive Board of the Society nominated the slates for both Officers and Councillors, with the President empowered to make substitutions if nominees did not accept. The collective pool of individuals who thus at one time or another influenced such nominations from the beginning of SEM until the elections at the sixth annual meeting in 1961 included Rhodes, Kolinski, McAllester, Merriam, Sachs, Densmore, Brandel, Kurath, Herzog, Waterman, Burrows, Hood, Kunst, Seeger, McCollester, and Nettl. The 1955 and 1956 "elections" of officers were preplanned, and the first twenty-five Councillors who were asked to serve were determined by the Board alone on 22 March 1957 (Society for Ethnomusicology 1957a). Twenty-three of them accepted. Once the draft constitution went into effect, Councillors nominated by the Executive Board were submitted to the Council for election. Candidates for the Executive Board were expected to be current or former Councillors; Councillors were to be scholarly members who had made contributions to the objectives of the Society. Executive Board records show that in only one case was an early female collector viewed as not scholarly enough to warrant nomination to the Council, an opinion that was objectively justifiable at the time.

4) While a number of men, including Sachs, Chase, Herzog, Seeger, and Nettl were identified by some of the ten women as influencing their schol-

arly interests, two others were important as recruiters of women into Society work. Rhodes secured Densmore's agreement to serve as 2d Vice-President and also recruited Rose Brandel on 25 March 1957, after Board approval on 22 March 1957 (unrecorded in the minutes). A student of Sachs, Brandel was asked initially to finish out McAllester's term as Secretary-Treasurer starting on 1 July 1957 when the latter resigned, having secured Guggenheim support for a sabbatical. Merriam, in his role as Editor of the early *Newsletters/Journals,* brought in Kurath, Krader, and McCollester. Only two of the women mentioned being recruited by other women: Chilkovsky was brought in by Kurath and then proposed for Council membership by both Kurath and Rhodes. Spector credited McCollester for interesting her in service work.

5) In the cases of the two pioneers, Densmore and Roberts, the recruitment efforts appear to have been mainly motivated by a desire to be associated with their professional names and prestige, as well as, perhaps, a wish to honor them. In the other eight instances, the women nominated for Council and/or Executive Board service were scholars who possessed special skills (linguistic, choreographic, ethnographic, teacher education, editorial, public service, or whatever), or had important connections at home or abroad with individuals, other professional societies, and, sometimes, other resources.

6) Although there were a number of well-known women actively involved in ethnomusicology abroad during this same time period, those who were brought into early administrative work for SEM, especially on the Executive Board which Merriam called "the inner circle," were based in the United States. Of them, Krader and Spector were out of the country most frequently, with McCollester a close second.

7) The women who were asked to serve came from a variety of backgrounds. All except Spector and Chilkovsky were born in the United States. Four—Kurath, Spector, Chilkovsky, and Smith—were concert artists in their own right. Some were single; others were married or widowed. All had graduate degrees, including some which were honorary, and together they hailed from a variety of disciplines, including musicology, anthropology, art history, dance, and Slavic languages and literature. Some of the women were also actively involved in service work in other societies. Kurath, for example, was just finishing the first of two terms as President of the Michigan Folklore Society, and Korson was on the Council of the American Folklore Society. Then, too, five were "founders" in their own right. Kurath founded the Rhode Island Creative Dance Guild and, later, the Dance Research Center in Ann Arbor. Chilkovsky founded the Philadelphia Dance Academy. Roberts was one of the founders of the American Society for Comparative Musicology. Brandel founded the graduate ethnomusicology program at Hunter College, and Spector,

the ethnomusicology department at the New York Jewish Theological Seminary.

8) While all of the women contributed news to SEM publications, and all, except Roberts, Densmore, and Korson, participated regularly in annual meetings, the women who became involved followed a variety of paths in their service during the early years of SEM and, thus, made different contributions. As both an indicator of the hospitality of the discipline and the tone of the formative years in SEM, instead of a stereotypical parade of female secretaries, one finds the nine women who agreed to serve in a variety of jobs and considered for everything, including the Presidency. Given the diversity, it is appropriate to provide a brief outline of their individual paths:

As noted above, *Frances Densmore* went directly on the Executive Board, but declined nomination to the Council when named in the first group of nominees only a few months before her death. Her input was essentially by correspondence.

Rose Brandel joined the Board on 1 July 1957 to complete McAllester's term as Secretary-Treasurer. She had been simultaneously proposed for the Council and the Secretary-Treasurer's slate on 22 March 1957 (Society for Ethnomusicology 1957a), and in the time period under consideration, served two terms on the Council, and a second term as Secretary, when the combined job was split. Although Board minutes suggested that Kurath was the opposing candidate in 1957, Kurath's statements as well as the 1957 ballot[10] show Brandel's opponent was Barbara Krader. When elected to her second term in 1959, Brandel ran against Johanna Spector. While on the Board, Brandel chaired the Membership Committee and made significant contributions to membership recruitment. She also successfully negotiated the Journal's new printing contract with Braun and Brumfield.

Gertrude Kurath began Council service with the first group nominated in March of 1957, serving two terms during this time period. She also began what became sixteen years of service as Dance Editor with *Ethno-Musicology Newsletter* 7 (April 1956). At the first annual meeting in 1956, she became one of three Members at Large added to the Executive Board. She also noted that she ran opposite Kolinski in the 1957 presidential election. Early ballots confirm this and show that she was one of six on the ballot for Member at Large in the 2 February 1959 election. The other candidates were Herzog, McAllester, Merriam, Nettl, and Spector. Kurath also ran against Merriam for 1st Vice-President in the December 1959 election. She served a second term as Member at Large (1960–62) as a result of a constitutional change to a system wherein the two candidates not elected to the 2d Vice-President's job automatically became Members at Large. On that ballot, 28 December 1960, the candidates were Bruno Nettl and Willard Rhodes, in addition to Kurath. Kurath's major contributions during this period were made through her work as Dance Editor and regular participation at meetings, as well as by bringing Nadia Chilkovsky into the Society, and actively arranging panels on music and dance at anthropology meetings.

Barbara Krader also started Council service with the first group nominated in March of 1957 and ran against Brandel in the Secretary-Treasurer election at the end of that year. Krader contributed bibliographies of Herzog and Schaeffner, and helped with Densmore's before becoming Record Review Editor for the journal in 1961. At the sixth annual meeting in 1961, she was elected Treasurer over William Malm and thus joined the Executive Board. Krader's main contributions in the early period stemmed from her editorial work, linguistic skills, and contacts with Eastern European ethnomusicologists. She should also be thanked for her suggestion to McAllester, as Journal Editor, that brief sketches of officers, councillors, and authors be included in *Ethnomusicology*. (The practice was followed from 1960 through the first issue of 1965.)

Roxane Connick McCollester helped with the Densmore bibliography and then began compiling the Recordings section with *Ethnomusicology Newsletter* 9 (January 1957). Although I have not been able to locate the Executive Board minutes for the meeting which took place during the third annual meeting in Boston in December 1958, McCollester was evidently nominated for the Council at that time. She appeared as the only woman among five nominees on the 2 February 1959 Council ballot and was duly elected. At the 8 June 1959 Executive Board meeting (Society for Ethnomusicology 1959a), she was nominated to run for Treasurer, when the Board decided to split the Secretary-Treasurer job. Charles Haywood was the other candidate. Upon becoming Treasurer, McCollester took charge of the legal incorporation of the Society in the State of New York. The process, completed by November of 1961, was initially handled by her husband's law firm. Described by colleagues as an active, influential, socially prominent person who had important contacts abroad, it is important to note what Krader (p.c. 9/20/87) said, namely, that McCollester "took care of the legal work and paid the full costs of our incorporation, and probably other things, too." During the early years, in addition to her contributions as Treasurer and Editor for Recordings (through *Ethnomusicology* 4 (3), 1960), she assisted with membership recruitment efforts and represented SEM at international conferences. Although asked by the Executive Board on 13 May 1961 (Society for Ethnomusicology 1961a) to be on the 1961 ballot for another term as Treasurer, McCollester said the matter had to be given further thought, and later declined.

Nadia Chilkovsky was proposed for the Council on 28 December 1957 (Society for Ethnomusicology 1957b) and was elected, and she served two terms during the formative years of the Society. She also ran as the candidate opposite Mantle Hood for 2d Vice-President in the 2 February 1959 officers election. During the early period, Chilkovsky was on the Membership Committee chaired by Brandel, as well as the 1961 Program Committee. She represented SEM at international conferences and was cited for her efforts in recruiting new members. Equally important was the contribution she made by introducing SEM scholars to dance notation through her own papers and the training sessions she conducted at annual meetings.

Johanna Spector was also among the first group of Councillors nominated in March 1957, and served two terms during this early period. The 2 February 1959 ballot for Members at Large showed that she was among the six on that slate (see above), and Executive Board minutes for 8 June 1959 (Society for Ethnomusicology 1959a) show that she was nominated to run as the candidate opposite Brandel for Secretary in the 1959 election. The December 1959 ballot confirms this. Spector (p.c. 3/22/88) defined her early input in SEM as "teaching ethnomusicology courses at the Jewish Theological Seminary, recruiting members for the New York Chapter of SEM as Secretary-Treasurer [1960–64], and corresponding with [and contributions to] the Journal." It should also be noted that Spector was cited for her membership recruitment efforts for the Society at large and that she often represented SEM at international conferences.

Rae Korson, who became Head of the Archive of Folk Song, Music Division, Library of Congress in the 1956–57 fiscal year, was nominated to the SEM Council on 9 October 1960 (Society for Ethnomusicology 1960b) and duly elected. Her Council membership appears to have been related mainly to her job and connections, as well as to the collecting activities of her husband, George, a specialist on Pennsylvania mining songs.

The tenth woman, *Barbara Smith*, joined SEM in 1958 and then began reading papers at meetings and sending both institutional and personal news to the Journal. She was nominated for the Council at the 16 November 1961 Executive Board meeting (Society for Ethnomusicology 1961b) as the only woman on a list of seven. Duly elected, she began her service work in SEM right at the end of the period presently under consideration. However, we are all aware of the numerous contributions that were to unfold.

9) In addition to the variety evident in the service paths of the women who agreed to be involved in Society work during the formative years, it is also clear that diversity characterized their experiences in the new Society. Many reported harmony and supportive collaboration with fellow workers; interestingly, however, to date Chilkovsky and Kurath are the only individuals in the group to note a close personal as well as professional friendship. The two first met in 1926, when Kurath gave a concert supported by the Riva Hoffman dancers, a group which included Chilkovsky. Later, Kurath asked Chilkovsky to present a paper for her at the 1956 SEM meeting, and the two began a professional collaboration, in which Chilkovsky did the Labanotation for

Kurath's publications. Only two women, Roberts and Brandel, reportedly had confrontations with male coworkers during the formative years or earlier, which led either to exclusion from Executive Board service or a gradual shift in personal priorities away from such work. Of the eight women still alive in the group of ten, some remain both vitally interested in the discipline and active in the Society; others maintain their professional interest but have withdrawn from active participation because age, injuries, or other physical conditions of self or spouse have curtailed travel, or because of other reasons.

10) Gender-balancing was *not* discussed during the formative years of the Society, nor did I think it would have been. It is clear, however, that some of these women experienced discrimination in both their personal and professional lives. For a few, country of origin and ethnic heritage led to deep personal suffering during World War I and/or II, and later suffering because of the suspicions and prejudices of others. Some of the women who were married had to shift to a "legal name," or redefine or interrupt careers respectively because of funding-agency rules, nepotism laws, or geographic moves determined by spouses. Some also experienced other kinds of discrimination in their work, losing salary support, jobs, opportunities to publish, or being expected to be an organization's all-serving Secretary. Given the group's first-hand acquaintance with various forms of discrimination, it is a credit, at least on the surface, to the Society for Ethnomusicology that to date, none of the women have reported any discrimination on the basis of sex in the Society's formative years. However, by 1961 at least some Councillors were becoming concerned about gender-balancing and other related issues.[11]

11) Finally, some, but not all, of these women have been honored by the Society in one way or another, such as through bibliographies (Kurath, Densmore, Roberts), awards (Kurath), and invitations to give the Distinguished Charles Seeger Lecture (Krader and Smith). I would like to close with the thought that we can honor them further by making sure that their service contributions to the formative years of SEM, be these editorial, educational, financial, or in the areas of recruitment and representation abroad, *are* recognized in any histories that we write about ourselves and the Society for Ethnomusicology.

Notes

1. The present work is a revised and expanded, September 1988 version of a paper, "Women and the Society for Ethnomusicology, 1952–1961," given at the con-

ference "Ideas, Concepts, and Personalities in the History of Ethnomusicology" held at the University of Illinois at Urbana-Champaign on April 14–17, 1988. I would like to thank Kay Shelemay, Gertrude Kurath, Ted Frisbie, and Joyce Aschenbrenner for their comments on the earlier, oral version.

2. Archival work was made possible by a 1988 summer-research fellowship from Southern Illinois University at Edwardsville, for which I am grateful. Thanks are also appropriate to a number of people at various archives for facilitating this work: among them are Tony Seeger, Dorothy Sara Lee, Marilyn Graf, and Ruth Stone at the Archives of Traditional Music, Indiana University; Elizabeth Swaim and Shaozong Ma at Special Collections and Archives, Olin Library, Wesleyan University; and Judith Schiff and Nancy Lyon at Manuscript and Archives, Sterling Memorial Library, Yale University. One of the results of this work is Frisbie (1989).

3. A copy of this letter and the list of individuals to whom it was sent were among the materials in the George Herzog papers, Archives of Traditional Music, Indiana University. Early *Newsletter* accounts set the number of recipients at "approximately 70" and "approximately 75" (*Ethno-Musicology Newsletter* 1:1 (December 1953), and 6:4 (January 1956)).

4. Correspondence showed that both Seeger and McAllester proposed Roberts, valuing the prestige of her name and her support. Rhodes originally proposed Densmore because of respect for her work and her seniority in the field.

5. Executive Board minutes for 22 April 1960 (Society for Ethnomusicology 1960a) included the recommendation that the following changes be made in the previous (12/28/59) minutes: "Omit Helen Roberts and also omit Strunk and Roberts were nominated under the category of 'Honorary Member.'" President Seeger's point was that, constitutionally, there was no such membership category on the Council. The first "omit" signifies that Roberts had declined when asked after the 28 December 1959 meeting.

6. There were other officers in the American Society for Comparative Musicology. For example, in 1936, in addition to Seeger as President and Herzog as Treasurer, Cowell and Spivacke were serving as Vice-Presidents, Roberts as Corresponding Secretary, and F. C. Lathrop as Recording Secretary (Roberts 1936).

7. McAllester (1953) made reference to this in a letter to Seeger on 24 February 1953, saying that during a phone conversation with Roberts, he gathered "that she feels she was left at the end of the ASCM doing all the work without much help while it slowly collapsed." That Seeger (1953) felt no animosity toward Roberts is clear in two letters to McAllester. In one, bearing the same date, Seeger referred to "Miss Roberts (who is indeed a fine and lovable person) . . . "; in the other, of 25 February 1953, Seeger included the following: "Just a word about the old ASCM. It is more than true that Miss Roberts did practically all the work—and damned well, too."

8. The portions of the chronology of the Nootka manuscript story from 1936 to 5 May 1946, and 7 May 1946 to 1953 still need clarification. From materials in the Roberts collection at Yale, it is clear that Roberts transcribed the ninety-nine songs, at the request of Edward Sapir, for the National Museum of Canada in 1923 before departing for her Hawaiian fieldwork. In a short autobiography, loaned to me by her niece (cf. Frisbie 1989), she listed the Nootka manuscript as among those she

was completing in the 1931–35 period. In a report to Sapir, dated 29 May 1935, Roberts (1935) describes the situation as follows:

> A report of Nootka Indian music was completed for publication in 1925–26 in the Institute of Psychology, but was shelved for completion of another part by a collaborator. This has recently been subject to revision (still going on) owing to drastic changes in modern linguistic orthography, and because of opportunity to work directly with a visiting Nootka Indian [Alex Thomas, who visited New Haven in 1934–35]. An effort is being made to complete this report soon, for publication by the National Museum of Canada.

Roberts's correspondence showed that the completed manuscript was sent to Jenness in 1936. The next reference to it in the correspondence appeared in a letter from Marius Barbeau (1946), on 6 May 1946, telling Roberts that the manuscript was in the files of the National Museum of Canada and could be released. Various letters Roberts wrote in 1954 indicated that at that time, she was redoing the transcriptions, thus duplicating work done earlier. While I found nothing that said that the transcriptions had been lost, such must have been the case. In this same year, Roberts reported, in *Ethno-Musicology Newsletter* 3:4 (1954), that the manuscript, which had been "lost for eighteen years," would be published in 1955.

Roberts's introduction to the published work (Roberts and Swadesh 1955:199) states that

> The records were originally transcribed in the early 1920s and the music manuscript completed, with texts drawn in, at that time, in conformity with spellings supplied by Dr. Sapir. The actual study of the music was not undertaken until 1934–36, during which years the music manuscript had to be re-drawn to conform to changes made in American phonetic usage which had been adopted by the American Anthropological Association in the interim. However, by this time, the 'phonemic' approach was crystallizing among scientific linguists all over the world, and led logically to a few further modifications.

Other information, in Swadesh's section (Roberts and Swadesh 1955:310), showed that "A first draft of the entire manuscript was seen by Sapir, and corrected by him for matters of content about 1935. . . . A final stylistic revision was done by Swadesh in 1953."

Although Roberts, in conversations with McAllester and others, clearly blamed Herzog for "losing" the Nootka manuscript, no confirming documentation was located in either the Herzog papers or the Roberts collection. According to McAllester (p.c. 7/16/88), since Swadesh and Herzog were good friends, Herzog may very well have been asked to review the manuscript during the publication consideration process, and then either "lost" it or delayed his comments interminably, as he was known to do by his colleagues.

Letters at the Archives of Traditional Music showed that Marian Smith, editor, American Ethnological Society, was seeking publication support funds from ACLS for both the Barbeau Tsimshian manuscript and the Roberts-Swadesh manuscript in May of 1947 and that Swadesh was working on Sapir's and his own Nootka notes with Guggenheim support in both 1947 and 1948. In one letter to Swadesh, dated 29 January 1953, Herzog inquired about the fate of the Nootka manuscript and asked for clarification of Swadesh's part in it, in order to write a recommendation in support of its publication by the American Philosophical Society. In part, that letter suggested that the manuscript "was around" at the end of November 1952, but never reached Herzog, who was then on sick leave. Herzog continued that he would be interested in knowing "the status of the MS, since it goes back to Sapir, and thus represents much good and hard work on the part of Miss Roberts who is now practically retired; her eyes aren't very good, I understand." Herzog made no reference to any earlier reading of the manuscript, and his papers do not include copies of the letters he told Swadesh (on 29 January 1953) he would write to both Esther Goldfrank and the American Philosophical Society about the Nootka manuscript.

9. That no great friendship existed between Roberts and Herzog is clear in conversations with Roberts reported to me by both McAllester (p.c. 7/16/88) and Krader (p.c. 4/2/88), as well as in Roberts (1979, tape 3) and in comments Helen made during an interview with Frank Gillis, to which Herzog (1970) referred in a letter of 20 June 1970 to Sam Chianis. There is minimal correspondence between Roberts and Herzog in the Roberts collection at Yale. The Herzog papers at Indiana contain what appears to be the first letters between the two, 3 March and 16 March 1932, before Herzog went to Yale. These were cordial and showed an exchange of publications. Records of Herzog's work as a Research Associate at the Institute of Human Relations showed that both he and Roberts turned funds over to each other during summers when one was doing fieldwork or was absent from the Institute for other reasons. Voluminous correspondence during the summer of 1933, which eventually also involved Sapir, revealed basic disagreement over what type of recording/transcribing equipment should be acquired at Yale, and is perhaps indicative of the Roberts-Herzog relationship from then on.

Although Roberts never addressed the causes of the rivalry, it is more than possible that she felt like the underdog because Herzog had a Ph.D., a teaching assignment in Yale's Anthropology Department, and a higher title and salary at the Institute than she. That he also perceived her as a rival and a threat is clear, although the reasons are not. How much sabotaging on his part ensued is hard to document; in addition to the Nootka manuscript story discussed above, Roberts held Herzog responsible for the loss of her Yale position in 1936. Although that was not the case, as shown in Frisbie (1989), it should be remembered that Herzog was known for sabotaging many he perceived as rivals, including Ph.D. candidates at Columbia such as Willard Rhodes, Martha Huot, Bruno Nettl [sic], and Jane Belo (McAllester p.c. 7/17/88). Remarks from David Burrows (p.c. 6/10/88) about his father, Edwin Grant "Ted" Burrows, suggested that such behavior was also characteristic of Herzog during the 1932–36 period when he was at Yale. Ted Burrows, who earned an M.A. there in 1932 and a Ph.D. in 1937 (McAllester 1959:15), obviously was working with Herzog before changing dissertation advisors and finishing under Peter Buck. In response to queries, David Burrows (p.c. 6/10/88) reported:

> My father regarded Helen Roberts as his mentor in ethnomusicology, and continued in touch with her long after [cf. Frisbie 1989]. I have no knowledge of his contacts with Herzog. The story in the [Burrows]

family was that Herzog vetoed his [Ted's] first completed dissertation because of his [George's] rivalry with Roberts. Charles Seeger confirmed this in conversation with me at an SEM meeting in Albuquerque (late 60s), adding that he had tried to intercede with Herzog on my father's behalf, without result. Eventually the aborted dissertation, *Songs of Uvea and Futuna,* was published as Bishop Museum Bulletin 183 [1945]; the substitute dissertation, *Western Polynesia,* had already appeared before the war (Göteborg 1938).

10. The 1957 ballot is the earliest one that I have located to date. For the historical record, the Officers and Council ballots from 1957 through 1961 are shown below; names of successful candidates are italicized for Officers, and identified in the text for the Council.

December 1957—President: *Mieczyslaw Kolinski* and Gertrude Kurath; 1st Vice-President: *Richard Waterman* and Mantle Hood; 2d Vice-President: *Edwin G. Burrows* and Bruno Nettl; Secretary-Treasurer: *Rose Brandel* and Barbara Krader.

2 February 1959 (noted as late because of certain delays in nominations in report of 3d Annual meeting, Boston)—2d Vice-President: Nadia Chilkovsky and *Mantle Hood;* Members at Large; *George Herzog,* Gertrude Kurath, *David P. McAllester, Alan P. Merriam,* Bruno Nettl, and Johanna L. Spector.

December 1959—President: *Charles Seeger* and Richard Waterman; 1st Vice-President: Gertrude Kurath and *Alan P. Merriam;* Secretary: *Rose Brandel* and Johanna L. Spector; Treasurer: Charles Haywood and *Roxane McCollester.* (Board minutes for 8 June 1959 (Society for Ethnomusicology 1959a) show a slightly different slate: Honorary President: George Herzog and Jaap Kunst; President: as above, 1st Vice-President: Willard Rhodes and John Ward; Secretary: as above; Treasurer: Bruno Nettl and Roxane McCollester. Later minutes, from 2 October 1959 (Society for Ethnomusicology 1959b), show substitutions because of the unavailability of certain people. Board minutes for 28 December 1959 (Society for Ethnomusicology 1959c) show that the Board elected Jaap Kunst as Honorary President rather than including that office on the 1959 ballot as originally planned.) At the 1959 annual meeting, three amendments to the constitution passed: the office of Honorary President became optional; the form of the annual slate was changed so that the candidate for President receiving fewer votes automatically became 1st Vice-President, and on a triple slate, the two candidates for 2d Vice-President receiving fewer votes automatically became Members at Large; and a Corresponding Member category was added.

December 1960—2d Vice-President: Gertrude Kurath, Bruno Nettl, and *Willard Rhodes;* the other two automatically became Members at Large. During the 1960 annual meeting, five amendments to the constitution passed: a Nominating Committee was added, the Editor was added to the Executive Board, presidential appointments to committees were made subject to Board approval, the deadline for dues payment was changed, and old Article VII-D concerning leave of absence for committee members as well as the provisions governing the first annual meeting were deleted from the constitution.

November 1961—President: Boris Kremenliev and *Alan P. Merriam* with the candidate not elected automatically becoming 1st Vice-President; Secretary: Robert Brown and *George List;* Treasurer: *Barbara Krader* and William P. Malm. (Board minutes (Society for Ethnomusicology 1961a) for 13 May 1961 show a different slate: President: Hood and Merriam with the other becoming 1st Vice-President; Secretary: Brandel and __; Treasurer: McCollester and __.)

The use of ballots for the Council began after the first group was selected in March of 1957 by the Executive Board. That group included: Bertrand Bronson, E. G. "Ted" Burrows, Rose Brandel, Gilbert Chase, Daniel Crowley, Melville Herskovits, George Herzog, Mantle Hood, Otto Kinkeldey, Mieczyslaw Kolinski, Barbara Krader, Gertrude Kurath, William Lichtenwanger, Edward Lowinsky, David P. McAllester, Bruno Nettl, Fred Ramsey, Willard Rhodes, Curt Sachs, Charles Seeger, Johanna Spector, John Ward, and Richard Waterman. Two others, Frances Densmore and Alan Merriam, declined the 22 March 1957 invitation; both were already on the Executive Board as were Herzog, Kolinski, Kurath, McAllester, Rhodes, and Sachs.

16 February 1958: Nadia Chilkovsky, Charles Haywood, and Vernon Taylor; all approved.

2 February 1959: Jan LaRue, George List, William P. Malm, Roxane McCollester, and Gustave Reese; all approved.

The 28 December 1959 Council meeting minutes stated, "The recommendations of the Executive Board for three new Councillors were approved by the Council. Additional nominees were also submitted as follows: Laura Boulton, Robert Brown, Sam Chianis, Robert Garfias, Rae Korson, Harold Powers, Darius Thieme, and Eric Werner" (Society for Ethnomusicology 1959d). (Executive Board minutes (Society for Ethnomusicology 1959c) for 28 December 1959 show the three Board nominees to be Nicholas England, Oliver Strunk, and Helen Roberts, the latter two under the category "Honorary Member.") These names were sent to the whole Council on 10 January 1960 on a ballot to determine whether they should be nominees. At the Executive Board meeting on 22 May 1960 Roberts was removed from the Council ballot (she had declined), and the Honorary Member category was deleted (Society for Ethnomusicology 1960a).

The December 1960 Council ballot for the 1961–63 term included, under new: Robert Brown, Sam Chianis, Nicholas England, Hormoz Farhat, Robert Garfias, Rae Korson, Boris Kremenliev, Leonard Meyer, Harold Powers, Oliver Strunk, Darius Thieme, and Eric Werner. Under reelection were: Bertrand Bronson, Gilbert Chase, Daniel Crowley, Melville Herskovits, George Herzog, Mantle Hood, Otto Kinkeldey, Barbara Krader, William Lichtenwanger, Edward Lowinsky, Frederic Ramsey, Jr., Johanna Spector, John Ward, and Richard Waterman. (This reelected list was comprised of original Council members minus deceased individuals and those presently on the Executive Board or on an officers' ballot.) All the names on the 1960 Council ballot had been nominated at the Executive Board meeting of 9 October 1960 (Society for Ethnomusicology 1960b), and all nominees were duly elected in December 1960.

In December of 1961, the Council voted on whether or not to reelect those whose terms were expiring, including Rose Brandel, Nadia Chilkovsky, Charles Haywood, Mieczyslaw Kolinski, Jan LaRue, George List, William P. Malm, David P. McAllester, Roxane McCollester, Gustave Reese, and Vernon Taylor. It also voted on the individuals nominated by the Board at its 16 November 1961 meeting: Robert Stevenson, Barbara Smith, Sirvaert Poladian, Theodore Grame, Laurence Petran, Peter Etzkorn, and Harold Spivacke (upon joining the Society) (Society for Ethnomusicology 1961b). Only Spivacke and Taylor were not duly elected or reelected to the Council.

11. While the Officers ballots for 1957–61 show the inclusion of women as well as men, they do not convey what was evident in the correspondence of the founding fathers, namely, that McAllester, Merriam, Rhodes, and Seeger put much thought into planning the leadership of the Society, especially the makeup of the Executive Board, during the formative years. Discussions were ongoing with regularity, always including all four even when one or more were no longer on the Board, were out of the country, were on sabbatical, etc. The founders computed when it would be most appropriate for each of them to serve and, as might be expected in such a context, gave equally careful thought to the identity of those who would be asked to run as opposing candidates. It is clear that sometimes individuals were selected to be the opposing candidates because the founders believed the individuals would not have a chance of being elected. These discussions are not evident in Executive Board minutes, and to date, I have found no indication that any of the women candidates during this time period were aware of these discussions and "master plans."

The following presents a numerical breakdown of women and men involved in SEM leadership from 1955, the year of the first officers, through the end of 1961, including the election of that year reported in print in *Ethnomusicology* 6 (3) (1962). The percentage of women serving in leadership capacities is given at the end of each year's entry. It is clear that although the Council grew during the formative years, the number of women in leadership positions in SEM did not.

1955—4 Officers	4 men	0 women (0%)
1956—9 Officers	6 men (1 in 2 jobs)	2 women (22%)
1957—Council of 23,		
including above 8	19 men	4 women (21%)

1958—Council of 15—2 women; plus Executive Board of 9—2 women. Total leadership (Council included Executive Board): 24—4 women (16%).

1959—Council of 21—4 women; plus Executive Board of 8—1 woman. Total leadership (Council plus Board): 29—5 women (17%).

1960—Council of 19—3 women; plus Executive Board of 10—2 women. Total leadership (Council plus Board): 29—5 women (17%).

1961—Council of 32—4 women; plus Executive Board of 8—3 women. Total leadership (Council plus Board): 40—7 women (18%).

1962—Council of 38—6 women; plus Executive Board of 9—2 women. Total leadership (Council plus Board): 47—8 women (17%).

Works Cited

Barbeau, Marius
1946   Letter to Helen Roberts, 6 May. Roberts Collection, Yale University.
Burrows, David
1988   Personal communication, 10 June.

Chilkovsky (-Nahumck), Nadia
1987   Personal communication, 18 October.
Densmore, Frances
1957   Letter to Willard Rhodes, 18 April.
Ethnomusicology: Journal of the Society for Ethnomusicology
1958   Vol. 2 (2).
1960   Vol. 4 (3).
1962   Vol. 6 (3).
1967   Vol. 11 (2).
Ethno-Musicology Newsletter
1953   No. 1, December.
1954   No. 2, August.
          No. 3, December.
1955   No. 4, April.
1956   No. 6, January.
          No. 7, April.
Ethnomusicology Newsletter
1957   No. 9, January.
          No. 10, May.
Frisbie, Charlotte J.
1988   "Frances Theresa Densmore (1867–1957)," in *Women
          Anthropologists, A Biographical Dictionary*, Ute Gacs, Aisha Khan,
          Jerrie McIntyre, and Ruth Weinberg, eds. (Westport, Conn: Greenwood
          Press), pp. 51–58.
1989   "Helen Heffron Roberts (1888–1985): A Tribute," *Ethnomusicology*
          33 (1):97–111.
n.d.   *Women and the Society for Ethnomusicology, 1952–1961.*
          Monograph currently in preparation.
Herzog, George
1970   Letter to Sam Chianis, 20 June. Herzog Papers, Archives of Traditional
          Music, Indiana University.
Koskoff, Ellen (ed.)
1987   *Women and Music in Cross-Cultural Perspective*. Westport, Conn.:
          Greenwood Press.
Krader, Barbara
1987   Personal communications, 19 July and 20 September.
1988   Personal communication, 2 April.
Kunst, Jaap
1959   *Ethnomusicology*. 3d ed. The Hague: Martinus Nijhoff.
McAllester, David P.
1953   Letter to Charles Seeger, 24 February.

1959   "Memorial to Edwin Grant Burrows," *Ethnomusicology* 3 (1):14–17.
1963   "Ethnomusicology, the Field and the Society," *Ethnomusicology* 7 (3):182–86.
1987   Personal communications, 4 May, 29 June, 16 July, 11 August.
1988   Personal communications, 16 July and 17 July.

Nettl, Bruno
1983   *The Study of Ethnomusicology: Twenty-nine Issues and Concepts.* Urbana: University of Illinois Press.

Rhodes, Willard
1963   "A Decade of Progress," *Ethnomusicology* 7 (3):178–81.

Roberts, Helen Heffron
1935   Report to Edward Sapir, 29 May. Roberts Collection, Yale University.
1936   Notes reporting a meeting of the American Society for Comparative Musicology on 4 April at the home of Mrs. E. F. Walton, 25 Washington Square North, New York City, at which Helen presided. Roberts Collection, Yale University.
1979   "Interview." Done for Federal Cylinder Project by Maria La Vigna and David P. McAllester on 5 December at Roberts's home, 1200 Ridge Road, North Haven, Conn. Tape recording, American Folklife Center, Library of Congress, Washington, D.C.

Roberts, Helen H., and Doris Cousins
1969   *A History of the New Haven Symphony Orchestra Celebrating Its Seventy-Fifth Season, 1894–1969.* New Haven: Yale University Press for the New Haven Symphony.

Roberts, Helen H., and Morris Swadesh
1955   "Songs of the Nootka Indians of Western Vancouver Island," *Transactions of the American Philosophical Society,* n.s. 45 (3).

Seeger, Charles
1953   Letters to David P. McAllester, 24 February and 25 February.

Society for Ethnomusicology
1956a   Draft Constitution, part 4: Provisions to Govern First Annual Meeting.
1956b   Executive Board minutes, 5 September.
1957a   Executive Board minutes, 22 March.
1957b   Executive Board minutes, 28 December.
1959a   Executive Board minutes, 8 June.
1959b   Executive Board minutes, 2 October.
1959c   Executive Board minutes, 28 December.
1959d   Council minutes, 28 December.
1960a   Executive Board minutes, 22 April.
1960b   Executive Board minutes, 9 October.
1961a   Executive Board minutes, 13 May.
1961b   Executive Board minutes, 16 November.

Spector, Johanna L.
1988   Personal communication, 22 March.

Bruno Nettl

The Dual Nature of Ethnomusicology in North America: The Contributions of Charles Seeger and George Herzog

ON THE CHARACTER OF AMERICAN ETHNOMUSICOLOGY

ETHNOMUSICOLOGY HAS BEEN sometimes characterized as a North American field. I am not sure this is a correct appraisal, but while there is no doubt that a great deal of ethnomusicological work has been carried out in the United States and Canada, it is more to the point that the concept of ethnomusicology as a separate discipline has been promulgated more in the United States than in Europe. In any event, the field of ethnomusicology developed in this part of the world in a unique fashion. Americans (native and naturalized) have devoted themselves to it in many different ways, but nevertheless as a group their approaches provide a configuration that is distinct from the practice of ethnomusicology elsewhere.

To some, ethnomusicology seems like a field especially made for the Americas. Joseph Kerman, in his generally critical view of the field, remarks upon the "magnetic force that ethnomusicology exerts upon Americanists" (1985:159). This essay comments on some aspects of this uniqueness and suggests that it is the result of certain characteristics of American culture, and goes on to propose that these characteristics are embodied in the work and the approaches of two of the most influential leaders of ethnomusicology in North America.

Anthropologists and historians who broadly characterize American culture focus on two processes. One concerns the essentially innovative character of the culture, both self-consciously and as seen from outside. For some two hundred years, Americans themselves as well as Europeans, and presumably also Asians and Africans, have perceived that there is something new and different, resulting from a unique opportunity, about the American concept of life. But just as much, American culture has been described as a melting pot, as a venue for the combination of values extant elsewhere, of syncretic mixing of cultural elements.

I am not qualified to go into a characterization of American culture and history. But in looking at the history of ethnomusicology in North America,

I am struck by a kind of opposition which expresses these two paradigms. On the one hand, ethnomusicology in the United States and Canada has developed independently of other cultures and other fields. On the other hand, a major characteristic of ethnomusicology in the United States has been its eclectic character and its tendency to sample from a variety of disciplines, theories, and approaches extant in Europe.

The two scholars who are usually cast in opposing roles are Alan P. Merriam and Mantle Hood, especially as represented in their classic publications *The Anthropology of Music* (Merriam 1964) and *The Ethnomusicologist* (Hood 1971). Merriam, without presenting his data in a revolutionary fashion, strikes out in behalf of a *discipline* of ethnomusicology associated with anthropology, the well-worn three-part model of music, the concept of the study of music in culture as an overarching umbrella which subsumes the detailed study of music itself. It is not in proposing the individual activities of the ethnomusicologist that he was innovative, but in establishing an attitude towards them. On the other hand, Mantle Hood—whose conception of bimusicality and special ideas about the use of participation in fieldwork and teaching were surely also unique and innovative—provides in his book a continuation of a number of European approaches, including those of Hornbostel, Sachs, and Kunst.

The dialogue between Merriam and Hood dominated American ethnomusicology in the 1960s and early 1970s, as recognized by Kerman (1985:163–64), and can be regarded as a paradigm of the dualism of American research. But the paradigm of American dualism is represented better by two individuals whose leadership in the American scene provided the personal and intellectual background for the generation of Merriam and Hood, by the work of George Herzog and Charles Seeger, and by the contrast between them. Seeger's contributions have been very widely acknowledged and hailed, but Herzog's, in part because they covered a short period of his life, have not always received appropriate attention. I would suggest that in a sense, the history of American ethnomusicology of the last sixty years can be seen as a kind of dialogue between the two approaches to research, the radical, represented by Seeger, and the syncretic, by Herzog.

CHARLES SEEGER (1886–1979)

Seeger did not at first consider himself an ethnomusicologist; indeed, perhaps he never did. But he was almost always one of the first to come to grips with issues that later became central to ethnomusicology. He came early to the problems facing those who study music as a part of culture, and to the comparative study of musical systems, as he presented the dichotomy of musical and linguistic communication about music in one of his earliest publications (Seeger 1925). It was a theme to which he was frequently to return (e.g., Seeger 1977:16–30). A second consistent theme of Seeger's involved the understanding of vernacular music, which he viewed much more broadly than the traditional concept of "folk" music. Prevalent in some of his publications of the 1930s and 1940s (see Seeger 1977:346 for bibliography), this interest coincided with his strong commitment to social and political reform and to the role music might play, a commitment which led him to composition and performance along with scholarship.

The 1950s saw Seeger take the lead in several directions: the founding and direction of the Society for Ethnomusicology, the development of the melograph (Seeger 1957b), the study of musical parameters not widely understood (Seeger 1958b), the investigation of the relationship of music with social and class structure (1957a). Beginning in the 1950s, but mainly in the 1960s and into the 1970s, we find Seeger (in several publications, e.g., 1970) holistically circumscribing the field of musicology, the aspect of it that might be called ethnomusicology squarely in the center. Along with all of this, of course, came specific studies involving tune families (Seeger 1966b), musical life in North America (1966a), the dulcimer (1958a), and much more.

Seeger is clearly one of the giants of the history of our field. But contrasting his stature with that of some other intellectual leaders, one would have to admit that a look at his publications shows a relatively modest set of contributions to the specific understanding of musics and musical cultures. There is a great deal about the field of musicology, but while it is writing that makes one think, "think big," it does not tell one precisely how to proceed. And so, it seems to me, Seeger's highly significant role in the history of American ethnomusicology has been greatest as stimulus and inspiration; inspiration in the sense that he spoke to the side of scholarship that espouses the radical, striking out in new directions without caring very much what others thought, ignoring the traditional canons. In my experience of him, Seeger was always a man ahead of his time, out in front, exhorting others to follow but perhaps not caring too much whether they did. Thus, while many regard him as a major teacher and a major influence, he did not spend much of his career as a classroom teacher. He did not guide many dissertations or review many books. He was busy with theoretical and organizational innovation.

Seeger's personal and political radicalism, going back to his experiences in California after 1912, are well known (see, e.g., Dunaway 1980). But he was radical as well in ethnomusicology. I would, for example, suggest that his development of the melograph (although there were of course concurrent projects) was an attempt to take the field from one stage of its development to another (see Seeger 1960). Likewise, his insistence on circumscribing musicology and its aims also had the role of moving us from one framework of thought to another (which has not yet been attained). His studies of vernacular musics, too, do not really fit into the framework of folk-music studies but, rather, are tailored to illustrate, perhaps somewhat dissonantly, his complex philosophical, social, and technological ideas. And so I am somewhat puzzled by Seeger's role in our history. Scholars are not really following his lead. The melograph has declined in influence. Vernacular musics are not treated as a unit. The philosophy of musicology has not emerged as a major area of discussion at meetings or in publications.

That we still see Charles Seeger as a great leader is due to his charismatic style. It has been important to American scholars to feel that they are led by someone who has a view of them all, who brings them to the new, takes a responsible social view, knows the European background of his culture and yet is willing thoroughly to disregard it at times, and exhibits, in some way, a characteristic Americanness. And they look to him more for inspiration than for substantive instruction.

In a memorial lecture in 1979, I pointed out (like Kerman in 1985:160–61) important similarities between Seeger and the composer to whom he felt very close, Charles Ives, and perhaps also other American figures in the arts of the same period such as Frank Lloyd Wright. There was the creative and innovative mind, the tangential connection to earlier European models, the insistence on striking out on one's own, a desire to be particularly though not aggressively American, the combination of artistic or intellectual ideals with the vernacular culture, and the use of all this for social reform at some level. A characteristic combination. I am not sure to what degree I can make it into a truly American model. To me, the quintessential work of Seeger is the critical restatement of Adler's model of musicology (Adler 1885; Seeger 1970) in form of a Platonic dialogue, concentrating on a specifically American problem, the distinction between historical musicology and ethnomusicology, drawing into it the problems of American composers, extolling the bimusical (and typically American) approach of Mantle Hood, but surrounding it with highly abstruse rhetoric derived from philosophy and mathematics. It is indeed a bit like a verbal version of a symphony by Ives.

GEORGE HERZOG (1901–1984)

Seeger did not forge a particular method out of his sources; much more, he continued to innovate idiosyncratically. It was sometimes hard to follow him, but easy to be inspired. George Herzog, instead, tried to establish a consistent methodology of a practical sort, with specific methods and techniques, which one could indeed follow, although his rhetoric was in most instances less inspiring than Seeger's. If Seeger is often cited but rarely read, Herzog is frequently emulated without really being well known.

Herzog's contribution, as I suggested, comes from the systematic combination of extant approaches. He studied first in Budapest and became acquainted with Bartók's and Kodály's approaches to folk-song research, study of the authentic, transcriptional and analytical techniques, and a sense of repertories and styles as segments of history. Moving to Berlin to work with Hornbostel, he absorbed the methods of comparative musicology as established in the early 1920s, including a hunger for archiving and a comparative perspective. Going on to Columbia University, he added to his arsenal the concepts of extended fieldwork, of anthropology as an empirical and historically oriented discipline (McAllester 1985). These were a kind of troika pulling his intellectual chariot. But he also added the study of anthropological linguistics, particularly as developed in the United States, with the use of nonwritten languages; the study of folk music as developed by the early students of Anglo-American song such as Phillips Barry, including the particular implications of genetic relationships of tunes (see Barry 1939); and the field of folkloristics as brought to America by Stith Thompson, combining Boasian anthropological perspectives with the historical-geographic method of Scandinavian and Finnish scholarship (e.g., Thompson 1946). These influences combined to produce a large number of seminal studies in the period from 1928 to 1950, and this particular combination was very much in evidence when I was studying with Herzog around 1950. But I feel that it was in the 1930s, a period falling between two eras during which Seeger's influence was greatest, that Herzog was most influential.

I must confess that when I began my undergraduate studies, I had never heard of George Herzog, but I had heard of Curt Sachs and Erich von Hornbostel, and when Herzog was appointed to teach at Indiana University, it was explicitly as Hornbostel's direct and, in the United States, only successor. Herzog's self-view at the time was not only that of a leader of an established profession, but as the only person carrying on a thin tradition. It was not an unrealistic view, although by about 1950 he was really not acting like a leader. He had gradually, beginning in the late 1940s, begun to succumb to an emotional illness which was effectively to end his career some twenty-five years before his death. And so I want to remind us that earlier, he really did hold a role of leadership. Perusal of his papers at the Archives of Traditional Music at Indiana University show, in the period 1930–50, a steady stream of correspondence with virtually everyone who might be contributing to the development of ethnomusicology, either directly or in the role of patron, recordist, supporter, or ally. I cannot reproduce the list, but a sampling produces Carl Seashore, Ruth Benedict, Ernst Ferand, Béla Bartók, Zellig Harris, Manfred Bukofzer, George Pullen Jackson, A. L. Kroeber, Claude Lévi-Strauss, Bertrand Bronson. There is curiously little correspondence with Seeger, except for a burst of letters involving the founding of the American Society for Comparative Musicology in 1933, in which both participated.

Herzog kept careful track of his letters, thoughtfully (for us in posterity) providing carbons, and we see in the 1930s and 1940s a man who was determined to get the field of comparative musicology onto its feet. He wrote to colleagues who were involved and to students, giving advice, encouraging, making recommendations on recording techniques, supporting, helping people get jobs, commenting on publications and manuscripts. One has the feeling that he wanted to have a true overview of everything that was happening, that he wished to make things happen in his chosen way. And above all, he wrote letters that concerned the establishment of archives, in particular the archives that he was building at Columbia and later at Indiana. He kept in close touch with many, writing perhaps a dozen rather long letters each week. Throughout the correspondence one sees the hand of Hornbostel, the comparativist and the archive-builder, of Bartók the careful processor and analyst concerned with authenticity, of Boas the methodical fieldworker, of the confluence of folkloristics, linguistics, and ethnography. And one notes the attitude that there is one broad kind of methodology, without much in the way of alternatives. While Seeger struck out in different directions throughout his life, constantly innovating, Herzog made it clear that to him there was a single if eclectic method.

Despite his great network of contacts, Herzog is today frequently considered a somewhat misanthropic and unpredictable loner, due to his later years of illness when his behavior frequently appeared unreasonable and even paranoid. Yet it is important to emphasize the degree to which he was a leader not only by what he wrote, but in his direct interaction with people of many disciplines. The multidisciplinary nature of American ethnomusicology is in part due to his many-sided reach.

These things turn out to be true also if we look briefly at Herzog's publications. I can only say a word about a few, but a number of them were seminal in establishing genres of study. His study of the Yuman musical style (1928) was probably to that point the first comprehensive, style-centered description of a tribal repertory. "Speech-Melody and Primitive Music" (1934) took up the special relationship between tone languages and the accompanying musical styles and signaling systems. "Special Song Types in North American Indian Music" (1935b) took ideas from age-area approaches to look at an historical problem, but also dealt with the concept of stylistic subdivisions of tribal repertories. "Plains Ghost Dance and Great Basin Music" (1935a) may be the first properly ethnohistorical study in ethnomusicology. Herzog's dissertation, "A Comparison of Pueblo and Pima Musical Styles" (1936a), seems to me to be the first properly comparative study of two contrastive yet related repertories. His small book *Research in Primitive and Folk Music in the United States* (1936b) is a landmark for what later became a genre of state-of-research publications and directories dealing with the special problems of ethnomusicological archives. Perhaps most relevant lately has been his very short and obscure article "Music in the Thinking of the American Indian" (1938), which modestly began the trend of dealing with the conceptual part of Merriam's model and resulted in the well-known works of Merriam, Steven Feld, Hiromi Lorraine Sakata, Daniel Neuman, and others.

In other works Herzog attacked in innovative ways such diverse issues as the nonuniversality of the language of music (1939), the use of linguistic techniques for musical analysis, West African "talking drums" (1945), and the commonalities of European folk music (1950). Much of what he did has become our common practice. Possibly the relative neglect and ignorance of Herzog's work comes about in good measure because it is sensible and practical, combines approaches already extant or in other works, and does not markedly depart from earlier models. Its innovation lies in the way it combines methods from various sources, and its leadership, from its published presentation of practical, evenhanded, and comprehensive models.

CONCLUSION

Not so in the case of Seeger. His answer to problems was to forge ahead, hardly looking back, trying occasionally to combine incompatible ideas—musical class structure and type of transmission, the use of the melograph to study genetic relationships of "Barbara Allen" tunes, the analysis of European traditions in the New World with the presumably coordinate use of cultural dynamics, verbalization, and acculturation. To me, his analyses have always seemed "right." But I doubt that Seeger would have cared whether his analyses were always accepted, for his purpose it seems to me, was to write to make people think, to try many solutions, to experiment, and to test the untried. His radicalism was balanced by Herzog's conservatism. The tendency for American ethnomusicologists to think of their work, and of themselves as a population, in dichotomies—sound and context, anthropology and musicology, theory and application—harmonizes with the dualism represented by these two major figures: one radical and the other conservative; one an intellectual loner, the other a master of disciplinary fusion; one an intellectual frontiersman, the other a scholar combining and promulgating the orthodoxies of European authorities. Seeger, more charismatic, had the gift of inspiring many through his style and the soaring quality of his thought. Herzog brought his influence to bear through practical rather than theoretical service to the profession, teaching by example.

Note

I am grateful to Anthony Seeger for making available the materials in the George Herzog papers housed in the Archives of Traditional Music, Indiana University, and for permitting me to use the manuscript *An American Musicologist*, prepared in the Oral History Program of UCLA in 1972.

Works Cited

Adler, Guido
1885   "Umfang, Methode und Ziel der Musikwissenschaft," *Vierteljahrsschrift für Musikwissenschaft* 1:5–20.
Barry, Phillips
1939   *Folk Music in America*. National Service Bureau Publication no. 80–S. New York: Works Progress Administration, Federal Theatre Project.
Dunaway, David K.
1980   "Charles Seeger and Carl Sands: The Composers' Collective Years," *Ethnomusicology* 24:159–68.
Herzog, George
1928   "The Yuman Musical Style," *Journal of American Folklore* 41:183–231.
1934   "Speech-Melody and Primitive Music," *Musical Quarterly* 20:452–66.
1935a   "Plains Ghost Dance and Great Basin Music," *American Anthropologist* 37:403–19.

1935b   "Special Song Types in North American Indian Music," *Zeitschrift für vergleichende Musikwissenschaft* 3 (1–2):23–33.

1936a   "A Comparison of Pueblo and Pima Musical Styles," *Journal of American Folklore* 49:283–417.

1936b   *Research in Primitive and Folk Music in the United States.* Washington: ACLS (Bulletin 24).

1938   "Music in the Thinking of the American Indian," *Peabody Bulletin* (May):1–5.

1939   "Music's Dialects—A Non-Universal Language," *Independent Journal of Columbia University* 6:1–2.

1945   "Drum-signaling in a West African Tribe," *Word* 1:217–38.

1950   "Song," in *Funk and Wagnall's Standard Dictionary of Folklore, Mythology, and Legend*, M. Leach, ed. (New York: Funk and Wagnall), vol. 2, pp. 1032–50.

Hood, Mantle
1971   *The Ethnomusicologist.* New York: McGraw-Hill.

Kerman, Joseph
1985   *Contemplating Music: Challenges to Musicology.* Cambridge: Harvard University Press.

McAllester, David P.
1985   "George Herzog (1901–1984)," *Ethnomusicology* 29:86–87.

Merriam, Alan P.
1964   *The Anthropology of Music.* Evanston: Northwestern University Press.

Seeger, Charles
1925   "Prolegomena to Musicology: The Problem of the Musical Point of View and the Bias of Linguistic Presentation," *Eolus* 4 (2):12–14.

1957a   "Music and Class Structure in the United States," *American Quarterly* 9:281–94.

1957b   "Toward a Universal Music Sound-Writing for Musicology," *Journal of the International Folk Music Council* 9:63–66.

1958a   "The Appalachian Dulcimer," *Journal of American Folklore* 71:40–51.

1958b   "Singing Style," *Western Folklore* 17:3–11.

1960   Review of Carl Dahlback, *New Methods in Vocal Folk Music Research, Ethnomusicology* 4:41–42.

1966a   "The Folkness of the Nonfolk and the Nonfolkness of the Folk," in *Folklore and Society: Essays in Honor of Benj. A. Botkin*, Bruce Jackson, ed. (Hatboro, Pa.: Folklore Associates), pp. 1–9.

1966b   "Versions and Variants of 'Barbara Allen' in the Archive of American Folk Song in the Library of Congress," *Selected Reports in Ethnomusicology* 1 (1):120–67.

1970   "Toward a Unitary Field Theory for Musicology," *Selected Reports in Ethnomusicology* 1 (3):171–210.

1977   *Studies in Musicology 1935–1975.* Berkeley and Los Angeles: University of California Press.

Thompson, Stith
1946   *The Folktale.* New York: Dryden Press.

IV
Nourished by a Variety of Disciplines

Kay Kaufman Shelemay

Recording Technology, the Record Industry, and Ethnomusicological Scholarship

"Not even time shall efface the bent disk . . ."
John Ashbery, *Three Madrigals,* copyright for Eric Salzman's *The Nude Paper Sermon,* Nonesuch H71231, 1969.

T HE CYLINDER PHONOGRAPH with recording and playback capabilities was first marketed commercially in 1888, initiating a new age of "transmitted" (Rösing 1984) or "mediated" (Keil 1984) musical experience, of which several disciplines, including ethnomusicology, were primary beneficiaries. A considerable literature exists concerning the management and use of recording technology in the field from the earliest days of the discipline (Fewkes 1890; Abraham and Hornbostel 1904a, b; Herzog 1936), and its continuing application in that context for analytical purposes (Arom 1976; Stone and Stone 1981). Studies have been published about the record industry in various locales (Denisoff 1975, 1986; El-Shawan 1987; Gronow 1973, 1975, 1981, 1982, 1983; Racy 1976; Spottswood 1982; Sutton 1985; Wallis and Malm 1984). Other recent publications evaluate the impact of aspects of recording technology, in some cases introduced by researchers, on specific traditions (Dyen 1982; Goldstein 1966, 1982; Shelemay 1988; Sutton 1985). Yet there has been little general discussion concerning the broader relationship of recording technology and its associated industry with the history of ethnomusicology beyond straightforward acknowledgments of its impact.[1] Jaap Kunst once wrote that "ethnomusicology could never have grown into an independent science if the gramophone had not been invented" (1959:12). In *Theory and Method in Ethnomusicology* (1964:16–17), Bruno Nettl discusses the importance of sound recording, stressing its use in collecting and preserving musical sound, as an aid to the analytical process, and as the impetus for sound archives. Charles Keil has more recently suggested that recordings "may have been the single most important factor in getting . . . ethnomusicology started . . ." (1984:91). This paper seeks to build upon and complement the existing literature by providing an overview of ethnomusicology's relationship to the broader world of recording technology.

The following discussion will utilize three major technological transitions to provide an historical framework for analysis of events in both the record industry and the world of ethnomusicological scholarship. The first period, dated from the earliest days of the discipline until approximately 1940, is here termed the "phonograph era," since it was a period during which a series of different phonographs and gramophones were developed to record and play an array of cylinder designs and the 78-RPM disk.[2] After the hiatus in record production and technological development due primarily to World War II, the "LP era" begins in 1948, also incorporating the introduction of the first commercial magnetic tape machines in 1949. Finally, the third major transition discussed here is the start of the cassette revolution in the late 1960s. Although the entry of the LP and magnetic tape marked a major transition in the format and nature of ethnomusicological publications and source material through introduction of lengthier examples, LP technology had a relatively minor impact outside the American and European arena, and limited effect on musical processes and traditions cross-culturally. In contrast, the phonograph and cassette eras had major impact both on our discipline and the musical traditions it sought to study; paradoxically, the phonograph and cassette eras also raise analogous issues and problems.

Although many of the intellectual leaders in early ethnomusicology were European scholars, the contribution of recording technology and its first application in the field were American initiatives (Hickerson 1982). Perhaps this invention of American science and its embrace by American ethnographers have not been the subject of more scrutiny because the new technology was greeted with some reservations even by individuals who employed it effectively in their own research (Brady 1985:124–25). Distrust, or at best ambivalence, has dogged the utilization of recording technology throughout the century of its existence and still survives today, if a recent description by one scholar of his lifelong view of recording technology and its associated industries is representative of others in the discipline. In prefatory remarks to his valuable study of the use of mediated sound in Japan, Charles Keil comments:

> In my own case I know I have nurtured a deep ambivalence, at times masking outright hostility, toward all media for many years. I treat records badly; they aren't real music. I resent all

the accumulated tapes I haven't listened to since the day I recorded them. . . . Until a few years ago my position on all the electronic media was basically Luddite, a desire to smash it all on the grounds that it substituted machines for people, replaced live music with canned, further alienated us from our already repressed sensoria, enabled capitalists to sell us back our musical and emotional satisfactions at a profit. (1984:92)

Keil's confessional touches on several major issues characterizing the complicated relationship between recording technology, its industry, and ethnomusicological thought until the last decade. In particular, the nature of ethnomusicologists' reservations concerning both the use and study of recording technology has changed over the course of the century in response to new technologies, a growing record industry, and a shifting intellectual climate. Initially enthusiastic attitudes during the early phonograph era toward the tendency of recording technology to separate music from its performance context were transformed to concern about decontextualizing musical performance as the century progressed and ethnography became the central research methodolgy of the discipline. The expansion of the Western record industry and its impact upon musical traditions worldwide sparked a response among scholars, most prominently after the beginning of the LP era.

Despite the presence of a literature concerning the impact of technological reproduction and mass distribution on popular music and the arts (Benjamin 1969), the study of the record as source and influence has become an accepted area of ethnomusicological inquiry only in the last decade.[3] Recording technology has been aptly termed the "silent partner" or "third presence" (Brady 1985:7) in the field. Discussion of the interaction between ethnomusicology, changing technologies, and the record industry may well provide an unwritten chapter in the intellectual history of our discipline.

THE "PHONOGRAPH ERA"

In its relationship to early recording technology in the late nineteenth century, ethnomusicology clearly stands "among the disciplines," since a diverse group of folklorists, anthropologists, philologists, and independent scholars began to use the phonograph for scholarly purposes within a year or two of its entry into the commercial market. There is no doubt that the intellectual climate of the time encouraged early collectors to regard the recording of songs as a process analogous to the gathering of scientific specimens (Brady 1985:119). Jesse Walter Fewkes, whose generally acknowledged status as the first to use the cylinder phonograph in the field has recently been questioned,[4] discussed recording technology as a method of preservation, as a check on the fieldworker's objectivity, and as a source of material for comparative studies (Fewkes 1890:268–69). It seems likely that the notion of the musical artifact and the resulting focus on the song as the main unit of study were reinforced during the phonograph era by the physical constraints of the equipment. By 1890 four-inch cylinders accommodated a maximum of three-to-four minutes of recorded sound, while the six-inch cylinder had a nine-minute capacity (Brady 1985:27). Additionally, and almost paradoxically from the modern view, scholars such as Hornbostel and Abraham saw the ability of the phonograph to *separate* music from its context as a *positive* development that removed a primary distraction in the analytical process. They wrote that the phonograph enables one to "record a piece of music and study it at leisure in the studio, where attention is not so much distracted visually as it is at performances by exotic peoples." They further valued the machine for its ability to speed up or slow down music for transcription purposes and to split a piece into fragments for measurement (Abraham and Hornbostel 1904b:192, 195–96).

During the phonograph era, the recording activity of early ethnomusicologists could not be easily differentiated from that of the commercial record industry by either the technologies used or by musical content. Both used the same Edison crank-wound phonographs that had appeared in 1896; they were fairly cheap ($40.00)(Read and Welch 1976:63) and portable. Individuals such as John Lomax used an Edison phonograph as early as 1907 (J. Lomax 1937:57); in 1932 he had the trunk of his car modified to accommodate a half-ton, electrically-driven machine (Brady 1985:32–33). Commercial recordings also played a role in scholarly research, although early disks were criticized as both fragile and of limited utility because they contained only one performance of a given musical excerpt (Abraham and Hornbostel 1904a:123).

If early ethnomusicologists and the record industry shared technologies through the first decade of the twentieth century, they also shared working methods and interests in a diverse repertory for an even longer period. In many instances, representatives of the early record companies preceded ethnomusicologists into the field, themselves functioning as fieldworkers in locating and then recording local talent. For example, the activities of the Gramophone Company's representative Fred Gaisberg during his first recording trip to India in 1901 (Gronow 1981:251) must be appreciated not only as a pioneering effort in the record industry but as one of the early ethnomusicological field trips as well. John Lomax wrote that by 1933, "the big record companies sent trucks through the South . . . looking for singers of the old ballads and folk songs" (1937:58). Through much of the phonograph era, the major record companies published ethnic recordings (Spottswood 1982), sometimes collaborating with ethnomusicologists. Hugh Tracey published "The Sound of Africa" series in cooperation with Eric Gallo, a commercial record manufacturer in Johannesburg, South Africa.[5] The task of the early scholars making field recordings differed little from that of the early commercial record industry in part because from its inception, the cylinder phonograph carried both recording and playback capabilities. The early record companies also sold cylinders, 78-RPM records, phonographs, and gramophones, which wedded cylinder and disk to their respective machines in a combined marketing strategy.

In the first decades of the recording industry, several technologies overlapped: the cylinder, first introduced in 1888, was quickly supplemented by prerecorded 78-RPM disks in 1895. The wire tape recorder, invented in 1898 by a Danish scientist, Valdemar Poulsen, had to be used with earphones, since it lacked means of amplification, and therefore did not become an important competitor in the commercial recording industry (Read and Welch 1976:158). However, it was used often by fieldworkers through the 1940s. Entry of 78-RPM disks did not substantially alter time constraints described above since they, too, could only accommodate short segments of music, although they did improve the quality of recorded sound.

However, a critical transition on another level did take place with the entry of the 78-RPM by Emile Berliner in 1895, which allowed the gramophone to be marketed only with playback capabilities. This historic invention conclusively separated the acts of recording and playback in the commercial market, and necessitated more sophisticated recording facilities to achieve "professional" sound recordings; the era of the studio recording had commenced. Additionally, by the late 1920s and early 1930s, the depressed economic climate as well as the growing focus on mass entertainment led the major record companies to begin to withdraw from the ethnic record market (Spottswood 1982:63–64). Thus by the end of the phonograph era in the late 1930s, an irreversible divide separated the record industry from the world of ethnomusicological field recording. The dichotomy was deepened by growing scholarly interest in preservation, especially of rural cultures, and encouraged by scholarly skepticism of urban areas

increasingly perceived as environments encouraging "interruption and de-
struction of ancient traditions" (Redfield and Singer 1969:212–13). The
record industry and its products were largely thought to be vehicles of entertainment, not worthy subjects for the ethnomusicologist seeking to salvage rural musical traditions under pressures brought in part by this very industry.[6]

The distribution of recordings of American and other Western popular
styles by the record industry in Third World locations like Africa as early
as 1908 (Coplan 1979:143) had also served to alter the relationship of ethnomusicologists to the record industry. Klaus Wachsmann wrote of the
ambivalence of Africanists, who while acknowledging processes of change
in music, were disturbed over introduction of Western musical traditions
on 78s. He wrote that the African Music Society "opposed the extravagant
claims of the 'entertainment-first' school" when the record companies in
Africa offered music, "with a strangely exotic flavour . . . featuring for the
most part selections of popular American and European origin" (Wachsmann c.1961:77).

On yet another level, the phonograph era saw the establishment of archives by both ethnomusicologists and the record industry. The
Phonogramm-Archiv in Berlin was founded in 1900, the Archive of Folk
Song at the Library of Congress in 1928, and the Archives of Folk and
Primitive Music at Indiana University in 1948 (Nettl 1964:17–18). The
archive at Columbia Records dates from 1890, incorporating virtually all
label recordings, including cylinders, 78s (and their metal parts), 45s, LPs,
and CDs (Shelemay 1986). Both the scholarly and commercial archival efforts were driven by the need to preserve, although scholars for the sake of
eventual study, the record industry for potential commercial use. Ironically,
changing technologies rendered this strategy equally effective in both cases, as
processes for converting recordings into new formats assumed great importance both in generating reissues in the commercial record industry and in aid-
ing preservation of early field collections in ethnomusicology.[7] Finally, even as
their paths diverged in the 1920s, the record industry, notably the Edison
Company, continued to support scholarship indirectly by making blank cylinders available for use long after they were withdrawn from the commercial market in 1913, thus lengthening the life of the cylinder phonograph
until the late 1930s.

THE "LP ERA"

The beginning of the "LP era" in 1948 marked the entrance of a
technology able to accommodate longer segments of music. The growing

distinction between the major, commercial record firms owned by multinationals and the small, independent, specialty record companies was further solidified. With the changing shape of the record industry, ethnomusicologists not only began to consider the LP as a viable route for publications, they began to structure their field experiences to accommodate it. A new genre of "scholarly" ethnic recordings intended for a market beyond the ethnic community begins to emerge at this time.[8]

Some, such as Hugh Tracey, saw the LP as the venue for saving ephemeral traditions that would otherwise be lost (Wachsmann c.1961:77–78), and making recordings became his primary activity. LP technology, however, remained an elite one because of the necessary investment in both production equipment as well as new hardware for playback purposes. For these reasons, the LP gained limited popularity outside the United States and Europe. In contrast, the 78-RPM remained in widespread use in many Third World countries despite the relative scarcity of gramophones for playback purposes. The *African Music Society Journal* reported that a wide indigenous market existed for recordings of Western popular music, with individuals buying records that they heard on a friend's gramophone, or at a shop:

> A really good disc heard through the shop's loudspeaker will attract listeners out of the air and sell half a dozen copies in the time it takes to be played once. . . . It will probably be a 78 RPM record though the 45 RPM record is making headway. No 33 RPM has good prospects. . . . The great majority of Africans have hand-wound gramophones and it appears that recent substantial sales of transistorized players capable of taking slower discs may have made such inroads into the customer's budget that he cannot yet afford many. (Special Correspondent 1963:41)

Hugh Tracey also confirmed that "the African market at present is concerned almost exclusively with this size of record which can be played on portable gramophones. Long playing records offer a more generous time limit, but if the intention is to make the item available to Africans on their standard equipment, then the 78-RPM time limit must be accepted" (Tracey 1948:8).[9]

Although for economic reasons the LP era had lesser impact outside Europe and the United States, sound recordings at this juncture became firmly established in the mainstream of the ethnomusicological research process.

The increased length and fidelity of the LP, and, by the 1950s, the flexibility of newly developed magnetic tape, led to the increasing application of sound recording to analytical methodololgy. Quantification of musical data such as that carried out by Freeman and Merriam was both inspired and enabled by the development of increasingly sophisticated recording technology. Although Freeman and Merriam do not specify which technology they used, they explicitly credit "a recording device" with making possible their statistical analysis (1956:465).

As technologies and the record industry changed, so did scholarly attitudes. While ethnomusicology became more dependent upon recording technology as an adjunct to ethnography and analysis, it remained skeptical of the enterprise. The Cantometrics project of Alan Lomax is one of the most complex and interesting exemplars of the cumulative impact of recording technology by the 1960s. Cantometrics, with its goal to link folksong style with its cultural setting, utilizes recording technology both to generate its data base of about 4000 songs and to mediate the rating system by which the songs are profiled (A. Lomax 1976:29). I am here concerned not with Lomax's methodolgy, which has been assessed in countless reviews and Feld's thoughtful article (1984:385), but rather with the impact of technology on multiple aspects of the project.

Cantometrics emerges from Lomax's interaction with and ideological response to a world of recording technology. In the introduction to the Cantometrics handbook and sound examples, he writes:

> Cantometrics is a response to the media explosion of the 20th century, when a myriad of inventions vastly increased man's ability to record, store, duplicate, and transmit his communications. In this period, receivers became inexpensive and universal, but the means of production and transmission of communication continued to be costly and have remained largely in the hands of big companies and rich countries. . . . Once a universal human attribute, communication has tended to become a monopoly, a one-way channel from the powerful center to the mute periphery. Man, the communicating animal, is frustrated. . . . The effect on audible culture has been cataclysmic. . . . For the groups without broadcasting facilities, the media all have one main message—"Keep still and listen to us." (1976:8)

Although Lomax also acknowledges what he terms the "positive side" of the media explosion (including access to a world of music and the ability of the scholar to carry out cross-cultural comparative studies), he explicitly presents his Cantometrics research as a system designed to combat the threatening deluge of broadcasts and recordings and a step to insure "the integrity of cultural systems" (1976:9). Lomax thus displays a different, if more explicitly negative, response to the recording industry than did his predecessors in the discipline. The shift reflects empirical changes in the recording industry that by the 1960s had resulted in transnationalization (Wallis and Malm 1984:300), the Euro-American domination of the LP industry, and a changing intellectual environment in the world of scholarship. Lomax's studies emerged during the 1950s and volatile 1960s, when the questions concerning the impact of political and economic processes on culture were of increasing importance to American anthropology and ethnomusicology (Marcus and Fischer 1986:119–21). Thus Lomax's use of technology exemplifies both the pervasiveness of its impact by the middle of the twentieth century, and the manner in which contemporary ideological debate informed its use in the academic enterprise.

THE "CASSETTE ERA"

The cassette revolution, which began in the United States and Europe in the late 1960s and spread throughout the rest of the world by the mid-1970s, returned technology for recording and playback to the individual. One is tempted to characterize this development as the essential democratization of the relationship between recording technology and music makers cross-culturally. In part because cassette technology was much more affordable than any preceding it, the cassette quickly had an almost equally marked effect on the record industry, the ethnomusicologist, and musical traditions worldwide. In its transfer of recording technology from the studio back to a vast public, the cassette has on many levels a role analogous to its venerable ancestor, the cylinder phonograph. A more recent change in the record industry, the purchase of Columbia Records by the Sony Corporation in November 1987, also moves a large segment of the industry back toward its early position as a supplier of recording materials, recorded sound, and the machines with recording and playback capabilities.

The advent of cassette technology has defused some long-standing ethical and political issues concerning the colonial aspects of at least the basic technologies of recording, while at the same time raising thorny new problems. Record companies and ethnomusicologists no longer fully control recording technology, although one can certainly argue that the industry controls the commercial process and distribution. However, the widespread distribution of the cassette cross-culturally has ensured that the ethnomusicologist is frequently greeted in the field by informants with their own equipment. Prerecorded cassettes have also become increasingly important primary sources for scholars (Sutton 1985:26, 40–42). Recording equipment has ceased to be the same symbol of external (Western) power that it was as late as the mid-1970s. The "colonial pattern" of ethnomusicological activity (A. Seeger 1986:267) may in fact have been diminished by these new and accessible technologies. The cassette revolution, too, has made it easier and cheaper to repatriate recordings removed from their place of origin. Yet as recording technology ceases to be merely a tool of scholarship or the instrument of an industry, it has become an independent player in the musical processes of virtually every musical tradition worldwide. Issues concerning ownership and remuneration that in the past might have been resolved by individual negotiations have given way to complex legal and ethical problems involving copyright and international piracy.[10]

Conclusion

This brief discussion cannot do justice to the extraordinary impact of recording technology on our discipline, its methods, and the materials we study. I have not been able to discuss the impact of recording technology and its industries on other related disciplines, most notably musicology, where recordings have begun to influence research on performance practice in areas as diverse as the period-instrument revival and Verdi operas (Winter 1984; Crutchfield 1983). I have also purposefully omitted discussion of what may be considered the latest "eras" of technological change, those of the compact disk and digital tape, because their impact on either ethnomusicology or world music is as of yet minimal. The development of the video camera, which unites sound and image in the field and laboratory, has had a major impact upon the ethnomusicological research process outside the purview of this essay (Stone and Stone 1981).

A most crucial issue resulting from changing technologies past and future is their cumulative impact on individual perception. Some have begun to question in what way our perceptual abilities have changed in the course of this century because of the increasing need to discern and block sounds (Rösing 1984). Certainly an ear accustomed to the ubiquity of recorded sound, and a lot of passive listening, may have to sort out sounds differently in the field. Additionally, many modern musical traditions now have something approaching a one-hundred-year history on recordings that is accessible on commercial disks or in archives. For several generations, ethnomusicologists have not gone into the field as auditory *tabula rasa,* but rather with preconceptions and expectations predicated on exposure to sound recordings.

The use of recording technology has further altered the potential for studying musical systems over time, primarily by enabling the scholar to juxtapose the past with the present. Our understanding of what comprises an historical process has been revolutionized by the capabilities of recording technologies, which make accessible a past otherwise lost and which collapse synchronic/diachronic distinctions. It seems likely that the concern with musical processes in current ethnomusicological research has been enhanced, if not generated, by the presence of technologies which themselves permit such investigation. Finally, as recording technology displaces musical notation as the primary mechanism for the preservation and transmission of music, it simultaneously dislodges notated musical traditions from the top of the ethnomusicological pecking order—and agenda.

Recording technology and its associated industry have irrevocably altered the course of the ethnomusicological venture during the last century. But has the discipline had an impact on either technological developments or the record industry itself? Ethnomusicologists have had what might be termed at best an interactive relationship with technological innovation, in some cases by modifying existing machines for their own use (Jairazbhoy and Balyoz 1977) or even by contributing their own inventions (C. Seeger 1951). However, nearly a century of ethnic recordings, many prepared by or in collaboration with ethnomusicologists or "ethno-recordists," has contributed to a growing trend for cross-cultural synthesis in musical composition and performance. The experimentation of Western composers with the music of other cultures is now extending to mass-audience repertories as diverse as the Broadway musical and the rock-music industry (Shelemay 1987). Much of the inspiration and raw musical material for these new fusions stems directly from the ethnomusicological presence in the university, public-sector agencies, and the music industry itself.

The advent and growth of recording technology has therefore had a cumulative impact that transcends any single event or change. A brief story illustrates this point. The *New York Times* reported that a man was honored as the World Champion Liar by the Burlington, Vermont, Liar's Club. His winning lie described how he once had received a record as a gift. He found the music on one side so pleasing that he kept playing that side hour after hour. Eventually the record became so thin that music from both sides played at the same time. The man cannot recall how he came up with the winning story. "I thought of this lie a long time ago," he said (12/31/87).

Perhaps recording technology has been with us so long that we, too, can no longer remember when it began. In a recent article on sound archives, Anthony Seeger has suggested that what may actually survive most of us are our field recordings on deposit in an archive (1986). If so, recording technology is not only an integral part of our discipline's intellectual history. It is an increasingly important part of our future as well.[11]

Notes

1. A notable exception is Porter 1974.

2. Periodization is problematic since although the commercial record industry turned almost exclusively to the 78-RPM by the end of the first decade of the twentieth century, the cylinder remained the primary field technology for ethnomusicologists until around 1935 and continued to be used in some locales well after that date. The cylinder went through a series of different configurations described in detail by Brady 1985 (chapter 2) and Read and Welch 1976 (chapters 7, 8, and 12). Edison termed his original "speaking machine" the phonograph (Read and Welch 1976:28B–28C), while Emile Berliner's patented machine introduced to play 78-RPM discs in 1895 was called the gramophone.

3. Norma McLeod's editorial in *Ethnomusicology* (McLeod 1973:v–vi) helped to encourage ethnomusicological publications concerning popular music and its associated industry in various cross-cultural settings. However, aesthetics and the impact of the recording industry on society have more often been treated by sociologists (Denisoff 1975, 1986). The utilization of commercial sound recordings for research purposes, including music, has been discussed by Flanagan (1979).

4. Evidence that ethnologist Frank H. Cushing may have been the first to use the phonograph is cited by Brady (1985:116). A diary entry of an early member of the American Folklore Society mentions having heard recordings of American Indian languages in May of 1889 at the Cushing home, a year before the Fewkes trip to record the Passamaquoddy cylinders in Calais, Maine.

5. I thank Carol Muller for this example, drawn from an unpublished term paper, "The Indispensability of Recording Technology to the Scholarly Study of African Music . . . With Particular Reference to the Work of Hugh Tracey and The International Library of African Music," January 1988, typescript.

6. Read and Welch observe that American and European perspectives of the recording industry differ. While "in America, potential of the phonograph record as a medium of cultural communication was slightly appreciated by musicians, musical writers, and critics, . . . in Europe, the situation was quite the reverse" (1976:419).

7. The Federal Cylinder Project at the Library of Congress (Brady et al. 1984) and a similar project at the Indiana University Archives (A. Seeger and Spear 1987) have been mounted to preserve and better utilize surviving cylinder collections.

8. The availability of quality, portable recorders also led to a new breed of "ethno-recordists," musical amateurs with good equipment. I thank Nazir Jairazbhoy for this observation.

9. A similar situation evidently existed in Bulgaria, where despite the introduction of the LP in 1958–59, 78-RPM recordings continued to be sold in areas where only the older gramophones were available (Atanasov 1967:141). J. A. Ellison brought this article to my attention and provided an English translation.

10. Jabbour (1983) provides a useful discussion of issues relating to copyright and legal protection of folklore.

11. An experience as faculty-in-residence at CBS Records during Summer 1986 provided the impetus for investigating this topic. I would like to thank members of the New York University Urban Ethnomusicology Seminar, Fall 1987, especially Rolf Groesbeck, Robert Kendrick, and Ingrid Monson, for their comments and suggestions upon the early drafts of this paper. In addition to the many colleagues acknowledged in the body of this paper or its bibliography, I would also like to thank Lawrence Gushee, Neil Rosenberg, Anthony Seeger, and Mark Slobin for comments or materials.

Works Cited

Abraham, Otto, and E. M. von Hornbostel
1904a "Phonographierte indische Melodien," in *Hornbostel Opera Omnia.* Edited by Klaus P. Wachsmann et al. Translated by Bonnie Wade. (The Hague: Martinus Nijhoff), vol. 1, pp. 115–82.
1904b "Über die Bedeutung des Phonographen für die vergleichende Musikwissenschaft," in *Hornbostel Opera Omnia.* Edited by Klaus P. Wachsmann et al. (The Hague: Martinus Nijhoff), vol. 1, pp. 183–202.
Arom, Simha
1976 "The Use of Play-Back Techniques in the Study of Oral Polyphonies," *Ethnomusicology* 20 (3):483–520.
Atanasov, Vergilii
1967 "Zvukozapis," *Entsiklopediia na bulgarskata muzikalna kultural* ["Recording in Bulgaria," *Encyclopedia of Bulgarian Musical Culture*], pp. 140–41. English translation by J. A. Ellison.
Benjamin, Walter
1969 "The Work of Art in the Age of Mechanical Reproduction," in *Illuminations,* Hannah Arendt, ed. (New York: Schocken Books), pp. 217–51.
Brady, Erika
1985 "The Box That Got the Flourishes: The Cylinder Phonograph in Folklore Fieldwork, 1890–1937." Ph.D. dissertation, Indiana University.
Brady, Erika, and others
1984 *The Federal Cylinder Project.* Vol. 1., *Introduction and Inventory.* Washington, D.C.: American Folklife Center, Library of Congress.

Coplan, David
1979 "The African Musician and the Development of the Johannesburg Entertainment Industry, 1900–1960," *Journal of Southern African Studies* 5 (2):135–64.
Crutchfield, Will
1983 "Vocal Ornamentation in Verdi: The Phonographic Evidence," *19th Century Music* 7 (1):3–54.
Denisoff, R. Serge
1975 *Solid Gold: The Popular Record Industry.* New Brunswick, N.J.: Transaction Books.
1986 *Tarnished Gold.* New Brunswick, N.J.: Transaction Books.
Dyen, Doris
1982 "New Directions in Sacred Harp Singing," in *Folk Music and Modern Sound,* William Ferris and Mary L. Hart, eds. (Jackson: University Press of Mississippi), pp. 73–79.
El-Shawan Castelo-Branco, Salwa
1987 "Some Aspects of the Cassette Industry in Egypt," *The World of Music* 29 (2):32–47.
Feld, Steven
1984 "Sound Structure as Social Structure," *Ethnomusicology* 28 (3): 383–409.
Fewkes, Jesse Walter
1890 "The Use of the Phonograph in the Study of the Languages of the American Indians," *Science* 15 (no. 378):267–69.
Flanagan, Cathleen C.
1979 "The Use of Commercial Sound Recordings in Scholarly Research," *Journal for Recorded Sound Collectors* 11 (1):3–17.
Freeman, Linton C., and Alan P. Merriam
1956 "A Statistical Classification in Anthropology: An Application to Ethnomusicology," *American Anthropologist* 58:464–72.
Goldstein, Kenneth
1966 "The Ballad Scholar and the Long-Playing Phonograph Record," in *Folklore and Society,* Bruce Jackson, ed. (Hatboro, Pa: Folklore Associates), pp. 35–44. 1980 reprint.
1982 "The Impact of Recording Technology on the British Folksong Revival," in *Folk Music and Modern Sound,* William Ferris and Mary L. Hart, eds. (Jackson: University Press of Mississippi), pp. 3–13.
Gronow, Pekka
1973 "Popular Music in Finland: A Preliminary Survey," *Ethnomusicology* 17 (1):52–71.
1975 "Ethnic Music and Soviet Record Industry," *Ethnomusicology* 19 (1): 91–102.
1981 "The Record Industry Comes to the Orient," *Ethnomusicology* 25 (2): 251–84.
1982 "Ethnic Recordings: An Introduction," in *Ethnic Recordings in America. A Neglected Heritage* (Washington, D.C.: American Folklife Center, Library of Congress), pp. 1–31.

1983   "The Record Industry: The Growth of a Mass Medium," *Popular Music* 3:53–76.

Herzog, George
1936   *Research in Primitive and Folk Music in the United States.* Washington, D.C.: American Council of Learned Societies (Bulletin 24).

Hickerson, Joseph
1982   "Early Field Recordings of Ethnic Music," in *Ethnic Recordings in America. A Neglected Heritage* (Washington, D.C.: American Folklife Center, Library of Congress), pp. 67–83.

Jabbour, Alan
1983   "Folklore Protection and National Patrimony: Developments and Dilemmas in the Legal Protection of Folklore," *Copyright Bulletin* 17 (1):10–14.

Jairazbhoy, Nazir, and Hal Balyoz
1977   "Electronic Aids to Aural Transcription," *Ethnomusicology* 21 (2): 275–88.

Keil, Charles
1984   "Music Mediated and Live in Japan," *Ethnomusicology* 28 (1):91–96.

Kunst, Jaap
1959   *Ethnomusicology.* 3d ed. The Hague: Martinus Nijhoff.

Lomax, Alan
1976   *Cantometrics: An Approach to the Anthropology of Music.* Berkeley: University of California Extension Media Service.

Lomax, John A.
1937   "Field Experiences with the Recording Machines," *Southern Folklore Quarterly* 1:57–60.

Marcus, George E., and Michael M. J. Fischer
1986   *Anthropology as Cultural Critique.* Chicago: University of Chicago Press.

McLeod, Norma
1973   "From the Editor. . . ," *Ethnomusicology* 17 (2):v–vi.

Nettl, Bruno
1964   *Theory and Method in Ethnomusicology.* New York: Free Press.

The New York Times
1987   "World Champion Teller of Tall Tales," 31 December 1987, C28.

Porter, James
1974   "Documentary Recordings in Ethnomusicology: Theoretical and Methodological Problems," *Association for Recorded Sound Collections—Journal* 6 (2):3–16.

Racy, Ali Jihad
1976   "Record Industry and Egyptian Traditional Music: 1904–1932," *Ethnomusicology* 20 (1):23–48.

Read, Oliver, and Walter L. Welch
1976   *From Tin Foil to Stereo.* 2d ed. Indianapolis: Howard W. Sams and Co.

Redfield, Robert, and Milton Singer
1969   "The Cultural Role of Cities," in *Classic Essays on the Culture of Cities,* Richard Sennett, ed. (Englewood Cliffs, N.J.: Prentice Hall),

pp. 206–33. Reprinted from *Economic Development and Culture Change* 3:53–73.

Rösing, Helmut
1984   "Listening Behaviour and Musical Preferences in the Age of 'Transmitted Music'," *Popular Music* 4:119–50.

Seeger, Anthony
1986   "The Role of Sound Archives in Ethnomusicology Today," *Ethnomusicology* 30 (2):261–76.

Seeger, Anthony, and Louise Spear, eds.
1987   *Early Field Recordings*. Bloomington: Indiana University Press.

Seeger, Charles
1951   "An Instantaneous Music Notator," *Journal of the International Folk Music Council* 3:103–06.

Shelemay, Kay Kaufman
1986   Journal. Summer Residency, CBS Records.
1987   "Musical Notes for the Year Ahead," *University* 7 (1):9–10.
1988   "Together in the Field: Team Research Among Syrian-Jews in Brooklyn, New York," *Ethnomusicology* 323:369–84.

Special Correspondent (of *The Star,* Johannesburg).
1963   [Untitled article], *African Music Society Journal* 3 (2):41–42.

Spottswood, Richard K.
1982   "Commercial Ethnic Recordings in the United States," in *Ethnic Recordings in America. A Neglected Heritage* (Washington, D.C.: American Folklife Center, Library of Congress), pp. 51–66.

Stone, Ruth M., and Verlon L. Stone
1981   "Event, Feedback and Analysis: Research Media in the Study of Music Events," *Ethnomusicology* 25 (2):215–26.

Sutton, R. Anderson
1985   "Commercial Cassette Recordings of Traditional Music in Java: Implications for Performers and Scholars," *The World of Music* 27 (3): 23–45.

Tracey, Hugh
1948   "Recording African Music in the Field," *African Music Society Journal* 1 (2):6–11.

Wachsmann, Klaus
c.1961 "The Sociology of Recording in Africa South of the Sahara," *African Music Society Journal* 2 (2):77–79.

Wallis, Roger, and Krister Malm
1984   *Big Sounds from Small Peoples*. New York: Pendragon Press.

Winter, Robert
1984   "The Emperor's New Clothes: Nineteenth-Century Instruments Revisited," *19th Century Music* 7 (3):251–65.

Albrecht Schneider
Psychological Theory and Comparative Musicology

IT CAN HARDLY be denied that comparative musicology in its early days was at least as much a psychological enterprise as it was an approach comprising the "The Ethnological Study of Music." We find this title employed as a definition of sorts by Charles Myers, who was, moreover, also an eminent psychologist devoting himself, among other topics, to the study of rhythm sense in so-called "primitive peoples." His ethnomusicological interests, furthermore, included his well-known work on the music of the Veddas and his writings—not unlike those of his Berlin colleague Carl Stumpf—on the "Beginnings of Music."[1]

The combination of ethnological, anthropological, and psychological aspects in the study of music seems to have been particularly favored and pursued by English, Austrian, and German scholars, including such leading pioneers in ethnomusicology as Herbert Spencer, Richard Wallaschek, Robert Lach, Géza Révész, Otto Abraham, and, of course, Erich Moritz von Hornbostel.[2] In the United States it was Benjamin Ives Gilman who recognized that the publications of Hermann von Helmholtz and Stumpf on the sensation and psychological properties of tone raised the possibility of taking a closer look at the "musical system of China, based upon observations of performances by native musicians." Gilman thus considered his investigations "as material for a comparative psychology of that element of our sensations of sound which is known as the quality of pitch" (Gilman 1892:54).

The view that any such investigations could contribute to a comparative psychology and aesthetics of music was, no doubt, central to comparative musicology and can be found in several of the methodological articles written by Wallaschek, Lach, Stumpf, Hornbostel, Révész, and S. Nadel. Gilman further asserts that these investigations might help to solve such intricate questions as the origins of music, its development, and the universal principles underlying music making (ibid.:54, n1; see also Spencer 1890).

Further strengthening the case for music's potential contributions to the study of psychology and perception, W. V. Bingham claimed that "the psychologist will be interested in the growing knowledge of primitive music, chiefly because of the accumulating light it throws on certain mooted questions in audition, for example, the nature of consonance" (1914:427). Still in the 1960s Mieczyslaw Kolinski emphasized the task of formulating a general theory of consonance by posing "the question whether it is possible to approach the phenomena of consonance and dissonance in an objective way giving these terms a universally valid meaning" (1962:66).[3]

STUMPF'S "TONPSYCHOLOGIE"

Rather than try to evaluate all approaches and contributions made by ethnomusicologists to the psychology of music or of psychologists to comparative musicology, I shall focus in this article on one central issue that I believe played an almost dominant role in both fields as a result of theories advanced by Carl Stumpf in his *Tonpsychologie* (1883 and 1890a) and several articles (e.g., 1890b). Stumpf, a disciple of the philosopher and psychologist Franz Brentano, postulated a rather complex theory of tone sensation with a primarily phenomenological basis. The theory focused on cognitive functions, such as judgment and comparison, mental analysis by means of similarity or difference, attention, and memory. Though Stumpf carried out a number of experiments, many based on introspection, it is quite obvious that his *Tonpsychologie* largely belongs to phenomenological traditions of philosophy, as well as to *Denkpsychologie* [thought-psychology], which, in turn, relates to both Gestalt theory and modern cognitive psychology. One can, therefore, trace Stumpf's ideas back to Brentano and find parallels in the writings of Ernst Mach, Alexius von Meinong, and Oswald Külpe. The work of Edmund Husserl also contains parallels, especially his *Readings on the Phenomenology of Internal Time-Consciousness* and his investigations of "experience and judgment" (Husserl 1928, 1939),[4] both of which relate to the thinking of Brentano and Stumpf.[5]

The *theory of relations*, the unifying principle in Stumpf's *Tonpsychologie*, was also the prevalent concept in Brentano and Meinong. Just as Hermann von Helmholtz concentrated on the physical properties of sound and the psychophysics of hearing,[6] Stumpf investigated the effects of tone sensation on the listener.[7] With the theory of relations as a background, and the doctrine of the relativity of apprehension (previously formulated by T. Fechner) as a guideline, Stumpf systematically discussed criteria governing sensory judgments as well as methods for arriving at such judgments.

One of the most universal and simple methods is *comparison*, which Stumpf treats at some length with respect to tonal stimuli and the theoretical issues of similarity, likeness, dissimilarity, diversity, and the like. Chapter 7 of *Tonpsychologie* addresses so-called *Distanz-Vergleichungen* [Distance Comparisons], which stem from the various degrees of likeness, for instance, between two notes separated by a "distance."

The notion of *distance* later became central to theories of scale formation favored by Stumpf himself, his coworker Hornbostel, and much more recent scholars (see especially Husmann 1961, Graf 1975 and 1980, Reinecke 1970, and the discussion of these in Schneider 1976). Stumpf first investigated the concept in his essay, "Über den psychologischen Ursprung der Raumvorstellung," where he stated that we are able (a) to recognize the dissimilarity of two places and (b) to measure the amount of difference, that is, to judge the "distance" between two places (m, n) (1873:17).[8] In *Tonpsychologie* Stumpf defines distance as the *degree* of dissimilarity (1883, 1:122ff).

Ellis and "The Musical Scales of Various Nations"

Only one year after Stumpf had published the first volume of *Tonpsychologie,* Ellis and Hipkins's "Tonometrical Observations on Some Existing Non-Harmonic Scales" appeared (1884). Ellis's more detailed "On the Musical Scales of Various Nations" followed soon thereafter (1885). In this seminal paper, Ellis claimed to have measured almost exactly scales that either were equidistant or used some form of equal temperament, with steps of 100, 150, and 200 cents. Ellis asserted that "this tempered form seems to have been that aimed at" (Ellis and Hipkins 1884:377), whereas other forms, such as that analyzed in Arabic music by the nineteenth-century theorist Mikhāil Meshakah, had "adopted an equal temperament of 24 quartertones, or 24 equal divisions of the octave, each containing 50 cents," which Ellis believed was a scale that was no more than "a pure survival of Zalzal's" (Ellis 1885:497).[9]

There is no need here to pursue the contributions of Ellis any further, for I have done so elsewhere (Schneider 1976, 1986, and 1988a). I should emphasize, however, that the measurements of Ellis (who, according to Jaap

Kunst, was "totally tone-deaf") seem a bit far-fetched and should be interpreted with the appropriate caution. The same holds true for his "final conclusion" (Ellis 1885:526), for one might think that Helmholtz had claimed to have found one "natural" scale based "on the laws of the constitution of musical sound." Actually, Helmholtz always insisted that while hearing is, to a certain extent, governed by physiological mechanisms present in every human (and, thus, "natural"), scales are dependent on human invention and, in fact, show a high degree of diversity when understood from historical and cultural perspectives (Helmholtz 1870:401ff, 568).

After all, it was Carl Stumpf who relied on the work of Ellis, even though he recognized that the scale measurements and published interpretations of them did not always concur and that there were considerable deviations in the data obtained by Hipkins with a set of tuning forks from scales claimed to be based on some kind of "temperament." Notwithstanding such minor objections, Stumpf agreed with Ellis that (a) tempered scales existed and (b) such temperament resulted from *intention* (Stumpf 1886b:513–17). This agreement made it possible to interpret the "Siamese" scale found on *ranāt* instruments (xylophones, metallophones) as comprising seven steps spaced equally at a distance of 171.43 cents each. With actual measurements revealing intervals between 90 and 219 cents, to speak of a scale built on equal temperament (7 × 171.43 cents) was anything but a case for naturalness. Still, Stumpf welcomed the work of Ellis and Hipkins because it served as "the first 'psychophysical' measurements of individuals from non-European nations" (1886b:517). Despite inconsistent data and interpretations, Stumpf could make use of the measurements to illustrate his claims. He took the Siamese equal-temperament hypothesis of Ellis (1885), for example, as a point of departure when he prepared his own special report on the "Tonsystem und Musik der Siamesen" [Scales and Music of the Siamese] (Stumpf 1901).

LOGARITHMS, ROOTS, GEOMETRICAL PROGRESSIONS

Stumpf regarded the "Siamese" scale as a series of steps, each of which can be mathematically defined as $\sqrt[7]{2} = 1.1040895$. The intervals calculated by Stumpf as mean values on the basis of Ellis's measurements and those he made with Otto Abraham approximate the theoretical norm, but still contain the rather considerable standard deviation of

$(\gamma - 1) = 8.47$ cents. Stumpf declared "existence of the equal-tempered seven-tone scale with the Siamese" to be beyond all doubt (Stumpf 1901:84). He then faced the problem of finding a *psychological* explanation for how such scales could have come into existence with peoples unaccustomed to calculating with logarithms and/or roots of numbers.

With a mathematical foundation for the "Siamese" scale unlikely, Stumpf took refuge in a theory he and contemporaneous psychologists did not particularly like, the so-called Weber-Fechner Theorem,[10] one of the basic concepts of psychophysics. Fechner himself had declared that, with respect to tonal stimuli, Weber's "law" was self-evident and required no further experimentation: everyday experience revealed that equal-frequency ratios from oscillations corresponded to the sensation of a difference in tones with the same value in different octaves (Fechner 1860, 1:181). Perhaps with this in mind, Stumpf went on to explain the "Siamese" scale by stating the *assumption* "that the successive, geometrically equal steps will also be registered as equal tone-distances in sensation" (Stumpf 1901:91). Methodologically speaking, basing an explanation on an assumption is no proof, relying instead on the *petitio principii*.[11]

Seeking to establish hypotheses is, of course, always legitimate, and in a later article Stumpf wrote at length to explain this strange scale phenomenon. Drawing on the Weber-Fechner Theorem, he pointed to the comparison of so-called *Übersgangsempfindungen* [transitional sensations], *Komplexqualitäten* [complex qualities], or *Kohärenzgraden* [coherence levels] or whatever principle (Stumpf and Hornbostel 1911:260). In other words, there was no easy way to find a psychological interpretation of the "Siamese" heptatonic scale or any other allegedly equidistant scale, which Hornbostel in 1906 had declared to be "the most important discovery of tonometrical research next to irrational intervals" (Hornbostel 1906).

Stumpf's position was attacked quite early on by his rival, Wilhelm Wundt, one of the foremost psychologists of the time, whose particular strength was experimental design. Wundt asked one of his disciples, Carl Lorenz, to undertake a large series of experiments on the problem of the perception and judgment of tone-distance, which challenged the unreserved application of the Weber-Fechner Theorem in the field of sound.[12] There is no need here to detail the controversy between Stumpf and Wundt.[13] Instead, let me close this section with Stumpf's claim, namely that humans are capable of judging pure pitch distances as long as they are not conditioned by the principle of consonance or hindered by "false experiments in psychological laboratories" (Stumpf 1901:94).

TONE-DISTANCE, TONAL BRIGHTNESS, AND THE THEORY OF PITCH

Stumpf's insistence on a principle of tone-distance independent of pitch and interval relationships (*Tonverwandtschaft*) first appeared in *Tonpsychologie*, where he stated that domains of musical notes could exist in only one dimension. This supposition is necessary if one is to assign pitch relationships an aspect of "distance" that is measurable in a *linear* fashion. Stumpf's own investigations into the nature of "Siamese" music (1901:96) had revealed that, even with a presumed equidistant scale, intervals influenced by consonances were present. Experimental work done from 1905 to 1914 by Stumpf's coworkers, Abraham and Hornbostel, produced similar results (Abraham and Hornbostel 1925), namely that it is very difficult, if not impossible, to isolate the element of tonal "distance" from the "quality" (tone-chroma) perceived by the listener in a given interval.[14]

In his comprehensive study on "Konsonanz und Dissonanz" (1898), Stumpf himself had denied that a musical interval could be understood as two pitches a discrete "distance" apart. Drawing on communications with Franz Brentano, Stumpf declared almost categorically "that distance and interval are of two different kinds," the latter being defined by "fusion," while "distance" in the strict sense measured the *dissimilarity* between two sensations, caused, for instance, by musical notes (Stumpf 1898:68–69 and 1890a:199; for definitions of *Tondistanz* [tone-distance] see 1873:17 and 1883:122ff).

This study appeared only two years before Stumpf undertook research on the "Siamese" scales and music, making his shift in reasoning appear amazing. It is understandable, however, when seen as a corollary of a position originally stated in a book on the origins of space conception as well as of ideas in *Tonpsychologie* concerning the notion of "distance." As a philosophical idea this notion seems to have governed much of Brentano's thinking, as well as that of his disciple.[15]

Brentano, however, must be credited with being one of the first to recognize that neither is pitch a simply linear scale nor can it be reduced to one dimension. Quite the contrary, he regarded musical pitch as comprising certain "qualities" recurrent in each octave, and of two other elements which he discussed by analogy to colors and subsumed together under the concept of "brightness" (*Helligkeit*).[16] Brentano, thus, belongs among the "fathers" of modern *pitch theories* who, since Géza Révész's *Zur Grundlegung der Tonpsychologie* (1913), always incorporated at least two dimensions, *Tonigkeit* and *Helligkeit*, thereby pairing a recurrent element with a more linear one.[17]

To be fair to Stumpf, I must add that he later (1914:309ff) accepted the so-called "two-componential theory of pitch," whose validity Révész had demonstrated. Stumpf admitted that the concept he developed in *Tonpsychologie* was too narrow to account for the necessary distinction between tone quality (chroma) and "brightness" (*Helligkeit*). Furthermore, the view of *pitch* reduced to a single dimension expressed in terms of "distance"[18] would make sense only for *pure tones,* which were not present, anyway, in the music he was investigating, for instance, Javanese or "Siamese" instrumental pieces. However, when Stumpf changed his view on the concept of interval size and the theory of pitch in 1914, his influential paper on "Siamese" scales and tunings had been around for some time. Hornbostel, moreover, had adopted the *Distanzprinzip* not only to explain the *pélog* tuning but also intervals in Tunisian music, which he believed were governed by the same *psychologischer Tatbestand* [psychological fact] of *equidistance* that Stumpf had been unable to explain (Hornbostel 1906:33f).

EVOLUTIONARY THOUGHT AND TONAL DIMENSIONS

Adding further complexity to Stumpf's concepts was evolutionary theory, which not only pervaded much of the writing on the psychology of music before the turn of the century,[19] but figured strongly also in some of Stumpf's and Hornbostel's essays. In his article on the songs of the Bellakula Indians, Stumpf had suggested that a tonal system with stable steps required "an intellectual development . . . whose consecutive stages and inner properties no one has yet demonstrated for us in a psychologically credible way" (Stumpf 1886a:426), a task to which he later devoted himself in his book on the "origins of music" (Stumpf 1911). With historical records unavailable for the "early stages," the "line of development" sketched by Stumpf quite naturally employed both ethnographic parallels and psychological hypotheses.[20]

Stumpf's scheme for the development of melodies commenced with arbitrary, small steps showing no tonal relations (cf. Stumpf 1911; Stumpf and

Hornbostel 1911:265), followed by what he called *Distanzleitern* [distance scales], which he again defined not by tonal relations, but by fixing "distances" between notes. Only then—at a third stage—could one envisage the principles of consonance and "fusion." Abraham and, to an even greater degree, Hornbostel accepted this basic scheme. Hornbostel was of the opinion that the principle of "distance" seemed to be much more important than consonance in music yet lacking harmony (Hornbostel 1905:91f).

Abraham and Hornbostel then ventured to generalize that with respect to steps between two notes (m, n), "distance" would be equivalent to "*Helligkeit*" as a constituent of a single tone, while the element of "*Tonigkeit*" would be equivalent to a musical interval. In this way, the single pure tone is defined by its "*Helligkeit*," the musical note by both "*Helligkeit*" and "*Tonigkeit*" [tone height/brightness plus chroma], while arbitrary two-tone complexes (comprised of two tones with different "brightness" and "*Helligkeit*") may cause the perception of a certain "distance," though not the sensation of a distinct interval (intervals being defined by two musical sounds, both of which should have chroma and tone height). Thus, aspects of *quality* that define tone *chroma* also define the musical *interval*, whereas "distance" is a numerical value measuring difference and dissimilarity of any two tones as a *quantity* (*Abstandsmaß* [measure of difference] and *Maß der Unähnlichkeit* [measure of dissimilarity]). Abraham and Hornbostel claimed that for "primitive" singers (1925:249)—by "primitive" they meant both certain non-Western as well as nonspecialist European singers—the musical interval seems to be no more than a "distance" (according to the overall "contour" of a melodic line or gesture): "only at somewhat higher stages of development musical intervals having a distinct quality (that is, fourths and fifths) can be observed" (ibid.). Figure 1 illustrates central aspects of the pitch theory advanced by Stumpf, Abraham, and Hornbostel.

Hornbostel in particular considered *Helligkeit* to be a "more primitive and, from an evolutionary standpoint, much older and more general property of sound" than *Tonigkeit*.[21] *Helligkeit*, moreover, was thought to have equivalents in other fields of sensory perception, and Hornbostel, a chemist by training, even investigated the problem of "olfactory brightness" and published an article on the problem, where he argued that *Helligkeit* was an intermodal quality found in all sensory phenomena, forming a one-dimensional continuum stretched between two poles (Hornbostel 1931:517–19).

In a lecture entitled "Geburt und erste Kindheit der Musik" [Birth and Early Childhood of Music] (Hornbostel 1973), Hornbostel declared *Hel-*

a) "Helligkeit" (tonal brightness) according to Stumpf (1883), Abraham & v. Hornbostel (1925)

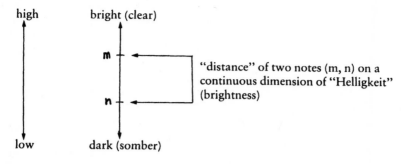

b) elements of musical tone relevant to "pitch"

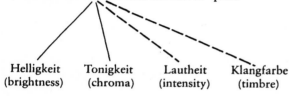

FIGURE 1. Part *b* illustrates that musical tones (notes of a scale played by any instrument) have more than one dimension relevant to the sensation of "pitch." Because of "fusion" (claimed by Stumpf 1883/1890a and 1898), intervals of tones arranged according to small-integer ratios could cause a sensation analogous to "Tonigkeit" to be termed "Intervallqualität" (that which distinguishes a fourth from a fifth; see Jacques Handschin, *Der Toncharakter,* Zurich 1948).

ligkeit much older than *Tonigkeit* and to be prevalent in "primitive" music, while at the same time expressing reservations about linear evolution. With *Helligkeit* assigned to tone-distance, musics making use of "distances" were considered "primitive" and to be automatically "older" than any musical culture based on simple interval "structures." Hornbostel summed up his theory thus: "Primitive music is to a large degree distance-music, and during an extensive period of development distance maintains predominance over tonal relationships or consonance."[22]

This point of view was unconvincing for several reasons. Even the music of the Vedda, whose music served Hornbostel as a good example of *Distanzmusik* based on *Helligkeit*,[23] was reported by both Wertheimer and Myers to contain no "unclear, fluctuating pitch structures, rather precise, clearly

specified pitches" (Wertheimer 1909/10:306), that is, "not a single example of that *glissando* from note to note, which one frequently finds among
certain primitive peoples" (Myers 1911:360). Also, if one looks at those
tribes described as most "primitive" in the anthropological literature written by Hornbostel's contemporaries, Bushmen and Pygmies are almost certainly "on any list." However, neither Bushman nor African Pygmy music
demonstrates aspects of *Distanzmusik,* and certainly musical styles in these
cultures are far from "primitive."[24]

Perhaps the most conclusive objection to Hornbostel's approach, however, would be that "distance" itself, at least in Stumpf's original concept,
was not regarded so much as "primitive," but rather as an *independent*
principle complementing interval structure.[25] It was only because *Helligkeit* had been subjected to an evolutionary interpretation and then had
been confounded with the dimension of "distance" that both could be conceived of as characteristics of "primitive" music. As a consequence of this
view, the "Siamese" orchestral piece "Thai oi Kamēn" that Stumpf, Abraham, and Hornbostel recorded and transcribed (Stumpf 1901, Hornbostel
1920) would be considered "primitive" music because it is a genuine example of *Distanzmusik* in the strict sense of the word (the term had been
coined by Stumpf and Hornbostel). *Distanzmusik* was thus only a consequence of theories advanced by Stumpf, Abraham, and Hornbostel following Ellis's initial gospel of "equal temperament" in Southeast Asia, a view
which enjoyed early popularity, but has been shown to be without real
foundation.[26]

ACOUSTICAL NOTES ON TONOMETRICAL RESEARCH

Theories about "Siamese" and other allegedly equal-tempered scales
have been based mostly on measurements taken from xylophones and metallophones, tuned sets of wooden or metal slabs, and bell-type instruments, such as the "Siamese" *kong* (Stumpf 1901:77ff) and the Javanese
bonang (Ellis 1885:512f). For purposes of measurement Ellis used a set of
tuning forks and "the ear of Mr. Hipkins"; Stumpf used the so-called
"Appunn'scher Tonmesser" (a set of tuned metal reeds for the octave from
400 to 800 vibrations per second) and the support of several students.
Only a few years after Ellis had published his articles, J. W. Strutt, better
known as Lord Raleigh, delivered a paper "On Bells" (Strutt 1890), in
which he investigated "a so-called hemispherical metal bell" resembling
the shape of a single *bonang-gong*.[27] Lord Raleigh was able to determine
four partials from the spectrum that did not correspond to a single harmonic series.

Thus, the analysis of "pitch" is far from easy, for, unlike conventional sounds—those produced by strings or vibrating columns of air—there is no clearly marked "fundamental" with an adjunct series of partials whose frequencies would be integer multiples of the lowest component like $1:2:3:4:5: \ldots :n$. Because there is no clearly discernible "fundamental," it is usually not possible to obtain a "frequency" by measurement and then equate this with "pitch." For instance, if we look at the following graph obtained from spectral analysis of a *saron demung* of the Javanese *sléndro,* we find a rather dense and quite inharmonious spectrum. The most prominent component occurs at 4,412.5 Hz (see graph 1), which, of course, cannot be called the "fundamental" of that particular sound; the same data resulted from several measurements. Even when we represent the scale with "distances" measured as "fundamental" frequencies of the slabs of a *saron,* we will not find five equal steps in such a *sléndro* tuning (cf. Hood 1954 and 1966); however, some approximation may be determined from the following data obtained from recent measurements:[28]

(Slab)	I	II	III	IV	V	VI
Interval (Cents)	234.4	244.5	223	256	235.5	
Scale (Cents)	0	234.5	479	702	958	1193.5

The single step does not seem that far from the theoretical value of 240 cents. The "pure" fifth, however, cannot be overlooked. With the standard deviation no less than 14.077 cents, "equal temperament" as envisaged by Ellis and others becomes even statistically unlikely.

The actual "pitch" the listener perceives, however, has little if anything to do with the lowest component in such complex spectra as those produced by slabs and bells (see the reasons above and Schneider 1986:161–65; 1988a; Schneider and Beurmann 1989). Sounds from such instruments quite often cause significant "uncertainty" in pitch perception, a fact only recently demonstrated in experiments undertaken on Balinese *gender-wayang* metallophones (Deutsch and Födermayr 1986).

I myself have obtained similar results when using either synthetically produced sounds similar to "tubular bells" or original sounds obtained from *saron*s and a *bonang* in *sléndro* tuning. The reasons for "auditory uncertainty" are quite easily detectable. First, most of the notes produced are

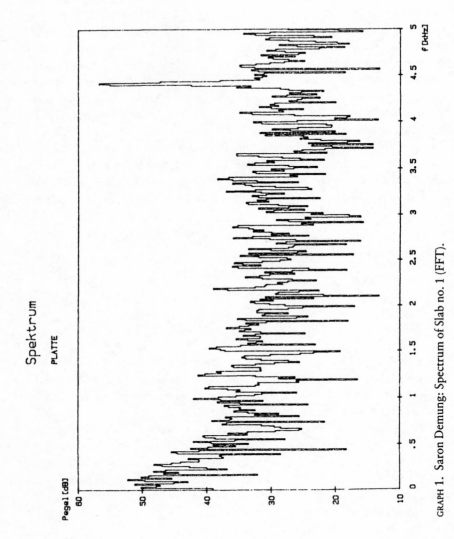

GRAPH 1. Saron Demung; Spectrum of Slab no. 1 (FFT).

rather short in duration, with only a fraction of a second for the listener to judge "pitch" (see graphs 2a and b, where from the moment of articulation to the point where decay is almost complete, little more than 0.4 seconds elapses).[29] Second, because we are working with slabs and bells, we find, on one hand, very complex vibration patterns but, on the other, no stationary (that is, quasi-stationary) section, a requisite for reliable "pitch" judgments. The problem is obvious in graphs 3a and b, which give parts of the unstable vibration patterns produced by a *saron* and a *bonang*. As a consequence of this vibration pattern, the spectral content shifts as a function of time (see graphs 4a and b) so that once more the auditory impression is that of fluctuation and "uncertainty." Graphs 4b and c clearly illustrate this effect with marked shifts in "pitch."

I leave it to the reader to imagine what Ellis, Stumpf, and others may have actually "measured" or taken as the "pitch" of xylophones and metallophones. It should be clear, however, that, since "pitch" is not equatable with any single "frequency" (Deutsch and Födermayr 1986), the idea of "tone-distances" (measured in hertz and expressed in cents) as a linear *Abstandsmaß* (measurement of difference) between notes spaced on *one* dimension was surely inadequate from the very beginning, whether or not the single dimension is identified with *Helligkeit*. Although some tuning patterns, such as those observed in Africa, do balance pitch relations in a way one might rightly call "temperament," there is no evidence that such procedures consciously yield exact frequency "distances" like $\sqrt[5]{2}$ or $\sqrt[7]{2}$ (see Schneider and Beurmann 1990).

Notwithstanding the various methods of measuring vibration patterns and spectral characteristics of idiophones such as xylophones and metallophones, technology that singles out one component designated as "pitch" has heretofore often produced erroneous results or given way to misinterpretation.[30] The "exactness" of the science of comparative musicology was probably no more or less than that of many sciences, which, at the end of the nineteenth century, attempted to turn new technologies toward the solution of humanistic and psychological problems. The early speculation about non-Western scales and tone-systems is today obsolete, even if it did provide some of the fundamental tenets for the growth of comparative musicology. It is, no doubt, worthwhile to reexamine critically a good deal of the former research on tuning and temperament. In this essay I have suggested one possible framework within which to undertake such historical reexamination, namely by investigating historically yet another set of theoretical issues, those derived from the psychological or even philosophical thinking[31] that exercised an influence on comparative musicology virtually since it was established some one hundred years ago.

Signal Display:

Sampled data

File SARON   (50.000 kHz)
Length: 6.000 620 Sec.
Cursor: 0.124 000 Sec.
Level: Volts

(Compressed)

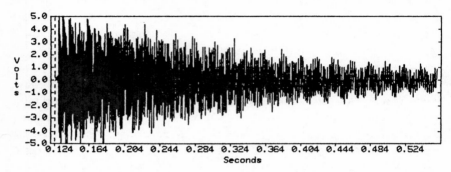

GRAPH 2A

Signal Display:

Vibration pattern of Bonang/Sound 5b

File BONANG5B (50.000 kHz)
Length: 0.889 000 Sec.
Cursor: 0.033 000 Sec.
Level: Volts

(Compressed)

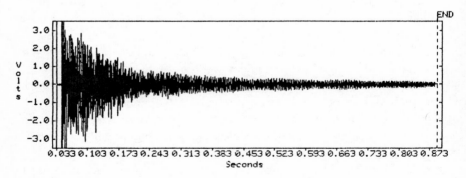

GRAPH 2B

Signal Display:

Sampled data

```
File SARON      ( 50.000 kHz)
Length:     6.000 620 Sec.
Cursor:     0.128 000 Sec.
Level:                Volts
```

(Compressed)

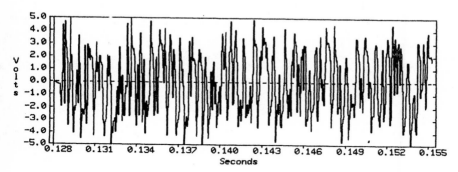

GRAPH 3A

Signal Display:

Vibration pattern of Bonang

```
File BONANG2A  ( 50.000 kHz)
Length:     1.575 000 Sec.
Cursor:     0.010 000 Sec.
Level:                Volts
```

(Compressed)

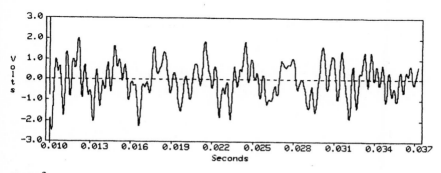

GRAPH 3B

Spectral Display

Sampled data

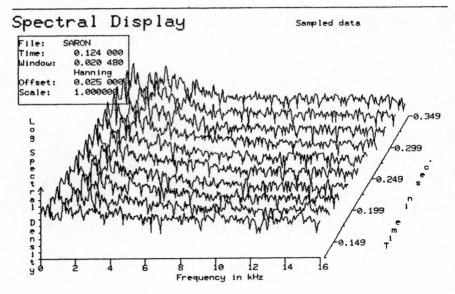

GRAPH 4A

Spectral Display

shifts of spectral components ./. time

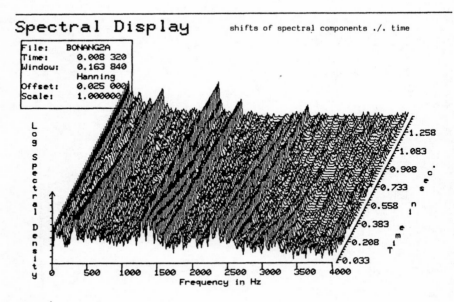

GRAPH 4B

Spectral Display

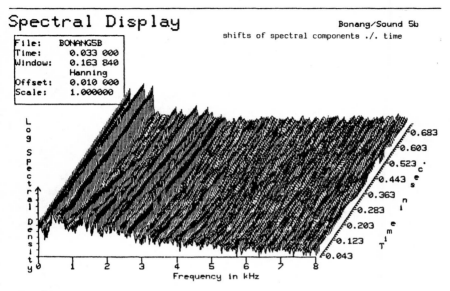

Bonang/Sound 5b
shifts of spectral components ./. time

File: BONANG5B
Time: 0.033 000
Window: 0.163 840
Hanning
Offset: 0.010 000
Scale: 1.000000

Log Spectral Density ↑

0.683
0.603
0.523 c
0.443 e
s
0.363
n
0.283 i
0.203 e
m
0.123 i
T
0.043

Frequency in kHz

GRAPH 4C

Notes

1. Charles Myers was a physician and held a position as Professor of Psychology in King's College, London, and at Cambridge University. As to his contributions, see Myers 1905, 1907, 1911, 1913.

2. As to the history of comparative musicology, see Graf 1975 and 1980, Schneider 1976, Nettl 1983, and Wachsmann 1973. In his book on *Musikpsychologie und Musikaesthetik* (Frankfurt am Main: Akademische Verlagsgesellschaft, 1963, p. 154–55), Albert Wellek, a psychologist and a musicologist who had studied at Vienna with Robert Lach, states that the foundations of a scientific psychology of music are owed to comparative musicology (mentioning R. Lach, C. Stumpf, S. Nadel, G. Révész).

3. See also Kolinski 1936:43–44, where he discusses most of the major conceptions of consonance and dissonance until 1935, including those of Helmholtz, Stumpf, Lipps, and Hornbostel.

4. Edmund Husserl, *Vorlesungen zur Phänomenologie des inneren Zeitbewusstseins,* in *Jahrbuch für Philosophie und phänomenologische Forschung 9,* M. Heidegger, ed., (Halle 1928):367–496. (English edition, Bloomington: Indiana University Press, 1964); also his *Erfahrung und Urteil: Untersuchungen zur Genealogie der Logik,* L. Landgrebe, ed. (Prague 1937). Among Mach's writings, see his *Die Analyse der Empfindungen und das Verhältnis des Physischen zum Psychischen* 4th ed., Jena: G. Fischer, 1903 (first published 1886). Among Meinong's many interesting studies, *Über Gegenstandstheorie* is recommended; see *Untersuchungen zur Gegenstandstheorie,* A. v. Meinong, ed. (Leipzig: J. A. Barth, 1904),

pp. 1–50. Külpe's thought is condensed in his *Grundriss der Psychologie* (Leipzig: W. Engelmann, 1893).

5. For those interested in the philosophical background as well as the history of ideas in psychology, the books of Metzger (1954), Pongratz (1967), and Bergmann (1967) are worth reading. For background to Stumpf's *Tonpsychologie*, see *Psychologie vom empirischen Standpunkt* by Franz Brentano (first published 1874; see the edition by Oskar Kraus in 3 volumes (Leipzig: F. Meiner, 1924–28)), and William James's *Principles of Psychology* (1981; see note 18).

6. See Helmholtz 1863, 3/1870, 4/1877, 5/1896. Helmholtz's basic concept was put forward in a speech of 1857 delivered at the University of Bonn, titled "Über die physiologischen Ursachen der musikalischen Harmonien" (in *Vorträge und Reden von Hermann von Helmholtz*. 4th ed. (Braunschweig: F. Vieweg, 1896), vol. 1, pp. 119–55). See also Schneider 1988a.

7. The respective theories of consonance quickly clarify the difference. Although both of them are derived from ratios of small integers, Helmholtz stressed the importance of beats or their absence (a *physical* phenomenon with effects in audition), while Stumpf emphasized *Verschmelzung* [fusion] as a criterion of consonance based on the listener's perception and *psychic* pleasure.

8. Again, for thorough understanding, the reader is referred to Brentano 1874 (see note 5), and to papers published posthumously in *Franz Brentano: Philosophische Untersuchungen zu Raum, Zeit und Kontinuum* (Körner and Chisholm 1976). Of course, the notion of *distance* still plays a major role in "multidimensional scaling" (MDS); see Shepard 1986 (note 17).

9. A critical examination of Ellis's speculations is found in Schneider 1976:105–6. Of course, Meshakah did *not* advocate a scale of twenty-four equally tempered steps. A new and reliable translation of the treatise of Meshakah was given recently by Gabriele Braune in her M.A. thesis, *Übersetzung und Kommentierung eines arabischen Musiktraktates,* (University of Hamburg, 1983).

10. In a strict sense, of course, there are *two* distinct theorems which have been formulated by Ernst Heinrich Weber (who worked on the sense of touch and found out that the just-noticeable difference between two weights used as stimuli is almost constant, thus $\frac{\Delta S}{S}$ = const.) and Gustav Theodor Fechner (1860, 1:134ff; 2:9ff). The latter transformed Weber's "law" into his own *Maßformel* [Measurement formula] $E = k \times \log R$, thus stating a logarithmic relationship between the increase of sensation (E) and the necessary increase of the stimulus (R). Both "laws" have been tested and found to be valid only in certain parts. See S. S. Stevens, "On the Psychophysical Law," *Psychological Review* 64 (1957):153–81, and Jean-Claude Falmagne, *Elements of Psychological Theory* (Oxford: Clarendon Press, 1985).

11. To evaluate Stumpf's reasoning, the reader is referred to Stumpf 1901:81–107. The difficulties occasioned by any such explanation, with similar problems in psychophysical scaling, cannot be denied. See also Fechner 1860, and the commentary by L. L. Thurstone, "Fechner's Law and the Method of Equal Appearing Intervals," *Journal of Experimental Psychology* 12:214–24 (1929), as well as the remarks in Hornbostel 1910:477.

12. See Lorenz 1890, whose investigations were based on no less than 111,000 single judgments of stimuli. However, along with some solid results this study contains some untenable conclusions.

13. See Lorenz 1890, Stumpf 1890b, and Wundt 1890. Wundt (1890:612) saw rather clearly that it is almost impossible to expect individuals to look for tone-distances exactly "half" or "twice as big" as a given one.

14. In the only experiment in which Abraham and Hornbostel came close to the result they had expected (i.e., the isolation of "distance"), they used a cluster of twenty-four narrowly spaced tones and interpreted the resulting phenomenon of *Klangbreite* [sound breadth] as being analogous to "distance" (which is doubtful); see Abraham and Hornbostel 1925:238, 245–46.

15. Cf. Bergmann 1967, section 17, and particularly pp. 321–27, and for first-hand knowledge, the writings of Brentano in note 16. One should bear in mind that Stumpf worked as a professor of *philosophy* at the University of Berlin. The notion of "distance" was also discussed with respect to the basic principles of geometry (see Schneider and Beurmann 1989).

16. Brentano's rather complicated theory may be found in large measure in his lecture "Von der psychologischen Analyse der Tonqualitäten in ihre eigentlich ersten Elemente," *Atti del V. Congresso intern. di psicologia Roma 1905* (Rome, 1906), pp. 157–65; reprinted in F. Brentano, *Untersuchungen zur Sinnespsychologie,* 2d ed., R. M. Chisholm and R. Fabian, eds. (Hamburg: F. Meiner, 1979), pp. 93–103. A short discussion of Brentano's view is contained in Révész 1913:36ff.

17. See Révész 1913. Révész later wrote a critical report on the various efforts to establish an adequate theory of pitch, in "Zur Geschichte der Zweikomponentenlehre in der Tonpsychologie," *Zeitschrift für Psychologie* 99:325–56 (1925). Regarding the dimensions of pitch, *Tonigkeit,* in English and American terminology, is usually translated as "chroma," while German *Helligkeit* corresponds to "tone height" (cf. Bachem, "Tone Height and Tone Chroma as Two Different Pitch Qualities," *Acta Psychologica* 7:80–88 (1950)). Meanwhile, pitch is often considered to incorporate more than two dimensions; see, for example, C. Monahan and E. C. Carterette, "Pitch and Duration as Determinants of Musical Space," *Music Perception* 3:1–32 (1985/86); R. N. Shepard, "Structural Representations of Musical Pitch," in *The Psychology of Music,* Diana Deutsch, ed. (New York: Academic Press, 1982), chapt. 11.

18. Cf. W. James, *The Principles of Psychology,* edited by F. Bowers and I. K. Skrupskelis (Cambridge: Harvard University Press, 1981), vol. 1, pp. 500ff. James obviously knew the *Tonpsychologie* very well and gives a lucid discussion of the concept of "distance." See also vol. 2, chapt. 20.

19. For a critical review see Stumpf 1885, who deals especially with theories on the origins of music put forward by Darwin, Spencer, Sully, and Gurney.

20. Cf. Stumpf 1911, chapters 2 and 5. See also the review of Edward Sapir in *Current Anthropological Literature* 2:275–82 (1913). Sapir points out the hypothetical nature of Stumpf's outline. The concept to which not only Stumpf but others adhere (see, for example, Frances Densmore, "Scale Formation in Primitive Music," *American Anthropologist* 11:1–12 (1909)) is that of *Entwicklungsgeschichte,* a mixture of "historia naturalis," plain "facts," and evolutionary ideas that govern much of nineteenth-century anthropology.

21. See Abraham and Hornbostel 1925:249: "Untersuchungen der neueren Zeit haben ergeben, daß die Helligkeit eine primitivere, entwicklungsgeschichtlich äl-

tere und allgemeinere Eigenschaft von Schällen ist, die ihre Entsprechung in einer analogen, wenn nicht identischen Eigenschaft der Erscheinungen anderer Sinnesgebiete hat." Regarding Hornbostel's conception of *Helligkeit* and *Tonigkeit*, see his contribution, "Psychologie der Gehörserscheinungen" (1926) where "distance" is correctly defined as "die Spannweite der Bewegung" (in melodic movement).

22. This lecture, delivered on invitation at the "Kant-Gesellschaft" of Rostock in 1928, is most interesting as it provides insights into Hornbostel's methodological thought. The sentence reads in the original German, "Primitive Musik ist wesentlich Distanzmusik und auf lange hinaus behält die Distanz die Vorherrschaft vor der Tonverwandtschaft oder Konsonanz."

23. The other material was of course the music of the Fuegians. In his famous article, Hornbostel turns to the *Helligkeit/Tonigkeit* dichotomy but points to the fact that even the singing of the Yámana (Yahgan), which he considered to be the most primitive of the Fuegian groups under review, had already made a transition from simple alternation of two tones to melodic movement based on fixed intervals wherein tones have melodic "functions" (see Hornbostel 1948:68ff).

24. Much of the relevant literature to 1970 is listed in Charlotte J. Frisbie, "Anthropological and Ethnomusicological Implications of a Comparative Analysis of Bushmen and African Pygmy Music," in *Ethnology* 10:265–90 (1971). Among available recordings, those of the Ba-Benzélé (Bärenreiter BM 30 12303) and of the Bibayak (Ocora OCR 558504) give a clear impression of the "contrapuntal" techniques employed in such "primitive" music.

25. See Stumpf 1883, 1898, 1901. Moreover, even when there are "neutral" intervals in musical styles, these may not result from "distance" alone but from a deformation of larger framing intervals; for examples, see Chailley 1963.

26. See Barbour 1963; Hood 1966; Schneider 1976, 1986, and 1988a. The view that *pélog* is based on a division of the octave into nine equal steps of 133 cents each has been brought forward by Rahn (1979). Jan Pieter Land had already noted that *pélog* literally means "irregular" (Land 1889).

27. With respect to acoustics, the term "bell" would perhaps be more adequate, although it is customary to speak of "gongs" and *Gongspiele* because of the usage of the Hornbostel/Sachs system (see also Simbriger 1939).

28. Measurements of spectrum (FFT) have been made with the Bruel and Kjaer Narrow Band Spectrum Analyzer 2033. For technical support, I would like to thank H. Stoltz (Phonetisches Institut, Universität Hamburg) and the acoustical department of the Staatl. Institut für Musikforschung of Berlin (West), especially Mrs. Prigrann. The instruments investigated all belong to the collection of the Museum für Völkerkunde, Hamburg.

29. Graphs 2–4 are from measurements made with a Synclavier II by Dr. E. Beurmann (Hamburg), whom I would like to thank for all of his support.

30. Many of the measurements published have been exercised by means of a strobo-tuner (Stroboconn), which by construction (see R. W. Young and A. Loomis, "Theory of Chromatic Stroboscope," JASA 10:112 (1938)) is directed to a comparison of two frequencies, one of which is that of an "unknown sound," the other provided by the device. Extensive measurements such as those published by W. Surjodiningrat, P. J. Sudarjana, and A. Susanto (1972:10ff, 26) again were

directed to detect "fundamental frequencies" while "pitch" of course is a psycho-acoustical category most likely comprised of several dimensions (see note 17). Regarding the acoustical properties of xylophone—and metallophone—sounds, the perception of "pitch" seems to be related very much to spectral content; to this problem, see also G. Stoll, "Spectral-Pitch Pattern: A Concept Representing the Tonal Features of Sound," in *Music, Mind, and Brain,* M. Clynes, ed. (New York: Academic Press, 1982), pp. 271–78.

31. As to Hornbostel's thought, a critical review has been supplied by Veit Ernst in his unpublished *Habilitationsschrift,* "Die Vorstellungen vom 'Phänomenalen' in Hornbostels systematischer und vergleichender Musikwissenschaft," Humboldt-Universität, Berlin, 1970. The criticism contained in this study concentrates (as far as psychological theory is concerned) on phenomenology and Gestalt theory. For an evaluation of Hornbostel's achievements, see also Schneider 1988b.

Works Cited

Abraham, Otto, and Erich M. von Hornbostel
1925   "Zur Psychologie der Tondistanz," *Zeitschrift für Psychologie*
          98:233–49.
Barbour, John Murray
1963   "Mißverständnisse über die Stimmung des javanischen Gamelan," *Die Musikforschung* 16:315–23.
Bergmann, Gustav
1967   *Realism: A Critique of Brentano and Meinong.* Madison: University of Wisconsin Press.
Bingham, W. Van Dyke
1914   "Five Years of Musical Progress in Comparative Musical Science," *Psychological Bulletin* 11:421–33.
Chailley, Jacques
1963   "L'Égalisation (les éléments de formation des échelles extérieurs à la résonance)," in *La résonance dans les échelles musicales,* E. Weber, ed. (Paris: Edition CNRS), pp. 191–96.
Deutsch, Werner, and Franz Födermayr
1986   "Tonhöhe versus Frequenz: Zur Frage der indonesischen Tonsysteme," *Musicologica Austriaca* 6:197–226.
Ellis, Alexander J.
1885   "On the Musical Scales of Various Nations," *Journal of the Royal Society of Arts* 33:485–527.
Ellis, Alexander J., and A. J. Hipkins
1884   "Tonometrical Observations on Some Existing Non-Harmonic Scales," *Proceedings of the Royal Society* 37:368–85.
Fechner, Gustav Theodor
1860   *Elemente der Psychophysik.* 2 vols. Leipzig: Breitkopf und Härtel.
Gilman, Benjamin Ives
1892   "On Some Psychological Aspects of the Chinese Musical System," *Philosophical Review* 1:54–71, 154–78.

Graf, Walter
1975   "Die Vergleichende Musikwissenschaft in Österreich seit 1896,"
         Yearbook of the International Folk Music Council 6:15–43.
1980   *Vergleichende Musikwissenschaft: Ausgewählte Aufsätze.* Edited by
         Franz Födermayr. Vienna-Föhrenau: Stiglmayr.
Helmholtz, Hermann von
1863   *Die Lehre von den Tonempfindungen als physiologische Grundlage für
         die Theorie der Musik.* Braunschweig: F. Vieweg. Third edition 1870.
Hood, Mantle
1954   *The Nuclear Theme as a Determinant of Patet in Javanese Music.*
         Groningen: J. B. Wolters.
1966   "Sléndro and Pelog Redefined," *Selected Reports in Ethnomusicology*
         1:28–37.
Hornbostel, Erich M. von
1905   "Die Probleme der Vergleichenden Musikwissenschaft," *Zeitschrift der
         Internationalen Musikgesellschaft* 7:85–97.
1906   "Phonographierte tunesische Melodien," *Sammelbände der
         Internationalen Musikgesellschaft* 8:1–43.
1907   "Über den gegenwärtigen Stand der Vergleichenden Musikwissenschaft,"
         *Bericht über den 2. Kongress der Internationalen Musikgesellschaft Basel
         1906* (Leipzig: Breitkopf und Härtel), pp. 56–60.
1910   "Über vergleichende akustische und musikpsychologische
         Untersuchungen," *Zeitschrift für angewandte Psychologie* 3:465–87.
1920   "Formanalysen an siamesischen Orchesterstücken," *Archiv für
         Musikwissenschaft* 2:306–33.
1926   "Psychologie der Gehörserscheinungen," in *Handbuch der normalen und
         pathologischen Physiologie,* A. Bethe et al., ed. (Berlin: J. Springer), vol.
         11, pp. 701–30.
1931   "Über Geruchshelligkeit," *(Pflügers) Archiv für die gesamte Physiologie
         des Menschen und der Tiere* 227:517–38.
1948   "The Music of the Fuegians," *Ethnos* 13:61–102.
1973   "Geburt und erste Kindheit der Musik," *Jahrbuch für musikalische Volks-
         und Völkerkunde* 7:9–17. First published in 1928.
Husmann, Heinrich
1961   *Grundlagen der antiken und orientalischen Musikkultur.* Berlin: de Gruyter.
Husserl, Edmund
1928   *Vorlesungen zur Phänomenologie des inneren Zeitbewusstseins,* in *Jahrbuch
         für Philosophie und phänomenologische Forschung,* Martin Heidegger, ed.,
         vol. 9, pp. 367–497. English edition, Bloomington: Indiana University Press,
         1964.
1939   *Erfahrung und Urteil: Untersuchungen zur Genealogie der Logik.* Edited by
         L. Landgrebe. (4th ed. Hamburg: F. Meiner, 1972).
Kolinski, Mieczyslaw
1936   *Konsonanz als Grundlage einer neuen Akkordlehre.* Vienna:
         M. Rohrer.
1962   "Consonance and Dissonance," *Ethnomusicology* 6:66–74.

Körner, S., and R. M. Chisholm, eds.
1976   *Franz Brentano: Philosophische Untersuchungen zu Raum, Zeit und Kontinuum.* Hamburg: F. Meiner.

Land, Jan Pieter Nicolaas
1889   "Über die Tonkunst der Javanen," *Vierteljahrsschrift für Musikwissenschaft* 5:193–215.

Lorenz, Carl
1890   "Untersuchungen über die Auffassung von Tondistanzen," *(Wundt's) Philosophische Studien* 4:26–103.

Metzger, Wolfgang
1954   *Psychologie: Die Entwicklung ihrer Grundannahmen seit der Einführung des Experiments.* 2d ed. Darmstadt: Steinkopf.

Myers, Charles
1905   "A Study of Rhythm in Primitive Music," *British Journal of Psychology* 1:397–406.
1907   "The Ethnological Study of Music," in *Anthropological Essays Presented in Honour to Edward Tylor* (Oxford: Oxford University Press), pp. 235–53.
1911   "Music of the Veddas," in *The Veddas,* C. G. Seligman and B. Z. Seligman, eds. (Cambridge: Cambridge University Press), pp. 341–65.
1913   "The Beginnings of Music," in *Essays and Studies Presented to William Ridgeway* (Cambridge: Cambridge University Press), pp. 561–82.

Nettl, Bruno
1983   *The Study of Ethnomusicology: Twenty-nine Issues and Concepts.* Urbana: University of Illinois Press.

Pongratz, Ludwig J.
1967   *Problemgeschichte der Psychologie.* Bern: Francke.

Rahn, Jay
1979   "Javanese Pelog Tunings Reconsidered," *Yearbook of the International Folk Music Council* 10:69–82.

Raleigh, Lord (see J. W. Strutt)

Reinecke, Hans-Peter
1970   "Zum Problem der musikalischen Temperatur in außereuropäischer Tonsystemen," in *Speculum musicae artis: Festgabe für Heinrich Husmann,* H. Becker and R. Gerlach, eds. (Munich: Fink), pp. 271–75.

Révész, Géza
1913   *Zur Grundlegung der Tonpsychologie.* Leipzig: Veit.

Schneider, Albrecht
1976   *Musikwissenschaft und Kulturkreislehre: Zur Methodik und Geschichte der Vergleichenden Musikwissenschaft.* Bonn: Verlag für Systematische Musikwissenschaft.
1986   "Tonsystem und Intonation," *Hamburger Jahrbuch der Musikwissenschaft* 9:153–99.
1988a   "Musikwissenschaftliche Theorienbildung, außereuropäische Musik und (psycho-)akustische Forschung," in *Festschrift Martin Vogel,* H. Schröder, ed. (Bonn-Bad Nonnef: Schröder), pp. 145–74.

1988b   Review of Erich Moritz von Hornbostel, *Tonart und Ethos*, in *Jahrbuch für Volksliedforschung* 33:90–95.

Schneider, Albrecht, and Erich Beurmann

1989   "Tonsysteme, Frequenzdistanz, Klangformen und die Bedeutung experimenteller Forschung für die Vergleichende Musikwissenschaft," *Hamburger Jahrbuch der Musikwissenschaft* 11.

1990   "Okutuusa amadinda: Zur Frage äquidistanter Tonsysteme und Stimmungen in Afrika," in *Musik-Kulturgeschichte: Festschrift für C. Floros*, P. Petersen, ed. (Wiesbaden: Breitopf und Härtel).

Simbriger, H.

1939   *Gong und Gongspiele*. (*Internationales Archiv für Ethnographie* 36). Leiden: Brill.

Spencer, Herbert

1890   "The Origin of Music," *Mind* 60:449–68.

Strutt, J. W. (Lord Raleigh)

1890   "On Bells," *Philosophical Magazine* 29:1–17.

Stumpf, Carl

1873   *Über den psychologischen Ursprung der Raumvorstellung*. Stuttgart: S. Hirzel.

1883   *Tonpsychologie*. 2 vols. Leipzig: Hirzel.

and

1890a

1885   "Musikpsychologie in England," *Vierteljahrsschrift für Musikwissenschaft* 1:261–349.

1886a   "Lieder der Bellakula-Indianer," *Vierteljahrsschrift für Musikwissenschaft* 2:405–26.

1886b   Review of Alexander J. Ellis, "On the Scales of Various Nations," *Vierteljahrsschrift für Musikwissenschaft* 2:511–24.

1890b   "Über Vergleichungen von Tondistanzen," *Zeitschrift für Psychologie* 1:419–62.

1898   *Konsonanz und Dissonanz*. Leipzig: J. A. Barth.

1901   "Tonsystem und Musik der Siamesen," *Beiträge zur Akustik und Musikwissenschaft* 3:69–146.

1911   *Die Anfänge der Musik*. Leipzig: J. A. Barth.

1914   "Über neuere Untersuchungen zur Tonlehre," in *Bericht über den 6. Kongress für experimentelle Psychologie Göttingen 1914* (Leipzig: J. A. Barth), pp. 305–48.

Stumpf, Carl, and Erich M. von Hornbostel

1911   "Über die Bedeutung ethnologischer Untersuchungen für die Psychologie und Ästhetik der Tonkunst," in *Bericht über den 4. Kongress für experimentelle Psychologie Innsbruck 1910* (Leipzig: J. A. Barth), pp. 256–69.

Surjodiningrat, W., P. J. Sudarjana, and A. Susanto

1972   *Tone Measurements of Outstanding Javanese Gamelans in Jogjakarta and Surakarta*. Jogjakarta: Gadjah Mada University Press.

Wachsmann, Klaus P.

1973   "Spencer to Hood: A Changing View of Non-European Music," *Proceedings of the Royal Anthropological Institute of Great Britain and Ireland* 1973:5–13.

Wertheimer, Max
1909/10 "Musik der Wedda," *Sammelbände der Internationalen Musikgesellschaft*
         11:300–309.
Wundt, Wilhelm
1890   "Über Vergleichungen von Tondistanzen," *(Wundt's) Philosophische Studien*
         4:605ff.

Doris Stockmann

Interdisciplinary Approaches to the Study of Musical Communication Structures

A music communicates itself qua fact and value;
but it does not "say" so.

Charles Seeger 1977:48.

DURING RECENT DECADES of musicological as well as ethnomusicological research, there have been various attempts to develop ideas and programs to tackle communication problems in music. When dealing with this topic one cannot avoid getting involved with many rather basic questions about our subject, questions which, at least partly, would need more thorough investigation than heretofore available, including interdisciplinary research. This seems to be one of the reasons for the great disparity of approaches to the field of musical communication which, in the present state of affairs, is rather difficult to summarize in a representative and at the same time understandable way, at least within the limited scope of this essay. The topic of musical communication structures is, nevertheless, essential in a volume on the intellectual history of ethnomusicology.

There are other reasons, of course, for the difficulties intrinsic to this endeavor, not least the fact that music, or different kinds of music, as humanly structured systems of communicative sound bearing some kind of "meaning" for the people who use a music, functions normally as an alternative to speech communication: it mainly communicates or "expresses" what language does not or cannot do (and vice versa), thus, to some extent, resisting any verbal explanation.

About twenty-five years ago, in 1964, Alan Merriam explained the communication problem in the following, rather simple, way: "To view music as a communicative device is clearly one of the purposes of ethnomusicology, though it has been little investigated" (1964:13). A few pages before this Merriam stated that "the question remains as to what we mean by *communication*" . . . but "there is little understanding of how this communication is carried on. The most obvious possibility is that communication

318

is effectuated through the investiture of music with *symbolic meanings* which are tacitly agreed upon by the members of the community" (ibid.:10).

Interestingly enough, Merriam later separated this "*function of symbolic representation*" from the communicative one, as well as from the *functions of enjoyment, entertainment, physical response, enforcing conformity to social norms,* and some others, thus revealing that the whole complex of communication was something akin to a black box in those days, despite the fact that some musicological, psychological, and linguistic studies had already begun to investigate the problems, albeit from different viewpoints (see, e.g., Besseler 1926 and 1959, Meyer 1956, Springer 1956, Nettl 1958, Meyer-Eppler 1959a, Seeger 1962, Bright 1963).

Let us pursue Merriam's considerations a few steps further, for he writes that

> there is also *verbal communication about music,*[1] which seems to be most characteristic of complex societies in which a self-conscious theory of music has developed. But little is known about these processes, and without such knowledge it is difficult to talk intelligently about music as communication. . . . The major problem is that while we know music communicates something, we are not clear as to what, how, or to whom. Music is not a universal language, but rather is shaped in terms of the culture of which it is a part. In *song texts* it employs, it communicates *direct information* to those who understand the language in which it is couched. It *conveys emotion,* or something similar to emotion, to those who understand its idiom. The fact that music is shared as a human activity by all peoples may mean that it communicates a certain limited understanding simply by its existence. (Merriam 1964:10–11, 223; emphasis mine).

Merriam concludes with the assertion that "of all the functions of music, the communicative function is perhaps least known and understood," a statement to which Charles Seeger some years later added the qualification, "limited speech understanding," with four words: "least known and understood *in terms of speech*" (Seeger 1966:23–24 and 1977:157).

We shall repeatedly touch upon this important issue in ethnomusicology, and musicology in general, to which Seeger dedicated much of his most penetrating systematic thinking. Even today, this issue, at least partly, produces obstacles in dealing intelligently and successfully with musical and other nonverbal communication, although the research situation has changed radically since Merriam's remarks in the early 1960s. In the meantime a tremendous amount has been written about the topic—a virtual explosion—mainly during the 1970s, not only from different fields of musical research (psychological, sociological, reception studies, pedagogical, anthropological, aesthetic, and semiotic, including structural analysis), but also from nonmusical disciplines (information theory and communication research, philosophy, general semiotics and aesthetics, psychology, linguistics, and others). Considered as a whole, the disparate conclusions drawn by this research are often controversial, if not contradictory. Not all of such research deserves serious consideration, for some is simply trendy or an attempt to demonstrate control over a new jargon. Still, many of these rather different issues are worthy of further consideration.

Today, it has therefore become more complicated to talk about musical communication for reasons quite different from the earlier ones; rather than a lack of information, we now face a divergence of available information. At the very least, it has become increasingly difficult to survey the multitude of approaches, concepts, methods, terminologies, and results, and to do this while accounting for the necessarily subtle factual details and theoretical problems involved in the analysis of communicative processes in music.

On one hand, negotiating the jungle of problems will hardly be possible without serious shortcomings, caused mainly by the complex view of the producer-music-receiver relation within its social, cultural, and environmental conditions of time and space. These include the semiotic relations between music and nonmusical reality, whatever such relations may be like. Consequently, one must employ sociological interpretation, as well as some basic theory of music as process, structure, and function, on one side, and as concept, effect, and object of valuation, on the other, a theory, as Charles Seeger put it succinctly, of "music as fact and value" (1977:48).

On the other hand, it still remains difficult to discern clear lines or trends that could easily serve as some kind of cicerone through the thicket of fundamental problems. This is hardly astonishing since communication theory in general, including semiotics, is still a science under construction. Applied to verbal and nonverbal systems of human and nonhuman communication, which were previously so widely neglected, it remains an interdisciplinary branch of research in a process of continuous change. Thus, any report on the field, as the Finnish semiotician Eero' Tarasti observed, "does not imply an unambiguous solution based on the safe application of an established method and school" (1985:99). Despite the variety, or even disparity, of approaches, assumptions, methods, and terminologies, every attempt to survey or review even parts of the multitude of studies available by classifying and evaluating them should look for overlap and possible concordance. Above all, one should attempt to show which would be valid or indispensable for further programs of research and would lead to promising future work toward a general theory of musical communication upon the further development of their basic concepts. What now seems to be the crux of the communicative approach to music is that it has to take into account the "entire phenomenon" of music making: music as a system within a nest of systems, and "the musical process as a function in a context of functions" (to use the title of an article by Charles Seeger (1966)). Achieving this end could very well turn out to present both ethnomusicology and historical musicology with a significant opportunity.

Given the difficulties we have introduced above, this essay will serve to attempt the following topics: to identify some questions crucial in the general topic, to touch upon a few of the more important trends of research, and to present some approaches in greater detail. For the latter I shall draw mainly from studies in the German-speaking areas, including recent research in my own country, which may not yet be well known in English-speaking countries. At the same time, however, I shall bring in parallel ideas and concepts from the American literature. Curiously, scholars concerned with communication in music have often not taken notice or even known of each other, though they were dealing with the same subject, sometimes in a very similar way, thus yielding conclusions fairly close to each other.

*

Let me begin with some remarks on the word *communication*. To my knowledge it has been and still is rather often used, in ethnomusicological writings and elsewhere, without reflecting its proper meaning and implications. When defining the term as applied to music and nonverbal communication in general, one has to bear in mind its restricted scientific meaning and usage during the 1940s and 1950s as components of *information theory* (or *theory of communication*) and the rise of intelligence techniques, characterized by dealing mathematically with statistics and problems of information transfer. The application of information theory to the problems of general linguistics at this time became the main subject of communication research. Together with *cybernetics* (the theory of systems) and *semi-*

otics (the theory of signs), and strongly supported by structural linguistics, information theory helped to clarify the relations within the so-called *"speech chain of communication."* This chain of communication was valid for natural language and its derivatives, and it was characterized mainly by the *"double representation"* of items of reality on the *semantic level* of understanding. This linguistic form of coding and decoding meanings and understanding messages is a purely cognitive strategy that may occur with music, but is by no means, as we have long known, the essence of music or musical "understanding," no doubt the reason that some musicologists do not bother at all with coding or decoding meaning or message. Since this attitude seems hardly suitable for expanding our limited knowledge of the complex ways of communicating by music, many scholars think it more useful to learn as much as possible about the functioning of semantics in general, which, in turn, might lead to a *new definition of the term communication with respect to music.*

A short analysis of "double representation" and how it came into being may help to clarify some of the questions posed in this essay. This rather fantastic function of speech semantics is the kernel of the term communication in its narrow scientific sense, which is used to comprehend referents of all kinds, most commonly those that are not in the art of speech, but also, of course, those about speech or speech reference itself. Charles Seeger refers to double representation as "informational" relative to the *extrinsic* or *outward meaning* present in speech contexts, which, in turn, is dependent upon another kind of reference in speech composition, called "operational" with respect to the *intrinsic* or *inward meaning.*

Thus, double representation means that *structure of notions* (that is, mnemonically encoded representations of behaviorally relevant sets of features, including their possible transformations) are related arbitrarily to the structures of special *speech names* (*sound figures* or *sound patterns*). The stable or relatively stable relations and their continued combination constituted the major evolutionary step from higher animal societies (unable to survive without bioacoustic and other systems of communicative intercourse)[2] to communication in human societies (Klix 1980). With the introduction of this new quality to and its development within the acoustic systems of communication, the doors opened to the immense possibilities of dealing cognitively with matters of reality. Language, finally, was recognized as the central instrument of human communication as we know it today, inseparable from its impact on all other nonverbal, communicative activities, music being a prime example.

We should bear in mind that verbal communication has achieved its new status by combining two independent and totally different mechanisms in animal behavior, one classificatory, the other communicative. The former was developed for categorizing and classifying the environmental items and conditions, and was acquired during the action-motivated exchange with them. The communicative mechanisms are a device for momentarily contacting or communicating with, thus influencing, the behavior of some partner (be it a youngster, sexual partner, rival, enemy, or someone in the local community).

Let me summarize this historical excursus in the following way. First of all, thorough investigation of speech structures and examination of earlier stages of communication are by no means superfluous for our studies. Quite the contrary, they may clarify some of the questions of mutual differentiation between music and language throughout history. At the semantic level of communication systems, music may have preserved elements or traits of early human stages of information transfer because music, to some extent, is able to carry or embody some kind of symbolic "meaning," though in quite another way as language. This was especially the case when only a few "informational items"[3] were not only repeated fairly often to be understood, but also accompanied, grounded, supported, surrounded, or intermingled with affective/emotional, motivational qualities, expression, and utterances, as known from communication among primates. The most archaic kinds of speaking, known as "affective language," presumably functioned in that way. Though of limited semantic differentiation, they must have been very effective in mediating an holistic impression of a need or situation. In the development of natural language (except poetry) the *levels of emotional expression* and *diagnostic understanding*[4] became less important or, at least, subordinant to the *semantic level*. In modern language derivatives, moreover, they have been dropped totally for the benefit of purely intellectual qualities.[5] Music, in contrast, has elaborated them considerably because they were worthy of preservation. A communicative device therefore emerged whereby humans, psychologically and emotionally, could manage the needs and conflicts of life, not least among these the enormous changes within the species's own evolution, which required more than cognitive understanding and technical know-how.

Second, my short analysis of speech semantics has already demonstrated that the restrictive use of the word communication by information theory and its adherents is rather artificial. One has to question seriously whether research on music and dance, for example, should continue to bother with this language-related meaning of the term, which, anyway, does not fit properly into nonverbal information transfer. But does this necessarily mean that mediating anything other than speech information—qualities of sensitivity, feelings, or values bound to them—is less important or less communicative? I don't think so, especially when we keep in mind the original, broader meaning of the word "communication." Its archaic sense is *"to share."* In today's colloquial language, in addition to the meaning *"to transmit information, thought, or feeling*[!], so that it is satisfactorily received and understood" (*Webster's New Collegiate Dictionary* 1976:228), we encounter the following semantic field: *"to make contact," "constitute connection," "to open into each other," "to take part/participate," "to do in joint action/act together"* (ibid.). Since sharing and active participation in a very direct, physical sense are so basic for music and dance, for "understanding" and appropriating them, we might well make use of this preexisting, more complex meaning,[6] including it in our theoretical considerations. This seems to me preferable to denying any communicative effect for music or chasing after speech-specific applications of a term that is only marginal in musical contexts. Otherwise we would miss our subject. I could quote several prominent scholars, among them Carl Dahlhaus (1973) or Johan Huizinga (1955), who would support the idea in one way or another. Theodor Adorno described one aspect of the problem in this way: "Sprache interpretieren, heißt Sprache verstehen; Musik interpretieren, Musik machen" [To interpret speech means to understand speech; to interpret music means to make music] (1963:12). The whole problem is, of course, not that simple. But information transfer or, better, communication in music and the arts in general is surely not achieved primarily by signs in the sense of speech semantics, nor only by activities and experiences that can be verbalized.

When reading again through the studies of Charles Seeger recently, I was really not astonished to find him among those who recommend a similar approach:

> It is possible that use of the word "communication" in a broader sense[7] might put the matter upon a firmer footing. Such a broader sense might comprehend impacts upon any one or several senses of an individual receiver or group of receivers. Such impacts might range from a caress to a blow upon a sense of touch, through the comparatively undeveloped (occidentally, at least) senses of taste and smell, to the highly refined, varied

and organized impacts upon sight, from posture and facial expression to reading and writing, and upon hearing. (1962:157–
58)

And in still another context he explains:

The relationships of the different systems of communication
among men, tactile, auditory, and visual, are prime subjects for
musicological investigation. The aim ... is to develop this
broader sense of the word communication, both as a concept
and as a referent, by providing a minimal roster of necessary
basic concepts in whose terms and operational employment in
speech its music referents may be described a) in a context,
b) in itself.[8]

Development of this broader sense of the word is also achieved by exploring two kinds of referents, one arising from the relation of the parts of music among themselves, and the composition of those parts in phrases, periods, and so on.[9] This is a predominantly *music-operational approach*. The
other arises from relations between music or musical patterns and nonmusical as well as musical reality.[10] This would produce a *music-
informational approach*. Concerning the former, Seeger and certain
others[11] believe "that all known musics make use" of it (ibid.:157).

Seeger is rather sanguine about the *music-informational approach*,
which, though controversial, is at least discussed with respect to Western
art music, while data for non-Western musics are still rather spotty. He
states: "it is not impossible that we might eventually isolate a body of data
to which we could give the name 'music information' " (ibid.:156). When
analyzing types of musical signs, one can see precisely how far one can get
with this approach, at least until the present time. In any case, it could be
helpful for further research to distinguish explicitly between information
and operational aspects of music communication and to be aware of the
narrower, speech-oriented, and the broader meaning of the term in nonverbal contexts.

My third and final remark in this context concerns the differences between music and language considered as systems. In short, music is constructed, in general, as a much less coherent system of communication than
language. As we know, it is quite open to different kinds of adaptation and
combination, mainly with speech (in vocal music), which constitutes a second level of, as Merriam put it, "direct information," and may thus reduce
music more or less to what I have called "*sign accompanying*" or "*sign

supporting means" (Stockmann 1980:137). This may happen, too, with dance, the other frequent companion of music, or with other kinds of less stylized body movement. These occur, for the most part, when using sound tools, the third major factor in music making, which may be parts of the body, environmental objects, or artifically produced instruments. The construction of such instruments may materialize and fix the basic features of a musical system, and their shape and function, moreover, may signify extramusical meaning, for example, the male and female principle, fertility, or an animistic or totemic concept, most of these apparent already during the arts of the Ice Age. In more differentiated cultures the construction of instruments may be attributes or symbols of a deity, of wisdom, of some social class, of political and economic power, or of legal authority, which was the case during the Central European Middle Ages.[12] Thus, musical instruments add different kinds of meaning to a musical performance and its purely musical "message," and those who know about it will include this additional information in their decoding strategies. Such tools and tool use are absolutely unique among arts and in nonverbal communication in general.[13]

Seeger clearly argues for a broader concept of the term communication in music by recognizing that not only visual components are frequently included in music through dance, musical theater, and manipulation of instruments, but also tactile ones through playing instruments, dancing in groups, celebrating ritual, nursery communication, musical education, and other activities, mainly those contexts which I refer to as *interactive communication*.[14] One could not ask for a more persuasive argument for the necessity of including the study of musically relevant visual and tactile behavior/information transfer into ethnomusicological research.

Let me now briefly touch upon a few attempts to survey different aspects of musical communication. I have already mentioned several names, ideas, and concepts, for instance, those starting from *information theory, general communication research,* and *structural linguistics.* There are, additionally, some works by *philosophers and aestheticians* who touch upon musical problems, for example, Adam Schaff, Max Bense, Georg Klaus, and L. O. Resnikow. I have summarized these early works in my article, "Musik als kommunikatives System" (1970); in later articles I included selected bibliographies (e.g., 1978b).

Steven Feld has published a very thorough and critical review of the abundant writings from the 1960s and 1970s that assume a *linguistic-oriented approach to musical analysis,* though he was largely concerned with contributions in English (Feld 1974). The serious problems, obstacles, and traps involved in a purely formal transfer of theories and methods from one discipline to another have been criticized repeatedly by several scholars, for example, John Blacking (1970 and 1971), although their work tended to concentrate on the first decade of research,[15] thus making the thrust of Feld's criticism understandable. Feld's article is unquestionably worthy of reexamination, not least because of its bibliography. Feld himself has since provided an interesting and stimulating example of how to employ musical communication ethnotheoretically in his book *Sound and Sentiment: Birds, Weeping, Poetics, and Song in Kaluli Expression* (1982).

Another kind of summary or set of readings on the divergence of approaches to musical understanding appears in *Musik und Verstehen* (Faltin and Reinecke 1973), a volume that includes articles on semiotics, aesthetics, and the sociology of musical reception, with contributors coming from quite different scholarly backgrounds, for example, Carl Dahlhaus, Adam Schaff, Ingmar Bengtsson, Hans Heinrich Eggebrecht, Peter Faltin, Zofia Lissa, Vladimir Karbusicky, Jean-Jacques Nattiez, Tibor Kneif, Gerhard Kubik, Otto Laske, Harry Goldschmidt, and Dénes Zoltai.[16]

Finally, Eero Tarasti's "Music as Sign and Process" (1985) is a notable survey of semiotic approaches, which examines the literature concerned with structuralism as well as the iconic approaches to music, mainly in French and English. The structuralists, like Tarasti himself in *Myth and Music* (1978), search for the smallest significant units in a sign system or proceed "in the depth, i.e., from the surface level towards deep structures," thus representing "reductionism, the reduction of sensory reality into a small number of categories" (ibid.:99). Those concerned with icons "are anti-reductionist in essence: they argue . . . that the significance of music is based upon itself; this view emphasizes the *gestural nature of music* as something sensory, as a process" (ibid.), an approach also used by Charles Seeger. Seeger, in general, referred to music as "paraphrastic" or "paradromic," that is, accompanying the processes of individual and social life (1977:165). He was convinced that "music has . . . its own peculiar semiotics, study of which, with modern methods of investigation, can hardly be said to have begun" (1977:5). As early as 1960, however, Seeger had presented an influential attempt at systematic description—or better, "iconisation"—of basic units in the musical process, which he called "moods" (Seeger 1960).

While dealing with the role of time and memory in musical semiosis,[17] Tarasti surveys the structuralist and iconic semiotic approaches by including their forerunners, thus undergirding the importance of continuity with musicological thinking. From Heinrich Schenker, Tarasti cites the concept of reductionism; from Ernst Kurth, the concept of iconicity ("the kinetic, energetic, and process nature of music" (Tarasti 1985)); and from Boris Asafiev, the "intonation concept." Tarasti is one of the few Western scholars conversant with Soviet semiotics, the most influential representative of which is today perhaps the Estonian, Juri M. Lotman. Although music plays a minor role in Lotman's thinking, his valuable ideas and concepts hold much that is worthwhile for the study of musical communication.[18]

*

In the final section of this essay I shall turn to some individual approaches developed in the German Democratic Republic during the past two decades. Scholars there are dealing with aesthetics, semiotics, structural analysis, and communication in music, some of them working with considerable cooperation, both among themselves and with scholars working in linguistics, bioacoustics, ethology, cognitive psychology, and other disciplines. These "communicative" activities have taken several forms, for example, a special lecture series in 1978/79 organized by the late Harry Goldschmidt and by Georg Knepler, which was later published as *Musikästhetik in der Diskussion* (1981), a volume in which the eight contributors advanced rather different concepts. There was also a working circle on music and language at the Humboldt University in Berlin, which included linguists and aestheticians, and an interdisciplinary project at the Berlin Academy of Sciences on the appropriative function of the arts, which will appear as a book written by contributors from musicology, ethnomusicology, aesthetics, and art history (Franz and Feist 1990).

It is, of course, impossible to touch upon all of the important issues, as does, for example, Georg Knepler's book *Geschichte als Weg zum Musikverständnis* (1977), which uses interdisciplinary chapters to focus on such subjects as the early development of communicative devices, for example, the concept of *biogenic elements in music,* an approach rather close to my own ways of thinking.

I would like here to deal with, or at least discuss critically, two (or two-and-a-half) different approaches, along with my own attempts to investigate some of the basic problems in musical communication. The first approach was developed during the 1970s by a linguist from the German Democratic Republic, Manfred Bierwisch, and is a very systematic investigation well worth the attention of all those interested in musical communication (Bierwisch 1978). Like many semiotic approaches of this decade, Bierwisch's deals with a thorough comparison of language and music.[19]

Though aware of the aspects and features both systems have in common or exhibit as similarities, Bierwisch primarily searches for the fundamental differences between the two, pointing out the simple fact that distinctions like that between speech and poetry/literature do not exist in music, which even when not artistically expressed (e.g., signals or work songs) is subject to some kind of aesthetic valuation. Another difference is that musics make much greater use of "natural," or, as Bierwisch calls them, "*extra-communicative*" means, for example, the so-called *primer effect* (or *effect of inflammation*). For Bierwisch "extra-communicative" derives from the *restrictive meaning* of the word communication, indeed, the normal usage for a linguist. But if we keep in mind our plea for the broader (original) sense of the word, a meaning yielding a better understanding of what is communicated musically, these extracommunicative effects turn out to be important means of musical communication. This does not necessarily imply an *explicit sign character* for musical patterns (in the sense of a signaling structure, or *symbol*). Knepler had recognized that *effects of the primer type*[20] were quite basic for music, for example, *establishing a special mood or emotional status*. I should emphasize that they are typical for musical behavior within social groups, for example, in ritual or dancing, as well as for anonymous mass communication. The same communicative distinction between music and speech may prove relevant for the role of *symptomes,* or *indexical signs* (in the sense of Peirce), which are somewhat distinct from normal signs by their *causal relation* to what they signify or denote. Charles Seeger, too, refers to the importance of the *cause-and-effect relation* in music (1977:164), in which the reactions of the receiver may result from stimuli coming from the personality of a performer/producer and his or her musical abilities (*mechanism of identification* for sound-source features). Seeger also regards this as an aspect of the context and function of music, and when these are loosened from their contextual conditions (a lament from actual death and its rituals, a march or dance from a situation of real marching or dancing), they refer to the original reality more in the sense of a symbol. Christian Kaden has called them *abgelöste Symptome,* "detached or loosened symptoms" (1984:126). This is but one example of the *flexible borderlines between different types of musical signification* and historical change in the sign characteristics of music.

Another important designation established by Bierwisch during several intermediate steps of comparative inquiry[21] is the distinction between the *speech mode's "saying or stating something"* (*Aussagemodus,* "mode of statement") and the *music mode's "showing something"* (*Zeigemodus,* "mode of display"). It is the latter that is relevant for the arts in general.

According to Ludwig Wittgenstein, "saying" and "showing" as modes of human activity or attitudes toward reality are mutually exclusive. Even though Augustine had already made a case for a third attitude, namely "acting," which could be combined with each of the other two, neither Wittgenstein nor Bierwisch refers to this third mode.[22] Again, Seeger joins those whose observations turn in this direction when he states "music communicates itself qua fact and value, but it does not 'say' so" (1977:48). Or, to quote Zoltán Kodály, "to say something substantial about music which music cannot express by itself is either impossible, or superfluous."[23]

It is only a small step from qualifying music as a mode manifesting features of reality to, as Tarasti put it, the *iconic approach of musical semiotics*. Charles Morris, one of the early great figures of semiotics, was the first to recognize the inclination of the arts toward the *specific nature of iconic signs* that are related by similarity to reality or aspects of reality. Bierwisch uses the iconic approach in distinguishing between speech and music by referring to the *"logical form of language meaning"* (or meaning of language signs), as opposed to the *"gestural form of music meaning."* The latter are *"motivated syntactic structures,"* while the former are *"conventional"* ones, chosen arbitrarily. Bierwisch proves these designations by investigating elementary types of signs in both systems. "Saying" that is conventionally conditioned and "showing" that is structurally motivated are assumed to be opposite poles of a continuum along which intermediate positions are possible. One could learn more about them by examining the different amounts of analogous and discrete coding in music and language according to the different kinds and conditions of speaking and music making.

Bierwisch raised another question in his article: What are the aspects of reality to which music refers by "showing" them? He claims they are the *totality of emotional, affective, and motivational conditions and processes* (as opposed to the *cognitive structures and processes* referred to by speech). While the *logical proposition of language* refers to a *conceptual representation*, *musical gesture* (German, *Gestus*) refers to the *structure of a coherent emotional pattern*.

This assumption, which, by no means fundamentally new, is nonetheless tackled by Bierwisch in a new and stimulating way, seems to me worthy of serious consideration by musicologists and ethnomusicologists. We must question, nevertheless, whether the thorough emotional grounding in or reference to musical processes is the only kind of reference deserving consideration. In my opinion, there are other aspects of reality to which music refers directly, even if thoroughly mediated by affective qualities. I would place these under a distinctive heading: *processual, qualitative, and relational aspects of reality*, that is, any kind of movement—including its properties, relations, and their transformations—for any matter of substance, including the most highly developed, namely biotic, organismic, social and societal, or even mental. The particular aspects of reality represented by a concrete musical item can only be expressed by one of the partners of music, explicitly only by speech. If one considers the specific means of musical patterning and structuring, and its techniques of syntactical composition,[24] one might go so far as to say that humans have developed no better device for *showing* or *embodying* the dynamic aspects of reality. I might be permitted to quote Charles Seeger once again: "What can be communicated by Music [and] cannot . . . by Speech [is] *world view as the feeling of reality*" (1977:35; emphasis mine); and later in the same article: "World view, Weltbild, Weltanschauung is, by necessity, bipartite: on the one hand a looking outward to a totality that may or may not be a unit, on the other, a looking inward to a totality that we deeply believe to be a unit" (ibid.:42). "Both speech and music communicate much of whatever it may be: speech, by symbolizing it; music, by embodying it" (ibid.:43).

Although Bierwisch's approach merits much more extensive treatment, I must turn now to my final topic, an *approach to communication in music coming from a sociological or contextual viewpoint*. For this I shall turn to the work of the German musicologist and medievalist, Heinrich Besseler, who already in the 1920s had postulated valuable approaches by classifying the different forms of music making and listening during European history (cf. 1926 and 1959). In his studies, where classificatory concepts were far more complex than I can detail here, he was attracted by two fundamental and totally different types of musical communication (a term, of course, not in his vocabulary). These he called *Umgangsmusik* and *Darbietungsmusik*. The former describes musical communication in which all of the participants, very often a coherent social group, are actively involved, for example, in dancing or other kinds of tribal, folkloric, and popular or even private artistic music making. *Darbietungsmusik* describes all kinds of *presentational music making,* mainly by professionals, before a more or less passive audience. This we could label *stage-audience communication,* such as that typical of a Western concert situation, though I believe with deep roots in mythical and epic narration. More recently, I have referred to *Umgangsmusik* (e.g., 1978b) as *interaktive Gruppenkommunikation* (interactive musical communication within social groups), a type characterized by its limited number of participants, usually acquainted with each other, and its coherence in space and time. This situation contrasts with the anonymous audience in a recital and with communication through the modern mass media, where not only the unit of space is suspended, but, very often, also that of time. The interactive musical processes include, as a special form, *partnership communication,* that is, dialogue types. Furthermore, one should, in my opinion, also pay attention to *hybrid forms* that combine both of Besseler's classes, such as variants of interactive communication on stage in folklorismus, or in opera and other genres of musical theatre. One must also take into account *autocommunication,* which is much more frequent in music than in speech and not by accident a topos since antiquity (the lonely herdsman with his flute!). This may be due, at least partly, to the necessity of instrumental skill and a uniqueness resulting from the use of sophisticated tools in music. We know, of course, of other reasons, such as influencing, calling, calming, or frightening cattle, suggesting that an apparently autocommunicative behavior turns out to be a special kind of *interactive communication between humans and animals.* Still, there may be also purely subjective needs inherent in human music making.

Having studied in recent years the music of an Arctic herding culture, the Sami, a music characterized in part by what one might call the loneliness of music making, namely *yoiking,* I have come to recognize acutely social implications of singing alone. Yoiking is a means of detailing the native environment—the mountains, lakes, and animals—and its human inhabitants—the family members, who are often separated from each other by labor, friends, and neighbors, including the deceased. Singers try to remember, memorize, and realize social ties, which may mediate the feeling of belonging to a social group in native surroundings and in its continuity between a known past and a yet unknown future.

Besseler's concepts have been discussed and advanced by a number of musicologists in the German Democratic Republic, especially those interested in anthropological or sociological problems (e.g., Konrad Niemann (1974) and Christian Kaden (1984)). In my own work, I have expanded upon Besseler's concepts by using ideas and concepts developed recently within ethology and biocommunicative research.[25] Ethologists analyze communicative behavior, acoustical as well as nonacoustical, as a distance-regulating mechanism whereby, for example, two opposite forms of basic, life-protecting behavior, conditioned primarily by motivation and emotions (*appetency* and *aversion*), can be easily distinguished. Knepler was the first to consider this mechanism from a musical point of view, and I also incorporated it on several occasions to find more convincing interpretations of certain musical practices.[26] Two opposite types of sound characterize this double mechanism: on one hand, attracting, enticing, alluring utterances, and the respective acoustic structuring, called *affine;* on the other, frightening utterances, showing quite different types of structures, called *defensive* (German, *diffug*). Their influence on music and their important role in coding and decoding musical patterns can hardly be emphasized enough. From early signal forms (e.g., protecting against danger) to recent kinds of composition (including movie music, where they support the sequences of pictures in an eye-catching way), the contrasting forms of the double mechanism can be decoded by any receiver without difficulty. In their immediate social function they are, indeed, highly reliable and effective, not only because they automatically produce the correct (positive or negative) evaluation, but because they directly diminish or increase spatial distance between the receiver and environmental objects or processes.

These mechanisms assist considerably in the structuring of space and time in human communication.[27] Ethologists claim that auditory as well as visual communication happens mainly within the so-called *field of distance (Distanzfeld)*, an area defined by great uncertainty. This is, in fact, the case for Besseler's first type of musical communication (presentational or stage-audience communication). The ethological *fields of closeness and contact* are characterized by increasing determinance, with the field of contact reducing acoustic exchange to a minimum and expanding tactile communication to a maximum.

From my own ethnomusicological viewpoint, a good deal of interactive musical communication, whether interaction between partners or communication within social groups, is not primarily performed within the field of distance, but usually at the borderlines of the fields of distance and nearness, showing a strong tendency to overcome distance and reach the behavioral fields of closeness and contact. In another way, this seems to be true, too, for certain aspects of autocommunication, for example, the functions of Sami yoiking I previously described. Seeger summarizes the problem thus: "Tactility is what we need to be more aware of. Closeness. Tactility holds us closest to what we try to communicate" (1977:43).

Obviously, there are different intentions and different degrees of showing or expressing the need for closeness that music provokes and makes possible, from pure imagination to physical contact; moreover, either musical or other reasons may dominate these. Concerning the musical reasons Seeger states:

> The ... musician who is near—within touching distance—of another ... musician communicates also by fact of that nearness and all the more if they actually touch. One has seen this— and, perhaps, felt oneself—in the kind of vocal quartet singing in the United States called "close harmony" or "Barbershop Quartet" singing in which the shoulders of the singers are pressed as closely as possible against each other, so that the tensions, tonicities, and detensions of each tonal, rhythmic, and formative progression are felt as if it were, by precise "tuning" of touch as well as that of pitch, loudness, and phrasal agogic. Often as not, the eyes are closed, as if one were seeing and feeling, as well as hearing, inwardly. (1977:39)

Many more examples of music making could substantiate this point, say, different kinds of ensemble playing and singing, for example, Albanian polyphony, where the bourdon group always maintains tactile contact, and the two or three soloists sing their overlapping parts face to face in the closest position possible. Similarly, certain conducting attitudes (for example, Karajan with closed eyes) indicate nearness to the musical structure, its contents, expression, and *Gestus*.

The spatial fields of closeness and contact further offer some specific kinds of musical communication and behavior. These mix music with verbal, visual, and tactile elements, such as lullabies, cozy songs, and the improvised soft, intimate singsong performed to a small child, as well as many children's games, dances, and rituals, those important "enculturative mechanisms" that not only teach the individual musical behavior but, at the same time, shape "his world view and ... his system of values" (Waterman 1956:41). Many of these kinds of music making serve as a means to get into the same mood or emotional state, may it be for some special task (for example, a hunting ritual) or for reasons of emotional integration that strengthen and stabilize the social connections among the members of a group or community. The ethologist Konrad Lorenz describes such efforts as validation for *fastening the social ties* (*Festigung des sozialen Bandes*), certainly a value that in itself is worthwhile to achieve (Lorenz 1980:79ff; see also Klix 1980:160). This would, I suspect, be quite impossible without music.

Two additional and final remarks, the first one concerning the *time aspect of the space-time concept*. All of the musical contexts I have described here—especially those involving communicative interaction—make use in one way or another of the *primer effect,* which is characterized by its persistent influence. It is at a future moment that the primary efficacy emerges, for example when a hunting ritual strengthens the participants for the real hunt, which takes place the next day or week. This produces a *temporal field of distance (zeitliches Distanzfeld),* a quality arguably of great importance for music in general.[28]

To close with a second remark, I wish to point out that I have not tried here to examine the different kinds of *feedback structures* that include the producing/performing and receiving/interacting subsystems of musical communication. By integrating the advanced methods of cybernetics, one could generate valuable insights into this complex of problems (Kaden 1984:174ff). A systematic investigation of sociocultural systems[29] that comprises these feedback structures, the musically relevant space-time concepts, and, of course, the different types of musical communication and information transfer surveyed historically in this essay seems to be one of our most stimulating future tasks. In the end, it might well lead to a better understanding of our common topic of interest: *music.*

Notes

1. This could refer to the verbal explanations of producers, or to exchange of impressions among receivers (as some special kind of feedback), as well as to critical and musicological treatment.

2. Already, by the way, bearing germs of symbolic elements.

3. For example, "danger!", "here I am, where are you?", "come here!", "go away!"

4. Levels which have been referred to as *paralinguistic* or *ektosemantic levels.* See Meyer-Eppler 1959a:3.

5. As in scientific metalanguages (including mathematical signs or chemical symbols), computer programming, etc.

6. Perhaps by differentiating the two ways of communicating with the use of special indexical signs added to the term.

7. Seeger does not refer explicitly to the dictionary evidence of the broader meaning of the word.

8. That is concerning (a) the physical and cultural environment in which the music communication is cultivated, and (b) the music as a text.

9. In linguistics this kind of reference is known as *syntactical meaning.*

10. This would be some kind of equivalent to speech semantics, but in music would probably have to include the musically relevant items of the pragmatic context.

11. See, among others, Meyer-Eppler 1959b, Klaus 1969, D. Stockmann 1970, Bierwisch 1978.

12. See, e.g., D. Stockmann 1973, 1974, 1978a, 1985a, 1985b; E. Stockmann 1975.

13. Only the mask of an actor, magician, or dancer in visual communication may, at least to some extent, be comparable.

14. See D. Stockmann 1978b, 1980, 1985b.

15. Feld includes also the French structuralist approaches of C. Lévi-Strauss, N. Ruwet, J.-J. Nattiez, and others, but excludes, for example, the generative attempt of B. Lindblom and J. Sundberg (1970).

16. Essentially the same may be learned from the relevant studies in the *International Review of the Aesthetics and Sociology of Music,* or from a survey-annotated bibliography collected from several countries by J.-J. Nattiez during the 1970s. As concerns the controversies surrounding the role of communication or semiotics in musicology, Reinhold Schneider's summary book of 1980 dealing with some of the German and French literature contains some useful statements. Schneider strongly defends the old traditions of music analysis and interpretation, while attacking all attempts to make use of cross-disciplinary approaches and knowledge. The unconvincing state of affairs around 1975, where Schneider's bibliography stops, may have been responsible for his view.

17. By developing a concept of the French structuralist A. J. Greimas on "isotopy" and the functions of "temporal, spatial, and actional shifters."

18. See his recently translated collection of papers, *Kunst als Sprache: Untersuchungen zum Zeichencharakter von Literatur und Kunst* (1981). There is more which has to be omitted here, for example, the "Prague School" and other semiotic activity in Czechoslovakia, with its grand tradition and names such as Jakobson and Mukařovsky. Concerning Lotman, I have referred to his musically relevant ideas in my contribution to a recently finished volume of the Academy of Sciences in Berlin (Franz and Feist 1990).

19. Referring, by the way, mainly to Western art music, and thus slightly inclined to underestimate, or ignore, some basic traits in other kinds of musical activity.

20. Another one is the so-called *releaser effect.* See Tembrock 1971, 1977, 1978.

21. Concerning, among other things, cognitive and emotive structures, patterning of time and segmentation in both systems, kinds of coding, and the like.

22. Special concepts would have to be developed for music and dance research to be included. Jürgen Habermas's use of the term in his widely discussed, recent book *Theorie des kommunikativen Handelns* is purely language-oriented.

23. Transcribed from a television interview in the early 1960s with the late conductor, Ferenc Friscay.

24. Such as repetition, sequencing, variation, *Fortspinnung und Entwicklung* (in the sense of Friedrich Blume), developmental techniques in a sonata, motivic treatment, decomposition, crushing of patterns, transposition, modulation, contrasting (in melodic or harmonic sequence, or through foreground-background opposition), cadencing, etc.

25. See Tembrock 1971, 1982, D. Stockmann and Tembrock 1983, and Stockmann 1985b.

26. See Knepler 1982, and D. Stockmann 1980, 1982b, 1983.

27. A topic to which Ludwik Bielawski (1976) contributed valuable insights.

28. See also Knepler 1982, who referred to it repeatedly, using the terms, *Einstimmung* or *Umstimmung*.

29. The term "systematic" here means investigating dynamic systems and subsystems.

Works Cited

Adorno, Theodor W.
1963   "Fragment über Musik und Sprache," in *Quasi una fantasia* (Frankfurt am Main: Suhrkamp).

Bengtsson, Ingmar
1973   " 'Verstehen'—Prolegomena zu einem semiotisch-hermeneutischen Ansatz," in *Musik und Verstehen*, Peter Faltin and Hans-Peter Reinecke, eds. (Cologne: Arno Volk), pp. 11–36.

Besseler, Heinrich
1926   "Grundfragen des musikalischen Hörens," *Jahrbuch Peters für 1925* 32:35–52.
1959   *Das musikalische Hören der Neuzeit: Berichte über die Abhandlungen der Sächsischen Akademie der Wissenschaften zu Leipzig.* (Philosophische-historische Klasse, series 155, vol. 6). Berlin: Reclam.

Bielawski, Ludwik
1976   *Strefowa teoria czasu i jej znaczenie dla antropologii muzycznej.* [The Theory of Time Zones and Their Importance for Musical Anthropology]. Cracow: Polskie Wydownictwo Muzyczne.

Bierwisch, Manfred
1978   "Musik und Sprache: Überlegungen zu ihrer Struktur und Funktionsweise," *Jahrbuch Peters 1978:* 9–102.

Blacking, John
1970   "Deep and Surface Structures in Venda music," *Dyn* 1:69–98.
1971   "Towards a Theory of Musical Competence," in *Man: Anthropological Essays Presented to D. F. Raum*, E. J. DeJagger, ed. (Cape Town), pp. 19–34.

Bright, William
1963   "Language and Music: Areas for Cooperation," *Ethnomusicology* 7:26–32.

Dahlhaus, Carl
1973   "Das 'Verstehen' von Musik und die Sprache der musikalischen Analyse," in *Musik und Verstehen*, Peter Faltin and Hans-Peter Reinecke, eds. (Cologne: Arno Volk), pp. 37–47.

Eco, Umberto
1972   *Einführung in die Semiotik.* (German edition of *La struttura assente*.) Translated by Jürgen Trabant. Munich: Wilhelm Fink.

Faltin, Peter, and Hans-Peter Reinecke, eds.
1973   *Musik und Verstehen: Aufsätze zur semiotischen Theorie, Ästhetik und Soziologie der musikalischen Rezeption.* Cologne: Arno Volk.

Feld, Steven
1974   "Linguistic Models in Ethnomusicology," *Ethnomusicology* 18:197–217.
1982   *Sound and Sentiment: Birds, Weeping, Poetics, and Song in Kaluli Expression.* Philadelphia: University of Pennsylvania Press.

Franz, Michael, and Hans Peter Feist
1990   *Zur Aneignungsfunktion der Künste.* Berlin: Akadamie Verlag.

Goldschmidt, Harry, and Georg Knepler, eds.
1981   *Musikästhetik in der Diskussion.* Leipzig: Deutscher Verlag für Musik.

Guilbault, Jocelyne
1987   "The La Rose and La Marguerite Organizations in St. Lucia: Oral and Literate Strategies in Performance," *Yearbook for Traditional Music* 19:97–115.

Herzog, George
1941   "Do Animals Have Music?" *Bulletin of the American Musicological Society* 5:3ff.

Huizinga, Johan
1955   *Homo Ludens: A Study of the Play-Element in Culture.* Boston: Beacon Press.

Jakobson, Roman, and Morris Halle
1960   *Grundlagen der Sprache.* (German translation of *Fundamentals of Language.*) Translated by Georg Friedrich Meier. Berlin: Akademie-Verlag.

Kaden, Christian
1984   *Musiksoziologie.* Berlin: Verlag Neue Musik.

Keil, Charles, and Angeliki Keil
1966   "Musical Meaning: A Preliminary Report," *Ethnomusicology* 10:153–73.

Klaus, Georg
1969   *Semiotik und Erkenntnistheorie.* 2d revised ed. Berlin: Deutscher Verlag der Wissenschaften.

_____ , ed.
1976   *Wörterbuch der Kybernetik.* 4th revised ed. Berlin: Dietz Verlag.

Klix, Friedhart
1980   *Erwachendes Denken: Eine Entwicklungsgeschichte der menschlichen Intelligenz.* Berlin: Deutscher Verlag der Wissenschaften.

Knepler, Georg
1982   *Geschichte als Weg zum Musikverständnis: Zur Theorie, Methode und Geschichte der Musikgeschichtsschreibung.* 2d ed. Leipzig: Reclam.

Kubik, Gerhard
1973   "Verstehen in afrikanischen Musikkulturen," in *Musik und Verstehen,* Peter Faltin and Hans-Peter Reinecke, eds. (Cologne: Arno Volk), pp. 171–88.

Kurth, Ernst
1947   *Musikpsychologie.* 2d ed. Bern: Krompholz.

Lindblom, Björn, and Johan Sundberg
1970   "Towards a Generative Theory of Melody," *Svensk Tidskrift för Musikforskning* 52:71–88.

Lomax, Alan
1968   *Folk Song Style and Culture.* Washington, D.C.: American Association for the Advancement of Science.
Lorenz, Konrad
1980   *Das sogenannte Böse: Zur Naturgeschichte der Aggression.* 7th ed. Munich: Deutscher Taschenbuch Verlag.
Lotman, Juri M.
1981   *Kunst als Sprache: Untersuchungen zum Zeichencharakter von Literatur und Kunst.* Leipzig: Reclam.
Merriam, Alan
1964   *The Anthropology of Music.* Evanston: Northwestern University Press.
1969   "Ethnomusicology Revisited," *Ethnomusicology* 13:213–29.
Meyer, Leonard B.
1956   *Emotion and Meaning in Music.* Chicago: University of Chicago Press.
1960   "Universalism and Relativism in the Study of Ethnic Music," *Ethnomusicology* 4:49–54.
Meyer-Eppler, Werner
1959a   *Grundlagen und Anwendung der Informationstheorie.* Berlin: Springer.
1959b   "Informationstheoretische Probleme der musikalischen Kommunikation," *Revue Belge de Musicologie* 13:44–49.
Morris, Charles W.
1972   *Ästhetik und Zeichentheorie.* (German translation of *Esthetics and the Theory of Signs.*) Translated by Roland Posner, with Jochen Rehbein. Munich: Carl Hauser.
Nattiez, Jean-Jacques
1973   "Y a-t-il une diégèse musicale?" in *Musik und Verstehen,* Peter Faltin and Hans-Peter Reinecke, eds. (Cologne: Arno Volk), pp. 247–57.
1975   *Fondements d'une sémiologie de la musique.* Paris: Union générale d'éditions.
Nettl, Bruno
1958   "Some Linguistic Approaches to Musical Analysis," *Journal of the International Folk Music Council* 10:37–41.
Niemann, Konrad
1974   "Mass Media: New Ways of Approach to Music and New Patterns of Musical Behaviour," in *New Patterns of Musical Behaviour,* J. Bontinck, ed. (Vienna: Universal Edition), pp. 44–53.
Schaff, Adam
1966   *Einführung in die Semantik.* Berlin.
1973   "Das Verstehen der verbalen Sprache und das 'Verstehen' der Musik," in *Musik und Verstehen,* Peter Faltin and Hans-Peter Reinecke, eds. (Cologne: Arno Volk), pp. 276–88.
Schneider, Reinhold
1980   *Semiotik der Musik.* Munich: Wilhelm Fink.
Sebeok, Thomas A., ed.
1968   *How Animals Communicate.* Bloomington: Indiana University Press.

Seeger, Charles

1960 "On the Moods of a Music-Logic," *Journal of the American Musicological Society* 13:225–61.

1962 "Music as a Tradition of Communication, Discipline, and Play," *Ethnomusicology* 6:156–63.

1966 "The Music Process as a Function in a Context of Functions," *Yearbook of the Inter-American Institute for Musical Research* 2:1–36.

1969 "On the Formational Apparatus of the Music Compositional Process," *Ethnomusicology* 13:230–47.

1971 "Reflections upon a Given Topic: Music in the Universal Perspective," *Ethnomusicology* 15:385–98.

1977 *Studies in Musicology 1935–1975.* Berkeley and Los Angeles: University of California Press.

Springer, George P.

1956 "Language and Music: Parallels and Divergencies," in *For Roman Jakobson: Essays on the Occasion of His 60th Birthday* (The Hague: Mouton), pp. 504–613.

Stockmann, Doris

1970 "Musik als kommunikatives System: Informationszeichentheoretische Aspekte insbesondere bei der Erforschung mündlich tradierter Musik," *Deutsches Jahrbuch der Musikwissenschaft* 14:76–95.

1973 "Deutsche Rechtsdenkmäler des Mittelalters als volksmusikalische Quelle," *Studie musicologica* 15:267–302.

1974 "Der Kampf um die Glocken im deutschen Bauernkrieg: Ein Beitrag zum öffentlichrechtlichen Signalwesen des Spätmittelalters," *Beiträge zur Musikwissenschaft* 16:163–93.

1976 "Zur Analyse schriftlos überlieferter Musik," *Beiträge zur Musikwissenschaft* 18:235–55.

1977 "Some Aspects of Musical Perception," *Yearbook of the International Folk Music Council* 9:67–79.

1978a "Die Erforschung vokaler und instrumentaler Praktiken im mitteralterlichen Rechtsleben," *Deutsches Jahrbuch der Musikwissenschaft* 18:115–34.

1978b "Zum Problem einer Klassifikation der kommunikativen Prozesse," in *Philosophische und ethische Probleme der modernen Verhaltensforschung,* G. Tembrock et al., eds. (Berlin: Akademie-Verlag), pp. 157–76.

1979 "Musik-Sprache-Tierkommunikation," *International Review of the Aesthetics and Sociology of Music* 10:5–45.

1980 "Die ästhetisch-kommunikativen Funktionen der Musik unter historischen, genetischen und Entwicklungs-Aspekten," *Beiträge zur Musikwissenschaft* 22:126–44.

1982a "Interdisziplinäre Aspekte bei der Untersuchung musikethnologischer Probleme." Unpublished paper.

1982b "Musik und Sprache in intermodaler ästhetischer Kommunikation," *Yearbook of Traditional Music* 13:60–81.

1982c   "Musik, Sprache, Biokommunikation und das Problem der musikalis-
         chen Universalien," *Beiträge zur Musikwissenschaft* 24:103–11.
1983   "Universals in Aesthetic Valuation of Music?" *The World of Music* 25
         (3):26–45.
1985a   "Music and Dance Behaviour in Anthropogenesis," *Yearbook of Tradi-
         tional Music* 17:16–30.
1985b   "Grundtypen musikalischer Kommunikation und ihre rezeptive Bewer-
         tung," in *Musikhören als Kommunikationsprozess (7th Musicological
         Congress of the German Democratic Republic)*, Union of Composers
         and Musicologists, ed. (Berlin: Verband der Komponisten und Musikwis-
         senschaftler), pp. 7–20.
1985c   "Perception and Valuation Processes of Music in Cross-Modal Aesthetic
         Communication," in *Analytica: Studies in the Description and Analysis
         of Music, in Honour of Ingmar Bengtsson*, Hans Åstrand et al., eds.
         (Stockholm: Publications of the Royal Swedish Academy of Music 48),
         pp. 35–48.
1986   "Musikethnologie und interdisziplinäres Denken heute in Relation zu
         Guido Adlers Konzept der Musikwissenschaft," *Musicologica Austriaca*
         6:157–72.
_____ , and Günter Tembrock
1983   "Interdisziplinäre Probleme zwischen Musikwissenschaft und Bioakus-
         tik," *Beiträge zur Musikwissenschaft* 25:171–95.
Stockmann, Erich
1975   "Trommeln und Pfeifen im deutschen Bauernkrieg," in *Der arm man
         1525*, H. Strobach, ed. (Berlin: Akademie-Verlag), pp. 288–308.
Tarasti, Eero
1978   *Myth and Music: A Semiotic Approach to the Aesthetics of Myth in Mu-
         sic*. Helsinki: Suomen Musiikkitieteellinen Seura (*Acta Musicologica Fen-
         nica* 11).
1985   "Music as Sign and Process," in *Analytica: Studies in the Description and
         Analysis of Music, in Honour of Ingmar Bengtsson*, Hans Åstrand et al.,
         eds. (Stockholm: Publications of the Royal Swedish Academy of Music
         48), pp. 97–115.
Tembrock, Günter
1971   *Biokommunikation*. Berlin: Akademie-Verlag.
1982   *Tierstimmenforschung*. 2d ed. Wittenberg: A. Ziemsen.
_____ , ed.
1978   *Verhaltensbiologie (Wörterbücher der Biologie)*. Jena: Gustav Fischer.
Waterman, Richard A.
1956   "Music in Australian Aboriginal Culture—Some Sociological and Psy-
         chological Implications," *Music Therapy* 5:40–50.
Webster's New Collegiate Dictionary
1976   Springfield, Mass.: G. and C. Merriam Co.

Anthony Seeger
Styles of Musical Ethnography

CHARLES'S CONSPECTUS

T HE PAST CAN be conceived as a series of discontinuities—moments of decisive change—or as a set of continuities—the more things change, the
more they remain the same. Ever since Thomas Kuhn's influential book,
The Structure of Scientific Revolutions (Kuhn 1970), ethnomusicologists
have used a model of successive changes of central paradigms to argue that
ethnomusicology has undergone a series of "paradigm shifts" or fundamental reformulations over the past few centuries (for a recent example
see Bohlman's essay in this volume). Such proposals provide ethnomusicology with direction and coherence. It is equally possible, however, to argue
that there have been no such major shifts in theoretical conceptualization,
but rather, simple differences in the way the same questions have been
asked, decade after decade and century after century. While one might argue that the different approaches to the history of ethnomusicology are essentially a disagreement over whether a glass is half-full or half-empty, I
believe that the different conceptualizations of the history of ethnomusicology reflect profoundly different understandings of the field. In this paper I will examine the nature of musical ethnography, and point out some
of the continuities that link our work with that of our predecessors. In so
doing I shall argue that the unity of the discipline comes from the questions
it asks. I shall suggest that the possibilities for musicological communication between traditions lie in our acknowledgement of the *questions* and
not the way we have researched the *answers* to them.

Charles Seeger's "Conspectus of the Resources of the Musicological
Process" (presented in C. Seeger 1977:125–27) is a major ahistorical presentation of ethnomusicology, and my treatment of the styles of musical ethnography will refer to his diagram. Frustrated by the limitations of narrative
time and the inflexibilities of radical dualism, Seeger devoted considerable
time and attention to the designing of charts on which all possibilities could be

placed and (ideally) explored simultaneously, or at least at the reader's own pace. The diagrams, however, were often accompanied by a dense prose that erected an edifice around them that discouraged interpretation. The "Conspectus" was a complex diagram that indicated as many of the influences on musicology as Seeger could imagine, from the acoustical physics of the sounds themselves to the historical influences of tradition and the ultimate values and concepts that may be expressed in or influence music. His diagram, reproduced in my figure 1, divides musicology itself into a systematic and an historical orientation, each of which is further subdivided into sections that had been treated separately in different articles. Whether the diagram is complete or not is less important here than its usefulness for mapping an alternative interpretation of the ethnography of music.

Charles Seeger tried to make his chart dynamic through the reader's use of it.

> By its nature such a schema is static and makes the field it represents—a dynamic, functional thing—appear static. . . . In limiting myself to the two dimensions of the conspectus, the best I can do is ask you to begin at the top and as you read down to remember that you are tracing your own progress over the terrain. When you come to a fork you must decide which path to follow first, but not to stay on it so long that you forget to go back and follow the other fork; for it is the drawing of the two together that is essential to the reading of the table. (C. Seeger 1977:125)

ETHNO-GRAPHY AND ETHNOGRAPHY OF MUSIC

What is music? Audio recordings of music may lull us into thinking of music as sound, but it is more than that. Elsewhere I have defined music as an intention to make something called music (or structured sounds similar to what *we* call music) as opposed to other kinds of sounds. It is an ability to formulate strings of sounds accepted by members of a given group as music (or whatever *they* call it). Music is the construction and use of sound-producing instruments. It is the use of the body to produce and accompany the sounds. Music is an emotion that accompanies the production of, the appreciation of, and the participation in, a performance. Music is sound, but it is also the intention as well as the realization; it is emotion and value as well as structure and form (A. Seeger 1987:xiv). Music is composed, learned, performed, and reacted to by members of societies. Music, then, is a system of communication involving structured sounds

FIGURE 1. Charles Seeger, Conspectus of the Resources of the Musicological Process.

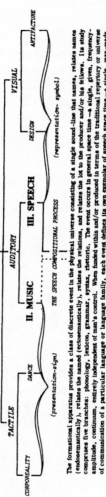

I. WORLD VIEW

Its formation by response to and appetite for communication,
and
for communicating in traditional norms of semiotic behavior

TACTILE — AUDITORY — VISUAL

CORPOREALITY — DANCE — **II. MUSIC** — **III. SPEECH** — DESIGN — ARTIFACTURE

(presentation-sign) — (presentation-symbol) — (representation-symbol)

THE SPEECH COMPOSITIONAL PROCESS

The formational apparatus provides a class of discrete event in the physical universe consisting of a single sound-line that names, relates names (endosemantically), relates the named (ectosemantically), relates the relations, and relates the lot to the producer and/or his fellows. Its study comprises five branches: phonology, lexicon, grammar, syntax, rhetoric. The event occurs in general space time —a single, given, frequency-amplitude, continuum, entirely independent of man's control. When funded within and/or produced in terms of the traditional repertory or universe of communication of a particular language or language family, each event defines its own individual space time —a single, man-made, discontinuum, entirely within man's control. A universe of speech communication may be conceived as a synchrony of ideation, more multitary than unitary, that serves as part of the reference and, hence, of the content of each discrete event in the two space times, viz.:

Mathematics Logic	Physical Sciences	Biological Sciences	Anthropology Sociology Psychology	Economics Political Science	Philosophy Communication Theory	Ethology Aesthetics	Belles Lettres Poetics	Religion Folklore	Myth Mysticism Ecstatics

THE MUSIC COMPOSITIONAL PROCESS

The formational apparatus provides a class of discrete event in the physical universe consisting of single and/or multiple sound-lines that do not name, that is, that do not symbolize, represent, but embody, present. Its study comprises a phonology basically identical with that of the study of speech in the principal concepts and laboratory devices employed; but the music analogs of the speech lexicon, grammar, syntax, logic and rhetoric (only recently so named) are heterologous and possibly complementary in most respects. Like the speech event, the music event occurs in general space-time —a single, given, frequency-amplitude continuum entirely independent of man's control. When funded within and/or produced in terms of the traditional repertory or universe of communication of a particular music or music family, each event defines itself as an exemplar of music space-time —a single, man-made discontinuum entirely dependent upon man's control. A universe of music communication may be conceived as a synchrony of ideation, more unitary than multitary, that serves a part of the reference and, hence, the content of each discrete event in the two space-times. It is present, that is, presented, in direct proportion to the extent and elaboration of each discrete event in the two space-times.

IV. MUSICOLOGY

a cross-communicatory, cross-disciplinary, cross-cultural speech study in whose terms the student competent in both arts aims to produce results as valid for the one as for the other. One phenomenology, one axiology and one evolutional-historical theory may serve both.

Single sound-line	Successive sound-lines	Simultaneous sound-lines	Successive simultaneous sound-lines

A. SYSTEMATIC ORIENTATION
Speech and music processes in their own space-times

B. HISTORICAL ORIENTATION
Speech and music processes in general space-time

THE COMMUNICATORY CONTINUUM

THE BIOCULTURAL CONTINUUM

As Fast — As Value — Music and Speech — Human Beings

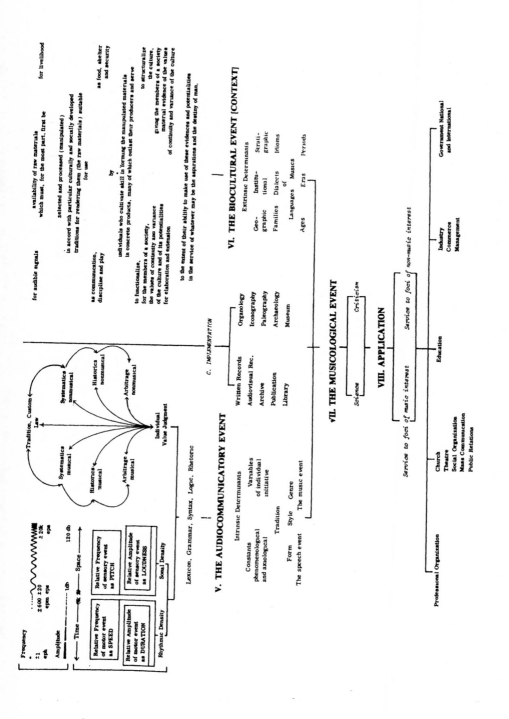

produced by members of a community who communicate with other members. This is a definition very similar to John Blacking's of music as humanly organized sound (1973), and to Alan Merriam's of music as culture (1964).

Charles Seeger defined musicology as the "cross communicatory, cross disciplinary, cross cultural *speech* study" of music (see figure 1), and devoted considerable attention to the kinds of difficulties that using speech to deal with music has gotten us into. Yet the field is not simply based on words (*logos*) about music, it is based on writing (*graphein*) about music. And since ethnomusicology is (cross) cultural, it is by definition ethnography (from the Greek *ethnos* = folk, people). We are thus above all engaged in an "ethno-graphy" of music. The work of ethnomusicologists is fundamentally to *write* about *music* using words and other forms of graphing, such as transcriptions of sounds, to communicate concepts.

The ethnography of music is quite distinct from an anthropology of music. The anthropology of music is the application of a particular set of theories about human action and history to musical processes; the ethnography of music is the writing down of ideas about people's musics without any required theoretical referent—except for the postulate that writing about music is possible and desirable.

The ethnography of music is also a literary genre, typically expressed in articles exceeding twenty-five pages and in books ranging from 150–600 pages about the musical traditions of a single group of people. Just as the genre of the novel gained ascendancy over other literary forms during the past seven centuries and for a while dominated our understanding of literature, so ethnography has dominated our approach to music, at least for the past one hundred years. Different disciplines use different means to publish findings. In some fields, such as chemistry and physical anthropology, practitioners publish many short articles, often in conjunction with other scientists. In others, such as social anthropology and history, books and longer articles with a single author are the rule. Ethnomusicology is more like history and anthropology in its approaches as well as in much of its theoretical framework.

There are different styles of musical ethnography that to a certain extent reflect different questions being emphasized by different writers. Rather than our having a developing series of conceptually different questions over time in a Kuhnian sense, I believe ethnomusicological writings have instead given different weights to the same questions, resulting in the impression that we have changed our basic premises, while in fact these have remained the same. The questions include (1) What are the principles that organize the combinations of sounds and their arrangement in time when people make music? (2) How are these sounds similar to or different from other musical traditions? (3) Why does a particular individual or social group perform or listen to the sounds he/she/it does in any given context? To demonstrate the antiquity of these questions, let us return to an early systematization of music often referred to in the literature, Jean-Jacques Rousseau's *Dictionnaire de musique*.

ROUSSEAU'S DICTIONARY

Dictionaries and encyclopedias were a preferred scientific genre in eighteenth-century France. In his dictionary of music, translated as *A Complete Dictionary of Music* (1975 [1779]), Rousseau gathered into one volume both classical and contemporary information, arranged by entries in alphabetical order. The entry on music is an early systematic use of non-Western music to make generalizations about music as a whole, and for that reason alone is worth investigating.

Rousseau's initial definition of music is performative: music is "the art of combining tones in a manner pleasing to the ear." This definition stresses a performance, the sounds produced, and an audience that hears them. But further on in the text, "to put the reader in a way to judge the different musical accents of different people," Rousseau presents musical transcriptions of a Chinese Air, a Persian Air, a Song of Savages in Canada, and the Swiss *Ranz des Vaches,* and draws two important conclusions. The first is about the possible universality of musical rules, or physical laws of music. "We shall find in these pieces a conformity of modulation with our music, which must make one admire the excellence and universality of our rules" (Rousseau 1975:266). In other words, musical transcriptions reveal certain similar sound processes governed by laws of acoustics. This affirmation underlies virtually all cross-cultural studies of musical sounds to the present day. The careful transcription of musical sounds has been a hallmark of entire schools of ethnomusicology, as highlighted in some of the papers on the Berlin School in this volume.

Rousseau's second observation about the examples he transcribed is that the effects the songs have on people are not limited to the physical effects of the sounds themselves but include their cultural interpretation. To make this point he describes how a certain song was outlawed among Swiss troops because of its effect on the listeners:

The above celebrated Air, called *Ranz des Vaches,* was so generally beloved among the Swiss, that it was forbidden to be play'd in their troops under pain of death, because it made them burst into tears, desert, or die, whoever heard it; so great a desire did it excite in them of returning to their country. *We shall seek in vain to find in this air any energetic accents capable of producing such astonishing effects. These effects, which are void in regard to strangers, come alone from custom, reflections, and a thousand circumstances,* which retrac'd by those who hear them, and recalling the idea of their country, their former pleasures, their youth, and all their joys of life, excite in them a bitter sorrow for the loss of them. *The music does not in this case act precisely as music, but as a memorative sign. . . .* So true it is, that it is not in their physical action, we should seek for the great effects of sounds on the human heart. (1975:267, italics mine)

In other words, to understand the effects of music on an audience, it is necessary to understand the ways musical performances affect performers and audience. Music is indeed more than physics. The quotation above could be considered one of the earliest justifications for the ethnographic study of music. If we are to understand the "effects of sounds on the human heart," we must be prepared to explore "custom, reflections, and a thousand circumstances." This is impossible to achieve through the transcription of sounds alone, difficult to do in a short article, and therefore book-length descriptions are more common. Many of the divergences in the history of ethnomusicology—among them the musicological approach and the anthropological approach referred to in the opening pages of *The Anthropology of Music* (Merriam 1964)—can be traced to the dual approaches of Rousseau. Descriptions of a universal acoustic system have been a central focus of interest for many, while the effects of sounds on human groups have been a central concern for others. These are not sequential but rather parallel concerns in the study of music.

These two complementary approaches to music did not remain static over the centuries. The increasing amount of information about other traditions and the development of different theoretical approaches in other branches of the human sciences led to various efforts to further systematize our understanding of musical processes. One ethnographic approach to musical traditions seeks to organize the diversity of traditions by reducing them to a few broadly defined categories.

WALLASCHEK, STUMPF, SACHS

Increasing amounts of data from around the world and borrowed scientific questions led to the establishment of several distinct approaches to music in the nineteenth century that included studies of the origin and development of music, usually phrased in terms that are characterized by "stratigraphic" in Charles Seeger's Conspectus.

Such works took examples from many different traditions and organized them into a coherent developmental sequence. A nineteenth-century example of a stratigraphic approach was Richard Wallaschek's *Primitive Music: An Inquiry Into the Origin and Development of Music, Songs, Instruments, Dances and Pantomimes of the Savage Races* (1893). The system through which the diversity was organized is clear in the title. The book privileged evolutionary questions over others, and expressed what became a popular approach to musical diversity that reappeared in a more sophisticated form in Alan Lomax's works on Cantometrics and Choreometrics.

Although Wallaschek's book has been dismissed as mainly of historical interest (Nettl 1964:28), it made a number of points that continue to characterize ethnomusicological writing today. One of these was that studying non-European music can be useful because we can see among other communities aspects of music less obvious to ourselves in music of our own traditions (Wallaschek 1893:163). Wallaschek also anticipated a great deal of subsequent writing when he argued that (primitive) music is not an abstract art, but one deeply entrenched in the rest of life. He wrote that dancing and music making increased group solidarity, organized collective activities, and facilitated association in action (1893:294). If we ignore the social Darwinism of certain passages, Wallaschek anticipates a great deal of the work that took its inspiration from the French sociologist Emile Durkheim's *The Elementary Forms of the Religious Life* (1965 [1914]), written twenty-five years later.

In spite of some of his prophetic emphases, Wallaschek's work is dated—as much of the anthropology of that day was—by a tendency to view the late nineteenth century as the epitome of development. The treatment of the different societies is to take their music out of context and compare the forms according to one parameter or another. In spite of Franz Boas's convincing criticisms of the methodology employed (Boas 1896), the collection of the world's music in order to present a natural history of the development of musical structures and forms continued for another half century. It appears in Carl Stumpf's *Die Anfänge der Musik*

(1911), and in modified forms in Curt Sachs's books on music, musical instruments, and dance. For Sachs, in "primitive" music "imitation and the involuntary expression of emotion precede all conscious sound formation. . . . Ecstasy in the broadest meaning of the word dominates the throat as well as the limbs" (1937:175). But the massive accumulation of music from around the world caused Sachs and his generation of comparativists to recognize the inherent problem of an historical model in which musical development—or maturity—followed a path from simple to complex. Such interpretations were, furthermore, inconsistent with the growing presence of scientific method in ethnomusicological investigation, disabusing those using comparative methods from judging other cultures and mentalities by their own criteria.

But if the history of music was not to be so easily discerned, how could the diversity be organized? There were two answers. One was the study of the diffusion of traits over space, which organized the diversity into historical patterns. This usually involved the definition of culture areas, which organized diversity into a homogeneity of areas larger than the individual culture, community, or society, and smaller and less unified than large nations, states, or empires, and traced influences among them. The second answer was the intensive study of single groups in monographs.

MONOGRAPHIC STUDY

In the first half of the twentieth century a number of researchers, again influenced by developments in anthropological theory, thought that the questions being asked by Wallaschek and others were fundamentally wrong. They proposed that we address different questions, ones whose answers would stress history and the diffusion of styles through space over time. These included the studies of culture areas and diffusion by Clark Wissler (1917), Helen Roberts (1936), George Herzog (1936), Bruno Nettl (1954), as well as more recent studies such as those of Lomax (1968) and McLean (1979). On Charles Seeger's Conspectus these could be grouped under geographical approaches. These overview studies have both advantages and disadvantages. Advantages include that the researcher can speak of style units larger than the individual culture, some elements of history are included, and a world style map can even be attempted. The disadvantages include the unreliability of the data, the privileging of similarities over differences, and issues of sampling. Even the descriptive vocabulary used by specialists does not always mean the same thing over time. McLean found that different ethnomusicologists mean different things by the word "recitative" in Oceania. If one draws general lines of similarity, what status does one give to things that are different among traditions, and how much music must one analyze in order to have a good sample?

Rousseau suggested that we look for "a thousand circumstances." While it is true that history and contact among groups are a few of the circumstances, the exclusive concentration on these parameters ignored many other factors, ones that were treated more extensively by other authors. To say that Swiss music is related to the broader European forms may classify it, but it does not explain why the *Ranz des Vaches* had such an effect on Swiss troops at a certain period of Swiss history.

Those authors who concerned themselves with the meaning of the signs of music have usually employed a different genre of writing. Here each tradition is usually taken as a separate unit, with the author possessing intensive knowledge of the tradition based on first-hand experience. An early example would be A. H. Fox-Strangways' *The Music of Hindostan,* published in 1914. The book is striking for the clarity of its focus, its admiration of Indian music, and its constant comparison between Western music (including that of the author's contemporaries) and Indian music. Fox-Strangways argued that Indian music was worthy of study because of the lack of influence of the European concepts of harmony, and therefore its similarity to song in medieval Europe or ancient Greece. He argued that understanding of music is necessary to aesthetic appreciation of it, but that understanding can be difficult to achieve because we do not know what to make of what we hear (1914:2). While admitting that music might be called a universal language, he observes,

> Just as no one language can be really common to all peoples because it will be pronounced differently in different mouths, so the very same notes will be sung by different throats in such a way as to be unrecognizable to us. This is conspicuously the case with Indian singing, in which all the distinctions of colour which we should get from notes in simultaneity (harmony) has to be extracted from notes in succession. (Fox-Strangways 1914:181; parentheses mine)

Fox-Strangways's volume on Indian music has been followed by many others that describe a single musical tradition, among them Blacking (1967), Berliner (1981), Stone (1982), Feld (1982), and A. Seeger (1987).

Where did the single-volume ethnography come from? Scientific literary genres are as culturally defined and developed as musical genres, and I suspect the relationship between the novel of the self and the ethnography is more than skin deep. The presentation of our data owes a great deal to the novel. Although everything we write may not qualify as fiction, it is narrative.

At the start of any book, everything is potentiality. The author has a simultaneous understanding of the interrelated "thousand circumstances" that can explain the meaning of music, but these have to be presented in a temporal and essentially narrative sequence, although Charles Seeger used graphs (1977) and Steven Feld employed a photograph (1982). Even the tense in which one may write it is a point of contention and reduction of possibility (Fabian 1983). Should one use the past tense to indicate that the events are past, and possibly distance the reader and trivialize the described events (which unless they are generalizable may become in the reader's eyes unworthy of interest)? Should one use the present tense and risk removing the events from the group's history and possible future as Fabian suggests in his critique of the ethnographic present? Should one insert oneself in the narrative (as Dante did) or pretend that one was a fly on the wall rather than an equipment-laden giant in the living room during the research process? Every decision reduces the potentiality until the finished product is a single approach among what might have been many, trying to convey an understanding that is not necessarily narrative but that must use narrative to be presented. When I set out to write *Why Suyá Sing* (A. Seeger 1987), for example, I decided to limit the manuscript to no more than 270 pages so that the book would be reasonably accessible to specialists in other fields. I decided to begin at the opening of a ceremony and conclude at its closing in order to impose a temporal narrative structure on what need not have been a narrative. I chose to use the present tense in two chapters and the past tense in the rest in order alternately to stress the evolving, unfolding nature of events while they are happening and their historicity when they are being analyzed. I prepared a master tape for a cassette that provided the original data for all the examples that I discussed in order to give the reader the means to criticize my own analyses, and I only considered publishers who would distribute a tape as well as a book. The questions I approached were best discussed in narrative form, but the structure was a construction (in the sense that I could have developed several others, and did while I was in the early stages of writing).

Contemporary ethnographies of music indicate a variety of approaches of their authors, but all relate to Rousseau's statement that music functions as a sign. Some authors focus on native concepts of musical phenomena.

These might be grouped under Charles Seeger's heading of "semantic density," for example Ames and King (1971), Zemp (1971), and in different ways Keil (1979), Stone (1982), Feld (1982), and A. Seeger (1987). Another group of authors began their research with an enthusiasm for a particular instrument, and then moved on to concepts. We might say they began with an interest in traditions as "aesthetic density" but moved on to study "semantic density." These included Berliner (1981) and Chernoff (1979).

Using Charles Seeger's Conspectus we can see that the ethnography of music can be located in several places, depending on the kinds of approaches the authors begin with and what kinds of answers they end up with. The approaches are not necessarily grouped chronologically, but rather may reappear over and over again. Although he did not mean it to be a history of the discipline, the Conspectus contains its history in an appropriately nondevelopmental presentation. No sequential paradigms are presented, and readers are encouraged to consider all the approaches for themselves, rather than relegate some to a mythical past.

Conclusion

The styles of musical ethnography are the results of approaches to a few questions about music presented in historically determined narrative forms. Most research over the past two centuries can be related to the dual observations of Rousseau about music. The different ways these questions have been approached owe much to the conceptual developments of related fields and the development of sound recording technology. However, whatever we do, certain questions appear to be more the same than different, and no matter what we write, we suffer the constraints of language and the necessity of narrative. These are factors that transcend smaller changes in approach, and demonstrate the major continuities in the history of ethnomusicology.

Note

Some of the ideas in this paper will appear in the forthcoming *New Grove Handbook of Ethnomusicology* (A. Seeger, in press), but are employed to different ends.

Works Cited

Ames, David, and Anthony King
1971   *Glossary of Hausa Music and its Social Contexts.* Evanston: Northwestern University Press.

Berliner, Paul F.
1981   *The Soul of Mbira.* Berkeley and Los Angeles: University of California
         Press.
Blacking, John
1967   *Venda Children's Song: A Study in Ethnomusicological Analysis.* Johan-
         nesburg: Witwatersrand University Press.
1973   *How Musical Is Man?* Seattle: University of Washington Press.
Boas, Franz
1896   "The Limitations of the Comparative Method," *Science* 4:901–8.
Chernoff, John M.
1979   *African Rhythm and African Sensibility.* Chicago: University of Chicago
         Press.
Durkheim, Emile
1965   *The Elementary Forms of the Religious Life.* Translated by J. W. Swain.
(1914)   New York: Free Press.
Fabian, Johannes
1983   *Time and the Other: How Anthropology Makes Its Object.* New York:
         Columbia University Press.
Feld, Steven
1982   *Sound and Sentiment: Birds, Weeping, Poetics, and Song in Kaluli Ex-
         pression.* Philadelphia: University of Pennsylvania Press.
1984   "Sound Structure as Social Structure," *Ethnomusicology* 28:383–409.
Fox-Strangways, A. H.
1914   *The Music of Hindostan.* London: Oxford University Press. Reprinted
         1965.
Herzog, George
1930   "Musical Styles of North America," *in Proceedings of the 23rd Interna-
         tional Congress of Americanists* (New York), 455–58.
1936   "A Comparison of Pueblo and Pima Musical Styles," *Journal of Ameri-
         can Folklore* 49:283–417.
Keil, Charles
1979   *Tiv Song.* Chicago: University of Chicago Press.
Kroeber, Alfred L.
1947   *Cultural and Natural Areas of Native North America.* Berkeley and Los
         Angeles: University of California Press.
Kuhn, Thomas
1970   *The Structure of Scientific Revolutions.* 2d edition. Chicago: University
         of Chicago Press.
Lomax, Alan
1968   *Folk Song Style and Culture.* Washington, D.C.: American Association
         for the Advancement of Science.
McLean, Mervyn
1979   "Towards Differentiation of Music Areas in Oceania," *Anthropos*
         74:717–35.
Merriam, Alan P.
1964   *The Anthropology of Music.* Evanston: Northwestern University Press.

1977   "Definitions of 'Comparative Musicology' and 'Ethnomusicology': An
          Historical-Theoretical Perspective," *Ethnomusicology* 21:189–294.

Nettl, Bruno
1954   *North American Indian Musical Styles.* Philadelphia: American Folklore
          Society (Memoirs of the American Folklore Society, vol. 45).
1964   *Theory and Method in Ethnomusicology.* New York: Free Press.
1983   *The Study of Ethnomusicology: Twenty-nine Issues and Concepts.* Ur-
          bana: University of Illinois Press.

Rhodes, Willard
1958   "A Study of Musical Diffusion Based on the Wandering of the Opening
          Peyote Song," *Journal of the International Folk Music Council* 10:42–
          49.

Roberts, Helen
1936   *Musical Areas in Aboriginal North America.* New Haven: Yale Univer-
          sity Press (Yale University Publications in Anthropology, no. 12).

Rousseau, Jean-Jacques
1975   *A Complete Dictionary of Music.* New York: AMS Press. Reprint of the
          1779 edition.

Sachs, Curt
1937   *World History of the Dance.* Translated by Bessie Schönberg. New York:
          W. W. Norton.
1940   *The History of Musical Instruments.* New York: W. W. Norton.

Seeger, Anthony
1987   *Why Suyá Sing: A Musical Anthropology of an Amazonian People.* With
          accompanying audio cassette. Cambridge: Cambridge University Press.
In   "The Ethnography of Music," to appear in *New Grove Handbook of
press   Ethnomusicology,* Helen Myers, ed. (London: Macmillan).

Seeger, Charles L.
1977   *Studies in Musicology 1935–1975.* Berkeley and Los Angeles: University
          of California Press.

Stone, Ruth M.
1982   *Let the Inside be Sweet: The Interpretation of Music Event among the
          Kpelle of Liberia.* Bloomington: Indiana University Press.

Stumpf, Carl
1911   *Die Anfänge der Musik.* Leipzig: J. A. Barth.

Wallaschek, Richard
1893   *Primitive Music: An Inquiry into the Origin and Development of Music,
          Songs, Instruments, Dances and Pantomimes of the Savage Races.* Lon-
          don: Longmans, Green and Co.

Wissler, Clark
1917   *The American Indian.* New York: McMurtie.

Zemp, Hugo
1971   *Musique Dan: la musique dans la pensée et la vie sociale d'une societé
          africaine.* Paris: Mouton.

Philip V. Bohlman

Epilogue

DIVERSITY, VARIETY, PLURALITY; interdisciplinary, multidisciplinary, cross-disciplinary; abiding issues, competing ideologies, intertwining histories. Writ large across the pages of this book is the impressive abundance of the constituent parts of a larger history of ethnomusicology, the sheer weight of a multifaceted ethnomusicological literature, the bewildering polyphony of disparate scholarly voices and conflicting texts. Even the title of the book has the dubious distinction of identifying three distinct disciplines, four when one admits "history" to the fray. Still, despite the multitude of smaller histories, no author argues that his of her chapter lies outside the subject of the book. The more frequent apologia bemoans insufficient space to include even more, not the burden of ferreting out moot relations among a surfeit of artificially mustered parts.

That these essays have a common subject, then, appears unproblematic to their authors. The precise identity of that common subject, however, may be somewhat more difficult to pin down. It is, on one hand, ethnomusicology, though there can be little doubt that the authors apply that term to rather different scholarly pursuits. On the other hand, the common subject is the *intellectual history* of ethnomusicology, not the field itself. Linking these essayists, at least for the purposes of this volume, is their common role as intellectual historians, perhaps even more so than as ethnomusicologists.

The common subject of these essays does not so much take shape as a uniformity of theme as of purpose. Whatever the peculiarities of their academic homes, whatever the distinct dialects necessitated by their diverse specialties, the essayists have rallied around the historical theme with a surprising effortlessness. It is as if they were accustomed to the task of writing intellectual history, as if the historical agenda were inseparable from their other activities as ethnomusicologists.

The historical impetus of this book has clearly captured the spirit of common purpose that unifies ethnomusicology. One is tempted to think,

furthermore, that the ability of different issues and disciplines to cohere because of an historical impetus is somehow basic to the field. Is it possible
that the intellectual history of ethnomusicology unifies it far more than we
have heretofore recognized? Could one go so far as to suggest that the intellectual history of the field is not simply observation at a distance or
meta-historical stocktaking, rather that it is intrinsic to the way ethnomusicologists identify their central issues and construct channels of communication with other ethnomusicologists? And might the self-critical and self-
reflexive preoccupation of the field be a corollary of a fundamentally
historical epistemology? These essays, quietly yet convincingly, seem to answer such questions in the affirmative.

It may seem remarkable to some who read this book that ethnomusicologists communicate among themselves with such ease. The book illustrates
clearly that, despite their different perspectives and disciplines, ethnomusicologists do share a common language. A simple explanation of this common language would be that ethnomusicologists share a subject, namely
music, that is superordinate to their academic training and institutional
home. This explanation is, however, too convenient, and its pretense that
music simply stands at the center of our conceptual universe is too facile.
Moreover, the willingness to communicate and the urge for a common language do not in themselves serve as metaphors for the essential logocentrism of the field, a logocentrism most fully evident in and expressed by the
historical impetus. It is this privileging of language, however, that has the
power to focus the field and the activities of its practitioners by encouraging the formulation of related questions about tone systems by psychologists, linguists, acousticians, and musicologists at the beginning of the
twentieth century. Comparative musicologists depended on the mediating
function of language to reduce musical phenomena in different cultures to
a universally valid vocabulary. But linguistic mediation also has its unset-
tling role, for, by its very tendency to spin off new questions and to identify
new problems, it finds little repose in the answering of universal questions
or establishing all-embracing theorems. In the history of the field, it was
the relentless diversity of questions, rather than the ready acceptance of
convenient answers, that expressed the ultimate concern for a common
ethnomusicological language.

History, of course, assumes many different forms in the areas embodied
by the larger domain of ethnomusicology. Each subdiscipline examined
here has its own history, its own issues, and the intellectual forebears who
animated them. The centrality of ideology in these essays, too, summons

up historical moments and the arguments that tie ideas to time and place. Even the very concept of the "world's cultural diversity," so significant as a force that draws ethnomusicologists into the field, exhibits an infinite range of possible meanings, constantly tempered through time by what we consider "us" and "them" to be. The diversity of which ethnomusicology is so duly proud nevertheless demands that it accept the inevitability of describing that diversity rather nervously, always keeping in mind the fallacies of our ancestors and looking not to eliminate such fallacies, but to beware of their new permutations in the historical present.

These are, unquestionably, among the primary concerns of the intellectual historian. What is so surprising in this volume is that so many of these concerns should arise and then demonstrate such a natural affinity and kinship. Although it is perhaps too early to say, these concerns surely suggest that the field's unity is greater than its surface diversity would suggest. At the very least, the essays share historiographic themes, if their specific personalities, issues, and disciplinary foci are different.

The theme of *representation,* for example, looms rather large in these essays. The early ethnomusicologists were interested in representing the music of the "other," both as a means of extending a political and social hegemony and as an attempt to discover common origins. Systems of representation emerge as "abiding issues" in questions of terminology or ideology. These systems become competitors among the "variety of disciplines," whether through communication systems, modes of musical ethnography, or the uses of recording technology. The roles of semiotics, linguistic modeling, and transcription achieve their persistent relevance to ethnomusicology because they undergird ethnomusicological thinking over time.

The *use of language* to translate the meaning of music to something meaningful for the reader is also a theme that recurs throughout the essays. Here, too, we witness the emergence of a leitmotif that symbolizes the historical backdrop for the coherent development of the field. Language and its diverse uses constitute the essential tool of the intellectual historian. To understand what someone in the seventeenth century really believed about music, to gain some sense of what Native American or African music meant to the missionary of the eighteenth century or the ethnomusicologist of the nineteenth, we must look more closely at their texts. At the same time, we succeed in determining the historical contexts without which musical meaning did not exist. Language, therefore, specifies the texts for the ethnomusicologist-intellectual historian, relativizing them and unifying their position in the vast landscape occupied by the field.

The recognition that the physical essence of music—its sound—exists only within a larger system of *musical thought,* with its constellation of cognitive, psychological, and emotional factors, is yet another theme treated historically by these essays. Early ethnographers may have misunderstood the "structure" of the music they encountered, and early acoustic specialists may have misunderstood the tuning data produced by nascent technologies, but it wasn't really structures and measurements they were after. Instead, they hoped to identify the components of a rational, human system that they could relate to a culture's way of thinking about its own music. The concern for musical thought historically had many names and employed many strategies, but it was no less relevant for the eighteenth-century debates about the naturalness or artificialty of music than for twentieth-century attempts to situate music in culture or as culture.

Comparison inescapably is a common theme in the underlying historicism of this book. Various scholars may have espoused comparison or eschewed it, but few could or did ignore it. We might even say that there has been an historical tendency to alternate between elevating and subverting the influence of comparison. If nothing else, comparison necessitates historical posturing. More important for our concerns, comparison permits, even encourages, a plurality of histories. Comparison serves as the link between the portraits of individuals and issues and the larger panorama of ethnomusicology that the book forms. It is an approach that we employ as individual scholars, but rely on to bind us together as a field.

The theme of *ideology* is so omnipresent in these essays as to assert forcefully that it plays an indispensable role in ethnomusicology's intellectual history. Again, we find a theme that at different times inspires and disturbs, that both engenders new theories and too quickly dismisses the old. Yet ideology as a theme is impossible to ignore when writing the history of the field. To understand why eighteenth-century *savants* pondered non-Western musical systems, why nineteenth-century philologists constructed elaborate historical models to chase down an elusive past, and why comparativists juxtaposed the values of one culture on another, the ethnomusicologist asks hard ideological questions. And they are even harder for being as relevant to one historical moment as another. Indeed, they link many historical moments to each other, not least to our own. Surely, this historical concern for ideology—one's own as powerfully as another's—looms large in each critical reexamination of the field and in our seemingly obsessive self-critique. The disquieting presence of ideological issues in ethnomusicology poses far more questions than answers. But it is precisely these abundent questions that so effectively quicken our historical debate.

In the opening pages of his introduction Bruno Nettl makes a strong case for the uniqueness of ethnomusicology. There is no other field in the humanities quite so explicitly concerned with non-Western art forms; no other field bridges the humanities and social sciences quite so consciously, depending on the catalytic potential of anthropological theory to spawn new ways of understanding the arts; and there is no other field whose practitioners can come from just about any other field. In his characteristically restrained way Nettl links the field's uniqueness to its history, formulating from this the motivating credo of the book: "This uniqueness in particular requires an understanding of ethnomusicology's history." Of course, Nettl is claiming a great deal more about the relation between the field's uniqueness and its history, and the following essays further exemplify, document, and argue the often improbable manifestations of such a relation.

Improbable? Perhaps, but again we find that the abundance of evidence militates against the hastiness and ease of deferring to improbability. Uniqueness? Indeed, but by no means can uniqueness be construed as unlikelihood or anomaly. Quite the contrary, everything about these essays suggests that the intellectual history of ethnomusicology resulted from reasoned responses to the phenomena of music and culture by a community of scholars. Whatever their other differences, the issues of ethnomusicology served as a rallying point for these scholars. Whatever their contributions to other disciplines and institutions, the history of ethnomusicology unified their endeavors and ideas.

Intellectual historians have in recent years spoken rather hopefully about the potential for their discipline to shape discourse about the common ideas shared by disciplines that in other ways differ. The essays here would indicate that ethnomusicology has been doing this all along. Whether ethnomusicologists are any better at it for the experience is another issue. But, at least at this point in our extensive experience we are no less optimistic that our intellectual history can summon up common ideas and provide a unified discourse. The hopeful enjoinder of modern intellectual historians conveys a message so evident in all these essays, namely that ethnomusicology can most effectively determine its future while taking critical stock of its past.

Contributors

Carol M. Babiracki studied at the Universities of Minnesota and Illinois and has done fieldwork in Bihar, India, and with ethnic groups in the American Midwest. Her research interests include tribal music in India, musical instruments, and dance ethnography, and her publications include articles on Indian folk instruments in *The New Grove Dictionary of Musical Instruments*. She has taught at the University of Illinois at Chicago and is Instructor of Music at Brown University.

Gerard Béhague studied at the University of Brazil, the Sorbonne, and Tulane University, taught at the University of Illinois at Urbana-Champaign, and is Professor of Music at the University of Texas at Austin. His principal fields of research are musical nationalism in Latin America and Afro-Bahian cult music, and he is the author of *Music in Latin America* (1977) and the editor of *Performance Practice: Ethnomusicological Perspectives* (1984).

Stephen Blum studied at Oberlin and the University of Illinois and did field research in Khorasan, Iran. Among his other research interests are North American hymnody and the history of tonality. He is coeditor of *Ethnomusicology and Modern Music History* (1990), has taught at Western Illinois University, the University of Illinois at Urbana-Champaign, and York University (Toronto), and is Professor of Music at the City University of New York Graduate Center.

Philip V. Bohlman studied at the Universities of Wisconsin and Illinois and has done field research in Israel and the American Midwest. He is the author of *The Study of Folk Music in the Modern World* (1988) and *"The Land Where Two Streams Flow": Music in the German-Jewish Community of Israel* (1989) and, having previously taught at the University of Illinois at Chicago, is Assistant Professor of Music at the University of Chicago.

Charles Capwell studied at Brown and Harvard and has done field research in Bengal, India. He is the author of *The Music of the Bauls of Bengal* (1986) and editor of the journal *Ethnomusicology*. He is Associate Professor of Music and Chairman of the Division of Musicology at the University of Illinois at Urbana-Champaign.

Dieter Christensen studied at the Free University of Berlin (where he also taught), was director of the Berlin Phonogramm-Archiv, taught at Wesleyan University, and is now Professor of Music and Director of the Center for Ethnomusicology, Columbia University. He is the author of *Musik der Kate und Sialum* (1967) and *Musik der Ellice-Inseln* (with Gerd Koch, 1964), and editor of the *Yearbook for Traditional Music*.

Oskár Elschek   studied at Comenius University, Bratislava (Czechoslovakia) and is Head of the Ethnomusicology Laboratory of the Slovak Academy of Sciences. Among his areas of research are organology, systematic musicology, and Slovak folk music, and his publications include *Die slowakischen Volksmusikinstrumente* (1983) and *Hudobná veda súčastnosti* [Contemporary Musicology Research] (1984).

Charlotte J. Frisbie   studied at Wesleyan University and the University of New Mexico and is Professor of Anthropology at Southern Illinois University at Edwardsville and a past president of the Society for Ethnomusicology. With extensive fieldwork among the Navajo, she is the editor of *Explorations in Ethnomusicology: Essays in Honor of David P. McAllester* (1986) and, with McAllester, of *Navajo Blessingway Singer* (1978), and the author of *Navajo Medicine Bundles or Jish* (1987).

Nazir Ali Jairazbhoy   studied at the University of Washington and with Arnold Bake at London University, where he also taught. He is Professor and Chairman of the Department of Ethnomusicology and Systematic Musicology, University of California at Los Angeles. His areas of research include the music of India, methods of transcription, and ethnomusicological filmmaking, and he is the author of *The Rāgs of North Indian Music* (1971).

Bruno Nettl   studied at Indiana University with George Herzog, has done fieldwork in Iran and with the Blackfoot, taught and worked as a librarian at Wayne State University, and is Professor of Music and Anthropology at the University of Illinois at Urbana-Champaign. He is the author of *The Study of Ethnomusicology* (1983), *The Western Impact on World Music* (1985), and *Blackfoot Musical Thought: Comparative Perspectives* (1989).

James Porter   studied at the Universities of St. Andrews and Edinburgh and is Professor of Ethnomusicology and Folklore at the University of California at Los Angeles. His main research has been on the singing traditions of the Scottish Travellers, and he is the author of *The Traditional Music of Britain and Ireland* (1989) as well as coeditor of the forthcoming *Garland Encyclopedia of World Music*.

Regula Burckhardt Qureshi   studied at the Curtis Institute, the University of Pennsylvania, and the University of Alberta. With fieldwork in India and Pakistan, her research centers on performance traditions of South Asia, especially Islamic musical traditions and Hindustani art music. The author of *Sufi Music in India and Pakistan* (1986), she is Associate Professor of Music at the University of Alberta.

Alexander L. Ringer   studied at the University of Amsterdam (with Jaap Kunst), the New School for Social Research, and Columbia University. His research interests include medieval organum, music of the French Revolution, nineteenth- and twentieth-century music, and music of the Middle East. He is Professor of Music at the University of Illinois at Urbana-Champaign and the author of *Arnold Schoenberg: The Composer as Jew* (1990).

Albrecht Schneider studied at the Universities of Cologne and Bonn. He is the author of *Musikwissenschaft und Kulturkreislehre* (1976)—one of the first books devoted to the subject of this volume—and *Analogie und Rekonstruktion: Zur Methodologie der Musikgeschichtsschreibung und zur Frühgeschichte der Musik* (1984). He is Professor of Systematic Musicology at the University of Hamburg.

Anthony Seeger, grandson of Charles Seeger, studied at Harvard and the University of Chicago. He has done fieldwork with peoples of Amazonian Brazil, has taught in Brazil and at Indiana University, and is Curator of the Folkways Collection and Director of Smithsonian/Folkways Records at the Smithsonian Institution. He is the author of *Early Field Recordings* (with Louise Spear, 1987) and of *Why Suyá Sing: A Musical Anthropology of an Amazonian People* (1987).

Kay Kaufman Shelemay studied at the University of Michigan and has done field research in Ethiopia, Israel, and the United States. Her areas of research include Ethiopian Christian chant, music of the Falashas, music in the recording industry, and urban ethnomusicology in New York. The author of *Music, Ritual, and Falasha History* (1986), she has taught at Columbia and New York Universities, and is Professor of World Music at Wesleyan University.

Doris Stockmann studied at the Music Academy of Dresden, the Stern Academy of Berlin, and Humboldt University. Her areas of research include German, Albanian, and Sami folk music, methodologies of scholarship, and medieval music. She is the author of *Der Volksgesang in der Altmark von der Mitte des 19. bis zur Mitte des 20. Jahrhunderts* (1962) and holds the position of Research Scholar in the Academy of Sciences of the German Democratic Republic, Berlin.

Christopher A. Waterman, son of Richard A. Waterman, studied at the Berklee School of Music and the University of Illinois. He has done fieldwork in Nigeria, and his research interests include African and African-American societies and musics and popular music. He is Assistant Professor of Music at the University of Washington and the author of *Jùjú: A Social History and Ethnography of an African Popular Music* (1990).

Isabel K. F. Wong studied at University of Melbourne, Northwestern University, and Brown, and has done fieldwork on *kunqu* in the People's Republic of China. The author of the article on East Asia in the *New Harvard Dictionary of Music,* she is Lecturer in Music and directs East Asian Exchange Programs at the University of Illinois at Urbana-Champaign.

Index

Abraham, Otto: African ethnomusicology by, 169; and development of the phonograph, 280; and general laws, 194; as pioneer ethnomusicologist, 244, 293; and quantitative research, 296, 298, 299, 300; and recording of Thai music, 204, 302
Abrahams, Roger, 114
Acculturation, musical, 23, 60
Adisura (Bengali king), 231
Adler, Guido, 18–19, 269
Adorno, Theodor, 324
Africa, distribution of Western musical recordings in, 282, 283. *See also* African music
African-American music: application of European musical terminology to, 3–10; sources of, 22–23
African-Americans, acculturation of, 172. *See also* African-American music
African ethnomusicology, development of, 169–81 passim. *See also* African music
African music: application of European musical terminology to, 3–10, 25–26; as categorically transitional, 18–19; early study of, 14–15; influence on Latin American music, 57, 63–64; and musical instruments, 14; recordings of, 14, 15, 170–71, 172; rhythm in, 170–75; variation in, 169–70; viewed as different from European music, 171
Allami, Abual-Fazl, 165 n.17
Alvarenga, Oneyda, 60, 62
Aman, Father Hugo, 81
American folk songs, contrasting paradigms in the study of, 113–26 passim
American Indian music: Anglo-American research on, 191; Frances T. Densmore's interest in, 248; George Herzog's interest in, 272; Helen H. Roberts's interest in, 249, 250; and Latin American music, 29 n.9, 57, 64; musical system of, 22; recordings of, 248–50
American Indians, representation of, 131, 137–38. *See also* American Indian music
American Society for Comparative Musicology, 250, 253, 271
Ames, David W., 176, 353
Ames, Russell, 122
Amiot, Jean-Joseph-Marie, 141, 146, 191
Anderson, Lois Ann, 27
Ankermann, Bernhard, 15
Appunn'scher Tonmesser, 302
Araújo, Alceu Maynard de, 62, 63
Archer, W. G., 79, 82, 83
Aretz, Isabel, 59–60
Aristotle, 189
Asaf'yev, Boris, 328
Atanasov, Vergilii, 96
Augustine, Saint, 330
Ayyangar, R. Rangaramanuja, 71
Azevedo, Luiz Heitor Corrêa de, 62

Bachmann-Geiser, B., 97
Bake, Arnold Adriaan, and study of Indian music, 7, 210–22 passim
Bake, Cornelia ("Corry") Timmers, 210–12, 214, 216, 219–21, 224 n.16, 225 n.29, 226 nn.36, 39, 40
Baker, Theodore, 9, 191, 244
Ballová, L'uba, 99
Bandiwdekar, Kalpana, 220
Banerjee, Nikhil, 165 n.24
Barbeau, Marius, 9, 258–59 n.8
Baring-Gould, Rev. Sabine, 120–21
Barni, Ziauddin, 156
Barrow, John, 191